Human Resource Management
A Concise Analysis

Pearson Education

We work with leading authors to develop the strongest educational materials in Human Resource Management, bringing cutting-edge thinking and best learning practice to a global market.

Under a range of well-known imprints, including Financial Times Prentice Hall, we craft high quality print and electronic publications which help readers to understand and apply their content, whether studying or at work.

To find out more about the complete range of our publishing, please visit us on the World Wide Web at: www.pearsoneduc.com

Human Resource Management
A Concise Analysis

EUGENE McKENNA

NIC BEECH

FINANCIAL TIMES
Prentice Hall

An imprint of **Pearson Education**

Harlow, England · London · New York · Reading, Massachusetts · San Francisco · Toronto · Don Mills, Ontario · Sydney
Tokyo · Singapore · Hong Kong · Seoul · Taipei · Cape Town · Madrid · Mexico City · Amsterdam · Munich · Paris · Milan

Pearson Education Limited

Edinburgh Gate
Harlow
Essex CM20 2JE
England

and Associated Companies throughout the world.

Visit us on the World Wide Web at:
www.pearsoneduc.com

First published 2002

© Pearson Education Limited 2002

ISBN 0273 65510 8

British Library Cataloguing-in-Publication Data
A catalogue record for this book is available from the British Library

10   9   8   7   6   5   4   3   2   1
06   05   04   03   02

Typeset in Great Britain by 3
Printed in Great Britain by Henry Ling Ltd., at the Dorset Press, Dorchester,
Dorset

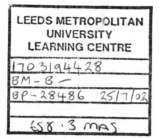

To Alison, Geraldine, Graham, Linda and Rosie

Contents

Preface

Our major aim in writing this book was to introduce the reader to the established topics and critical issues in the broad field of Human Resource Management (HRM) in a succinct way. The student, the HRM specialist and the line manager grappling with people problems will derive benefit from this text which is comprehensive, accessible and up-to-date.

Throughout there is analysis and reflection on both practical and theoretical issues in this growing area of study. In addition, a large number of case studies and vignettes are used to help the reader explore the connections between the relevant body of knowledge and its application. It is well recognised that HRM is vitally important for the success of the organisation. In order to achieve that success through HRM, managers must manage their employees effectively. This involves a good understanding of the topics and debate that are covered in this book, which are based on the relevant body of knowledge and practice. Of particular importance are issues related to coping with accelerating change, globalisation/internationalisation, fostering commitment, managing knowledge workers, use of technology, customer care, and going beyond the adversarial 'us and them' cultures so that the deployment of resources and necessary change are easily and promptly introduced. Also, the careful selection and use of HR techniques generally must not be understated.

The effective management of people is now acknowledged as a crucial factor in achieving organisational success. If people are to perform to their potential, the HRM systems and structures must be appropriate and in harmony with each other, but in addition management must be of sufficient quality to promote employee commitment. An adaptable and flexible workforce is also a necessary requirement in modern organisations, and certainly these strengths equip people to cope with change in an uncertain world. The use of well-conceived and properly implemented HRM policies will no doubt contribute to the development of such a workforce. Each chapter in this book explores an important topic that needs to be understood if organisations are to achieve successful performance through people. The approach adopted is to take a balanced and critical perspective and recognise the problematic nature of theory and practice in HRM.

Eugene McKenna
Nic Beech
August 2001

List of abbreviations

ABLE   Aptitude for Business Learning Exercises
ACAS   Advisory, Conciliatory and Arbitration Service
BA   British Airways
BBC   British Broadcasting Corporation
BP   British Petroleum
BPR   business process re-engineering
CBI   Confederation of British Industry
CEO   chief executive officer
CV   curriculum vitae
EAPs   employee assistance programmes
EFQM   European Foundation for Quality Management
EI   employee involvement
EU   European Union
EWCs   European Works Councils
HCM   high commitment management
HR   human resource
HRM   human resource management
HRP   human resource planning
IIP   Investors in People
ICT   information and communication technology
IDS   Income Data Services
IPM   Institute of Personnel Management (now Institute of Personnel and Development)
IRS   Industrial Relations Surveys
JIT   just in time
LSC   Learning and Skills Council
L Tips long-term incentives
MBO   management by objectives
MCI   Management Charter Initiative
MMS   Malin Manufacturing Services
MSF   Manufacturing, Science and Finance (union)
NIESR   National Institute of Economic and Social Research
NVQs   National Vocational Qualifications
OD   organisational development
OECD   Organization for Economic Cooperation and Development
OPQ   occupational personality questionnaire
PBR   payment by results
PRP   performance-related pay
QCs   quality circles
SBUs   Strategic Business Units
SIA   Singapore Airlines
16PF   Cattell's 16 personality factors
STARs   situations, tasks, actions and results
SWOT   strengths, weaknesses, opportunities and threats
T&G   Transport and General Workers Union
TEC   Training and Enterprise Council
TQM   total quality management
TUC   Trades Union Congress

Chapter 1

Introduction and overview

Human resource management (HRM) seeks to maximise organisational performance through the adoption of best practice in the management of people. In seeking to understand best practice HRM draws on theoretical foundations from disciplines such as psychology, sociology and industrial relations, and has developed a distinctive body of research over the years. The aim of this book is to conduct an analysis of HRM – the practice, theories and implications from research – in a concise and accessible way. The first chapter seeks to set the scene for such an analysis by introducing some of the key themes that will be revisited in more detail in subsequent chapters, and by showing how they can be integrated in practice.

Having read this chapter, you should:

- understand the general nature of HRM – its aims and practices;
- be aware of the development of HRM and its context;
- have a broad awareness of the various aspects of HRM that will be covered in greater depth in the book;
- be aware of some of the main topics of debate in the subject area.

Human resource management can be viewed as an approach to personnel management that considers people as the key resource. It subscribes to the notion that it is important to communicate well with employees, to involve them in what is going on and to foster their commitment and identification with the organisation. In addition, a strategic approach to the acquisition, management and motivation of people is heavily emphasised.

If HRM gets some of its basic sustenance from the practice of personnel management, this begs the question: what do we know about the origins of personnel management and its current standing? Before answering this question, a definition of personnel management would be useful. Personnel management assists with the management of people in an organisation. It is concerned with establishing, maintaining and developing systems that provide the framework of employment. These systems operate throughout an employee's membership of the company, starting with the system for entry (recruitment and selection) through the management of the employment relationship (reward, appraisal, development, industrial relations, grievance and discipline), finishing with the termination of the relationship (retirement, resignation, redundancy or dismissal). Ideally this management process is reinforced by the drive for efficiency and equality of opportunity.

■ Historical development

In the latter part of the 1800s the concept of welfare personnel developed. This was prompted by the humane concerns of certain families involved in business (e.g. Cadbury and Rowntree), and could be referred to as the Quaker tradition. Welfare personnel was concerned with the provision of schemes, considered progressive at that time, dealing with unemployment, sick pay and subsidised housing for employees. The introduction of these schemes could be viewed as a reaction to the harshness of capitalism at that period of British history. The motives of some industrialists adopting welfare schemes were questioned because there was a belief that some practices were intended as an alternative for realistic wages, and as a ploy to keep trade unions at bay.

Welfare personnel continued as a force until the Second World War, and later manifestations of it were the provision of canteens and company outings for workers. Even today it can be recognised that the welfare tradition has some significance in the practice of personnel management, for example health schemes and crèches for the children of employees.

The next phase in the development was the emphasis on personnel administration. This amounted to support for management and was basically concerned with recruitment, discipline, time keeping, payment systems, training and keeping personnel records. It came into its own in the period between the First and Second World Wars. The growth in the size of organisations is a factor to consider in connection with this development.

After the Second World War and up to the 1950s personnel management incorporated a wider range of services, including salary administration, basic training and advice on industrial relations, but the main focus was at the tactical rather than the strategic level. Again, increasing organisational size was notable in activating certain changes in industrial relations practices. For example, the movement from collective bargaining at industry level to the level of the company was apparent, resulting in the advent of the industrial relations specialist within personnel management.

The 1960s and 1970s saw a significant increase in the number of staff engaged in personnel work. This could be attributable in part to an increase in the amount of employment legislation. However, the state of the economy had a part to play as well. In conditions of full employment, up to the early 1970s, there was evidence of much recruitment, selection, training and payment system activity in the practice of personnel management. This was prompted to some extent by labour shortages, and was reflected in actions to retain skilled labour and increase the skill levels of the workforce. The approach to training was systematic and planned, heavily influenced by the establishment of the Training Boards, which exacted a training levy from industry and offered grants to companies that conducted training to acceptable standards. In turn this spawned a rapid growth in the number of training specialists within the personnel function. Related activities, such as performance appraisal (e.g. management by objectives) and management development, also assumed importance, as did forecasting manpower needs (manpower planning).

The prevalence of ideas and insights derived from behavioural science ought to be acknowledged as having a part to play as well. Also during this period the strength of the bargaining power of the trade unions at the workplace was conspicuous. The consequence of greater union influence was a substantial increase in the workload of the personnel specialists. The involvement of the personnel function in matters connected with industrial relations issues, and with productivity deals, elevated its concern to some extent to matters of strategic significance to the organisation, at a time when most of its activities could be considered tactical in nature. The emphasis on industrial relations heralded a delicate role for the personnel specialist interacting with both management and workers. This signalled a need to develop negotiation skills and to learn more about various systems of remuneration, and there was a tendency to identify the personnel function with management.

The 1980s saw personnel management entering the entrepreneurial phase, adapting itself to the market economy and enterprise culture. It was not uncommon to find senior personnel executives contributing to the debate within the company about future direction, the relevance of existing business objectives, and improved ways of achieving revised objectives. This era heralded a preoccupation with the management of change, the development of appropriate corporate culture, the acceptance of Japanese industrial relations practices, such as single unions to represent a company's workforce, and Japanese management practices in the form of quality circles and total quality management. A noticeable feature in the practice of industrial relations, in some but not all cases, was the shift in emphasis from workforce collective bargaining to centralised bargaining, and in the process a reduction in the involvement of personnel managers in negotiations at local level.

As the recession in the economy of the early 1980s began to bite, the role of the trade unions began to change. The threat of strike action became less effective as organisations could replace workers relatively easily. This resulted not only from the recession and high unemployment, but also from new legislation introduced at this time. The power of trade unions was reduced with the ending of closed shops, and changes in the rules about industrial action, including balloting and picketing.

The relative weakness in the power of trade unions signalled the need for less elaborate processes in collective bargaining and conflict management. It also culminated in swifter negotiated wage settlements. Also, organisations were better placed to make changes in work practices that resulted in increased productivity and a reduction in the numbers employed. There were also changes in personnel practices due to the large pool of available labour. For example, the emphasis switched from recruitment (attracting candidates) to selection.

The reduced volume of negotiations based on collective bargaining between unions and personnel specialists, together with the reduction in time devoted to recruitment and selection, provided personnel management with opportunities to manage redundancy programmes and enter negotiations to bring about lower wage settlements in a relatively calm industrial relations climate. Then the first signs of fundamental change to the nature of personnel management appeared on the horizon. Hunt (1984) speculated about the personnel function shifting in its emphasis. It was during the 1980s that the rise in HRM began to attract the attention of personnel practitioners. There was a move away from the traditionally adversarial industrial relations of the 1970s towards an approach that sought to achieve excellence in the organisation through a committed workforce. The reasons for this will be offered later.

The post-entrepreneurial phase for personnel management in the 1990s still saw HRM as the standard bearer, though some would argue that HRM would subsume personnel management. In fact the early 1990s witnessed a change in emphasis. The reaction to individualism and unjustifiable greed of the 1980s made way for the spirit of consent and the value of teamwork. There was concern for core workers who are essential to the operation of the organisation since high commitment is required from these workers. They are expected to be flexible about the hours they work and to work above and beyond their job descriptions. Wages tend to reflect the market rate rather than the rate determined by agreements with trade unions. The number of part-time and fixed-term contract workers as a proportion of the total workforce is increasing.

There was a continuing preoccupation with the value of a strategic approach to human resource management in the context of organisational success. Of course the challenges of the single European market had to be faced, and the significance of the Social Chapter in the practice of human resource management was considered, particularly by companies with European operations. (Amongst the issues covered by the Social Chapter are improved working conditions, equitable remuneration, equal opportunities, labour mobility, union representation, access to information and workers' involvement, and health and safety provisions). In this context, it should be recognised that Europe provides a different socio-technical and economic environment to that of the United States, where HRM took root, and this could influence the type of HRM that is pursued (see Table 1.1).

If one were to consider the application of the principles of HRM in an Asian context, it would be productive to note the following values in the population:

- Being polite and courteous;
- Not losing face, and placing value on personal relationships;
- Hard work and thrift;
- Harmony and avoidance of open conflict; strive for consensus;
- Group interests predominate over individual interests;
- Reciprocation in social relationships;
- Discipline and respect for authority (including elders);
- Normative system of control rather than a system of control externally imposed;

Table 1.1 Factors influencing HRM in Europe

The following features of the European scene should be recognised (Guest, 1994):

■ pluralism instead of unitarism (explained later, and reflected in the attitudes of trade unions and the nature of their role);

■ collectivism and social orientation instead of individualism (the emphasis is on national welfare schemes and group-based systems of work);

■ legal framework (e.g. the impact of the Social Chapter, constraints on hiring and firing decisions, changes to laws on employment and remuneration);

■ social partnership (e.g. industrial democracy, reasonable employment security, protection of workers' rights (e.g. health and safety, recognition of the role of the workers' representatives (unions), and the importance of the workforce as a stakeholder);

■ social responsibility (concern for the environment, and social obligations (e.g. training));

■ importance of community (interaction between industry and the community, the issue of subsidiarity reflected in degrees of local autonomy, community pressure on companies with respect to employment/environment);

■ toleration for diversity – cultural diversity (heterogeneity) as opposed to homogeneity (United States) – is prevalent and finds expression in many forms: organisational systems, vocational education, training and skills development, and the internal/external labour market);

■ recognition of complexity and ambiguity (e.g., influenced by a long European history and cultural diversity, there is less inclination to go for simple solutions, and there is a recognition of the complexity of the relationship between the various stakeholders in the organisation and the operationalisation of the concept of subsidiarity).

■ Trust and mutual help in business relationships;
■ Family business interests are to be protected;
■ Centralisation and authoritarianism;
■ Long-term view, with the guiding hand of government.

■ Personnel/HRM activities

In organisations of reasonable size one can expect to find a personnel function, just as one would expect to find a finance or marketing function. However, in the smaller organisation this level of specialisation may not prevail, and the personnel function is performed by a manager who handles personnel matters in conjunction with other duties. In very small organisations personnel activities could be carried out by all managers. Even where personnel management is normally seen as a specialist function it could be carried out by other managers where the amount of work did not warrant employing a specialist. Part of the concept of human resource management, by contrast, is that whatever the size of the organisation all managers should be involved. A number of activities can be identified with the personnel function, though not all the activities listed below may be carried out in some organisations.

Human resource planning

This process has developed from what was previously called manpower planning.

Human resource planning is concerned with matching the organisational demand for quantity and quality of employees with the available supply. The demand is derived from current and forecast levels of company operations. The supply side consists of human resources available both internally and externally. The internal supply, which has been a target for rationalisation in recent years, consists of the existing workforce and its potential to contribute. The external supply resides in the population outside the organisation and is influenced by demographic trends, developments in education and competitive forces in the labour market within the European Union (EU). The planning exercise outlines the manpower needs of the organisation and provides useful information for a number of activities listed below, e.g. selection, training and rewards.

Recruitment

Prior to recruitment, job analysis is undertaken. This is a process whereby the work to be undertaken by an employee is closely examined, and results in the preparation of a job description. Then a specification is produced of the attributes a suitable candidate will need in order to perform the job. The most appropriate means of recruitment, e.g. newspaper advertisement, employment agency or job centre, is specified with the intention of attracting suitable applications.

Selection

A variety of techniques, e.g. the application form, interviews, tests and assessment centres, are available to select the best candidate from a pool of applicants. It is likely that a shortlist of applicants will be produced as a first step in the selection process. This may be unnecessary where there are only a small number of job applicants. Some measure, i.e. criteria relating to the ideal candidate, is used to assist in making a selection decision.

Performance appraisal

This is a technique, not universally accepted, of assessing the performance of employees against agreed targets. The personnel practitioners would be most likely to be involved in designing the procedures, leaving the line managers normally to administer the process. This commonly takes the form of an interview following the completion of forms that facilitate assessment of achievement in the period since the last interview (often one year). Performance can be measured against criteria set previously. The outcome could signal the need for training, or in some cases remuneration.

Training

This is a process concerned with establishing what type of training is required and who should receive it. Training ranges from simple on-the-job instruction to educational and training courses offered by providers external to the organisation. Training, coupled with development, is apparent when organisations plan the progression of key employees through the company, in which case an attempt is made to reconcile organisational needs with individual career development.

Rewards

This covers a wide area incorporating rates of pay, trade union involvement where appropriate and other factors such as the use of job evaluation in the determination of rates of pay, methods for calculating pay (e.g. flat rate, piece-rate or performance-related pay) and fringe benefits.

Employee relations

Under this heading could be considered collective bargaining, grievance procedures and employment legislation. In collective bargaining the personnel/industrial relations specialist normally prepares and presents the employer's case in the negotiations with the employees' representative (trade union official). A responsibility of the personnel manager is to monitor the outcome of collective agreements.

With respect to grievance procedures, the personnel manager could be involved in preparing and implementing those procedures and be actively involved in trying to settle disputes that fall outside the collective bargaining process. Disputes within the gambit of collective bargaining could be considered to be group- rather than individual-based matters. The personnel specialist is normally involved in discipline cases, and has the function of gathering evidence and preparing the case, and also ensuring the employee is treated fairly.

The personnel specialist is likely to be called on to give advice on matters connected with employment legislation, and is expected to be conversant with the practical issues relating to the applicability of relevant legal provisions.

Employee communications and participation

This could amount to taking on board activities in connection with communicating relevant information to employees, and arranging for ways in which employees can participate in the processes of the company (e.g. suggestion schemes). In certain circumstances counselling could become part of the service under this heading. Increasingly, participation also incorporates aspects of Japanese management practices, such as quality circles and teamwork, in which operators take over certain aspects of production control such as quality control. In this way employees are involved in decision making that affects their work.

Personnel records

A record of the employee is likely to be kept centrally by the personnel department. This could contain information provided in the original application, with subsequent additions to reflect qualifications and experience gained, achievements and potential. The employee record could provide a useful input to personnel decisions. Records are normally computerised and can be used as part of the human resource planning process.

The personnel activities described above, which are expanded in subsequent chapters, can be executed in diverse ways (Needle, 2000):

- The personnel specialist or senior manager with responsibility for personnel matters can be involved at a strategic level at which policies are formulated.
- The personnel specialist or senior manager with responsibility for personnel matters provides an advisory service for line managers. For example, he or she could set up a performance appraisal system and advise managers on its use.
- The personnel specialist or senior manager with responsibility for personnel matters could join forces with a line manager in order to perform a specific function. For example, the line manager and personnel specialist could sit on the same interview panel when interviewing candidates for a job vacancy.
- The personnel specialist or senior manager with responsibility for personnel matters may engage in a specified number of activities, leaving line managers with a high level of autonomy for personnel matters close to their area of responsibility, e.g. selecting their own staff.

In practice, particularly in large organisations, personnel activities will often consist of several of the above roles. For example, if a production manager has a vacancy for a charge hand or team leader, there will be a planning exercise to consider the need for the job, the internal supply of labour and the cost of filling the vacancy. If there is a decision to appoint somebody the personnel specialist may support the production manager by provision of particular expertise, for instance by drawing up the job specification, preparing the advertisement and advising on the interview process. Normally you would expect the personnel specialist to issue the employment contract. This example indicates a high level of involvement on the part of the personnel function. In some organisations, and often for jobs that are lower in the organisation, the involvement of the personnel specialist is less, and may be confined merely to preparing the advertisement and employment contract. Nowadays there is a noticeable trend to avail of the services of outside consultants, particularly in the area of recruitment, selection and training. The involvement of the personnel specialist in this field is that of obtaining the services of the consultant and managing the process.

■ Personnel management versus HRM

Although personnel management shares a platform with human resource management on some key issues – a natural concern for people and their needs, together with finding efficient means to select, train, appraise, develop and reward them – there are some points of dissimilarity. Traditional personnel management tended to be parochial, striving to influence line managers, whereas HRM is integrated into the role of line managers, with a strong proactive stance and a bias towards business. Personnel management has a history of placing emphasis on bureaucratic control often in a reactive sense, i.e. control of manpower and personnel systems. To be fair it has had to respond to various bouts of employment legislation over the years and has been forced to develop adeptness in the design and use of administrative systems to cope with statutory and non-statutory matters. Some of this process was positive in a societal sense; for example the efforts against unfair discrimination based on sex or ethnic origin. Other legislation also had an effect on practice. For example, the Equal Pay Act (1970) (amended 1983) led to a growth in job evaluation in order to establish that people doing the same type of job would be uniformly rewarded. However, some would argue that personnel management represented a highly compartmentalised system, with thinking to match.

By contrast, as the commentary on HRM in the next section will show, HRM makes a determined effort to be a more integrative mechanism in bringing people issues into line with business issues, with a pronounced problem-seeking and problem-solving orientation, and a determination to build collaborative organisational systems where employee development features prominently. The role of top management in setting the agenda for change and development is very much in evidence in HRM. The typical concern here is offering good leadership and vision, with a commitment to creating and sustaining strong cultures that are compatible with evolving business needs. A strong culture is one in which there are clear organisational values and approaches that are held by all the members of the organisation.

Some personnel managers will no doubt see the growing influence of HRM as a threat, fearing that they may just become custodians of personnel systems. But the future for the personnel manager, referred to in the literature as the 'deviant innovator' (Legge, 1978), certainly does not look bleak. This type of personnel specialist, similar in outlook to the able human resource (HR) specialist, though unorthodox in some of his or her ideas, is a thinker, displays impressive professionalism and commands the respect of the line managers with whom he or she interacts (Torrington, 1989). These creative thinking skills are what is required if organisations are to be flexible and adaptive in the context of frequent and ongoing changes in the business environment.

In reality the type of HR specialist just described could be thin on the ground. Beer (1997) identified major obstacles in transforming the traditional administrative personnel function and moving to a fully fledged HRM system. In particular, he contends that one of the greatest obstacles in the transformation of the HR function is that most HR professionals do not possess the requisite analytical and interpersonal skills. In recent years others have called for an improved profile for the HR professional. There is the general view that HR must play a critical part in the success of the organisation in order to ensure its own viability (Ulrich, 1998); that HR professionals must be able to handle information technology proficiently and develop computer-based HR systems, as well as acting as agents of change by developing competence in managing and implementing change (Mohrman and Lawler, 1997); and that they need to become business partners of line managers so that the latter can acquire the competences needed to perform the HR tasks that are part of their jobs (Heneman et al., 1998). In addition, HR professionals will increasingly need to utilise 'outsourcers' to reduce costs in connection with running the HR system and it will be necessary to tap expertise not readily available in the organisation (Mohrman and Lawler, 1997). With reference to the 'knowledge age' and the needs of knowledge-intensive organisations, Despres and Hiltrop (1995) also call for HR professionals to develop high levels of competence in designing HR systems.

We have already characterised personnel management as a series of activities related to various aspects of an employee's relationship with the organisation. Human resource management is also concerned with these issues, but in addition stresses the primacy of business needs. Other points of departure are that HRM embraces individual flexibility and congruency between individual and organisational goals, whereas personnel management is concerned with systems applied to individuals and collectivism.

■ Distinctive features of HRM

Before looking at the distinctive features of HRM it seems appropriate to identify some of the factors that have led to the creation and popularity of HRM. Forces in the environment have influenced organisations to be responsive. This could be reflected in increased competitiveness, an emphasis on quality in staff and products/services, flexible modes of operation and a willingness to adapt to change. In such circumstances it would not be surprising to find organisation and management structures and systems responding to the new business conditions in the changed environment.

Examples of management and organisational responses would be increased decentralisation to facilitate a better reaction to market conditions, and greater autonomy and accountability for the efficient use of resources. Also, there could be a striving to inject flexibility into the roles employees play in teams (e.g. autonomous groups) and in getting people to adopt a wider range of skills (multi-skilling). A key point here is that these developments allow an increased speed of reaction which is vital if the organisation is to adapt to the changing environmental and market conditions that characterise the current situation. An example of this is the difference between IBM and Apple in their reactions to conditions in the personal computer market (Example 1.1).

EXAMPLE 1.1

Responding to the environment of the organisation

IBM had become a very large and successful company that dominated the large computer market. It was slow to meet the challenge of smaller organisations such as Apple that operated a team approach to creative thinking and product development aimed at the personal computer market. The teams at Apple were not subject to bureaucratic control and were flexible in the way they explored and exploited ideas. They were small, responded promptly to

events and displayed a high level of individual commitment and flexibility. \
petition of this nature was that IBM fell behind some competitors in the chan,
profitability was adversely affected.

IBM reacted by restructuring its organisation to decentralise and create busin
are closer to their markets and better equipped to react more quickly. To achieve
turing it had to cut labour costs, but such action brought the company into a collis
with its policies of lifetime employment. The company introduced a generous volunta
dancy scheme and helped ease the departure of employees with various forms of as   ..ce
(e.g. counselling and time off to get another job). At the same time the company did not want
to lose key staff, and to facilitate this process it produced manpower planning models to iso-
late the staff it wished to retain and encouraged them to stay. At all times it used a variety of
communication channels to put people in the picture as to why its strategy was necessary and
what it was proposing to do. In a six-year period IBM reduced its global workforce by 110,000.
It was clear that the high trust built up by the company over the years ensured the smooth
operation of its cost-cutting policy. It should be borne in mind that a large-scale redundancy
programme was alien to the IBM culture and its HR policies, and of course there were some
staff who were aggrieved by what was going on. In 1998 IBM set up a multi-country HR centre
to address global strategic issues as proof of its commitment to globalisation and HRM.

A major theme running through HRM is the acknowledgement that employees
are valued assets of the company, that there should be an interplay between a strategy for human resource and the main strategy for the business, that national culture is influential in shaping HR practices (Budhwar and Sparrow, 1997), that
corporate culture should be managed so as to make it compatible with the requirements of corporate strategy (Beer and Spector, 1985), and that seeking the commitment of employees to the organisation is of far greater value than forcing
compliance to the demands of the organisation. The value of commitment is that it
binds employees to the organisation. But one has to recognise that commitment to
an organisation is not something that springs out of thin air with little prodding.
Individuals have attitudes and attachments to their own values as well as values
connected with membership of the family, the trade union or professional body,
and these could clash with commitment to organisational values. Therefore changes
in attitudes and behaviours have to be contemplated.

One can view employee commitment as part of the 'psychological contract'. This
is an unwritten contract between management and employees whereby management offers challenging and meaningful tasks and employees reciprocate with loyalty and commitment (Tichy et al., 1982). In today's world there is reason to
believe that commitment on the part of employers is not what it used to be because
of rationalisation and pruning of costs with the inevitable discarding of the services
of people (Guest, 1998). One should add that commitment on its own, without
competence, may be an empty shell. There is further comment on commitment in
Chapter 5.

To elicit commitment, reference is often made to mutuality. This stands for HRM
policies that provide mutual goals, mutual influence, mutual respect, mutual

rewards and mutual responsibility (Walton, 1985). But mutuality may be a tender creature, as it is not uncommon to find a situation where the employee is short-changed by the employers. In a climate of mutuality the cause of commitment is advanced, with the consequence of both improved productivity and the development of people. A method used to foster mutuality is the 'development appraisal' discussed in Chapter 8. The aim of this approach is not to control the employee by judging past behaviour alone, but to offer encouragement by examining how the employee can contribute to organisational goals, and to specify the nature of the individual's development needs in order to achieve these goals.

Another feature of HRM that is often emphasised is the existence of the 'common interests' of management and employees in the profitability of the enterprise, which can lead to the tapping of a substantial reservoir of initiative and commitment within the work force. The objection raised to this view is that while it sounds good in principle, in practice there will be divergent interests. For example, the organisation could damage goodwill when the wages bill is cut following a cost-minimisation exercise.

The interaction between the HRM system and the corporate planning process is something that receives special attention. Proactive intervention on the part of the HRM system has been advocated here (Bird and Beecher, 1995). The guiding light comes from the strategic direction enumerated in the corporate plan. It is expected that the HRM policies and practices that develop as a result of identifying the human resource needs of corporate strategy can prove useful to managers (Gratton *et al.*, 1999; Guest, 1989; Legge, 1989). The following are examples of questions that might be asked with a view to establishing whether key facets of HRM are underpinning business strategy. Has the organisation the right calibre of employee to meet the demands of business strategy (Miles and Snow, 1984)? Are the techniques for selection, appraisal and promotion of people supportive of business strategy? Are managers as committed to human resource issues as they are to issues related to their primary specialism and function? Are the employment systems flexible enough to allow speedy adaption to change? (There is further discussion of strategic HRM in Chapter 2.) Other key considerations are as follows (Beer and Spector, 1985):

- People ought to be considered as social capital capable of development.
- Participation in decision making is of value, and people's choice of options or alternatives ought to be based on informed judgement.
- Power should be distributed throughout the organisation, rather than centralised, in order to foster trust and collaboration between people who are credited with a realistic sense of purpose.
- The interests of all parties with a stake in the organisation (e.g. employees, shareholders, suppliers and customers) should be harmonised.

The message coming across as a result of a serious consideration of the above issues is that properly conceived and applied HRM is beneficial in terms of individual and organisational performance. The performance theme has attracted the interest of a number of academics in recent years (e.g. Becker and Gerhart, 1996; Delery and Doty, 1996; Dyer and Reeves, 1995; Guest, 1997), and is expanded later in the section on the interaction between HRM and business strategy.

There are two models of HRM: one is called 'hard' and the other 'soft' (Storey, 1992), but this does not mean one is difficult and the other easy. (The models are used in the context of problem solving and decision making.) A hard problem is one that has a clear definition and an agreed method for working it out, and it will have a definite solution. For example, $2 + 2 = 4$ is a hard problem and solution. When one adopts a hard position there is a tendency to view people as a passive resource to be managed and controlled by adopting a rational, quantitative and calculative approach so as to ensure that the labour force is efficiently deployed in order to achieve a competitive advantage (Legge, 1995). Soft problems are less clearly defined, and there are alternative problem-solving methods and potential solutions. An example of a soft problem is how to motivate your subordinates or to suggest the best way to manage people.

In HRM the hard approach is concerned with costs and head counts, and tends to be associated with a unitarist view; that is that the goals of individuals and the organisation converge. (This is akin to the 'Michigan School' of HRM (Fombrun *et al.*, 1984), introduced in Chapter 2 in connection with strategy.) The following is an illustration of one aspect of the hard approach. In human resource planning the organisation will need to know its turnover rate. This gives the number of leavers in a given period as a proportion of the number of employees and is calculated by the following formula:

$$\frac{\text{Leavers in year}}{\text{Average no. staff in post during year}} \times 100$$

This statistical approach exemplifies the hard approach and naturally is less compatible with ideas derived from behavioural science that are ingrained in the soft approach. The soft approach will be concerned with the complexities behind this simple formula – for example, if there is a high turnover, is this because people are demotivated? If so, what can be done about this situation?

The soft model, which is similar to the 'Harvard School' of HRM (Beer *et al.*, 1984), includes the following features:

■ There is a view that individual needs and organisational needs will not always be the same (i.e. a pluralist view), but the organisation will endeavour to balance the different types of needs.
■ The uniqueness of the human resource must be recognised, and cannot be treated like any other resource. After all, people have feelings and emotions.
■ People are creative and responsible and can benefit from involvement in the participative management process.
■ A climate of consent features prominently.
■ There is a belief that commitment by employees to the organisation is nurtured when the organisation informs them of important matters, such as the mission

statement, the values it cherishes and trading prospects. In addition, it is considered wise to involve employees in decisions related to organisational and job design, and allow them to function in self-managing groups.

■ There is a recognition of the role of trade unions in representing the collective interests of employees, but at the same time it is important to respect the rights of management to liaise directly with individuals and groups within the organisation.

■ Objectives of an HRM system

The following list reflects the major items you would expect to find in a set of objectives relating to an HRM system (Armstrong, 1992):

1 The company's objectives are to be achieved through its most valued resource – its workforce.
2 In order to enhance both individual and organisational performance, people are expected to commit themselves to the success of the organisation.
3 A coherent set of personnel policies and practices geared towards effective organisational performance is a necessary prerequisite for the company to make the optimum use of resources.
4 An integration of HRM policies and business objectives should be sought.
5 HRM policies should support the corporate culture, where appropriate, or change the culture for the better where it is deemed inappropriate.
6 An organisational climate that is supportive of individual creativity and in which energetic endeavours should be created and nurtured. This will provide a fertile terrain for the promotion of teamwork, innovation and total quality management.
7 The creation of a flexible organisational system that is responsive and adaptive, and helps the company to meet exacting objectives in a competitive environment.
8 A determination to increase individuals' flexibility in terms of the hours that they work and the functions they carry out.
9 The provision of task and organisational conditions that are supportive of people trying to realise their potential at work.
10 The maintenance and enhancement of both the workforce and the product/service.

■ Implementation issues

Some time will now be given to an examination of selected issues associated with the implementation of a human resource management policy. Because of the selective nature of the examination, certain topics are excluded. For example, although some of the concepts and issues (e.g. commitment, mutuality) discussed earlier have features that relate to the implementation process, it is felt that enough has been said about them in this introductory chapter. The issues that will now be discussed are: *the role of management, the role of values and culture, the use of HRM/personnel management techniques and HRM–business strategy interaction.*

Management

There seems to be the view that it is important for management to display a strong interest in the continuing profitability of the organisation, with an appropriate vision for the future. The chief executive is said to be an important person when it comes to eliciting the commitment of employees. For example, it is he or she who sets the scene for change, takes responsibility for the change process, and by his or her actions reinforces the existing corporate culture, if appropriate, or reshapes it if not appropriate.

The responsibility for the implementation of HRM policy should rest with all managers who adapt it realistically to local circumstances. Although the personnel function may have been vocal in the setting of the guidelines contained in the HRM policy, it is the responsibility of all managers to implement the policy. The personnel function has the responsibility for monitoring and developing it. A stated policy of British Airways is that every manager should be a human resource manager. This emphasises the importance of people management in all managerial roles. An important feature is the management of human resources in a strategic way when managers are pursuing normal commercial and organisational objectives. It seems as if HRM is a frame of mind determining a behavioural perspective on everything a manager does, from policy making to normal everyday decision making (Armstrong, 1992). A valid question to ask at this stage is: to what extent do line managers embrace HRM? Apparently, there is evidence to suggest that HRM is not too popular among line managers because it does not excite them as an approach to managing people that offers instant solutions (Sparrow and Marchington, 1998).

Values and culture

The culture of an organisation is the collection of values, beliefs, attitudes and behaviours commonly held by the members. The culture is learnt and reinforced through interaction. Culture and its management are explicit features of HRM. Values expounded by top management have significance in gluing together policies and practices with respect to human resources. In this context, respect for people is crucial because without respect how can the necessary commitment be created? Commitment is a reciprocal process (Beer and Spector, 1985). To this would be added trust, and its operationalisation could be seen in the adoption of open management styles, particularly participative management.

Senior management is strategically placed to imprint its values on human resource policies and practices right across the spectrum of activities, ranging from selection practices to reward systems. In the process, considerable influence can be exerted in shaping corporate culture. Training is commonly used to shape cultures. When British Aerospace wanted to introduce autonomous teamworking at one of its production plants it undertook extensive training of all the workforce affected by the changes. The training was not just in the technical skills which would be needed but also in the culture and behaviour that needed to be developed. It necessitated a movement from a belief in hierarchical organisation to an acceptance of organisational roles where greater responsibility and involvement feature prominently.

Commentators who have examined HRM values from an industrial relations point of view refer to the existence of a unitarist perspective (Guest, 1989) in the sense that management and workers share a common interest, and that there is not much need for communication or negotiations between these two camps to be conducted by a representative system associated with the role of trade unions. This can be contrasted with a pluralist system – a voluntary system reinforced by collective bargaining at the local level – where the interests of the employers on one side and employees on the other, including many trade union members, are not seen as identical. The traditional industrial relations system in the United Kingdom and the rest of Europe is most likely to embrace a pluralist perspective, unlike the situation in the United States (although, as stated earlier, union power in the United Kingdom has waned somewhat in recent years). Perhaps a control strategy studded with adversarial industrial relations practice, where conflict of interests occupies a position high on the agenda, is akin to a pluralist perspective, while the unitarist perspective is more compatible with a commitment strategy that in its ideal form reflects mutual interests and respect in interpersonal and management–worker relations, where flexibility exists with respect to the nature of organisational roles, and participative management pervades the area of decision making.

A strong culture underpinning key aspects of organisational functioning (e.g. product quality, a climate of creativity, rapid response to environmental pressures) could be associated with an HRM system (du Gay, 1997; Legge, 1989). To some, this could be construed as a control system reinforced by internal propaganda and persuasion to exact commitment from people, irrespective of whether or not it serves their interests. The natural consequence would be to label HRM as a manipulative process. Supporters of HRM might retort by maintaining that HRM is manipulative, but only in a benign way. They might ask what is wrong with a system that offers realistic personal benefits and job security to those who commit themselves to the company's objectives and values, which encapsulate efficiency, innovation, quality products, customer service, etc. – the hallmarks of a potentially successful organisation. That is fine if the benefits, etc., are realistic and fairly dispensed!

Earlier in this chapter the virtue of flexibility was acknowledged as a key feature of an HRM system. But can the cause of flexibility be served by a potent, all-pervasive culture that requires employees to conform to specified values? Perhaps flexibility could be neutralised in such circumstances! Where a potent culture supports a prompt reaction to familiar events, because the prevailing ethos accommodates such an eventuality, it could be a different story when the organisation faces unfamiliar events (Legge, 1989, 1995). In such circumstances the organisation could benefit from flexibility to confront novelty and uncertainty but is denied it because of the strong culture. This was the situation in the IBM case described in Example 1.1. IBM had a strong culture and an established way of doing things. Apple was small, flexible and able to try out new ideas and innovate in a highly competitive market. Such a situation also raises the question of the tension between individualism, which flexibility supports, and collectivism, which is promoted by certain features of organisational life. Normally organisations try to tackle this tension, not always successfully, when on the one hand individual competence and achievement are recognised by a reward system, such as performance-related pay for individuals, and on the other the value of teamwork is advocated with reference to autonomous work groups. Further discussion of culture can be found in Chapter 5.

HRM/Personnel management techniques

The question to ask about techniques is: are they good enough to select the right calibre and mix of people, to develop them and to ensure that working relationships and incentives are of the required standard so that their services are retained in the implementation of a realistic corporate plan? Coherence in the application of personnel management techniques is something that is continually stressed. A set of techniques that do not fit neatly together is anathema to the serious HRM practitioner. What is not required is the application of isolated techniques that have more to do with practitioners displaying their technical prowess in their chosen field than tackling problems awaiting solution. The preferred action is the purposeful interrelationship and reinforcement of the battery of techniques in the service of the organisation's objectives (Hendry and Pettigrew, 1990). However, it must be acknowledged that it is no easy matter to develop a consistent and integrated set of personnel management techniques. It requires perseverance, managerial competence and a personnel function tuned into commercial thinking and sympathetic managerial attitudes and behaviour.

The internal coherence of HRM policies in practice could receive a fundamental challenge from the way the organisation is structured. (There is a discussion of organisation structure in Chapter 3.) In well-developed divisional structures authority can be delegated to business or divisional units with a high level of autonomy. The head office in such a structure might confine itself to overall financial control and setting broad guidelines, leaving the division to implement its own brand of personnel management. Some divisions may adopt a full-blooded HRM approach, but others may not because of an absence of firm guidance from top management at headquarters, in which case there is a lack of consistency in the use of HRM systems.

The role of reward systems is given pride of place in HRM. Reward systems are normally used as a change mechanism to create a more pronounced performance-oriented culture. Also, they can be used to encourage the development of new skills, and can be linked to performance appraisal schemes. A discussion of reward management appears in Chapter 9.

Another technique to consider is training and development because HRM embraces the notion of developing employees and enabling them to make the optimum use of their abilities for their own sake as well as in the interest of the organisation. Given the pivotal role of managers in the implementation of HRM policies, they should be targeted for training in this context. Training and development are considered in Chapter 10.

The Leading Edge Forum, a collaborative venture that includes the London Business School and organisations such as W. H. Smith, British Telecom and the National Health Service, suggested that personnel departments are failing to adopt a long-term view of their impact on business strategy because of organisational pressures to meet short-term goals, as well as their own natural predilection for short-termism. Personnel departments were, however, applauded by the Forum for developing close working relationships with line managers (Pemberton and Herriot, 1994). The practice of HRM is described in the case of Singapore Airlines (SIA) in Example 1.2, showing the integration of the different strands of HRM strategy and the link between corporate strategy and strategic HRM.

EXAMPLE 1.2

HRM at Singapore Airlines

Singapore Airlines (SIA) has experienced rapid growth over the past 22 years and currently employs approximately 23,000 people. The company has received high ratings in a number of market research surveys and has won a number of awards for quality service.

The business environment facing the company was challenging and volatile. Deregulation of the airline business in the United States and competition from carriers in the Asia-Pacific region, whose costs were lower, led to increased competition and fare reductions. SIA has differentiated the service it offered from that of immediate competitors by projecting an image of high quality in many spheres of its operations, ranging from global in-flight telecommunications at the disposal of passengers to the ticket reservations service.

The two major categories of operational costs are fuel and staffing. Efficiency through savings in fuel consumption is achieved by having a young fleet of aircraft. The average aircraft age in the SIA fleet is 5 years, whereas the industry average is 11 years. There is a determination to control costs through productivity increases and to maximise quality through linked human resource strategies of recruitment and selection, performance appraisal, career development and rewards. These strategies are considered to be equally important and mutually interdependent. The selection process is thorough and rigorous for all potential employees. Apart from the interview, there is a reliance on psychometric tests. The company places much emphasis on selecting applicants who are likely to fit the corporate culture, which is task oriented. SIA sees training and development as a very important HRM technique to equip employees to do their jobs better, as well as contributing to career development. Line managers play a key role in the orchestration of training related to job skills (e.g. computing skills). Training directed at the development of more general skills (e.g. management skills) is co-ordinated centrally. On average each employee receives 11 days of training each year.

There are two systems of performance appraisal: one for senior staff and the other for staff

generally. Assessment of an individual's potential and career planning is a distinguishing feature of the appraisal of senior staff. With regard to career development, there is a strong tendency to fill senior posts from the lower ranks. Therefore, those with good potential satisfy their
needs for advancement by progressing within the organisation, and many others are given the
opportunity to move horizontally to broaden their experience. In practice, most employees
have the chance to change jobs every four years. The staff turnover rate is rather low (between
3 and 6 per cent). Rewards consist of a package of benefits. Apart from pay, the benefits
include medical insurance, travel loans and share options. There are performance-related and
profit-related components built into overall pay. Total benefits are thought to be attractive, but
actual pay is not high by the standards of pay offered by other Singaporean employers.

(Chee, 1993)

In this case SIA faced an uncertain environment, and a clear message was to control costs. The company pursued a strategy aimed at market differentiation through
innovative approaches to the provision of quality services. To achieve these objectives the practice of HRM supported the drive for quality. This was evident in the
way the selection and appraisal processes were operated, and career development
plans and rewards were geared to fostering commitment and identification with the
organisation.

HRM–Business strategy interaction

Earlier there was reference to the importance of successfully integrating the HRM
strategy with the business strategy. It would be a positive advantage if the HRM
director or personnel director is involved in decision making with respect to normal
business issues at board level. In this way he or she is in a better position to orches-
trate the development of HRM strategies that flow from business strategy and to
put in place a coherent set of personnel strategies (Delery and Doty, 1996) related
to selection, training and development, rewards and employee relations.

HRM defines itself as strategic, with an emphasis on performance through
people. For example, Sisson (1990) sees the strategic aspect of HRM as being to
provide a workforce that is flexible, adaptable and cost effective, with one of the
means to this end being 'high commitment/involvement management'. Similarly,
Beer *et al.* (1985) link commitment with competence and cost effectiveness. Storey
(1995) encapsulates this view by saying that 'Human resource management is a distinctive approach to employee management which seeks to achieve competitive
advantage through the strategic deployment of a highly committed and capable
workforce using an integrated array of cultural, structural and personnel
techniques.'

The nature of the practices employed to achieve commitment and performance is
a matter of debate. Singh (1996) emphasises selection, performance management,
appraisal, collective bargaining and joint consultation as the basis for seeking to
achieve the desired HRM outcomes of strategic integration, commitment, quality,
flexibility and cost effectiveness. These HRM outcomes, it is hoped, will lead in

turn to overall performance outcomes of organisational effectiveness, congruence between objectives and performance, employees' well-being and harmonious employer–employee relations (Walton, 1985). Lawler (1986) presented the policies and outcomes as an exchange. The policies include participation, career flexibility, individual rights and performance-based rewards. They are designed to develop a highly skilled workforce who could operate using their discretion, and in return for so doing the employer would provide employment security, the potential for a satisfying career and good rewards.

As was stated above in connection with the difficulties of achieving coherency in the application of personnel management techniques, the successful integration of HRM strategy with business strategy may also be difficult to achieve for the following reasons: there may be a lack of determination to do so; the required managerial competence at all levels may not be available; the personnel or HR function may be too traditional in its outlook and operation; entrenched traditional managerial attitudes and behaviour may still prevail; and if traditional business strategy, with its primary emphasis on considerations such as marketing, finance, etc., receives the bulk of attention, human resource issues may be neglected.

However, more recent evidence (Becker and Huselid, 1999; Pfeffer and Veiga, 1999) has shown that there is a strong link between successful adoption of a 'bundle' of best HRM practices and organisational performance. Extensive empirical studies, particularly in the United States, but also in Europe, have substantiated the assertion of the HRM–business success link, and so development of best HRM practice is now seen as a crucial strategic consideration (Becker and Huselid, 1998). An example of this is provided by Vesuvius International, which is discussed in Example 1.3.

EXAMPLE 1.3

Strategic HRM in Vesuvius International

Vesuvius International is the ceramics division of the British-owned Cookson Group, which employs 8,500 people at 74 manufacturing sites in 21 countries (Arkin, 1999). It is located in Scotland and specialises in producing speciality ceramics for use in the steel industry. The Vesuvius plant in Scotland faced the prospect of closure by the parent organisation if it failed to perform to the highest possible standards at the lowest possible costs. In order to deal with this threat a change programme was introduced in 1994 with the aim of creating a culture in which all employees took responsibility for their performance. The HRM strategy had a series of elements:

- The traditional division of jobs and complicated wage structure were replaced with a single wage structure and flexibility of working, so that there were fewer barriers to job rotation.
- Self-managing teams were introduced.
- Training was enhanced so that all team members could carry out all the individual functions required of the team.
- Two-way communication was promoted through regular team meetings.

- A positive partnership was fostered with the trade union.
- The foremen were retrained to take on a new role as facilitators rather than supervisors.

The aim was to increase quality and performance through the management of the people. The outcomes were impressive. The Investors in People accreditation was awarded, and every employee had an individual development plan linking individual, team and organisational targets. Surveys of employee satisfaction produced an increase of the overall satisfaction score from 70 per cent in 1993 to 89 per cent in 1996. Customer complaints have decreased, and the market share enjoyed by Vesuvius has increased, while prices have been maintained. The introduction of self-managed teams has led to cost savings of £500,000 p.a. and turnover increased from £37 million in 1993 to £55 million in 1998. The company attributed this rise to the competitive edge it had gained through empowering its employees and giving them responsibility for quality.

(Arkin, 1999)

There is further discussion of the interaction of HRM strategy with corporate strategy in Chapter 2.

■ Conclusions

HRM can be seen as a development that originated from traditional personnel management and which has replaced it to some extent. Key managers and some professionals in the personnel function felt the old system was no longer functional and there was a need for a change in the status of personnel practitioners as well as for getting them more involved in business decisions. HRM also reflects changes in philosophies and practices with respect to the management of people in organisations.

In HRM there is a greater emphasis on strategic issues and on the way in which the human resource contributes to the achievement of corporate objectives. Amongst the natural concerns of the organisation are sensitivity to the needs of stakeholders, the development of human resources to meet future challenges, and ensuring that people's energies are sufficiently focused in order to add value to organisational inputs. HRM underlines the importance of flexibility and the ability to react and adapt quickly to changes in the organisation's environment. It is also concerned with quality management, where the requirements of the quality of both the operations of the organisation and the product or service trigger a need for high calibre staff to secure competitive advantage.

Although HRM unashamedly embraces a cost-effective business approach, it values employees for perfectly understandable reasons. Being concerned with the well-being of people is seen as a powerful way to motivate and inspire the workforce. HRM takes a systems approach to the analysis and management of organisations. It likes to see the different parts of the organisation functioning effectively and together moving cooperatively towards meeting the overall goals of the enterprise. This is facilitated through the management of systems such as human resource planning, recruitment and selection, appraisal, training and development, and rewards. These systems must be integrated and 'pull in the same direction'. In this way the HRM function assists the organisation to be more effective and profitable.

The rationale for the structure of the remainder of this book is that we will start with the strategic issues – those that determine the long-term future of the firm. Then three 'macro' issues that draw on a number of HRM practices and approaches will be explored. These are organisational structure, change and culture. Following the macro perspective, we will examine a series of specialist areas within HRM. First, employee resourcing – the processes of planning for and recruiting the workforce; secondly, employee development – focusing on performance, training and reward; thirdly, the topic of employee relations will be examined. We close by discussing how these areas of theory and practice might be integrated, and reflect on some of the theoretical and practical criticisms of HRM.

References

Arkin, A. (1999) 'Peak practice', *People Management*, 5, 57–59.

Armstrong, M. (1992) *Human Resource Management: Strategy and action*, London: Kogan Page.

Becker, B. and Gerhart, B. (1996) 'The impact of human resource management on organizational performance: Progress and prospects', *Academy of Management Journal*, 39, 779–801.

Becker, B.E. and Huselid, M.A. (1998) 'High performance work systems and firm performance: a synthesis of research and managerial implications', *Research in Personnel and Human Resources Management*, 16, 53–101.

Becker, B.E. and Huselid, M.A. (1999) 'Overview: strategic human resource management in five leading firms', *Human Resource Management*, 38, 287–301.

Beer, M. (1997) 'The transformation of the human resource function: resolving the tension between a traditional administrative and a new strategic role', *Human Resource Management*, 36, 49–56.

Beer, M. and Spector, B. (1984) 'Corporate transformations in human resource management', in Walton, R.E. and Lawrence, P.R. (eds), *Human Resource Management Trends and Challenges*, Boston, MA: Harvard Business School Press.

Beer, M., Spector, B., Lawrence, P., Mills, Q. and Walton, R. (1984) *Managing Human Assets*, New York: Free Press.

Bird, A. and Beecher, S. (1995) 'Links between business strategy and human resource management strategy in US-based Japanese subsidiaries: an empirical investigation', *Journal of International Business Studies*, First Quarter, 23–46.

Budhwar, P.S. and Sparrow, P.R. (1997) 'Evaluating levels of strategic integration and development of human resource management in India', *International Journal of Human Resource Management*, 8, 476–94.

Chee, L.S. (1993) 'Singapore Airlines: strategic human resource initiatives', in Torrington, D., *International Human Resource Management*, Hemel Hempstead: Prentice Hall.

Delery, J.E. and Doty, D.H. (1996) 'Modes of theorising in strategic human resource management: Traits of universalist, contingency, and configurational performance predictions', *Academy of Management Journal*, 39, 802–35.

Despres, C. and Hiltrop, J. (1995) 'Human resource management in the knowledge age: current practices and perspectives on the future', *Employee Relations*, 17, 9–23.

Du Gay, P. (1997) 'Organizing identity: making up people at work', in du Gay, P. (ed.), *Production of Culture/Culture of Production*, London: Sage.

Dyer, L. and Reeves, T. (1995) 'Human resource strategies and firm's performance: what do we know and where do we need to go?', *International Journal of Human Resource Management*, 6, 656–70.

Fombrun, C., Tichy, N.M. and Devanna, M.A. (1984) *Strategic Human Resource Management*, New York: John Wiley.

Gratton, L., Hope-Hailey, V., Stiles, P. and Truss, C. (1999) 'Linking individual performance to business strategy: the people process model', *Human Resource Management*, 38, 17–31.

Guest, D.E. (1989) 'Human resource management: its implications for industrial relations', in Storey, J. (ed.), *New Perspectives on Human Resource Management*, London: Routledge.

Guest, D.E. (1994) 'Organizational psychology and human resource management: towards a European approach', *European Work and Organizational Psychologist*, 4, 251–70.

Guest, D.E. (1997) 'Human resource management and performance: a review and research agenda', *International Journal of Human Resource Management*, 8, 263–76.

Guest, D.E. (1998) 'Beyond HRM: commitment and the contract culture', in Sparrow, P.R. and Marchington, M. (eds), *Human Resource Management: The new agenda*, London: FT/Pitman Publishing.

Hendry, C. and Pettigrew, A. (1990) 'Human resource management: an agenda for the 1990s', *International Journal of Human Resource Management*, June, 17–43.

Heneman, H., Metzler, C., Thomas, R., Donohue, T. and Frantzreb, R. (1998) 'Future challenges and opportunities for the HR profession', *HR Magazine*, 43, 68–75.

Hunt, J.W. (1984) 'The drifting focus of the personnel function', *Personnel Management*, February, 14–18.

Lawler, E.E. (1986) *High Involvement Management*, San Francisco: Jossey-Bass.

Legge, K. (1978) *Power, Innovation and Problem-solving in Personnel Management*, Maidenhead, Berks: McGraw-Hill.

Legge, K. (1989) 'Human resource management: a critical analysis', in Storey, J. (ed.), *New Perspectives in Human Resource Management*, London: Routledge.

Legge, K. (1995) *Human Resource Management: Rhetorics and reality*, London: Macmillan.

Miles, R.E. and Snow, C.C. (1984) 'Designing strategic human resource systems', *Organizational Dynamics*, 13, 36–52.

Mohrman, S.A. and Lawler, E.E. (1997) 'Transforming the human resource function', *Human Resource Management*, 36, 157–62.

Needle, D. (2000) *Business in Context: An introduction to business and its environment*, 3rd edn, London: Business Press–Thompson Learning.

Pemberton, C. and Herriot, P. (1994) 'Inhuman resources', *The Sunday Observer* (Business Section), 4 December, 8.

Pfeffer, J. and Veiga, J.F. (1999) 'Putting people first for organizational success', *Academy of Management Executive*, 13, 37–50.

Singh, R. (1996) 'Human resource management: a sceptical look', in Towers, B. (ed.), *The Handbook of Human Resource Management*, 2nd edn, Oxford: Blackwell.

Sissen, K. (1990) 'Introducing the *Human Resource Management Journal*', *Human Resource Management Journal*, 1, 7–24.

Sparrow, P.R. and Marchington, M. (1998) 'Introduction: is HRM in crisis?', in Sparrow, P.R. and Marchington, M. (eds), *Human Resource Management: The new agenda*, London: FT/Pitman Publishing.

Storey, J. (1992) *Developments in the Management of Human Resources*, Oxford: Blackwell.

Storey, J. (1995) *Human Resource Management: A critical text*, London: Routledge.

Tichy, N.M., Fombrun, C.J. and Devanna, M.A. (1982) 'Strategic human resource management', *Sloan Management Review*, Winter, 47–61.

Torrington, D. (1989) 'Human resource management and the personnel function', in Storey, J. (ed.), *New Perspectives on Human Resource Management*, London: Routledge.

Ulrich, D. (1998) 'The future calls for change', *Workforce*, 77, 87–91.

Walton, R.E. (1985) 'Towards a strategy of eliciting employee commitment based on policies of mutuality', in Walton, R.E. and Lawrence, P.R. (eds), *Human Resource Management Trends and Challenges*, Boston, MA: Harvard Business School Press.

Chapter 2

Corporate strategy and Strategic HRM

This chapter examines the nature of corporate strategy and strategic human resource management, and the interaction between the two. Different perspectives on strategy are outlined, as are the alternative models of strategic HRM. The developments in assessing the linkages between HRM and corporate performance are explored, and issues of implementation highlighted.

Once you have read this chapter, you should:

- be aware of the different schools of thought on strategy;
- understand the connections between strategy and HRM, and the implications of these connections for HRM;
- understand the connections between strategy and specific HRM topics, including involvement, empowerment, flexibility and training;
- be able to analyse critically the role and practice of HRM at the strategic level;
- understand the need for organisations to be adaptive to their environments, and recognise the importance of managing ongoing change in organisations.

■ Corporate strategy

Before entering into a discussion of strategic human resource management the concept of strategic planning in business should be examined. There are a number of generally agreed facets of strategy (Chaffee, 1985). First, strategy affects the overall direction and potential for success of the organisation; secondly, it is concerned with the fit between the environment and the organisation; thirdly, strategy deals with the non-routine activities and is seeking innovation and change in the organisation. In its simplest form it amounts to setting organisational objectives, and then deciding on a comprehensive course of action to achieve those objectives. Business strategy is concerned with the efficient use of resources, as well as ensuring that the mobilisation of those resources achieves the maximum impact. In this context a company could, for example, focus on the following:

- pursuing markets with high growth potential;
- improving channels of distribution;
- reducing the cost structure of the organisation through the application of modern technology.

At least five basic steps can be identified in the process of strategic planning (Walker, 1980):

1 *Definition of corporate philosophy and the preparation of a mission statement.* Nowadays it is fashionable to prepare a mission statement that deals with matters such as the values of the organisation and the reasons for its existence. A mission statement of a business organisation may make reference to the following points:
   (a) the customers/users to be served in a particular niche of the market; and
   (b) the actions necessary: first to serve the needs of customers, stressing, for example, the need for skilled and motivated employees, the pursuit of long-range profits and a commitment to meaningful and comprehensive employee development; secondly to serve the business, social and cultural needs of the communities in the area where the organisation is located; and thirdly to achieve levels of profitability equivalent to the leading companies in the organisation's industry.

2 *Scan environmental conditions.* This amounts to a systematic analysis of the technological, economic, environmental, political and social forces affecting the organisation's capability to pursue its mission. Questions that might be asked are as follows:
   (a) Are there advances in technology affecting the organisation's production technology, office technology or product design that should be seriously considered?
   (b) Are there changes in the economy likely to have an impact on the operation of the company?
   (c) Are there environmental requirements, such as reductions in waste or harmful emissions from processing, that need to be taken into account?
   (d) Are political circumstances conducive to the exploitation of market opportunities (e.g. market deregulation)?
   (e) Are demographic trends relevant with respect to future availability of labour?

3 *Evaluate the organisation's strengths and weaknesses.* Here the focus of attention is the internal resource base of the organisation, and a consideration of various facilitating or constraining influences. The following questions immediately spring to mind:
   (a) What distinctive strengths or advantages does the organisation possess?
   (b) What critical limitations (e.g. lack of managerial talent to undertake an ambitious project) does the organisation have?

4 *Develop objectives and goals.* Having assessed the internal and external factors affecting the capability of the organisation (as in 2 and 3 above), and given special consideration to the competitive advantage of the organisation in the marketplace on the basis of cost structure and product distinctiveness, there is now a movement towards determining specific goals and objectives aimed at fulfilling the mission of the organisation. Among the questions to pose at this stage are the following:

(a) What are the company's objectives for sales volume, profit and return on capital?

(b) How can performance be measured in areas such as customer service and employee development?

5 *Develop strategies*. Having gone through the four steps outlined above, the next step is to develop strategies. The types of question relevant at this stage are these:

(a) What specific changes of direction should the company take?

(b) What new or changed organisation structure and processes, technological development, financial arrangements and human resource policies should the company adopt?

This is the stage where the organisation begins to think strategically for human resources. It is acknowledged that unless decisions with respect to human resources are taken by top management we cannot expect a strategic plan for human resources (Purcell, 1992). When careful attention is paid at the top of the organisation to matters connected with acquiring, assigning, developing and rewarding employees, this is likely to set the scene for harmonising human resource planning with corporate strategic planning.

Prescriptive school

The approach outlined above is an example of what has been termed the 'prescriptive school' of strategy (Mintzberg *et al.*, 1998). The three areas emphasised in this school are design, planning and positioning. Design is concerned with the match between internal capabilities and external opportunities (Andrews, 1987), and this is echoed in the early approaches to strategic HRM (Fombrun *et al.*, 1984), which are considered in the next section. The purpose of planning is to predict and prepare for the future, for example through analysis of strengths, weaknesses, opportunities and threats (SWOT) (Ackoff, 1983). The third area of focus entails deciding on the position the organisation should adopt with regard to its suppliers, competitors and customers.

With regard to positioning, it has been argued that there are three main postures an organisation can take (Porter, 1980, 1985). First, 'cost leadership' entails the organisation seeking to produce output at low costs to enhance competitiveness, thereby making the market less attractive to competitors. Secondly, the organisation can seek to differentiate itself by producing a product or service that is unique and difficult to copy and offers higher profit margins. The third posture would identify the particular customer groups, products or markets (e.g. geographically defined) in which the organisation will specialise. In deciding on which position to adopt, organisations should consider the following (Porter, 1985):

- the threats of new entrants (how difficult it is for competitors to enter the market);
- the bargaining power of the firm's suppliers (the extent to which they are substitutable);

- the bargaining power of the firm's customers (for example, how easily customers could buy comparable goods or services from other suppliers);
- the intensity of rivalry amongst competing firms.

While the prescriptive school remains an important force in strategic management, it has been challenged (Mintzberg *et al.*, 1998). The challenge has come in part from theorists such as Lindblom (1969) and Quinn (1980), and also from practice found in successful organisations. For example, in the 1970s, adopting the tenets of the prescriptive school would have led to advising Honda, which at that time was mainly concerned with motorcycle manufacture, not to enter the car market that was already saturated with efficient competitors. Three decades later, however, Honda holds a significant position in the car market. Honda, and other such firms, did not always follow the advice of the prescriptive school, and yet they were still successful. This led to some doubts that the prescriptive school could accurately predict business outcomes in all cases.

From a theoretical perspective, it has been argued that strategic decisions are not fully rational, because managers suffer limitations with respect to the time they can spend on addressing issues, the information they can gather and the processes of decision making they employ (Lindblom, 1969). Typically, rather than carrying out a full analysis, organisations conduct a series of limited comparisons and adopt the most workable position that emerges within the restraints of the analysis. In addition, decision making and implementation are not entirely separate. So, while there might be a decision about the direction in which an organisation should go, in attempting to pursue their aims they may come across difficulties or new opportunities that lead them to alter their original decision. Although there may be an initial strategic plan, this is often altered and developed in response to external events and internal pressures as the implementation unfolds (Quinn, 1980); for example, employees may lack the skills that the organisation requires to develop in a particular direction, or customers may demand modifications to the nature of a service supplied. In this sense, strategy may be 'emergent' rather than fully planned in advance of taking any action. The strategy may be adapted to circumstances that arise at the operational stage.

Descriptive school

An alternative approach known as the 'descriptive school' has been proposed (Mintzberg *et al.*, 1998). This school has at least four important perspectives, namely vision, learning, power and culture.

Vision

The vision of the organisation, as discussed above, provides an image rather than a fully worked-out plan. It is typically concerned with change and providing a general direction (Drucker, 1970), and allows a certain degree of freedom within which employees can decide how to act. This can be particularly important in entrepreneurial organisations (Greiner, 1998) and for employees who deal directly with customers or users. Some organisations adopt a top-down approach to vision, with the direction coming from the top team or the entrepreneur. Others have developed visions by involving staff, for example through workshops in which they discuss the purpose of the organisation and their role within it; this has the characteristics of a bottom-up approach. In one example, Northern Foods set up consultation forums in each of its strategic business units in the UK, Ireland and the Netherlands. Employees are consulted on how the forums should operate, and the communication on strategic issues is becoming upwards as well as top down (Walsh, 2000).

Learning

The focus on learning has been highlighted by Prahalad and Hamel (1990), who argue that it is only through a collective learning process that an organisation will be able to compete effectively with others through speed of modifying standard processes or services in order to meet the demands of customers. Part of a strategic approach to enhancing learning is through deliberate planning, for example in enabling appropriate training and development in the organisation. However, a view from the other side of the coin indicates that employees must be able to move in a direction dictated by their own learning, rather than being required to adhere strictly to a formal plan. According to Senge (1990), the process is one of changing employees from being simply the implementers of plans to being problem solvers who will move the organisation forward. This implies a degree of bottom-up change and decision making. There is further discussion of the learning organisation in Chapter 10.

Power

The focus on power is justified when we acknowledge that organisations are co-alitions of individuals who have different beliefs, interests and information and may have different perceptions of reality (Bolman and Deal, 1997). Groups will naturally seek to influence decisions on organisational direction and resource allocation towards outcomes favourable to themselves. Eden and Ackermann (1998) see strategy making as intrinsically linked to organisational politics, which is a manifestation of the use of power. They argue that in formulating strategy one cannot merely reach rational decisions and expect them to be accepted. Rather, one needs to be aware of the interests and power of the different groups that may be affected by a decision and to take this into account. Sometimes it is possible to do this by incorporating representatives of powerful groups into the decision-making process so that there will be less resistance to the decision. On other occasions it may be necessary to negotiate the implementation of a decision with such groups. On some occasions manipulation or coercive pressure are used.

Culture

Strategy can be seen as a process of social interaction in which decision making is strongly influenced by culture (Johnson 1992). For example, some cultures are risk aversive and others support risk taking, therefore it is easy to conclude that the nature of decision making is dependent upon the prevailing culture. The strategy is likely to reflect the dominant values and taken-for-granted assumptions in the organisation. Culture is discussed in detail in Chapter 5.

The focus on vision, learning, power and culture has implications for strategic HRM. Of course, it is possible for an organisational culture to be authoritarian, and for the power orientation of leaders to be coercive. In such cases employees would normally be remote from the decision-making arena. However, in the way that the descriptive school is envisaged by Mintzberg, the following would be expected. First, a much greater degree of involvement and upward communication is envisaged. Secondly, attention must be paid to the employees' perceptions of their role in the organisation and the development of their skills and knowledge in order to become problem solvers. Thirdly, it is the incremental process of change that is seen as crucial rather than one-off grand strategic plans. The argument is not that rational analysis is unnecessary, or that top teams do not have responsibility for vision, direction and the welfare of the organisation. Rather the position is that, though all these are necessary, they are not sufficient in today's business environments, which require adaptability, responsiveness to customers and the commitment of employees.

It should be noted that the descriptive school could be subjected to criticism. Clearly, not all organisations and all environments lend themselves to thorough communication and employee involvement; for example, the required speed of decision making may prevent an extensive consultation process. In addition, there are examples of successful organisations that do not extend employee learning beyond the basics of operational training.

■ Strategic HRM

Nearly two decades ago a school of thought in HRM, known as the Michigan School (Fombrun *et al.*, 1984), arrived on the scene. This model of HRM placed much emphasis on the importance of the strategic approach, which involves relating corporate strategy to strategic HRM in areas such as structure (discussed in the next chapter), culture (discussed in Chapter 5), and employee resourcing and development (discussed in Chapters 6–10).

The model of HRM briefly outlined above can be viewed as the traditional model, also known as the matching model, which will be discussed shortly. Alternative models, known as the resource-based model and the processual view of human resource strategies, will be discussed later.

Matching model

The matching model focuses on strategic integration (Beer *et al.*, 1984). Integration in this sense means bringing about a good fit between the human resource policy and the company's policy with regard to strategic direction. For example, if the strategy of the company contains a focus on low cost with a high volume of output, then there will be a need to deploy the workforce in a way that minimises costs. The reduction in labour costs could be achieved by replacing skilled labour with greater application of technology. Conversely, if there is a strategy of producing high quality products to meet different customers' requirements, with the aim of charging a high price for the end product, then the implications in terms of a human resource management strategy would be to attract and use employees with high levels of skill who are able to command higher wages. One would expect this type of employee to be well able to address the needs of discriminating and demanding customers.

Another type of integration can be seen when the organisation uses various human resource management techniques in such a way that they complement each other. Consider for a moment the way the processes of recruitment and selection, and training and development, are handled, depending on whether one is looking at the situation in terms of high or low cost referred to earlier. A strategy advocating a low cost approach would only require rather basic approaches to recruitment and selection and less elaborate training and development. On the other hand, where high quality is emphasised (high cost) the approach would require greater effort to be devoted to recruitment and selection; for example, more time would be spent in two-way communication at selection interviews and, if necessary, at assessment centres, as well as putting more resources into well-targeted training.

Two other types of integration are highlighted by Bratton and Gold (1999). One is where line managers internalise human resource management as an important aspect of their approach to management. This is evident when they are actively involved in the implementation of the HRM strategy. The other type of integration can be seen in a situation where the workers identify with the objectives and values of the organisation and commit themselves when they perceive their interests and the organisational interests coalescing.

Guest (1987) endorses the matching model when he expresses support for the desirability of seeking a fit between corporate strategy and HRM strategy. Back in the late 1980s he argued that the typical corporate strategy focused on the quantitative aspects of organisational functions (e.g. finance, production, marketing), and generally had less to say about 'soft' issues such as values, culture and power. A failure to take such issues into account could be reflected in not being able to integrate corporate strategy and strategic HRM. As a result there could be significant problems in the formulation and implementation of corporate strategy. Also in such circumstances there could be a lesser likelihood of the development of mutual interests between employers and employees, and this raises the possibility of resistance to desired changes within the organisation.

Criticism of the matching model

The matching model has been subjected to criticism in at least four areas:

1 The matching model bears the features of a rational model of decision making. In other words it assumes that organisational decision makers can plan and act rationally and that those plans will be the ones that are executed in the organisation. But as Mintzberg *et al.* (1998) maintain there are other views of strategy, which are a better representation of the reality of organisational life. Also, the problematic nature of strategic decision making is recognised by Johnson (1987), who raises questions about constraining influences such as political processes in organisations, lack of consistency in management decision making and various manifestations of negotiating and bargaining ploys used by actors in the system. The existence of these constraints makes it very difficult to accept the idea of a rational 'linear' model of organisational decision making.

2 The matching model bears witness to a number of contradictions. It has been argued that in some circumstances there is a certain incongruity between corporate strategy and strategic HRM (Legge, 1995). This could arise when, for example, the corporate plan dictates cost minimisation through a reduction in labour costs following a pruning exercise such as downsizing. Putting such a plan into action could involve making staff redundant, and this could run counter to an HRM perspective that puts the accent on commitment to employees. As a result, the outcome could be lower satisfaction or dissatisfaction and poor organisational performance (Patterson *et al.*, 1997). Even though there may be a certain logic in pursuing the financial strategy stated above in the matching model, the outcome could be less than satisfactory or undesirable in human terms. There lies the contradiction!

3 It has been argued that the act of matching corporate strategy with strategic human resource management in a pronounced way may not be a good idea after all (Boxall, 1996). In seeking to gain competitive advantage through a strategic fit between corporate strategy and HRM strategy, the organisation could end up with structures and processes more inflexible than that of its competitors. The reality of the marketplace today indicates that flexibility is a central requirement for effective organisational performance, and flexibility based on organisational learning (see Chapter 10) is a valuable attribute (Boxall, 1996).

4 The matching model assumes a degree of freedom on the part of organisations, for example to reduce the number of employees as required. However, in reality, the freedom to change terms and conditions of employment are limited by employment law and custom and practice, not to mention the possibilities of industrial action if proposed changes are strongly objected to by the workforce.

Resource-based model

A noticeable feature of the resource-based model is its primary concern with what is going on within the organisational boundaries in order to be well placed to respond to opportunities in the external environment (Barney, 1991). This approach seeks to understand the distinctive competences of the workforce – which competitors would experience difficulty in imitating – through a process of analysing capabilities, knowledge and skills at the disposal of the organisation. The reason for doing so is to develop a sustainable competitive advantage for the organisation. Kamoche (1996) is of the view that it is important to align the distinctive competences of the organisation with the human resource competences if success in the marketplace is to be achieved.

Maintaining alignment of individual competences is particularly an issue where individuals have competences that are no longer relevant to the distinctive abilities of the organisation. In such circumstances there may be a need to retrain the individual, possibly redeploy them, or ultimately make them redundant where there is no other viable alternative. There may be situations where developments in a market mean that development in organisational competences is required. Under these circumstances it is necessary either to buy in new skills or identify training needs for employees. Maintaining alignment of competences is a dynamic process and has an impact on training and development (which is discussed in greater detail in Chapter 10).

Criticisms of the resource-based model

While it may be an attractive theory, there are relatively few overt examples in practice. It does not acknowledge sufficiently the potential for conflicts of interest between employees and their employer – the outcome of which can be that employees may have the necessary competences but they may choose not to employ them fully or effectively in pursuit of the organisation's ends (Bratton and Gold, 1999).

Processual approach

This approach has characteristics in common with the descriptive theories of strategy (Mintzberg *et al.*, 1998) discussed above. It conceives strategy as the outcome of both planned and unplanned activities. In its application to HRM this means that strategy is not simply concerned with setting policy in areas such as organisational structure, recruitment, training and so on. It is also concerned with the impact on the 'realised' strategy (i.e. strategy as it occurs in practice) as a result of the actions of managers and employees. For example, the way managers undertake recruitment at the local level can alter, in real terms, the 'espoused' or formal policy (Watson, 1999). This influence can be positive, for example when best practice is used as a benchmark for other managers to follow, but it can be negative, for example where an equal opportunities policy is subverted by personal bias on the part of a manager.

The processual approach often emphasises employee involvement, and in this regard it can have a strategic impact. For example, in recruitment and selection traditional approaches seek to match candidates to a pre-formed 'template' of the ideal employee designed by the organisation, but this approach (Newell and Rice, 1999) envisages selection as a two-way negotiation in which potential employees can have an input to the design of the job! This is carried out through informal and open discussion in which the candidates and the organisation get to know each other, and to understand what the possibilities and limitations of a match are. Subsequently, both sides have a choice in whether or not they take the process further to formalise application and selection. An advantage of this approach is that it increases the information both the individual and the organisation have of each other, but it can impose considerable costs on the organisation as employers will have to spend time with potential candidates, the majority of whom (in normal circumstances) will not end up as employees. Hence it is likely that such an approach cannot be used for all jobs, or in all organisations.

The processual approach can be criticised in a number of ways. Because it operates at the 'doing' level rather than the 'visioning' level it can be seen as 'downstream' of the 'real' strategy (Purcell, 1992) and as reactive rather than proactive (Legge, 1995). If a high degree of freedom is extended to managers then there is the potential for inconsistency and unfairness in the application of policy. For example, variable standards might be used by different managers in making selection decisions, and this would result in unfair treatment of job candidates. Hence there is a need for a framework of policy to ensure sufficient consistency.

■ HRM and organisational performance

High performance through people

Walton (1985) argued persuasively that the HRM model was composed of policies that promoted mutual goals, influence, respect, rewards and responsibility between employees and the organisation. The theory was that the resultant reciprocal positive attitude would lead to enhanced commitment on the part of employees, and that this would in turn lead to increased economic performance of the organisation. The practices Walton endorsed included the following:

- teamworking and undertaking the 'whole task' (rather than fragmentation of task and specialisation of skill);
- agreeing performance objectives that stretch people;
- a flat organisational structure with reduced supervision, coordination and communication through mutual influence, involvement and shared goals;
- group-based reward systems;
- a priority on training; and
- a joint problem-solving approach to employee relations.

He argued that such an approach can be applied in almost all organisational situations, and that it will result in enhanced commitment and performance.

There has been some debate over the detailed contents of the 'bundle' of best HR practice, with a variety of terms being employed, for example 'high commitment management' (HCM) (e.g. Wood, 1995) and 'high performance work practices' (Huselid, 1995). However, Delaney and Huselid (1996) offer a useful analysis that emphasises the logical flow of, and connection between the various practices. Their conceptualisation is as follows:

1 The *recruitment and selection* of employees can be improved in order to maximise the skills and knowledge that employees bring to the organisation.
2 The quality and contribution of current employees can be improved through *training and development*.
3 In order to encourage employees to deploy their skills and knowledge with enthusiasm in the direction of organisational objectives it is necessary to have an effective *reward system*. In addition, they argue that motivation also depends on employees believing that they will be treated fairly, that the *performance management* system will acknowledge their efforts, and that they will not be subject to arbitrary treatment by management.
4 The way that work is arranged has an impact on effectiveness.

The evidence of research marshalled by Delaney and Huselid (1996) indicates the benefits of organising work so that employees are directly *involved* in determining what the priorities are, and how work is carried out – for example, through *team-based working* and upwards *communication*. Pfeffer (1994, 1998) and Pfeffer and Veiga (1999) summarise the broad agreement amongst researchers on the make-up of the effective bundle of HR practices along the following lines:

■ employment security;
■ selective hiring;
■ teamworking and decentralised decision making;
■ comparatively high pay contingent on organisational performance;
■ extensive training;
■ reduced status distinctions;
■ sharing information.

Employment security

Although providing employment security may appear to be an anachronism in competitive conditions where a company may need to reduce costs by reducing the headcount, Pfeffer (1998) argues that it is important for a number of reasons. First, employees are unlikely to agree to increase their flexibility and cooperation in becoming more efficient and productive if there is not some assurance that they will not lose their jobs as a result. Secondly, if the first reaction to financial difficulties is to lay off staff, the effect is to put important strategic assets into the labour market for the organisation's competitors to employ. Thirdly, there are significant costs to reducing headcount, including redundancy payments. Fourthly, providing job security can be an important discipline for managers as it encourages considerable caution and care in recruitment and selection. The chief executive officer (CEO) of Southwest Airlines, quoted by Pfeffer and Veiga (1999), argues that the last approach has helped the company to maintain a smaller and more competitive workforce than their competitors over the long term. Additionally, the competitors have incurred the costs of a fluctuating headcount, both up and down.

Selective hiring

Pfeffer and Veiga (1999) highlight a number of steps in effective recruitment and selection. They advocate generating a large pool of applicants. Some would see dealing with large numbers as an unnecessary expense. However, the most successful companies in the research sample saw it as a necessary step. The selection process should focus on the most critical skills and attributes not only for the job but also for the future of the organisation. These include initiative, judgement, adaptability and the ability to learn, as well as more job-specific skills. Finally, selection, which is discussed in Chapter 7, should focus primarily on attributes that are difficult to change through training. For some organisations this includes finding a good fit between candidates and the organisational culture.

Teamworking and decentralised organisational design

Teamworking is advocated primarily because it replaces hierarchical control with peer-based control of work. This can lead to greater responsibility being taken by people at lower levels in the hierarchy and enables the reduction of supervisory layers of management. While this can result in cost saving it should be noted that there may be a tension between this approach and the approach based on the previous hierarchical model. This tension may be resolved in some companies by having an initial phase of change that reduces layers with a likely reduction in staffing levels or headcount reduction, but thereafter continuous improvement and change is pursued through the existing workforce. Pfeffer and Veiga cite many examples, but a telling one is that of Vancom Zuid-Limburg, the Dutch transport and bus organisation which has achieved rapid growth. It is able to win contracts because of its very low overhead costs based on a manager–driver ratio of 1:40 rather than the industry norm of 1:8. The self-managed teams of 20 drivers run their own lines and have budgeting responsibilities, and each driver has responsibilities for high levels of customer care and proactive problem solving.

Comparatively high pay contingent on organisational performance

Part of the argument for comparatively high pay is that it can refocus employees from worrying and complaining about their pay to improving performance. If the pay deal is favourable for employees, organisations have found that they can expect and achieve greater effort, particularly in the area of customer service, from their employees. Pfeffer and Veiga espouse share ownership, where employees hold shares in the company, and as a result they are more likely to act and think like owners. Other forms of reward that seek to achieve this outcome include profit sharing, gain sharing and various forms of team or individual incentives. These are issues which are discussed in Chapter 9.

Extensive training

Training is essential to the implementation of high performance work systems, as is argued in Chapter 10, because such systems rely on front-line staff being able to exercise initiative, solve problems, manage quality and initiate changes. Although it would be desirable to be able to evaluate clearly the contribution of training to performance in a cost/benefit analysis, this is difficult, if not impossible, as the isolation and identification of effects specifically due to training are problematic.

Reduced status distinctions

The basic premise of high performance work systems is that performance is derived from making use of the skills, ideas and efforts of all the people in the organisation. Strong status differentials are likely to obstruct such processes, and successful organisations have often sought to reduce such barriers both symbolically, for example through language, dress and physical space, and substantively through a reduction in the number of wage bands and distinctions.

Sharing information

Sharing information is vital to the establishment of trust in the workplace, and it is also crucial if employees are to understand the organisational objectives. In addition, if management are to understand and learn from employees on issues such as problem identification, improvements in systems and other suggestions, the sharing of information needs to be multi-directional rather than top down. Highly successful organisations seek to share information whether it is good or bad. If the organisation only propagates 'good news' employees are likely to think they are only getting part of the story, and will be less able to contribute solutions to real problems.

Evidence of the link between HRM and performance

Becker and Huselid (1999), surveying research findings, state that high performance HRM systems have now become a source of competitive advantage. In a major study in the United States covering more than 2,400 firms, Becker and Huselid (1998) found that considerable differences in organisational performance were attributable to the implementation of the bundle of high performance HRM practices. They devised an index including 24 items of HRM systems, and measured the correlation of this against various indicators of organisational performance. The general finding was that good HRM practice was positively correlated with increased performance. In particular, organisations placed 1 standard deviation higher than the norm on the HRM system index showed differences in performance measures as follows:

market value	+24%
accounting profits	+25%
gross rate of return on assets	+25%
sales per employee	+4.8%
staff turnover	−7.6%

In a study of five-year survival rates of newly quoted companies Wellbourne and Andrews (1996) found a correlation between company survival and HRM practices. When factors such as size, industry and profits were statistically controlled the survival rates varied by 20 per cent with a 1 standard deviation shift in the index of the value the firm placed on human resources. The difference in probability of survival between those organisations in line with best practice on employee rewards and those most distant from best practice was 42 per cent.

This research has been supported in the United Kingdom, where Patterson *et al.* (1997) found strong linkages between the acquisition and development of skilled people, job design stressing autonomy, flexible problem solving and positive employee attitudes and performance. They found that HRM practices correlated with 18–19 per cent variation in productivity and profitability, with good HR practice leading to increases, and lack of good HR practice leading to decreases in performance. Similarly, a strong link has been found between employee commitment and financial success of the business in the German banking sector (Benkhoff, 1997).

In these studies the relationship between an employee, their peer group and their supervisor was regarded as an important factor. For example, whether or not the bank managers were seen as committed had an impact on the commitment of others. This evidence would support the views of Guest (1998) that the 'psychological contract' is crucial in influencing effort and performance. As stated on page 11, the psychological contract concerns the expectations, rights and obligations the employee believes to exist between them and the organisation. Where there is a mutual understanding and perception of fairness performance is likely to be enhanced. For West and Patterson (1998) such factors are highly significant, because they contribute to the climate of satisfaction in a workplace. Their findings indicate that where there is a good climate then positively reinforcing cycles of attitude and behaviour occur with peer group relations and employee–supervisor relations supporting performance. Conversely, where there are problems, for example the psychological contract is not honoured due to poor communications or lack of involvement, then negatively reinforcing cycles can be expected. In such situations peer groups may expend considerable effort on discussing or worrying about the social situation and on ensuring their own future safety, rather than working together in order to perform. In a related argument Delaney and Huselid (1996) maintain that performance is higher in organisations in which there is a perception of job security. In other words expectations of a lower probability of future layoffs are associated with higher effort.

Criticisms and problems

While the benefits of high performance HRM systems have been stressed it is worth considering potential costs as well as benefits. Bratton and Gold (1999) note that there may be increased costs associated with training and investment in employees, and management will also lose some of its decision-making prerogative through devolved systems of management. From an employee's perspective there may be benefits of increased access to information, participation in decision making and sharing in shaping the work processes. However, there will also be the potential for increased stress associated with increased responsibility, and in many cases there is the loss of lifetime employment guarantees.

Another line of critique has questioned the extent to which the linkages have really been proved. Lam and Schaubroeck (1998) found such linkages applied only in a minority of their sample. They found that HRM policies, rather than being rational tools aimed at increasing organisational performance, were actually political tools, aimed at persuading top management to increase expenditure on HRM. Lahteenmaki *et al.* (1998) concluded from their study of Finnish organisations that there was 'hardly any link between the state of HRM and company performance'. They argue further that the linkages may be too complicated to be revealed other than in longitudinal in-depth studies.

Other studies have shown that HRM does have an impact on performance, but not uniquely so. For example, Wood and de Menezes (1998) argue from their analysis of the major UK survey of organisations – the Workplace Industrial Relations Survey – that high commitment practices do have some performance effects, but that alternative approaches (e.g. control oriented) can also be effective. They found that the high commitment management (HCM) workplaces had greater growth and financial performance than the two medium categories, but that the results for low HCM workplaces were not significantly different from those with high HCM. In other words good results seem to be achievable either through significant adoption of HCM or through a control-oriented approach (at least in the short term).

Finally, an example of a high technology company that is achieving high performance through people management is discussed in Example 2.1.

EXAMPLE 2.1

Strategic HRM at Quantum

Quantum was formed in 1980 and is a leading supplier of computer hard disks to manufacturers and end users. Its sales are in excess of $5.8 billion and it employs 6,800 people. It is based in California in Silicon Valley. The market it operates in has thin profit margins, and this pressure has led to consolidation, with a reduction from 55 firms operating in the area in the 1980s to 6 main firms now. Against that background, Quantum has grown and is seen as a leading example.

The culture is one of openness and flexibility. There are relatively few rules and little bureaucracy. For example, there is no formal flexitime scheduling, people come and go and manage their own time. This approach is complemented by being very task and action focused. The structure of the organisation is flat and team based, with teams changing in composition as new projects and tasks emerge.

The general goals of the organisation are stated as follows:

- Increase the value of the company.
- Increase market share.
- Build a company with an extraordinary work environment. This includes the following:

  achieving long-term business success; ensuring Quantum employees feel valued; ensuring a sense of pride in the company; instilling a sense of camaraderie; ensuring that each employee has the opportunity to reach their highest potential personally and professionally; generating a sense of excitement and fun.

There are nine associated 'key behaviours' that underlie performance management:

1 maintaining a results focus;
2 making decisions with the best interests of the company in mind;
3 working together collaboratively;
4 finding problems and fixing them;
5 setting high standards;
6 being open, honest and direct;
7 staying flexible and adaptable;
8 taking initiative for one's own development;
9 resolving issues in an objective manner.

Selection is conducted on the basis of a series of behaviourally based, structured interview tools (explained on page 154). The same tools are used to make decisions about team membership and promotion. Successful applicants are able to provide evidence of a willingness and ability to work in teams. The belief in the organisation is that if you get through the selection process you are one of the best.

Quantum forms teams around products and they will typically be located together for the length of a project or task, and will then move on to other work. Most teams are cross-functional, and there is a transfer of skills and knowledge between team members. Team formation is given priority, with roles and responsibilities being established during the first few days of working on a project. The aim is to ensure that customers get the new products they want on time and in the right quantities. This is referred to as 'time to volume' and the focus is on rapid product development without sacrificing quality.

Performance is managed through a five-step process – performance planning, coaching, reviewing performance, developing, and rewarding. Half of the bonus and merit pay is based on results and the other half is based on adherence to the desired company values. Team performance appraisals are based on input from managers on overall performance (50 per cent), peer feedback (25 per cent) and team leader feedback (25 per cent). Critical feedback is given, but employees are trained to make sure that it is constructive so that others can learn from it rather than feeling devastated by it. The bonus plan is transparent, and there is also a stock purchase plan available to all employees. This can generate as much as 60 per cent additional income on an annual basis.

Quantum believes that its approach to HRM has been fundamental to its success. While not everyone would be happy in such an environment, for Quantum it is important to attract and retain high quality employees who could easily find work with its competitors. The data that it has at its disposal is that staff are attracted to Quantum because the work is interesting and the environment created within the workplace reinforces the organisation's commitment to the way people are managed. The common culture of task focus and openness has resulted in teams being able to start functioning very quickly after forming, and this has been vital in getting products to market in competitive time spans at competitive quality. This has only been possible because much decision making is devolved to the teams, who are aware of the values of the organisation and are committed to them. The success of the approach is evident from Quantum's profitability and growth in a business environment where many firms have been taken over.

(Barber *et al.*, 1999)

■ Conclusions

Organisational environments are turbulent and change is always present. This places a great responsibility on the shoulders of strategic HRM to be proactive in developing the organisation's flexibility and creativity to capitalise on opportunities and to sustain competitive advantage. Interfacing corporate strategy with strategic HRM has significance in highlighting the importance of the human resource in contributing to organisational success. Therefore, having in place sound structures and processes, which allow people to pull together with commitment in a climate of mutual benefit, is a laudable aim. The links between individual and group performance and the achievements of the firm are now one of the central concerns of HRM.

The contribution of the management of people to the strategic aims of the organisation has been increasingly accepted over the last decade. Pursuing best practice in HRM can no longer be seen as a luxury, rather it is a necessity for new firms that want to survive and grow, and for established firms, particularly where high performance is required. There is some evidence that best practice models developed and tested in the United States are applicable in other areas of the world, particularly Europe. The basis of the high performance HRM models is the engendering of commitment in the workforce. This is achieved through involvement and mutuality, and the fostering of positive psychological contracts. However, questions can still be raised over how far such practices need to be adapted for implementation in different countries.

The role of managers in achieving a positive working environment and in establishing trust and open communications that underpin the psychological contract is central. It is not sufficient to have good HRM policies, and there will inevitably be difficulties in implementation. It is those companies which can develop their own solutions to such difficulties that will reap the benefits in achieving competitive advantage.

References

Ackoff, R.L. (1983) 'Beyond prediction and preparation', *Journal of Management Studies*, 20, 59–69.

Andrews, K.R. (1987) *The Concept of Corporate Strategy*, 3rd edn, Holmwood, IL: Irwin.

Barber, D., Huselid, M.A. and Becker, B.E. (1999) 'Strategic human resource management at Quantum', *Human Resource Management*, 38, 321–8.

Barney, J.B. (1991) 'Firm resources and sustained competitive advantage', *Journal of Management*, 17, 99–120

Becker, B.E. and Huselid, M.A. (1998) 'High performance work systems and firm performance:

A synthesis of research and managerial implications', *Research in Personnel and Human Resource Management*, 16, 53–101.

Becker, B.E. and Huselid, M.A. (1999) 'Overview: strategic human resource management in five leading firms', *Human Resource Management*, 38, 287–301.

Beer, N., Spector, B. and Lawrence, P.R. (1984) *Managing Human Assets*, New York: Free Press.

Benkhoff, B. (1997) 'Ignoring commitment is costly: new approaches establish the missing link between commitment and performance', *Human Relations*, 50, 701–27.

Bolman, L.G. and Deal, T. (1997) Reframing Organizations: Artistry, choice and leadership, 2nd edn, San Francisco: Jossey-Bass.

Boxall, P.F. (1996) 'The strategic HRM debate and the resource-based view of the firm', *Human Resource Management Journal*, 6, 59–75.

Bratton, J. and Gold, J. (1999) *Human Resource Management: Theory and practice*, 2nd edn, London: Macmillan.

Chaffee, E.E. (1985) 'Three models of strategy', *Academy of Management Review*, 10, 89–98.

Delaney, J.T. and Huselid, M.A. (1996) 'The impact of human resource management practices on perceptions of organizational performance', *Academy of Management Journal*, 39, 949–70.

Drucker, P.F. (1970) 'Entrepreneurship in business enterprise', *Journal of Business Policy*, 1, 3–12.

Eden, C. and Ackermann, F. (1998) *Making Strategy: The journey of strategic management*, London: Sage.

Fombrun, C., Tichy, N.M. and Devanna, M.A. (1984) *Strategic Human Resource Management*, New York: John Wiley.

Griener, L.E. (1998) 'Revolution as organizations grow', *Harvard Business Review*, May–June, 55–68.

Guest, D.E. (1987) 'Human resource management and industrial relations', *Journal of Management Studies*, 24, 503–21.

Guest, D.E. (1998) 'Beyond HRM: commitment and the contract culture', in Sparrow, P.R. and Marchington, M. (eds), *Human Resource Management: The new agenda*, London: Financial Times/Pitman.

Huselid, M.A. (1995) 'The impact of human resource management practices on turnover, productivity and corporate financial performance', *Academy of Management Journal*, 38, 635–72.

Johnson, G. (1992) 'Managing strategic change: strategy, culture and action', *Long Range Planning*, 25, 28–36.

Kamoche, K. (1996) 'Strategic human resource management within resource: capability view of the firm', *Journal of Management Studies*, 33, 213–33.

Lahteenmaki, S., Storey, J. and Vanhala, S. (1998) 'HRM and company performance: the use of measurement and the influence of economic cycles', *Human Resource Management Journal*, 8, 51–65.

Lam, S.S.K. and Schaubroeck, J. (1998) 'Integrating HR planning and organisational strategy', *Human Resource Management Journal*, 8, 5–19.

Legge, K. (1995) *Human Resource Management: Rhetorics and realities*, Basingstoke: Macmillan.

Lindblom, C. (1969) 'The science of muddling through', in Etzioni, A. (ed.), *Readings in Modern Organizations*, Englewood Cliffs, NJ: Prentice Hall.

Mintzberg, H., Ahlstrand, B. and Lampel, J. (1998) *Strategy Safari*, London: Prentice Hall.

Mowday, R.T., Porter, L.W. and Steers, R.M. (1982) *Employee–Organization Linkages*, New York: Academic Press.

Newell, S. and Rice, C. (1999) 'Assessment, selection and evaluation: pitfalls and problems', in Leopold, J., Harris, L. and Watson, T. (eds), *Strategic Human Resourcing: Principles, perspectives and practices*, London: Financial Times/Pitman.

Patterson, M., West, M., Lawthorn, R. and Nickell, S. (1997) *The Impact of People Management Practice on Business Performance*, London: Institute of Personnel and Development.

Pfeffer, J. (1994) *Competitive Advantage Through People*, Boston: Harvard Business School Press.

Pfeffer, J. (1998) *The Human Equation*, Boston: Harvard Business School Press.

Pfeffer, J. and Veiga, J.F. (1999) 'Putting people first for organizational success', *Academy of Management Executive*, 13, 37–50.

Porter, M.E. (1980) *Competitive Strategy: Techniques for analysing industries and competitors*, New York: Free Press.

Porter, M.E. (1985) *Competitive Advantage*, New York: Free Press.

Prahalad, C.K. and Hamel, G. (1990) 'The core competence of the corporation', *Harvard Business Review, 68, 79–91*

Purcell, J. (1992) 'The impact of corporate strategy on human resource management', in Salaman, G. (ed.), *Human Resource Strategies*, London: Sage.

Quinn, J.B. (1980) *Strategies for Change: Logical incrementalism*, Holmwood, IL: Irwin.

Senge, P. (1990) *The Fifth Discipline: The art and practice of the learning organization*, New York: Random House.

Walker, J.W. (1980) *Human Resource Planning*, New York: McGraw-Hill.

Walsh, J. (2000) 'Timing of Northern Foods' forum plan is coincidental', *People Management*, 6, 11.

Walton, R.E. (1985) 'From control to commitment in the workplace', *Harvard Business Review*, March/April, 77–84.

Watson, T. (1999) 'Human resourcing strategies: choice, chance and circumstance', in Leopold, J., Harris, L. and Watson, T. (eds), *Strategic Human Resourcing: Principals, perspectives and practices*, London: Financial Times/Pitman.

Wellbourne, T. and Andrews, A. (1996) 'Predicting performance of initial public offering firms: should HRM be in the equation?', *Academy of Management Journal*, 39, 891–919.

West, M. and Patterson, M. (1998) 'Profitable personnel', *People Management*, January, 28–31.

Wood, S. (1995) 'Can we speak of high commitment management on the shop floor?', *Journal of Management Studies*, 32, 215–47.

Wood, S. and de Menezes, L. (1998) 'High commitment management in the UK: evidence from the Workplace Industrial Relations Survey and Employers' Manpower and Skills Practices Survey, *Human Relations*, 51, 485–516.

Chapter 3

Organisation structure

Organisation structure is the infrastructure within which strategy is conceived and implemented. Structure can be seen as both the outcome of strategic decisions and a factor that influences strategy. Since HRM has an overwhelming interest in providing people with space and opportunity to utilise their abilities and skills to an optimum level, it pays particular attention to the way organisations and jobs are designed. In this chapter there will be an examination of theories and perspectives on organisation structure and design.

Once you have read this chapter, you should:

- be aware of alternative organisational structures, from highly regulated bureaucracies to looser networks;
- be able to reflect on the implementation of such structural designs in reality;
- understand the links between structure and other topics such as power, strategy and technology;
- be aware of the developments in structure, such as virtual and networked organisation, and some of the implications of these developments for management.

■ Classical bureaucracy

A concept of bureaucracy was developed by Weber (1947), a German sociologist. In its ideal form it was known as the legal–rational framework. This type of organisation is rational because it is specifically designed to perform certain functions, and it is legal because its operation is based on a set of rules and procedures for every position or job within it. Weber distinguished the legal–rational model from other models he had in mind, namely charismatic (leader driven) and traditional (influenced by custom and practice). The features of classical bureaucracy (legal–rational) are as follows:

- Clear definition of duties and responsibilities.
- Maximum specialisation.
- Vertical pattern of authority.
- Obedience to authority.
- Post-holders rely on expertise derived from technical knowledge.
- Maximum use of rules.

- Impersonality in administration.
- Remuneration is determined by rank and job responsibility.
- Promotion is determined by seniority or achievement as judged by superiors.
- Clear separation between ownership of the organisation and its control.

It is now apparent that bureaucratic organisation in its ideal form is heavily dependent on rules, procedures, well-defined duties, relationships and responsibilities. It is allegedly a rational, impersonal system of organisation, free from the whims and preferences of individuals who occupy roles within it.

Scholars who studied the blueprint of classical bureaucracy felt it had a number of shortcomings. For example, it was felt that the pressure placed on the individual to act methodically and cautiously, with strict adherence to rules and procedures, could create a situation where the preoccupation with the means to the end becomes far more important than the end itself. Also, there could be a ritualistic attachment to rules and procedures, with undue insistence on authority and status rights, which could have the effect of not advancing the interests of the organisation. In such a setting resistance to change could become a real issue. Finally, even if classical bureaucracy could be justified as functional, this is likely to happen only in conditions where tasks are simple and repetitive and are performed consistently over time. But where tasks become more complex and subject to change the conditions likely to be compatible with classical bureaucracy cease to exist.

■ Classical principles

The classical principles of organisation developed by theorists and practitioners many years ago still have some relevance when the structure of organisation is studied. In this section the classical principles will be acknowledged in their original form, but at the same time interpretations will be forthcoming in order to put them in a present-day context. The following classical principles are examined:

1 *Division of labour*. Economic benefits can result from the breaking down of tasks and allowing the employee to specialise in a narrow area. Specialisation makes it possible to apply technology to tasks, with potential for productivity gains, and facilitates ease of training. Although certain segments of the working population may be happy with routine jobs and repetitive tasks that flow from the division of labour and specialisation, others may have a preference for enriched jobs and can be more productive in such conditions. In the final analysis the negative effects of repetitive work have to be offset against the alleged economic benefits.

2 *Unity of command*. Subordinates report to only one superior from whom they obtain advice and guidance. Having access to only one official source of direction and assistance might be construed as restrictive, and could be a negative influence when coupled with the division of labour.

3 *Authority and responsibility*. Rights vested in the position occupied by the

employee are referred to as authority. The obligations placed on employees to perform are referred to as responsibility. Authority and responsibility are co-equal. Authority can be delegated within the organisational 'chain of command', but responsibility probably cannot, though this requires clarification. It is accepted that ultimate responsibility cannot be delegated, but there can be delegation of operational responsibility.

Authority can be referred to as line authority, that is the type of authority, which each manager possesses, and it flows through the chain of command. This should not be confused with the authority of the staff specialist (e.g. HRM specialist), whose role is to help line managers in executing their responsibilities.

The concept of authority had greater validity in the days when superiors were knowledgeable about all the jobs within their area of influence. Today over-reliance on authority could be dysfunctional if subordinates are well trained and superiors are not fully conversant with everything within their section. Also, it would be unwise to place reliance on authority to the exclusion of other factors, such as the persuasive skills and power base of the manager.

What is becoming more apparent in the age of HRM is the strengthening of the role of the line manager with the accent on its 'enabling' aspects in a climate of teamwork, participative management and availability of various specialisms, either internal or external to the organisation. Currently it is customary to refer to authority as part of a larger concept of power.

4 *Span of control.* The span of control refers to the number of subordinates reporting to one boss. It was originally suggested that the number should not be more than six. The span of control has an inverse relationship to the number of layers in the hierarchy (e.g. the narrower the span of control, the more layers there are in the hierarchy). When a conscious decision is made to widen the span of control it could be associated with a growth in the number of better qualified and more experienced employees. The flatter organisational structure that is created by the wider span of control is popular today.

The following factors are likely to influence the size of the span of control:
(a) job complexity (the more complex the job the greater the justification for a narrower span of control so that the supervisor has the capacity to assist subordinates);
(b) physical proximity of subordinates (a wider span of control is more manageable if subordinates are geographically closer to their boss);
(c) extent of formalisation and standardisation (it is easier to justify a wider span of control when the jobs of subordinates are governed by well-specified rules and procedures) – these will be examined again later;
(d) preferred managerial style (some managers feel comfortable and confident supervising a large number of people, and because of the wide span of control they resort to delegation of authority in a pronounced way; such a course of action could cramp the style of other managers who prefer a narrower span of control).

5 *Departmentalisation.* In effect this is a form of division of labour, whereby

certain cells of specialised activity are created that require overall coordination. This seems to be as far as classical theory goes in addressing the question of departmentalisation. If we take departmentalisation a stage further, the following groupings emerge:

(a) functional – there is a division of the organisation by function, such as finance, manufacturing, HRM and so on;

(b) product or service – there is a division by product, e.g. ICI's Paints Division, with associated functions such as production, marketing, etc., while a division by service is evident when a firm of chartered accountants is organised in accordance with service to clients, e.g. auditing, taxation, insolvency;

(c) customer – the nature of the customer base determines the structure used; e.g., in a particular company there could be a wholesale division as well as a retail division;

(d) process – in a manufacturing company production processes can be differentiated by section or department, e.g. a manager with responsibility for a particular production process would report to the manager of the plant;

(e) geographic – a part of the organisation, e.g. sales/marketing function, is fragmented on a regional basis.

The types of departmentalisation described can be combined to create a mixed structure. For example, one might find functional departmentalisation having within its boundaries process departmentalisation and a sales function organised by region. Within the region there could be departmentalisation by customer. (An important feature of HRM is giving pride of place to the customer.)

6 *Centralisation and Decentralisation.* Centralisation is referred to when a small number of people at the top of the organisation exercise significant authority and decision making. By contrast, decentralisation occurs when a lot of autonomy is felt by those working further down the organisation. Both have advantages and disadvantages, but it could be said that centralisation is complementary to a bureaucratic system of organisation, whilst decentralisation is more compatible with an organic system, which will be discussed latter.

■ Matrix organisation

This system of organisation integrates two groupings. For example, a project department (e.g. a Ford Vehicle Centre as shown in Example 3.1) is superimposed on the division by function described above. In practice this means that a particular employee belongs to a function (e.g. marketing) but also works on a project. Effectively the employee reports to two supervisors – one is the manager of the project and the other is the boss within the function. Matrix organisation can be a complex system and if it is to be effective it has to be operated with a certain amount of skill.

Among the problems to anticipate are role conflict among subordinates because of the dual system of reporting and power struggles about the use of authority in particular situations (Daft, 1998; Larson and Gobeli, 1987). Reflecting on the proposed global matrix structure for the Ford Motor Company, which is examined in Example 3.1, Lorenz (1994a) had this to say about matrices in general:

> the matrix organisation used by multinational companies in the 1960s and 1970s, especially by US companies, was, with a few notable exceptions, plagued by internal conflict, inefficiency, expense and delay, as divisional, geographic management debated and fought with each other. In many cases disputes were only resolved laboriously by powerful coordinators acting as matrix police.

You will notice in Example 3.1 that HRM techniques are mobilised to sustain the new form of organisation. The concept of the team (the project team) seems to be an important feature of matrix organisation. As we shall see later, in the spirit of HRM teams are created to cut across departmental boundaries to promote flexibility and innovation, with the needs of the consumer high on the agenda.

EXAMPLE 3.1

Global matrix at Ford

In early 1995 the Ford Motor Company merged its North American and European operations into a single global structure. A justification for the change is that the old 'command and control' culture promoted the power of departmental barons at the expense of innovation, prompt decision making and cross-functional teamwork. The company created five transatlantic 'Vehicle Centres', four located in the United States and one in Europe. Each centre has responsibility for designing, developing and launching a particular size and type of vehicle for the North American and European markets. In addition, the centres have responsibility for the cash flow and profitability of each product throughout its life. Ford's Asia-Pacific and Latin American operations remain separately organised for the time being.

The new structure consists of a matrix organisation, and as a consequence a large number of managers will have more than one boss. They will report to a manager from the 'Vehicle Centre' to which they are attached, but they will also report to a boss in their 'functional' department (e.g. manufacturing or marketing). Within the company there seems to be a lot of enthusiasm for the new matrix structure. It is suggested that it will promote flexibility, considerable informality, allow for improvisation as situations change, and is vital to global teamwork and organisational effectiveness.

Ford hopes to prevent the matrix organisation from being overcome by the problems stated earlier that have traditionally bedevilled this type of structure by proposing to take the following action:

- Take extra precautions to make sure that objectives are agreed precisely between the Vehicle Centres and the functional parts of the organisation.
- State clearly the roles and responsibilities of individuals in both arms of the matrix.
- Only appoint people to senior executive positions who have proved they are capable of working with colleagues on a collaborative basis.
- Train all those involved in developing cooperative modes of working implicit in operating a matrix system, in order to avoid the need for policing mechanisms.

■ Adjust the performance appraisal and reward management techniques in order to harmonise with the new system of organisation.
■ Introduce much more intensive and open communication than the organisation has been accustomed to.

Apart from the adoption of a matrix organisation, the transformation of the company, called 'Ford 2000', also includes measures such as delayering and business process re-engineering.

(Lorenz, 1994a)

■ Organisational configuration

The configuration or mode of arrangement of the organisation will be examined in the first instance from the angle of the five traditional features listed below. These features indicate the level of complexity within the organisation. Subsequently, there will be a brief acknowledgement of the six types of configuration identified by Mintzberg (1983).

1 *Vertical differentiation.* This is concerned with the number of levels or layers within the hierarchy through which control and coordination are exercised. Because information has to flow through a number of layers the potential for problems connected with the dissemination of information and the monitoring of operations is ever present.
2 *Horizontal differentiation.* This is akin to the division of labour and specialisation, whereby specialist activities are arranged in a lateral form and staffed by employees with specific orientations. For example, employees in the finance function could interpret commercial reality differently from those in the HRM function. This could give rise to communication difficulties that ultimately could affect modes of cooperation.
3 *Spatial differentiation.* If the organisation is fragmented in a geographical sense we refer to spatial differentiation.
4 *Formalisation.* The key characteristics of formalisation are job descriptions and well-defined procedures. When formalisation is rated highly employees have little opportunity to exercise discretion and use initiative in the job. The reverse is the case in conditions where formalisation receives a low rating. The position of a job within the hierarchy can determine the degree of formalisation. For example, we expect employees occupying positions in the higher echelons of the organisation to exercise more discretion in making decisions than employees located further down the organisation. The particular type of function might also be a factor influencing the degree of formalisation. For example, the production function may lend itself to a higher degree of formalisation than the marketing function. Finally, where formalisation is well established the terrain is fertile for standardisation to take root.
5 *Centralisation/decentralisation.* These were briefly mentioned earlier in connection with the principles of organisation; they occupy the opposite positions on

a continuum and reflect the location of decision making within the organisation. Factors likely to influence centralisation or decentralisation are as follows:

(a) The organisation is geographically dispersed (spatial differentiation) and this signals the need for decentralisation. However, if an organisation has sophisticated and comprehensive management information systems aided by information technology it would appear that there is a strong drive to go in the opposite direction and resort to centralisation.

(b) Where spatial differentiation is not an issue because the organisation is located on one site, decentralisation could be used for reasons connected with stated corporate policy or managerial preferences. A justification to adopt the opposite position and use centralisation could be an attachment to the notion of bureaucratic control or the existence of autocratic tendencies within the organisation.

Mintzberg (1983) identified six types of structure, each appropriate to the dominant needs of the organisation as follows:

1 *Simple structure.* This structure could apply to a recently created organisation where authority is centralised in the hands of the owner-manager or small group. The trappings of a bureaucratic organisation are minimal.

2 *Machine bureaucracy.* This structure has a number of the features of bureaucratic organisation referred to earlier and assumes the characteristics of the mechanistic system of organisation discussed later in the chapter. The organisation is large and long established and operates in a relatively stable environment.

3 *Professional bureaucracy.* This structure allows the exercise of professional expertise where autonomy and the absence of rigid status differentials prevail (e.g. the traditional hospital or college). There is a tendency not to place too much emphasis on bureaucratic practices.

4 *Divisional form.* This structure is appropriate for a large, well-established company with a number of different markets. The company could be organised by, for example, product or service referred to earlier, but there is a tendency to adopt machine bureaucracy.

5 *Adhocracy.* This structure could apply to a total organisation or a division within it. The organisation, which is designed to promote innovation, operates in a complex and dynamic environment. Employees with expertise, who tend to be attached to project groups with a market orientation, exercise a lot of power and influence. The attachment to the project group conjures up images of the matrix organisation examined earlier.

6 *Missionary.* This could be considered to be lacking in features of formal organisation; for example, division of labour and specialisation is not very pronounced. People are bound together by their shared values.

■ Formal and informal organisations

A distinction can be made between the formal and the informal organisation. Many of the features of organisation discussed earlier (e.g. span of control and hierarchy), coupled with the stated objectives of the organisation and the roles assigned to individuals, reflect the formal organisation. By contrast, the informal organisation is flexible with a fluid structure. In the informal organisation the degree of informality stems from the interaction of role occupants or employees and it can be harnessed to complement the aims of the formal organisation. For example, it could promote a sense of identification with the organisation, a sense of belonging and motivation. However, the informal organisation has the potential to undermine the effectiveness of the formal organisation.

■ Contingency perspectives

Over the years researchers have studied the form organisations take, and a general conclusion is that structure is determined by circumstances. The topics that will be examined in this section are: technology and structure, size and structure, strategy and structure, and power/control and structure.

Technology and structure

Burns and Stalker (1961) found that mechanistic (bureaucratic) structures had greater relevance when stability prevailed in markets and in the application of technology to operations within organisations. As you would expect, mechanistic structures are characterised by a pronounced vertical and horizontal differentiation, high formalisation, centralisation and limited upward communication.

Where conditions were unstable, that is markets were unpredictable and there was uncertainty with regard to the application of technology, organic structures were considered more appropriate. In the organic structure conditions opposite to those applicable to the mechanistic structure applied, as follows:

■ There was a lesser degree of horizontal differentiation, with greater collaboration between staff at different hierarchical levels and across functions.
■ There was a lesser degree of formalisation, and a greater degree of decentralisation.
■ Responsibilities were less clear-cut, with people interpreting and responding to events in the light of circumstances.
■ Communication was more likely to take the form of networks in which the giving of information and the exercise of control originated not from the apex of the organisation but from cells of the organisation where the greatest knowledge and expertise resided. Also, lateral communication between employees of different rank, resembling consultation more than command, was considered

more important than communication that flowed through formal channels organised on a hierarchical basis.

■ Community of interest – in current parlance 'shared vision and values' – was a more important influence on behaviour than contractual obligations.

■ Teams consisting of different specialists (e.g. design, engineering and production) operate better if they are located near each other, and the best way of managing innovative projects is through multi-functional teams led by the same manager from the idea generation stage through to completion.

The book containing the research evidence of Burns and Stalker has been reissued by the publisher 33 years after it was first released, and was praised by a respected journalist in the management field for the quality of its ideas, which he says had a profound impact on contemporary theory and practice (Lorenz, 1994b).

Another researcher interested in factors that determine organisation structures was Woodward (1965). She studied the influence exerted by technology. The term 'technology' can be broadly defined to embrace the activities associated with the transformation of various inputs into the output of the organisation. In a factory the production system is a technology. In Woodward's research companies were categorised by the types of production systems used; for example unit or small batch production, large batch or mass production, and process production.

Certain features of organisation – e.g. hierarchical level or vertical differentiation, span of control, formalisation and standardisation – moved in sympathy with the technology adopted. Successful companies in a particular category of production system tended to have similar organisation characteristics, and generally speaking organic structures were better suited to unit, small batch and process production companies, while mechanistic structures were most effective when aligned with mass production companies.

In later research Woodward and her colleagues studied the ways in which companies used control systems and how these influenced the design of organisations. Control was viewed from the standpoint of personal control (supervision) or impersonal control (administrative monitoring and control systems), and where it was located (i.e. localised or centrally focused).

Another way of looking at the influence of technology was proposed by Thompson (1967). The categories he used to classify all types of organisation are long-linked, mediating and intensive technologies:

1 *Long-linked* technology. Tasks or operations that flow in a particular sequence and are interdependent are referred to as long-linked. This type of production system is found on the assembly line in, for example, a car manufacturing plant, where one operation has to be completed before another starts.

2 *Mediating technology.* This type of technology includes the tasks and operations involved in linking clients using the services of two different functions of the organisation. For example, clients of a bank are treated as depositors in one function and as borrowers in another. The depositors are on the input side of the

organisation and the borrowers are on the output side. In this example the success of the bank depends on satisfying the needs of disparate groups, and it performs a mediating function in linking units or groups, which are otherwise independent.

3 *Intensive technology.* When tasks or operations are geared to tackling problems in conditions where the exact response or solution is unpredictable we enter the domain of intensive technologies. For example, a firm of management consultants has a number of specialists on its payroll. The firm is invited by a client to conduct an investigation into problems or difficulties experienced by the client. These could be messy problems requiring in the first instance a judgement on their nature and subsequently a decision on which consultant(s), e.g. from marketing, HRM or finance, to allocate to the assignment.

There is no direct link between the system of technology used and structural characteristics of organisation in Thompson's research. What he maintains is that the organisation arranges its structural characteristics in such a way as to protect the technology from the uncertainty surrounding it. To confront uncertainty, either in the sources of supply of raw materials or in the distribution network, a manufacturing company may adjust structure in a particular way. In these circumstances the technology used could be instrumental in shaping the structure of the organisation. There is also recognition of a connection between technology and structure when it is stated that mechanistic structures are more likely to be associated with companies using long-linked and mediating technologies, while the intensive technology could fit the organic structure.

A different interpretation of technology was advanced by Perrow (1970). He emphasised technology based on knowledge rather than production technology. The emphasis is on task variability and problem analysis. The interactions of these variables are shown in Table 3.1. Where there are a multitude of ways of performing tasks, i.e. there are many exceptions to the general rule, and the approach to the analysis of problems is ill-defined because of the complexity of the situation, the job is likely to be of a non-routine nature, as shown in Table 3.1 (Cell 4). By contrast, where there are few exceptions to the general rule on job performance, and the approach to problem analysis is well defined, the job is likely to be basic and

Table 3.1 Dimensions of technology based on knowledge

	Task variability	
Problem analysis	Few exceptions	Many exceptions
Well defined	Routine	Engineering
	1	2
	3	4
Ill-defined	Craft	Non-routine

clear-cut, i.e. routine as shown in Table 3.1 (Cell 1). An example of a routine job is that of a car park attendant who issues tickets in return for a stated sum of money. The job of a management consultant of some stature or a senior social worker who enjoys autonomy and a lot of scope to interpret situations in conducting assignments could be described as non-routine – Table 3.1 (Cell 4). The construction of a unique building uses engineering technology, and although it can be undertaken in a rational and systematic way there could be a large number of exceptions – Table 3.1 (Cell 2). Craft technology could be used by an electrical technician who could face a relatively difficult problem governed by few exceptions – Table 3.1 (Cell 3).

Activities falling into the upper part of the figure lend themselves to systematic analysis, while those in the lower part of the figure call for more discretion and intuition. The former are likely to be more compatible with mechanistic structures, and the latter with organic structures.

New technology

In recent years the impact of new technology on organisations has been analysed. Employees at the lower levels of the organisation have access to a greater quantity of information owing to the availability of information and communication technology (ICT) systems, and the justification for highly centralised structures is difficult to defend. As a result, the cause of decentralisation is advanced. However, one has to acknowledge that the growth of ICT systems could lead to the pendulum swinging in the direction of centralisation. This could arise because senior managers have access to information previously non-existent or difficult to obtain. Because senior managers are better informed about events throughout the organisation there is not the same need as in the past for a number of layers in the hierarchy. As a result, the organisation ends up with a simplified and compressed structure having removed layers of middle management that are no longer required (Huber, 1990; Reed, 1989).

In today's world new technology has created the intranet which is the fastest form of corporate networking, making it possible for the establishment of the 'virtual organisation'. In this type of organisation key activities are performed by the nerve centre of the organisation (i.e. headquarters), with other functions outsourced to separate companies or individuals connected electronically to the central office. Such an organisational system allows an expansion of operations and reduced costs.

In the ICT age it is also a live issue to support production technology by production systems based on 'just in time' (JIT). Japanese car firms were the first to develop JIT and a number of UK companies followed in their footsteps. JIT is a manufacturing and stock system whereby component parts arrive just in time to be used in the manufacturing process, thereby obviating the necessity to hold stock at the levels required under the old system. There are cost advantages arising from reducing buffer stocks in the warehouse, but because of the reduced stock levels employees are expected to be flexible and to solve problems as they arise, otherwise the next stage in the process will be adversely affected (Tailby and Turnbull, 1987). In effect JIT can promote employee flexibility and multi-skilling, but its introduction could necessitate a radical change in the culture of a factory, expressed as a display of serious interest in it by top management and a firm commitment of resources. Finally, there is a view that JIT is more applicable to manufacturing processes of a repetitive nature rather than to processes that are non-repetitive, e.g. production geared to the customers' specification (Collins *et al.*, 1997).

It has been argued that virtual workplaces will be the mode in the future. Such arrangements are facilitated by ICT and can include teleworking, dispersed networks of people working from their homes via ICT links to the central organisation, and 'hoteling', which involves employees combining working at home with meetings in convenient hotels. The virtual working trend has increased, and by 2000 it was estimated that 40 million people were teleworking on a global basis (Cascio, 2000). There are strong business reasons for such developments. For example, studies for IBM have shown savings on facilities costs of 40–60 per cent per site where virtual working has been implemented, and this has been combined with productivity gains of between 15 and 40 per cent. Similarly, Hewlett-Packard has doubled revenue per sales person and Andersen Consulting found that its consultants spent 25 per cent more face-to-face time with customers following moves to virtual working (Cascio, 2000). There are costs as well as benefits, for example the cost of setting up and maintaining ICT equipment in the homes of workers, limitations in effective communication and changes in the nature of team working. From an HRM perspective, one of the cost savings has been assumed to be a reduction of the need for supervisory management; however, Cascio argues that in practice managing people remotely actually calls for increased effectiveness of managers. Managers need to shift from a focus on time – overseeing the employees as they operate throughout the working day, to a focus on outputs or results. This requires sophisticated performance management systems in which specific and challenging goals are agreed with workers, measured and reviewed. In addition, the management style needs to be one of facilitating and encouraging performance, rather than trying to control it.

An example of a retailer seeking to implement an ICT-focused approach and some of the impacts of this for HRM and organisational structure are introduced in Example 3.2.

EXAMPLE 3.2

An ICT-focused approach at Sainsbury's

Sainsbury's, one of the UK's leading supermarkets, established its e-commerce outlet in 1999 with the aim of encouraging home shopping. At the time it was difficult to recruit staff with e-commerce expertise as Sainsbury's was regarded as a less attractive option than the many dotcom companies that were setting up at the time. In order to attract staff a reward system that paid bonuses for team, individual and company performance was established.

In 2000 Sainsbury's developed its Web presence with the 'Taste for Life' site, which was designed to provide ideas and inspiration about food and drink. Sainsbury's also formed a joint venture with Carlton Communications to create 'the Taste Network', which links Web sites and cable TV so that as TV technology becomes more interactive viewers will be able to watch a chef preparing a meal, and use their remote control to click on the site that provides the recipe and allows them to order the ingredients from the home shopping service. Half of the Sainsbury's Online team have now joined the Taste Network.

The impact on structure and staffing has been constant change, with staff numbers fluctuating between 60 and 120. Contractors, consultants and secondees have been regularly entering and leaving the various teams. As a result, achieving a shared sense of purpose has not been easy. The director of Taste Network coins the gymnast metaphor when referring to the management of the fluctuating staffing levels; that is, the organisation has to be able to move from one form to another quickly, to have people who can work either individually or in teams, and to be energetic in the way processes are managed.

An 'organisational charter' covering skills, knowledge, resource planning and management styles was used to identify the qualities expected, such as customer focus, receptiveness to new ideas, openness and integrity. Staff surveys and 360-degree feedback have been used to check how far managers and employees are able to meet these qualities. Initially there were some problems, with managers often scoring only 4 on a scale of 1 to 10. As a result, change agents were appointed to each team. The change agents were junior managers whose focus was on communications – upwards, downwards and laterally – with other teams. Initiatives have included 'lunch and learn' in which a team plays host to others, providing sandwiches and giving a presentation on their activities.

Over time there has grown an effective informal education process in which people get to know what makes the business function, and feedback scores have risen to an average of 8 out of 10. This type of flexible approach to communication was seen to be a key contribution to managing in the highly flexible and changing structure of the business. It is worth noting, however, that even though this is a high technology environment there is still a need for much face-to-face interaction.

(Arkin, 2001)

Size and structure

The outcome of the Aston Studies (Pugh *et al.*, 1968) indicated that it was size rather than technology which bore the strongest relationship to dimensions of organisation structure such as specialisation, formalisation and centralisation, though technology had an impact closest to its area of influence (e.g. the shopfloor). It is easy to appreciate the significance of size. Increasing the number of employees can lead to greater horizontal differentiation (i.e. more specialised activities) and greater vertical differentiation to facilitate the coordination of specialised functions. This sets the scene for greater reliance on rules and regulations (formalisation). With growing complexity owing to the above factors the exercise of personal control by management could become difficult, hence the need to resort to decentralisation. In recent years the opposite to the above trend – i.e. reducing the number of employees in organisations – has been associated with downsizing, and one effect of this approach is the creation of leaner organisations.

Strategy and structure

The main emphasis in this relationship is that changes in corporate strategy can lead to changes in the structure of organisation. It has been suggested that decision makers at top management level make choices about the strategic direction of the organisation and that this results in a reshaping of structure (Child, 1972; Child, 1997). A major proposition put forward by Chandler (1962) is that as corporate strategy shifts from a position where it is concerned with a single product to being preoccupied with product diversification, the management of the company will tend to develop more elaborate structures in order to achieve an optimum result. Effectively this means starting with an organic structure and eventually adopting a mechanistic structure.

In the light of recent evidence the strategy/structure proposition is taken a stage further. There is a view that organisations which have embraced an 'innovation' strategy need flexible systems normally associated with organic structures, where prominence is given to a loose structure, a low level of division of labour and specialisation and formalisation, and a pronounced emphasis on decentralisation. In different conditions an alternative arrangement could apply. For example, a mechanistic structure might be considered functional when a company goes through a period of rationalisation and cost reduction. In this case the suggestion is that there is a significant division of labour, with high levels of formalisation and centralisation. Finally, where a strategy of what is called 'imitation strategy' applies (where organisations try to capitalise on the best aspects of both an 'innovation' and 'cost minimisation' strategy), the result is a combination of both mechanistic and organic structures where tight controls apply to current activities and looser controls to new ventures or developments. Organisations adopting an imitation strategy move into new products or new markets after innovative competitors have proved that a market exists. In essence, they copy the successful ideas of innovators (Robbins, 1992).

Power/control and structure

Very briefly, the power/control explanation states that an organisation structure could be determined by the outcome of power struggles among influential competing factions within the organisation who are intent on advancing their personal interests. Power may also be derived from sources external to the organisation. For example, the funding levels of local government can be influenced by their readiness to adopt flexible structures (including a significant amount of contracting-out of work) approved by central government in the United Kingdom.

Power may operate in a number of ways. It may be centralised, in which case decision makers at the top of the organisation exercise a lot of influence. In such circumstances the structure of the organisation may be a tall organisation, with communications and decisions emanating from the apex. Alternatively, in smaller entrepreneurial organisations, the organisation's processes may all have to be ratified by the entrepreneur who is at the centre of a web of relationships with other organisational members. Power may also operate on a functional or expertise basis. Here power springs from being an expert or controlling access to being a technical function. For example, there is a tradition in the United Kingdom for accountants to be influential when making a contribution to discussions on the strategic direction of the enterprise, and accounting terminology has become part of the normal discourse between managers (Barber, 1997). The outcome of the latter is that problems and opportunities are framed in language and concepts, which tend to preserve the status quo in terms of power. The argument is that dominance of one professional language and set of concepts restricts the way problems and decisions are framed, and hence restrict the potential solutions that can be derived.

Finally, power has the capacity to be scattered along a range of stakeholders, including customers, shareholders, subcontractors and other companies with whom the organisation is collaborating, In this setting management becomes more of a process of negotiation and influence, and the structure may reflect points of contact with stakeholders. For example, an appropriate organisational unit is charged with acquiring and managing subcontractors. In such circumstances the importance of contracts and agreements on the level of service are underlined. This type of development has some of the features of Weber's legal–rational concept of bureaucracy referred to earlier.

■ Organisations as open systems

Organisations are not closed systems since they relate to an external environment, such as the financial and legal systems, customers or clients, suppliers, the labour market or regulatory bodies. Therefore they are open systems. As such, organisations can face stable or dynamic environments; the latter are more common nowadays and can create environmental uncertainty. In order to reduce or minimise uncertainty emanating from events such as changing customer tastes, serious challenges from new competitors, threats to sources of supply of raw materials and so on, the organisation could modify the way it is structured.

Emery and Trist (1965) examined four types of environment, which they referred to as follows:

1 placid randomised (relatively unchanging);
2 placid clustered (relatively unchanging, but there are clusters of threats of which the organisation ought to be aware);
3 disturbed reactive (more complex environment, with many competitors);
4 turbulent field (a rather dynamic environment with a high degree of uncertainty).

The disturbed reactive and turbulent field environments – a common sight at the present time – are more likely to be compatible with an organic structure, while the placid randomised and the placid clustered environments, which are becoming increasingly rare nowadays, could match a mechanistic structure.

Lawrence and Lorsch (1967) were also interested in the relationship between the environment and organisation structure. They studied companies facing different degrees of environmental uncertainty with reference to two dimensions of structure, namely differentiation (horizontal) and integration.

Differentiation exists when those who control different functional units or departments vary in their outlook and objectives. For example, the head of the manufacturing unit has objectives and an orientation at variance with those of the head of the finance unit and this is understandable because they relate to different external sub-environments. A particular sub-environment for the finance unit or function could be the regulatory agency controlling the disclosure of financial information, while for the manufacturing unit or function it could be externally prescribed technical specifications with regard to product quality or safety. Integration refers to the process of bringing activities together and achieving unity of effort within the organisation, and this function is even more important if there is pronounced differentiation.

Successful companies had structures more suited to the demands of their particular environments. Since an organisation could be relating to a number of sub-environments the key to success was to match particular sub-environments with organisational functions. For example, a certain type of functional activity within the organisation (e.g. product advertising) faces a dynamic sub-environment, and as a consequence adopts an organic structure; whereas a particular accounting activity interfacing with a relatively stable sub-environment operates within the confines of a mechanistic structure. Another finding from the Lawrence and Lorsch study was that the more diverse the environments faced by the company the greater the amount of horizontal differentiation within the organisation; and that successful companies were those which had established a high degree of integration for coordinating the various functions in the achievement of organisational goals.

When focusing on functions or sub-systems within organisations we could quite easily turn our attention to the socio-technical systems approach to studying organisations. This approach looks at the organisation as an open system structured in such a way as to integrate two major sub-systems, namely the technical (i.e. task) and the social sub-systems. The technical sub-system is concerned with transforming inputs into outputs and the social sub-system relates to the interpersonal aspects of life in organisations. The socio-technical systems approach developed from the research of Trist and Bamforth (1951) when they examined the effects of the introduction of new techniques in British coal mining many years ago. The expected productivity gains failed to materialise because of problems with the social sub-system due to the splitting up of well-established work groups. Here we see that improvements to the technical sub-system did not produce the desired result because of the adverse effect this development had on the social sub-system.

EXAMPLE 3.3

Autonomous work groups at Scottish & Newcastle Breweries

Fork lift truck crews, responsible for loading and unloading delivery lorries and conveying kegs to and from the production line, were closely supervised and had no discretion on how to perform their work. An experiment in job redesign took place in which each crew was formed into a team and allowed to organise how their work should be carried out. A crew would decide how work should be allocated amongst team members, and were briefed on such matters as the stock position and deliveries. The role of the foreman changed to that of a 'consultant' to the teams when they encountered problems they could not solve for themselves. Features of the new situation were improved communication, regular consultative meetings, better training, a more pleasant physical working environment and the introduction of a revised payment system. The experiment was considered to be very successful.

(Department of Employment, 1975)

The researchers suggested that the technical and social sub-systems could be integrated through the medium of autonomous work groups. These groups aim to facilitate cooperation between the two sub-systems so that they function for the good of the overall system. Autonomous work groups are related to task redesign, particularly job enrichment referred to in Chapter 10, and wider issues connected with group interaction, remote supervision and other aspects of organisation design (see Example 3.3). An important feature of the socio-technical systems approach to organisation design is the belief in the importance of harmony between the social and technical sub-systems.

■ Postmodern organisation

Clegg (1990) compares the modernist with the postmodernist organisation. The first is the type of organisation with which we are familiar and that has been analysed in the chapter up to this point. It tends to be rigid, caters for mass markets, and gives pride of place to technological determinism (as we found in contingency theory). There are also highly differentiated functions and jobs (as in classical theory), and a generous sprinkling of job demarcation and deskilling (Taylorism). There is reference to the work of Taylor, the father of scientific management, in the section on the utilisation of human resources in Chapter 6. Postmodernist organisations are flexible with niche markets, and are the opposite of modernist organisations with respect to differentiation, demarcation and skill, and actors (key employees) exercise choice as far as the use of technology is concerned (absence of technological determinism).

The postmodernist critique of organisations also recognises that there are multiple and competing views of organisation that are legitimate. It appears everything is open to question and there are always alternative explanations in conditions of diversity. Those advocating this approach have not much time for the modernist view of the existence of a universal objective truth that can be discovered by research methods, often referred to as rational and scientific, which the contingency theorists would like to think they use. The postmodernists recognise that we construct reality as we go along after indulging in self-reflection, aided by the use of language. Given the ambiguous and debatable nature of HRM, it is sometimes said that a postmodernist view of the organisational world is compatible with it. The impact of postmodernism on HRM will be examined further in Chapter 12.

■ Organisational trends

In recent years much has been said about the changes to traditional organisation structures that are considered necessary for companies to meet future challenges more effectively. Kanter (1989) maintains that future successful organisations will be post-entrepreneurial. By this is meant that organisations need to take entrepreneurship beyond its present position by combining the creative elements of the role of the entrepreneur and the more disciplined corporate approach which in an HRM sense would entail taking on board a commitment to cooperation and teamwork. There is a need for faster and more creative action within the organisation, and for closer partnerships with stakeholders, e.g. employees, suppliers and customers. Organisations need to be flexible and free from cumbersome bureaucratic structure if they are to cope well with changing markets and technology, and the external environment at large. In Kanter's terminology, 'corporate giants . . . must learn how to dance'.

Acceptance of the model of the post-entrepreneurial organisation would necessitate the adoption of three main strategies, with a consequent change in values, as follows:

1 *Restructuring to find synergies*. This means that there is an effective rearrangement of the constituent parts of the organisation so that the value added by the cooperative effort of the whole is greater than the sum of the individual parts. Such an eventuality could arise when a company goes through a process of downsizing (cutting numbers) of central corporate staff and the removal of layers at middle management level. In the Ford Motor Company's organisational transformation referred to in Example 3.1 there is expected to be a reduction in the average number of layers in several parts of the organisation, from 14 to 7 (Lorenz, 1994a).

   The manifestation of the restructuring could be seen in changes to the tasks previously carried out by the layer of management which has been removed. Authority could be delegated to lower levels of the organisation. This process could be facilitated by giving work groups more autonomy and by enhancing information technology systems to cope with the collection and exchange of information as well as the monitoring of operations.

In order to react more quickly, large corporations have set up small 'business units' within the organisation, and others have contracted out non-core activities (e.g. catering and security), which were previously carried out in-house. The results of these changes can be smaller organisations with flatter and more focused structures concentrating on 'core' business activity. The challenge facing HRM is to ensure that the changes described are introduced without demotivating the employees affected.

2 *Opening boundaries to form external strategic alliances.* As organisations concentrate on their core activities they can benefit from forming short-term strategic alliances with other organisations. These alliances assume various forms and, for example, may involve two organisations in a particular market collaborating on some aspects of research and development of mutual benefit to both of them, but too costly or difficult to undertake alone. In another situation a management consultancy firm and a hospital form an alliance to market consultancy services to other hospitals. The hospital, as part of the health sector, can establish contact with other health sector organisations more quickly and easily than the consultancy firm that supplies the services.

3 *Create new ventures from within the organisation* (i.e. ventures based on innovative practices). One way to promote innovation is to commission the formal research and development department (where one exists) to generate new ideas and projects. However, Kanter acknowledges another source from which fertile ideas can spring: essentially the flexibility built into the structure of the organisation and the workforce. For example, to encourage innovation the organisation could establish short-term interdisciplinary teams to undertake particular projects. In this arrangement team leaders would put a lot of emphasis on their advisory role, where they offer support to well-qualified team members, and would prefer empowering people rather than monitoring or controlling their activities in a traditional sense (see Box 3.1). These teams would then disperse on the completion of the projects and subsequently undertake a new set of tasks under a different arrangement.

Another observer of the organisational scene recognises that companies now operate in a tougher, more competitive and changing environment (Handy, 1989). He sees UK organisations as becoming less labour intensive and moving towards structures where a central core of knowledge-based workers controls the technology and operations of slimmed-down companies. Value is added not through the use of muscle power but through an input of knowledge and creativity. According to Handy, the future organisation will have a core of well-informed employees with ready access to relevant ideas and information (i.e. knowledge workers). This is similar to what Drucker (1988) called the information-based organisation. The core workers are referred to by Pollert (1988) as a group with permanent employment contracts and job security who are multi-skilled and able to perform a variety of functions (i.e. functional flexibility) that may cut across traditional occupational boundaries.

BOX 3.1

Empowerment

Empowerment is a comparatively recent management practice concerned with giving front-line employees more responsibility, resources and authority. It is something that is far more than delegation: in effect it means harnessing the creativity and brainpower of all employees, not just the chosen few such as managers. Properly empowered employees are well placed to maximise their potential, and in the process enhance the competitive advantage of their organisation. Empowerment is seen as supportive of a no-blame culture, where mistakes are seen as learning opportunities.

In an Industrial Society UK survey (1995) it was found that the managerial group most enthusiastic about the idea of empowering employees were senior managers. In some cases empowerment was introduced following the appointment of a new chief executive and had the effect of reducing the number of layers of management, normally at middle management level. In certain situations respondents noted other changes such as wider spans of control, managers exercising less control coupled with the use of supportive management, and a greater readiness to embrace HRM practices. Finally, the main motive for increasing empowerment at work was to make better use of people's skills, though customer service was also emphasised.

Surrounding the core of knowledge workers would be outside workers – a contractual fringe – operating on a subcontracting basis and paid a fee rather than a wage. The management of this group (periphery workers) is removed from the organisation that is receiving its services. A further consideration is the use of a part-time and flexible labour force. This group of temporary or casual workers is less costly for the organisation because their services will only be used to meet particular demands, and released when they are no longer required. In essence the organisation is using what Atkinson called 'numerical flexibility' (Pollert, 1988).

Another form of flexibility is called 'financial flexibility', where the organisation adapts its labour costs to its financial position (Pollert, 1988). Examples of this would be that the size of the pay packet would be determined by the profits made by the company (e.g. profit-related pay), and relating payment to the performance of specific tasks (e.g. the fees paid to a subcontractor for doing a particular job).

How do the different categories of workers respond to the demands of the flexible firm? From the results of a survey, Hunter *et al.* (1993) conclude that full-time employees were considered flexible, highly stable, committed to the organisation and easy to manage. Temporary employees were viewed as less stable and committed depending on the employment contract, and part-time permanent employees were believed to have higher commitment but were more difficult to use continuously because of the hours worked. Generally, it was noted that employers expected women to find part-time work attractive because of their domestic responsibilities (e.g. dependent children). But the opportunities to work part time are limited in managerial jobs; for example, in the late 1990s only 18 per cent of managers in the United Kingdom worked part-time (Sly *et al.*, 1998). Therefore it could be argued that women are at a disadvantage if they take advantage of 'family friendly' policies in the form of part-time work opportunities; in fact they run the risk of damaging their careers.

It is said that employees who choose to go down the part-time work route tend to miss out on factors vital to career advancement in management (such as visibility), have less time to establish relationships, tend to be allocated to marginal roles with a narrow range of duties, and carry the stigma of low commitment (Edwards *et al.*, 1999). It should be noted that there is a distinction between Edwards *et al.*'s (1999) reference to the 'stigma' of low commitment and Hunter *et al.*'s (1993) reference to actual high commitment amongst part-time employees. This may indicate an area where bias derived from unscientific assumptions (such as part-time workers being less committed than others) can have a negative impact on the validity of the recruitment and selection process. In other words recruiters may assume that part-timers will be less committed than full-timers, whereas this is not necessarily the case. This issue may be particularly significant for women as more women than men work part time.

The changes outlined above will have an impact on the management of human resources. The trend towards information-based organisations and the use of computer-aided production reduces the need for unskilled and semi-skilled production workers. There will be a changing pattern of employment and an increase in the proportion of the labour force devoted to short-term contract and part-time employees. As a result of pressure from the EU part-time workers can now benefit from rights to certain employment conditions, previously the preserve of full-time workers.

The appearance of flatter organisation structures will reduce the opportunities to improve pay through progression within the hierarchy, but such a development offers greater possibilities for the introduction of performance-related pay discussed in Chapter 9. The position of the 'core' workers warrants careful attention because their hours of work and the demands on them (e.g. greater flexibility with regard to working practices) are likely to be on the high side. However, we must not lose sight of the likely disadvantages of being a peripheral worker – lack of job security, which could adversely affect motivation and commitment (Feldman *et al.*, 1994), and perhaps very limited training opportunities.

Reflecting on the flexible firm, Hunter *et al.* (1993) conclude that the core–periphery contrast is too crude to be helpful with analysis. The so-called periphery has different strands (it gives the employer much scope for variation in the pattern of employment), and therefore is not unitary in its composition. This is a view similar to that taken by Barling and Gallagher (1996) when considering part-time employment. Overall, there is a mixed picture with regard to the adoption of flexible working patterns in Europe.

Finally, the 'network organisation' is likely to pose a different challenge to the management of the traditional organisation. For example, organisations could concentrate on things they do particularly well, outsourcing functions that can be done quicker and more effectively, or at lower cost, by other companies. One company in the network may research and design a product, another may engineer or manufacture it, and a third may handle distribution. This could allow for greater specialisation and encourage innovation; it could require less time and effort to be put into planning and coordination now that a number of functions have been hived off (Snow *et al.*, 1992). It should be stated that network organisations are not free of shortcomings. There may be a problem with control generally because of the existence of a number of subcontractors, and this could extend to the area of quality control. Equally, the subcontractor may take advantage of the dependency relationship to increase prices significantly, or prove to be unreliable in a number of ways, or there may be an unacceptable turnover in the number of subcontractors (McKenna, 2000). Miles *et al.* (1997), who previously were preoccupied with the intricacies of the network organisation, have attracted our attention to the cellular organisation, which is founded on the principles of entrepreneurship, self-regulation and member ownership.

In recent years organisational design in manufacturing companies has been influenced by developments such as lean production systems and high performance systems. In Japan lean production systems became popular and were influenced by the following principles: quality control, continuous improvement, minimum stock buffers, teamwork and customer focus.

An illustration of the impact of the application of lean production systems in the United Kingdom is provided by Wagstyl (1996). He put the spotlight on changes in management and organisation in certain British companies (e.g. Ford and Nissan UK) in the 1980s and 1990s, and reports on outcomes such as impressive productivity gains, improved work practices and management, a noticeable commitment to good quality standards and continuous improvement, greater cooperation between key constituents (e.g. workers, managers, suppliers), greater effort in detecting faults and taking appropriate remedial action, and an improved relationship with trade unions.

Although lean production systems have been used in the West, as we have seen above, one is more likely to find derivatives of these systems, called high performance systems, in use in advanced industrial countries such as the United States. The main reasons why they have been introduced are the highly competitive conditions in the marketplace and the demands of shareholders for greater returns on their capital. High performance systems are based on five principles, as follows (Useem, 1997):

1 *Customer-focused operating units*, where there is heightened sensitivity to reactions of customers, relying on market surveys and focus groups. This information would go directly to managers of operating units, and some of it could be used in HRM decision-making processes connected with the performance of employees and the determination of rewards.
2 *Devolved decision making*, where authority is pushed down the hierarchy to an extent that greater power resides in operating units (called Strategic Business

Units, SBUs). These consist of broad categories of products in which are placed appropriate functional specialisms (e.g. production, marketing). There is a similarity between this type of structure and the 'product grouping' referred to earlier in the chapter. SBUs are customer oriented, have responsibility for formulating strategy and are accountable for results, and this can provide a useful motivational spur to the management that runs them. The relationship between an SBU and the central controlling cell of the organisation varies; in some companies there are more centralised functions than in others.

3 *Streamlined management control/tighter financial control*, reflected in wider spans of control and flatter structures, arises as a result of downsizing and the removal of layer(s) of management. Although there are likely to be fewer policy directives sent from the nerve centre of the organisation to the operating units, tighter financial targets could be imposed on the latter.

4 *Business process re-engineering* (BPR), which amounts to a fundamental rethink and radical redesign of business processes and practices in order to bring about significant improvements in the quality and speed of the service to the customer as well as a dramatic reduction in costs (Hammer and Champy, 1993). The reader is invited to go to Chapter 5, where there is further discussion of BPR as a technique that can be used to change culture.

5 *Establishing a connection between organisational actions and decisions and shareholder value*. This amounts to assessing the effectiveness of management at producing wealth for shareholders. In HRM terms the link between management action and shareholder value can be seen in the connection between share option schemes and company performance.

Restructuring is an important feature of the organisational landscape in contemporary times and is likely to continue as an important activity in the future. Unilever, the Anglo-Dutch foods and detergent conglomerate, announced the formation of two global divisions, one for food and the other for home and personal care as from 2001. The heads of the two divisions will have both executive authority and profit responsibility for Unilever's operations across 88 countries. The company said that the rationale was to accelerate decision making and to strengthen the company's ability to harness innovation, and awaken the entrepreneurial spirit within the company. In addition, the move is designed to put brand management firmly at the centre of Unilever's focus and to speed up its responsiveness to the market (Killgren, 2000; Thornhill, 2000). An observer said that such an arrangement would allow the co-chairmen – Niall Fitzgerald and Antony Burgman – to concentrate more on strategy. It would appear that the newly created divisions are closer to the concept of an SBU than the Product Division, both of which were discussed earlier.

Ruigrok *et al.* (1999) conducted a survey of 450 European companies. The results indicated that over the period 1992–6 companies across Europe reported significant progress with features such as decentralising operational decision making, introducing project-based organisational forms and linking up with external agencies such as suppliers (e.g. outsourcing) and competitors (e.g. strategic alliances). The last point is a theme reinforced by Cravens *et al.* (1996) and Ferlie and Pettigrew (1996) when they state that the organisation's relationship with customers, suppliers and competitors has changed, with an emphasis on building partnerships, alliances and networks inside and outside the organisation. Increasingly initiatives are been taken to combine conventional work practices and settings with non-traditional ones (Apgar, 1998). More attention is being paid to the manner in which work is organised in order to take advantage of the deployment of flexible labour and the introduction of high performance work practices that can build on employee commitment and lead to a position of competitive advantage (Whitfield and Poole, 1997). Undoubtedly the above changes to organisational structures and work practices will necessitate changes to the nature and style of human resource management.

Is there a danger that we have gone too far with diluting the traditional hierarchy of organisation as a result of subscribing to principles behind the emerging forms of organisation referred to above? (See Box 3.2 for a possible answer.)

BOX 3.2

In defence of hierarchy: status

According to Adrian Furnham, Professor of Psychology, University of London, this could very well be the case. He is reported as saying that:

> there is a backlash against US-style management orthodoxy that has tried to tame the drive for status by flattening hierarchies. The desire for status is a powerful force, and companies should not try to suppress it. Status is all about one-upping the next person. The ego is a very powerful thing and companies must learn to exploit it. People are willing to trade down salary if it means trading up status. It is no coincidence that American companies tend to have dozens of vice-presidents.

John Hunt, Professor of Organizational Behaviour at the London Business School, makes the point that the contemporary 'egalitarian impulse behind dressing down (informal dress) has been subverted by status conscious workers who outdo their colleagues with designer labels' (Bilefsky, 2000).

In a recent research paper, Loch *et al.* (2000) argue that the drive for status is primordial and any attempts to tame it are futile. They go on to say that humans are genetically hard-wired to be status conscious, and that the drive for status can act as a catalyst to pursue success. Managers can encourage healthy competition by offering incentives such as a bigger office, invitations to lunch with the chief executive or a chance to work on high profile projects. Though recognising the validity of what has been said, it must be acknowledged that having a hunger for status can be destructive from the point of view of the organisation. In 1998 the first attempted marriage between Glaxo Wellcome and SmithKline Beecham collapsed because Richard Sykes and Jan Leschly could not decide who would get the top job.

(Bilefsky, 2000)

■ Conclusions

Strategy, discussed in Chapter 2, and structure are interrelated and together are crucial for the success of the organisation. Determining the nature of the structure of the organisation can be an important strategic decision where top managerial influence plays a key role. However, the various environments (e.g. technological, market, economic, political) to which the organisation is exposed also play a crucial role in the determination of strategy and structure. Ensuring that the structure does not militate against performance (the accusation levelled at bureaucracy) has led to increases in flexibility of structure.

Such changes present a challenge to HRM that seeks to determine the make-up of the workforce, and ensure that it is managed in such a way as to maximise commitment and performance. Greater flexibility and looser networks in organisational structure may bring advantages such as increasing the speed of response the organisation can make to changes in its environment, but there may be costs such as greater difficulty in achieving a shared vision amongst the workforce and in maintaining effective communication.

There is no one best way of structuring organisations, and it is important to find an appropriate fit between the structure, the business environment, the size of organisation, the available technology, the forces for change and the disposition of the employees. In seeking to find such a fit it is worth bearing in mind the development of structure from the classical theories to IT-inspired virtual organisations. Whatever the structure adopted there will still be a need for effective management of performance, communication and the interaction of employees. Some would argue that the need for excellence in these areas of management increases rather than decreases in modern organisational forms.

References

Apgar, M. (1998) 'The alternative workplace: changing where and how people work', *Harvard Business Review*, 76, 121–36.

Arkin, A. (2001) 'Playing the loyalty card', *People Management*, 7, 46–8.

Barber, P. (1997) 'Money talks: the influence of the accountant on organizational discourse', *Journal of Applied Management Studies*, 6, 35–46.

Barling, J. and Gallagher, D.G. (1996) 'Part-time employment', in Cooper, C.L. and Robertson, I.T. (eds), *International Review of Industrial and Organizational Psychology*, Chichester: Wiley.

Bilefsky, D. (2000) 'How to discover your inner chimp', *Financial Times*, 4 August, 14.

Burns, T. and Stalker, G.M. (1961) *The Management of Innovation*, London: Tavistock.

Cascio, W. (2000) 'Managing a virtual workplace', *Academy of Management Executive*, 14, 81–90.

Chandler, A. (1962) *Strategy and Structure: chapters in The History of the Industrial Enterprise*, Cambridge, MA: MIT Press.

Child, J. (1972) 'Organisation structure, environment, and performance: the role of strategic choice', *Sociology*, 6, 1–22.

Child, J. (1997) 'Strategic choice in the analysis of action, structure, organizations, and environment: retrospect and prospect', *Organisation Studies*, 18, 43–76.

Clegg, S.R. (1990) *Modern Organizations: Organizations in the postmodern world*, London: Sage.

Collins, R., Schmenner, R. and Cordon, C. (1997) 'Rigid flexibility and factory focus', in *Mastering Management: Module 9 Production and Operations Management*, 311–15, London: FT/Pitman Publishing.

Cravens, D., Piercy, N. and Shipp, S. (1996) 'New organizational forms for competing in highly dynamic environments', *British Journal of Management*, 7, 203–18.

Daft, R.L. (1998) *Organization Theory and Design*, 6th edn, Cincinnati, OH: South Western College Publishing.

Department of Employment (1975) *Making Work More Satisfying*, London: HMSO.

Drucker, P.F. (1988) 'The coming of the new organization', *Harvard Business Review*, January/February, 45–53.

Edwards, C., Robinson, O., Welchman, R. and Woodall, J. (1999) 'Lost opportunities? Organizational restructuring and women managers', *Human Resource Management Journal*, 9, 55–64.

Emery, F.E. and Trist, E.L. (1965) 'The causal textures of organisational environments', *Human Relations*, February, 21–32.

Feldman, D.C., Doerpinghaus, H.I. and Turnley, W.H. (1994) 'Managing temporary workers: a permanent HRM challenge', *Organizational Dynamics*, Autumn, 49–63.

Ferlie, E. and Pettigrew, A. (1996) 'Managing through networks: some issues for the NHS', *British Journal of Management*, 7, 81–99.

Hammer, M. and Champy, J. (1993) *Re-engineering the corporation: A manifesto for business revolution*, New York: Harper Business.

Handy, C. (1989) *The Age of Unreason*, London: Business Books.

Huber, G.P. (1990) 'A theory of the effects of advanced information technologies on organisation design, intelligence, and decision making', *Academy of Management Review*, 15, 47–71.

Hunter, L., McGregor, A., MacInnes, J. and Sproull, A. (1993) 'The flexible firm: strategy and segmentation', *British Journal of Industrial Relations*, 31, 383–407.

Industrial Society (1995) *Report*: 'Managing best practice', Issue No. 8 (London).

Kanter, R.M. (1989) *When Giants Learn to Dance: Mastering the challenges of strategy, management and careers in the 1990s*, London: Unwin.

Killgren, L. (2000) 'Unilever splits operations but denies plans for divorce', *Financial Times*, 5/6 August, 1.

Larson, E.W. and Gobeli, D.H. (1987) 'Matrix management: contradictions and insights', *California Management Review*, Summer, 126–38.

Lawrence, P.R. and Lorsch, J.W. (1967) *Organizations and Environment: Managing differentiation and integration*, Homewood, IL: Irwin.

Loch, C. *et al.* (2000) 'The fight for alpha position: channelling status competition in organizations', INSEAD

Lorenz, C. (1994a) 'Ford's global matrix gamble', *Financial Times*, 16 December, 13.

Lorenz, C. (1994b) 'Pioneers and prophets: Tom Burns', *Financial Times*, 5 December.

McKenna, E. (2000) *Business Psychology and Organizational Behaviour*, Hove: Psychology Press.

Mintzberg, H. (1983) *Structure in Fives: Designing effective organizations*, Englewood Cliffs, NJ: Prentice Hall.

Miles, R.E., Snow, C.C., Mathews, J.A., Miles, G. and Coleman, H.J. (1997) 'Organizing in the knowledge age: anticipating the cellular form', *Academy of Management Executive*, 11, 7–20.

Perrow, C.B. (1970) *Organisational Analysis: A sociological view*, London: Tavistock.

Pollert, A. (1988) 'The flexible firm: fixation or fact?', *Work, Employment and Society*, 2, 281–316.

Pugh, D.S., Hickson, D.T., Hinings, C.R. and Turner, C. (1968) 'Dimensions of organisation structure', *Administrative Science Quarterly*, 13, 65–105.

Robbins, S.P. (1992) *Essentials of Organizational Behaviour*, Englewood Cliffs, NJ: Prentice Hall.

Reed, M. (1989) *The Sociology of Management*, Hemel Hempstead: Harvester Wheatsheaf.

Ruigrok, W., Pettigrew, A., Peck, S. and Whittington, R. (1999) 'Corporate restructuring and new forms of organising: evidence from Europe', *Management International Review*, 39, 41–64.

Sly, F., Thair, T. and Risdon, A. (1998) 'Women in the labour market: results from the Spring 1997 Labour Force Survey', *Labour Market Trends*, 106, 97–120, London: Office for National Statistics.

Snow, C.C., Miles, R.E. and Coleman, H.J. (1992) 'Managing 21st century network organisations', *Organisational Dynamics*, Winter, 5–20.

Tailby, S. and Turnbull, P. (1987) 'Learning to manage just-in-time', *Personnel Management*, January, 16–19.

Thompson, J.D. (1967) *Organizations in Action*, New York: McGraw-Hill.

Thornhill, J. (2000) 'Unilever's rejig takes inspiration from its origins', *Financial Times*, 5/6 August, 12.

Trist, E.L. and Bamforth, K.W. (1951) 'Some social and psychological consequences of the Longwall method of coal getting', *Human Relations*, 4, 3–38.

Useem, M. (1997) 'The true worth of building high performance systems', in *Mastering Management: Module 8 Managing People in Organizations*, 288–92, London: FT/Pitman Publishing.

Wagstyl, S. (1996) 'Lifeblood from transplants: a revolution in British manufacturing has been heavily influenced by Japanese groups such as Nissan', *Financial Times*, 29 July, 15.

Weber, M. (1947) *The Theory of Social and Economic Organization* (trans A. Henderson and T. Parsons), New York: Oxford University Press.

Whitfield, K. and Poole, M. (1997) 'Organising employment for high performance: theories, evidence, and policy', *Organization Studies*, 18, 745–64.

Woodward, J. (1965) *Industrial Organisations: Theory and practice*, London: Oxford University Press.

Chapter 4

Organisational change and development

Change management is a topic that is rich both in theoretical perspectives and application to the practice of management. Important challenges for organisations are to react swiftly and effectively to external forces for change, and to capitalise on the potential for internally driven change and development.

Once you have read this chapter, you should:

■ understand why employees might resist change;
■ be aware of alternative approaches to overcoming resistance;
■ be able to discern the psychological stages that people can go through when they experience change;
■ understand and be able to judge the applicability of alternative approaches to managing change;
■ be aware of ways of executing change at the levels of the organisation, task and individual/group through organisation development techniques;
■ be able critically to reflect on the role of change and development in HRM.

Change is a phenomenon we encounter in life both inside and outside organisations and it is fair to say that the pace of change has accelerated in recent years. We have witnessed changes in the political landscape of the world with the disintegration of the communist system and the collapse of the eastern bloc. This has generated further changes, such as the creation of independent states within the old Soviet Union and of course the reunification of Germany. Change is visible in South Africa, where power sharing between blacks and whites replaced the previous system of rule by the white population, and hopefully recent international peace initiatives may bring about desired changes in Northern Ireland and in the Israeli-occupied territories.

At the economic level there will be greater competition as barriers to trade between EU countries are removed with the creation of the Single Market. This will be accentuated by the rapid development of global markets. The pace of technological developments is reflected in changes across a broad spectrum. For example, there have been impressive advances in the application of new technology to the office and the factory. Technological innovation also finds expression in the development of new products. Change will also impact on how people perceive careers. Already employee expectations are changing, because now there is recognition of the growing need to have a number of jobs throughout a working life, with much less attachment to the notion of a continuous association with one organisation.

As organisations seek to operate in global markets and to apply products and processes internationally, they may be faced with dealing with increased complexity. On the one hand, globalisation implies a unification to some extent – for example the same product can become sold more widely, or a particular management technique may be applied across national boundaries. However, it has been argued that internationalisation creates requirements for greater internal diversity of the organisation to deal with the external diversity. In some cases differences can be major and clearly identified. In others, differences between people in divergent national cultures (Rondinelli and Black, 2000), with histories of different forms of practice (Mintzberg and Markides, 2000), create subtle but important variation in perceptions of the reasons for, and the rationality of, change.

It is commonplace in today's world for organisations to bring about a variety of changes to their goals, structures and processes in response to both internal and external happenings or in anticipation of these events. At the strategic level corporate goals could be set or adapted (changed) so that the organisation is well placed to derive competitive advantage in its market. At the operational level responses or precipitative action to improve efficiency and effectiveness could be reflected in changes to working practices, contracts of employment, systems and structures. Given the degree of change at the social, political and economic levels the aim must be to achieve flexibility in response to external change at the operational level. Typically this will require employees to be flexible in their attitude to change and in the application of their skills and knowledge to new tasks.

■ Reactions to change

Change is not a painless process and it is often resisted by employees when they do not share the employer's view.

Resistance to change

The following are some of the reasons why change is resisted. These operate at the individual, group and organisational level and could be based on historical justifications (Bedeian and Zammuto, 1991; Katz and Kahn, 1978; Zaltman and Duncan, 1977):

■ People perceive that the proposed changes are likely to threaten their expertise, undermine their influence, dilute their power base and reduce the resources currently allocated to their department. If this negative view prevails efforts to introduce the change could be hindered.

■ There is a lack of trust between management and employees. This could have arisen because those likely to be affected by the proposed changes did not receive adequate explanations about what is due to take place, or they recall that past changes did not produce the promised benefits.

■ There are diverse views about the need for change and the anticipated benefits, and this creates some confusion. For example, management holds optimistic views about why the change is necessary and the expected results, whereas the workers are unable to share these views. Of course there could also be differences of opinion within each group. Whatever the reason, the lack of consensus acts as an impediment.

■ People have a low tolerance for change, though it is recognised that there are certain people who thrive on confronting change. Individuals with a low tolerance for change may feel anxious and apprehensive about the uncertainty that accompanies change, and as a result oppose it even though they recognise it is for the benefit of the organisation.

■ As creatures of habit people construe change as uncomfortable because it poses a challenge to established routines to which they have grown accustomed and to relationships developed over time. For example, there is a proposal to overhaul organisational processes and practices by resorting to business processing re-engineering and people feel uncomfortable about the prospect of a major upheaval that is likely to result in discarding established ways of doing things. If the proposed reorganisation leads to the break-up of established groups of colleagues people could feel sad at the disintegration of teams because of the impact it is likely to have on comradeship, mutual support and shared experience. Also, there could be a certain sadness at the prospect of severing contact with people who the organisation feels are superfluous to requirements and as a result are being made redundant.

■ There is a perception that the proposed change challenges cherished values and beliefs. For example, the proposal is to remove the system of promotion based on seniority that was considered an attractive HR practice in the past (e.g. as in Japan).

■ People harbour doubts about their ability to cope with the demands of the new situation.

■ People feel that their future job security and income could be adversely affected by the proposed changes, and this is compounded by fear of a future clouded with ambiguity and uncertainty (fear of the unknown).

■ People feel a sense of apathy due to powerlessness and are not well disposed to the proposals for change.

■ Individuals are influenced by group norms – for example, the group is critical of individualised incentive schemes (performance-related pay) – and as a consequence resist the proposed change.

■ Organisational systems are elaborate (i.e. entrenched bureaucratic processes and practices) with an inbuilt resistance to overhauling them even when justified (e.g. in the case of introducing total quality management (TQM) which disperses power); this is because of an attachment to the view that they are functional in maintaining stability. In fact there could be a certain inertia that acts as a counterbalance to change.

Overcoming resistance

A number of measures to overcome resistance to change have been proposed (Eccles, 1994; Kotter and Schlesinger, 1979). Some of the measures, which can be viewed as negative, are unlikely to appeal to the HRM specialist. These are 'coercion' in the form of direct threats or force to elicit compliance; or 'manipulation', which amounts to distorting facts and figures so that they look more attractive, or withholding negative data, so that the change scenario is more acceptable to the resisters. The following are the positive measures to overcome resistance to change.

Communication

If the source of resistance is poor communication, then action should be taken to communicate with employees specifying clearly the rationale for the change (e.g. change is crucial for the success of the organisation). It is a good idea to keep people fully informed by disseminating all relevant information; as a result, there is less likelihood of rumour or conjecture being a problem. It is also sensible to allow employees time to consider the proposals, and when they respond one should listen carefully to their reaction. When proposals for change are likely to challenge cherished organisational values (e.g. seniority-based pay), solicit the views of influential employees with relevant experience. As a general principle, it is not a bad idea to involve those likely to oppose the change in the decision-making process related to it, in particular those who can make a valid contribution to this form of participation, on the understanding that that they are more likely to accept decisions to which they have had an input (i.e. they own the problem). Also, opinion leaders and natural leaders could be targeted to assist with getting the message across to the rank and file. One could also target middle managers who are supporters of change.

Other factors

A bargaining process could be mounted where some position is conceded in return for more compliant behaviour on the part of the resisters. Those who initiate change will benefit from being flexible and adaptable because they need to be receptive to good ideas from those who are reacting to the change proposals. In the final analysis if people have strong fears and anxieties about the proposed changes some form of counselling and skills development could be beneficial.

■ Psychological impact

It is understandable that news of profound changes affecting the individual's job or place of work can arouse deep psychological feelings related to self-esteem and achievement, which in turn affect the level of motivation and performance. A 'cycle of coping', which covers five stages and traces the individual's reaction to change, has been proposed (Carnall, 1990). The pronouncements in the cycle of coping that now follow might be viewed as generalisations; however, reflecting on them when considering the management of change could be useful.

Stage 1 is 'denial' as the individual is confronted with the proposal for change. A typical reaction is that change is unnecessary, and there could be an enhancement of the person's self-esteem because of an attachment to the present way of doing things. Where a group is involved the threat posed by the proposal for change could lead to a reinforcement of the ties between members, and performance remains stable.

Stage 2 is 'defence' and at this stage the realities of the decision to institute change become apparent as early deliberations lead to the formulation of concrete plans and programmes. Faced with this outcome people become defensive in order to defend both their jobs and the way they have executed their duties and responsibilities. This stage produces an adverse effect, which manifests itself as a lowering of self-esteem, motivation and performance.

Stage 3 is 'discarding' and, unlike the previous stages, which emphasised the past, this stage puts the spotlight on the future. There is a change in perceptions as people realise that change is necessary and inevitable. Although performance is still on the decline, there are signs that self-esteem is improving as people get to grips with the new situation.

Stage 4 is 'adaptation', where people are beginning to come to terms with the new techniques and processes. Naturally it will be necessary to modify and refine the new system and if people are involved in this exercise they are likely to experience an increase in their self-esteem. However, performance still lags behind the growing level of motivation, particularly in situations where it was necessary to have an understanding of new methods and techniques.

Stage 5 is 'internalisation', where people finally make sense of what has happened, and the newly adopted behaviour is now becoming part of people's repertoire of behaviour. One could now expect an improvement in self-esteem and motivation and this coupled with the better use of people's abilities could give rise to raised levels of performance.

■ Managing change

An organisation must try to anticipate change, not merely respond to it. If so, the planning and management of organisational change must become part of the organisation's strategy. Before setting out to plan change it is well to recognise the existence of a state of equilibrium between the forces for change and the forces against change. In accordance with Lewin's (1951) force field model this equilibrium must be disturbed in a planned way in order to bring about change. This is done by strengthening the forces for change or weakening the forces against change, or taking both courses of action. However, at the beginning it is likely to be a difficult task to identify the forces for and against change. Lewin postulates a model that could be useful as a means of understanding the process of change from the old to the new situation. It consists of:

Unfreezing → Changing → Refreezing

People are not normally receptive to change when they are locked into a state where they are attached to traditional values supportive of the status quo (i.e. they are frozen). It is necessary to unfreeze this state before progress can be made in getting people to adopt new ideas and work methods. The unfreezing stage consists of a number of courses of action, such as highlighting the benefits of moving to the new situation, challenging the status quo and the attitudes that underpin it, using appropriate information and discussion in a supportive atmosphere to remove the psychological defences, and facilitating the movement from the status quo to the new situation by measures such as advice and skills training.

After the unfreezing has taken place we move to the changing stage, where the planned changes in the work situation are implemented. It is hoped that the anticipated benefits have materialised. If so, the final stage – refreezing – has arrived. At this stage the changes to structure (e.g. the development of a more focused and flexible organisation) or processes together with the underlying attitudes and behaviour need to be refrozen so that they can be sustained over time. If this stage is not successfully negotiated there is the danger of reverting to the previous equilibrium state. On the other hand, if the refreezing has gone ahead without a hitch, then the new situation is stabilised as the driving and restraining forces for change are balanced.

Another model of managing change – called the *continuous change process model* – puts particular emphasis on the role of top management and change agents. Top management specifies the changes that are necessary (e.g. the changes which are crucial in the realisation of corporate objectives), discuss with employees the alternatives available and what the outcome is likely to be (Kotter, 1995), and ensure that all parts of the organisation act in unison, supported by HRM strategies (Mabey *et al.*, 1998; Pfeffer, 1994; Storey, 1992). Obviously it would beneficial if top management had the right leadership skills, temperament, and commitment and that its proposals were unlikely to be seriously undermined by the prevailing organisational climate and culture (McKenna, 2000).

Change agents, who are either internal or external consultants, have the responsibility for managing the multitude of activities connected with bringing about the desired change. It stands to reason that they should be enthusiastic about the prospect of change and accept the challenges and opportunities it offers, and have the personal qualities and political skills to do a difficult job, which includes relating effectively with managers and others who are involved in the change process; the latter have to be convinced that the proposed changes are necessary and should be given appropriate help and encouragement, including training (Beer, 1980; Buchanan and Badham, 1999; Egan, 1994). Buchanan *et al.* (1999) call for a more effective role for the change agent because of their reservations about the way change management is normally handled.

While acknowledging the important part played by top management in managing change, there is a view that it is functional in dynamic and uncertain business environments to recognise the limited power of managers at the apex of the organisation to prescribe corporate renewal (Beer *et al.*, 1990). This view is encapsulated in the '*emergent approach*' to managing change, where it is conceded that there is scope for initiating and implementing change from the bottom up rather than the top down (Wilson, 1992). In such circumstances managers further down the organisation can make an important contribution to the change process, and senior managers can learn from those closer to the scene of action. In the emergent approach one has to recognise the existence of power relationships and the strength of interest groups, and acknowledge the need to reconcile the needs of the organisation with the varied interests of its members; also, participants have to recognise the imperfect nature of knowledge and the short attention spans of individuals (Burnes, 1996). In such an approach the role of the manager is likely to be one of facilitation, building-in a variety of views and enabling contributors to develop solutions to problems and new ways of working. This is in contrast to more traditional forms of leadership that typically focus on setting a vision and goals.

■ Organisational development

Organisational development (OD) is part of the process of planned change and has as its remit the improvement of organisational functioning. It relies on a number of interventionist strategies ranging from modifications to structure and processes to the use of therapeutic techniques and counselling. If it is properly applied, individuals and groups are likely to be better able to solve problems and the organisation ought to be better equipped to respond to the external environment. In the past OD was preoccupied to a significant extent with the improvement of interpersonal relationships, and placed less emphasis on organisational efficiency and effectiveness (Cummings and Worley, 1993). Today it is broader in its perspective and takes its cue from strategic planning. Normally you would expect OD techniques or interventions to apply at three levels: the organisation, the task and the individual/group.

Organisation

Some scholars (for example Thompson, 1990) believe that restructuring the organisation (e.g. delayering) is an effective way to bring about change. The result could be that employees are given revised or new duties and responsibilities and as a consequence pressure is put on them to change their attitudes and behaviour. Elsewhere in this text we have seen the application of various techniques and processes (TQM, BPR, new technology – see pages 105–7, 107–9 and 54–6 respectively) to bring about significant changes so as to improve the performance and competitiveness of the organisation. Other complementary methods for transforming organisations (e.g. changing culture and utilising the learning organisation – see page 240) are likely to be a useful means of bringing about change. Typically, such large-scale changes would utilise an 'unfreeze – change – refreeze' approach (Lewin, 1951).

Changes to the whole organisation have the advantage of being all encompassing. They can be used to generate a new mind-set and behaviour-set amongst the employees. Psychological denial of, and resistance to, change on this scale are difficult to sustain. However, disadvantages include that the resources required and the disruption caused are considerable. There is also a danger that repeated restructuring could have a detrimental impact on the attitudes of employees to change as they may start to experience 'change fatigue'. This has been the case for some employees in the British National Health Service, where they feel that they have not yet fully adapted to the last restructuring before the next one comes along (Beech, 2000). The result can be a degree of cynicism about how genuine and long lasting the changes will be. This phenomenon may become more general if organisations continue to be subject to increasing change in the social, political and economic arenas.

Task

It is felt that certain tasks are no longer as relevant as they used to be, and a strategy of job redesign is necessary. In this case job redesign is the intervention strategy. This could result in an enrichment of certain jobs and recognition that some tasks are superfluous to requirements. In Chapter 9 there is an examination of motivational techniques based on job redesign. Tasks are specified in the job description for a post. Traditionally, job descriptions would provide considerable detail, but nowadays they tend to be less specific and more open. The purpose behind this change is to establish an expectation from the outset that the tasks an employee has will not remain fixed throughout their term of employment. (These issues are discussed in relation to recruitment and selection in Chapter 7.) Changes in the nature of tasks may lead to training needs as there is a requirement for new skills or knowledge.

Individual/group

There are OD strategies or interventions aimed at changing the attitudes and behaviour of employees, apart from training and development discussed in Chapter 10. Among the well-known people-focused change techniques that put the accent on changing attitudes and behaviour are sensitivity training, process consultation, survey feedback, team building and intergroup development.

Sensitivity training

This technique is also referred to as encounter groups, or 'T'- (training) groups. Its objectives are to give people the opportunity to develop awareness of their own behaviour, how others see them, greater sensitivity to the behaviour of others and a better understanding of group processes. The main method used to change behaviour is group interaction in an unstructured setting. For example, a group of 10–15 members interact in an environment characterised by openness and frankness, and they discuss information about themselves and the dynamics of the group. A trainer or adviser is in attendance but refrains from taking a directional stand. Instead he or she creates a setting where people feel able to express their thoughts and feelings. An outcome from a successfully run 'T'-group would be that people are better able to empathise with others, are better able to listen to others, are less inhibited, are more tolerant of others' points of view and better equipped to confront conflict situations. However, some individuals could find the experience traumatic; also, the permanency of the benefits is questionable because of the difficulty of transplanting the changed behaviour to the place of work. This could be due to the fact that normal organisational conditions are not conducive to conditions of openness and trust (Makin *et al.*, 1989).

Process consultation

This technique bears some similarity to sensitivity training but is more task oriented, having as its major aim the resolution of interpersonal problems in order to improve organisational effectiveness. In process consultation an outside consultant helps a group (e.g. a management group), who is the client, to solve their own problems (Edmondson, 1996; Schein, 1969). The consultant will need to establish whether the project is of interest and one that he or she can handle, and that the client is interested. If so, together they diagnose the problem and explore the most likely solution. The able consultant, adept at devising pertinent questions and listening, uses the interview rather than the questionnaire for gathering information.

They use interventions, such as setting the agenda with the group, provide feedback and offer coaching or counselling. The consultant's role is a sensitive one because all questions asked can be viewed as interventions. The focus is on people-centred problems, helping the client to perceive and understand better key organisational problems but not suggesting solutions. Also, people are encouraged to come forward with their own solutions to the interpersonal problems they face. Generally, as stated above, the consultant does not offer solutions to technical problems; but there may be exceptional circumstances when technical advice is offered. It needs restating that the consultant's expertise is essentially in the domain of problem diagnosis and developing the most appropriate group dynamics. The consultant can help the group locate a technical expert if it is obvious that this type of help is needed. Important issues to consider in the relationship between the consultant and the client are the psychological contract between them, the question of trust, and the consultant not being viewed simply as the expert. Finally, a sensitive issue is the disengagement by the consultant and an evaluation of the effectiveness of the process consultation.

Survey feedback

This technique could be used to solicit views on a number of issues (e.g. communication, job satisfaction, supervision) from employees attached to particular sections or departments. At the outset a change agent interviews a cross-section of employees to establish the important issues (e.g. problems) before a questionnaire is prepared. The questionnaire is used to collect information. When the data is analysed a summary of the results are fed back to the participants in the survey (Franklin, 1978). The summary is used by the employees to help them with the identification and solution of the problem. The change agent organises feedback meetings (i.e. small 'family' groups) to promote interaction and discussion of the issues, and the feedback meetings are run by the managers. In fact the change agent's role is that of an expert and an information resource at the disposal of the group. Before the formal feedback meeting takes place, the change agent helps the manager when together they review the feedback data (e.g. communication, job satisfaction, decision making, leadership), and suggests ways of identifying and solving the various problems. At the formal feedback meeting the group discusses the issues raised by the survey data and, relying on the assistance provided by the change agent, states what they have learnt from the information presented. The next phase is when action plans for improvements are proposed; this stage could require a number of meetings. Finally, there is the implementation of the proposals for solving the problems.

Team building

It is natural to focus on team building as a technique because there are many situations in organisations where members of a team or group frequently work in an interdependent fashion. Interdependency is crucial in teamwork, and so is coordination of the efforts of the group members if a successful outcome is to materialise. The major objective of team building is to create a healthy climate of trust between members and to foster high levels of interaction with the ultimate aim of improving specific aspects of the performance of the team. In team building it will be necessary to make a serious examination of the group's goals and priorities, clarification of each member's role in the group, evaluation of the group's performance, analysis of the problems encountered by the group, and sensitivity to the overall dynamics of the group. During the team building process different perceptions will surface, and a critical perspective should apply to an appraisal of both the means and the ends in the context of group functioning. A change agent could be employed to facilitate the above activities and help with exploring action plans aimed at bringing about the necessary change. An example of a movement to teamworking appears in Example 4.1.

EXAMPLE 4.1

Teamworking at the Inland Revenue

Employees in the Inland Revenue worked for many years on an individual basis in their own particular areas in a unionised environment. When the manager of the main office of the Inland Revenue in Portsmouth was grappling with the idea of introducing team systems of working he was aware of that tradition. He was committed to teamworking because of a belief that this system of working would lead to greater employee involvement, job satisfaction and the realisation of people's potential for the benefit of the business. He was cognisant of the fact that teamworking was part of a much wider change programme launched by the Inland Revenue in the early 1990s and recognised that trying to enforce teamworking too quickly would not produce the desired effect.

He therefore formed a task group to establish whether teamworking was an appropriate vehicle to process work activities within his domain and, if so, the form it should take. After identifying likely difficulties, the task force felt that it would be desirable to pilot teamworking to a limited extent in the first instance. The services of a change agent were available at the conception and implementation stages of the scheme, and useful information (interpreted for the benefit of management) was provided as a result of his fact-finding exercises. Subsequently, when teamworking was in place it was found that the managers reporting to the overall office manager were operating as self-management teams, making their own decisions on operational matters without having to refer everything upwards, which was previously the case in the traditional hierarchy. These managers now enjoyed autonomy in the way the work was processed, although they had to operate within strict guidelines. The main guideline is that they must involve their subordinates when it comes to reorganising the work.

In this case the emphasis was on teamworking that cut across traditional functional (lateral) and hierarchical (vertical) lines, and it was done gradually in order to elicit support and to bring about a change in culture.

(Arkin, 1997)

An interesting example of team building is a model of management team development devised by Dyer (1984). The major objective of the team building session is to remove barriers to the smooth functioning of the team (i.e. to clarify roles, correct misunderstandings, advocate more sharing of information, be more creative). In the first instance data is collected to establish the causes of the problems. The change agent or consultant is committed to open discussion and acts as a catalyst – i.e. an observer/facilitator with a focus similar to the process consultation consultant – and the manager acts as group leader. To start with, the team assembles at a location away from the place of work. Before the team building session starts in earnest the following questions are asked:

■ What group practices are worth preserving?
■ What behaviour or practices are undermining or interfering with the effectiveness of the team?
■ What are the team's proposals for improving the quality of the working relationships within the team and its overall functioning?

At the meeting answers to these questions are discussed and, using a flip chart, the following points could be emphasised: identification of the barriers to individual and team effectiveness, the tasks people enjoy doing, and the suggestions made for improvements. The next step is for the problems facing the team to be prioritised; this forms the agenda for the remainder of the meeting. The objectives of the session will be re-examined in relation to what has happened. In practice certain issues will be resolved, others referred to a working party, and some will remain unresolved. Finally, strategies for action are stipulated, and in this context it is important to secure the commitment of the team leader (the manager) and the change agent (the consultant) to the implementation of the proposals.

The outcome of a serious research project into successful team performance underlined the importance of 'role heterogeneity' – that is, different group members are capable of performing different roles within a team (Belbin, 1993). For example, it would be functional to have members with the following skills: capable of chairing a meeting effectively, full of good ideas, a capacity to ensure that deadlines are met, an ability to put ideas into practice, able to inject useful information into a discussion and negotiate with external agencies, a facility to move the debate forward so that agreement can be reached, able to evaluate individual contributions and analyse complex situations, and able to provide social support to members. A team could consist of individuals each possessing a single but different skill, but it would be more realistic to assume that any one individual has the capacity to exercise more than one skill. If so, this would be useful resource in a small team consisting of a few members.

At this stage one may very well ask if teamwork penetrates the upper echelons of the organisation. It is sometimes said that senior executives sing the praises of teamwork at lower levels of the organisation, but when it comes to themselves, they often exhibit aloofness and blinkered perspectives (Hambrick, 2000). According to Hambrick, chief executives are resistant to teamwork at the top level, fearing that it amounts to an abdication of their leadership role, or that it runs counter to their organisation culture of unit accountability and initiative. What these executives do not understand is that an effective top management team greatly extends the capabilities of the chief executive; it rarely dilutes them. He goes on to say that a well functioning top management team is an important complement to individual effort directed at driving the business forward. An integrated senior management team is crucial not only to diagnose the company's current predicament, and formulating a plan for large-scale change, but also to engage in implementing change.

Intergroup development

The aim of this technique is to change attitudes and the perceptions that different organisational groups (e.g. finance, marketing) have of each other, so that they are better able to communicate and cooperate. If negative views prevail, this could undermine the quality of interactions and liaisons between teams, and perhaps adversely affect efforts to coordinate activities at the organisational level. If there are problems with intergroup relationships, one could take concrete action to solve them as follows (Liebowitz and De Meuse, 1982).

Teams, or their leaders, get together to attempt to solve the problem and in doing so promote better relationships. To start with the groups are located in different rooms and after initial deliberations each group comes forward with its perception of the other group, as well as speculating about what the other group is saying about it. Then the groups meet in a central location to share information, conveying to the other group their perceptions of that group. In this situation the consultant's intervention is confined only to the clarification of meaning. The groups retire to their respective rooms and discuss the insights that apply to themselves and the other group. This forum offers the opportunity to clear the air with respect to differences of opinion and friction between the groups. The groups return to the central location and meet and compare their lists of the issues that divide them. They cooperate in providing lists of outstanding issues (unresolved difficulties) and prioritise them. Action plans to solve the difficulties are created in the expectation that they will be implemented. It is important to evaluate the implementation of the plans.

Finally, in contemporary organisations the individual/organisational approach (i.e. people centred) to organisational development is not as important as it was in the past. The preferred overall approach nowadays is change management, and its strength is that it draws on a variety of approaches, including the three approaches examined above, to improve organisational performance (Worren *et al.*, 1999).

■ Role of change and development in HRM

Some have argued (e.g. Thornhill *et al.*, 2000) that managing change is now central to HRM. The HRM specialists are frequently cast as 'change makers' (Storey, 1992) who take on responsibility for leading the implementation of change through initiatives such as OD, structural change, and individual change through training or recruitment. A number of major challenges act as drivers of change, including the following:

- Cross-national boundary working requires people to work with different cultures and to be highly adaptive in the way they perform tasks and use management styles.
- Growth through mergers and acquisitions requires a blend of structures, processes and accepted ways of working.
- Increasingly, there is a need for organisations to work in partnership with their employees, which can entail significant changes in decision-making processes, communication and industrial relations (Armstrong *et al.*, 1998).
- There is a need for organisations to enhance performance and achieve competitive advantage through their HRM strategies.

To illustrate the link between HRM and change there will now be reference to a study of firms in Korea – a country that has been undergoing major change in recent history (Bae and Lawler, 2000). Bae and Lawler examined the relationships between placing value on HRM, high involvement and organisational performance. They found that in Korea, at the initial stages of export growth and economic emergence, firms typically adopted bureaucratic HRM strategies that complemented low cost production. However, as the country has gone through times of change and economic crisis there was a need to seek alternatives.

While some theorists have argued that in order to be coherent it is necessary for an organisation to have one unified HRM strategy, Lepak and Snell (1999) have argued that it is possible to mix strategies, such as developing staff internally and acquiring staff externally, and Bae and Lawler found a degree of mixed strategy in the Korean firms as they faced globalisation through what they termed the 'new human resource management'. This entailed high involvement strategies, and typically placing a strong value on HRM. People were now seen as a source of competitive success (realised advantage) and there was much greater effort to empower them. This turned out to be vitally important, because of time-based competitive advantage (Pfeffer, 1994) – i.e. beating the competition by the speed of the work. This required workers who had well-developed intellectual preparation to respond on the spot with speed and sophistication. These skills were fundamental to organisational performance, particularly in times of change. The ability of workers to learn quickly, adopt technologies and translate these into practice (Hobday, 1998) differentiated the high performance firms from those that struggled in the competitive external environment. Overall, the best performing firms were internally adaptive (i.e. have an ability to develop new practices and processes in response to new ideas and opportunities internally, as well as responding to forces of change externally). This could be achieved through their developmental HRM strategies, which focused on involvement and creating a workforce that perceived itself to be valued (Bae and Lawler, 2000).

In the modern organisational context change is ever present, and this presents HRM with both a challenge and an opportunity to be involved and add value. The challenge is to the traditional theories of HRM that sought consistency and coherence in a set of policies and practices, which would give employees a sense of stability and meaning over time. In changing market conditions it may be necessary to adopt mixed strategies (Lepak and Snell, 1999), which are contingent upon the strategic environment (e.g. variation in demand for products, changes in the number and type of competitors) but that, nonetheless, engender commitment in the workforce. It has been argued that such an approach could reduce commitment, as employees perceive themselves being treated as a contingent variable (Legge, 1995) – contingent variable in this context means that people perceive themselves to be secondary to the purposes of the organisation. As those purposes change so will people be required to change! For example, by using short-term contracts, people's services can be dispensed with when demand falls. Evidence from the United Kingdom indicates that organisations frequently do not adopt 'complete models', such as high commitment management; instead they use the mixed approach, which yields performance benefits for the firm (Wood and de Menezes, 1998).

The indications from studies such as those of Bae and Lawler (2000) are that mixed models can work as long as they incorporate involvement and equip the workforce for change through development. However, from the perspective of Pfeffer and Veiga (1999) – discussed in Chapter 2 – a fully integrated approach is preferable. This provides the opportunity for HRM to challenge traditional HRM perspectives and subscribe to individual, team and organisational development (i.e. change management through people).

■ Conclusions

In this chapter we have discussed some of the factors in putting change management through people into practice. It is necessary to understand potential psychological effects of change, resistance and various means of engaging with and overcoming such resistance. While in some forms of traditional management coercive strategies of change were popular, the more recent research evidence indicates that superior organisational performance is achieved through people-centred approaches to change. Coercion is likely to alienate the workforce and build up resistance. Involvement and development are more likely to equip employees to be flexible and adaptable in the face of the demands of globalisation, the need for rapid reaction to customers, the adoption of new technology and the enactment of emergent strategy (referred to in connection with the descriptive school of strategy in Chapter 2) that are associated with organisational success.

Communication plays a significant role in managing change. Effective communication has been highlighted in the high performance models of HRM (Becker and Huselid, 1999) and in the context of change it is crucial in ensuring that the various parties retain an open mind and perceive the messages that were really intended by others. Genuinely open communication is only likely to occur where there is a supportive organisational culture and an understanding by management of the implications of change for the workforce. For example, care is needed to match the appropriate management style with the 'stage of coping' or the level of resistance the workforce exhibits. Of course there are circumstances in which ideas for innovation occur not only in the management group but throughout the organisation. Various techniques of organisational development, such as process consultation, team building and intergroup development, can be used to encourage change and development and build on the potential of the whole organisation. Lastly, it is worth noting that change is likely to entail people thinking and acting differently, and so managing change plays a central role in HRM activities.

References

Arkin, A. (1997) 'Tax incentives', *People Management*, 3, 36–8.

Armstrong, P., Marginson, P., Edwards, P. and Purcell, J. (1998). 'Divisionalization in the UK: diversity, size and the devolution of bargaining', *Organization Studies*, 19, 1–22.

Bae, J. and Lawler, J.J. (2000) 'Organizational and HRM Strategies in Korea: impact on firm performance in an emerging economy', *Academy of Management Journal*, 43, 502–17.

Becker, B.E. and Huselid, M.A. (1999) 'Overview: strategic human resource management in five leading firms', *Human Resource Management*, 38, 287–301.

Bedeian, A.G. and Zammuto, R.F. (1991) *Organizations: Theory and design*, Orlando, FL: Dryden Press.

Beech, N. (2000) 'Narrative styles of managers and workers: A tale of star crossed lovers', *Journal of Applied Behavioural Science*, 36 (2), 210–28.

Beer, M. (1980). *Organizational Change and Development: A systems view*, Santa Monica, CA: Goodyear.

Beer, M., Eisenstat, R.A. and Spector, B. (1990) 'Why change programmes don't produce change', *Harvard Business Review*, November/December, 158–66

Belbin, R.M. (1993) *Team Roles at Work*, Oxford: Butterworth Heinemann.

Buchanan, D. and Badham, R. (1999) 'Politics and organizational change: the lived experience', *Human Relations*, 52, 609–30.

Buchanan, D., Clayton, T. and Doyle, M. (1999) 'Organization development and change: the legacy of the nineties', *Human Resource Management Journal*, 9, 20–37.

Burnes, B. (1996) 'No such thing as one best way to manage organizational change', *Management Decision*, 34, 11–18.

Carnall, C. (1990) *Managing Change in Organizations*, Hemel Hemstead: Prentice Hall.

Cummings, T.G. and Worley, C.G. (1993) *Organization Development and Change*, 5th edn, Minneapolis, MN: West Publishing Company.

Dyer, W.G. (1984) *Strategies for Managing Change*, Reading, MA: Addison-Wesley.

Eccles, A. (1994) *Succeeding with Change: Implementing action driven strategies*, Maidenhead: McGraw-Hill.

Edmondson, A.C. (1996) 'Three faces of Eden: the persistence of competing theories and multiple diagnoses in organizational intervention research', *Human Relations*, 49, 571–95.

Egan, G. (1994) *Working the Shadow Side: A guide to positive behind the scene management*, San Francisco, CA: Jossey-Bass.

Franklin, J.L. (1978) 'Improving the effectiveness of survey feedback', *Personnel*, May–June, 11–17.

Hambrick, D.C. (2000) 'Putting the team into top management'. Part 2, Mastering Management Series, *Financial Times*, 9 October, 6–7.

Hobday, M. (1998) 'Latecomer catch-up strategies in electronics: Samsung of Korea and ACER of Taiwan', *Asia Pacific Business Review*, 4, 48–83.

Katz, D. and Kahn, R.L. (1978) *The Social Psychology of Organizations*, 2nd edn, New York: Wiley.

Kotter, J.P. (1995) 'Leading change: why transformation efforts fail?', *Harvard Business Review*, 73, 59–67.

Kotter, J.P. and Schlesinger, L.A. (1979) 'Choosing strategies for change', *Harvard Business Review*, March/April, 106–14.

Legge, K. (1995) *Human Resource Management: Rhetorics and realities*, Basingstoke: Macmillan.

Lepak, D.P. and Snell, S.A. (1999) 'The human resource architecture: toward a theory of human capital allocation and development', *Academy of Management Review*, 13, 31–48.

Lewin, K. (1951) *Field Theory in Social Science*, New York: Harper & Row.

Liebowitz, S.J. and De Meuse, K.P. (1982) 'The application of teambuilding' *Human Relations*, January, 1–18.

Mabey, C., Salaman, G. and Storey, J. (eds) (1998) *Strategic Human Resource Management: A reader*, London: Sage.

McKenna, E. (2000) *Business Psychology and Organisational Behaviour*, Hove: Psychology Press.

Makin, P., Cooper, C.L. and Cox, C. (1989) *Managing People at Work*, London: Routledge/British Psychological Society.

Mintzberg, H. and Markides, C. (2000) 'Crosstalk', *Academy of Management Executive*, 14 (3), 31–45.

Pfeffer, J. (1994) *Competitive Advantage Through People*, Boston, MA: Harvard Business School Press.

Pfeffer, J. and Veiga, J.F. (1999) 'Putting people first for organizational success', *Academy of Management Executive*, 13, 37–50.

Rondinelli, D.A. and Black, S.S. (2000) 'Multinational strategic alliances and acquisitions in central and eastern Europe: partnerships in privatization', *Academy of Management Executive*, 14 (4), 85–98.

Schein, E. (1969) *Process Consultation: Its role in organizational development*, Reading, MA: Addison-Wesley.

Storey, J. (1992) *Developments in the Management of Human Resources*, Oxford: Blackwell.

Thompson, J.D. (1990) 'The structure of complex organization', in Pugh, D.S. (ed.), *Organisation Theory: Selected readings*, London: Penguin.

Thornhill, A., Lewis, P., Millmore, M. and Saunders, M. (2000) *Managing Change: A human resource strategy approach*, Harlow: Pearson.

Wilson, D.C. (1992) *A Strategy of Change*, London: Routledge.

Wood, S. and de Menezes, L. (1998) 'High commitment management in the UK: evidence from the Workplace Industrial Relations Survey and Employers' Manpower and Skills Practices Survey', *Human Relations*, 51, 485–516.

Worren, N.A.M., Ruddle, K. and Moore, K. (1999) 'From organizational development to change management: the emergence of a new profession', *Journal of Applied Behavioural Science*, 35, 273–86.

Zaltman, G. and Duncan, R. (1977) *Strategies for Planned Change*, New York: Wiley.

Chapter 5

Organisational culture

Culture is a central and important topic in HRM. It is concerned with the values, attitudes, beliefs, assumptions, actions and procedures that people adopt in organisational life. It encompasses the range of thought and action as they are reinforced in the corporate setting, and so underlies many of the specific issues of people management. It provides the social framework for the relationship between managers and employees and as such is an influencing factor on the psychological contract, employees' willingness to accept change and the ability of the organisation to be open about, and learn from, its experience.

After reading this chapter, you should:

- be aware of some of the main theories and models of national and organisational culture;
- understand the dimensions that are commonly used to analyse culture;
- be aware of the implications of culture for issues such as leadership style, teamworking and commitment;
- understand the problems and opportunities associated with managerial attempts to change culture
- be able to reflect critically on the interaction between culture and HRM, and on the issues for managers operating within a particular culture.

■ Societal culture

Goffee (1997) defines culture as guides for living and collective mental programming developed over time. These guides are based on assumptions reflected in the attitudes, values and behaviour of individuals and groups. The assumptions are learnt, they assume a pattern and are passed down through the generations. Culture, which can also be viewed as achievements in art, literature and music in society, has been a subject of investigation in social anthropology where researchers have sought to understand the shared meanings and values held by groups in society that give significance to their actions.

So, to understand actions and behaviour at a religious ceremony in a particular country, it would be most helpful to have an insight into the underlying system of beliefs. Nationality is an important factor to consider in the context of values and behaviour. For example, there is some evidence to indicate that the Americans adhere to values associated with individuality, the Japanese are partial to conformity and cooperation in groups, while Arabs tend to steer clear of conflict and place loyalty ahead of efficiency. In looking at differences between countries considerations other than national culture should be given due weight. For example, the legal system and political institutions can shape the national character.

Impact of national cultures

Cultural differences between nationalities were found when the views of a large number of employees spread over many countries but employed by the same organisation were solicited (Hofestede, 1980). Hofestede concluded that national cultures could be explained with reference to the following factors:

1 *Power distance.* This factor measures the extent to which culture prompts a person in a position of authority to exercise power. Managers operating in cultures ranked high in power distance (e.g. Argentina) behaved rather autocratically in conditions of low trust, and there was an expectation on the part of subordinates that superiors would act in a directive way. By contrast, in cultures ranked low in power distance (e.g. Canada) a closer and warmer relationship existed between superiors and subordinates, where the latter would be expected to be involved in decision making.

2 *Uncertainty avoidance.* This factor measured the extent to which culture encouraged risk taking and tolerated ambiguity. People in cultures that encouraged risk taking were inclined to take risks and were ranked low in uncertainty avoidance. Such people (e.g. in Hong Kong) encountered less stress from situations clouded with ambiguity and placed less importance on following the rules. By contrast, people in cultures ranked high in uncertainty avoidance (e.g. Iran) tended to be risk aversive. Features of the behavioural pattern of people displaying risk aversiveness when confronted by situations high in uncertainty avoidance are working hard, displaying intolerance towards those who do not abide by the rules and staying in the same job for a long time, in order to reduce the high levels of anxiety and stress stemming from conditions of uncertainty.

3 *Individualism–collectivism.* This factor gauged the extent to which culture measured an individual as opposed to a group perspective. In a culture with an individualistic bias (e.g. the United States) there would be a pronounced emphasis on the exercise of individual initiative and performance with a tendency to be preoccupied with the self and the immediate family. By contrast, in collectivist cultures (e.g. Singapore) there exists a broader set of loyalties to the extended family and, where appropriate, to the tribe. In return for loyalty the individual gets protection and support.

4 *Masculinity–femininity.* This factor measured the extent to which culture measured what were called 'masculine' as opposed to 'feminine' characteristics and would be reflected in the type of achievements that are valued. Masculine

cultures (e.g. Italy) place much emphasis on the acquisition of material pos-
sessions and an ambitious disposition, and there is a clear differentiation
between male and female roles. By contrast, the emphasis appears to be on concern for the environment, the quality of life and caring in feminine cultures (e.g.
the Netherlands).

As a result of more recent work, Hofestede (1994) puts forward a fifth dimension to his scheme. This dimension is called *long-term orientation vs short-term orientation*. A long-term orientation manifested itself as future oriented, with an
emphasis on perseverance and thrift, and high levels of adaptability to a changing
world. This orientation applied to societies in South-east Asia (e.g. Japan, Hong
Kong, Singapore), where the Confucian philosophy is prevalent. It was also applicable to Brazil.

Trompenaars (1993) also recognises the power of national cultures in the way
they influence the behaviour of managers. He identifies seven dimensions as follows, five of which are relevant in this context:

1 *Universalism vs particularism.* Universalism means that, for example, a solid
   principle can be applied everywhere, while particularism means that particular
   circumstances are influential in determining whether a principle or line of action
   should be adopted. Universalism would be more applicable to countries such as
   the United States and Germany, whereas particularism could apply to Indonesia
   and Venezuela.

2 *Individualism vs collectivism.* Individualism means that individuals experience
   personal achievement and assume personal responsibility for their actions, and
   is attributable to countries such as the United States and the United Kingdom. In
   societies where collectivism prevails (e.g. Thailand, Singapore and Japan) individuals function through groups and they assume joint responsibility for the collective output. This dimension has already been recognised by Hofestede.

3 *Neutral vs affective.* In societies where a neutral culture prevails expressing
   anger or happiness in the workplace is not really acceptable. Those with a neutral orientation in societies, such as Japan and the United Kingdom, do not like
   expressing themselves in an emotional sense in public. But those in societies (e.g.
   Brazil, Mexico) with an affective disposition openly express their emotions with
   an expressive face, body gestures and raised voice.

4 *Specific relationship vs diffuse relationship.* In societies with a specific relationship orientation (e.g. the United Kingdom, the United States) there is a preference for people to keep their public and private lives separate, particularly
   guarding their private lives. The tendency is to display mostly a public face. But
   in societies with diffuse relationships (e.g. Spain, Chile) it is possible to see more
   of the inner self of the person. Work and private lives are closely linked.

5 *Achievement vs ascription.* In societies with an achievement orientation (e.g.
   Switzerland, Germany, the United States) people work hard to improve themselves, they are ambitious and emphasise accomplishment. But in societies where
   ascription is found (e.g. Indonesia, Chile) there is a tendency to pay respect to

those with status in the community (e.g. respected and admired figures), quite independent of their achievement.

■ Cultural diversity: teams and leadership

Recognising the US roots of HRM, Guest (1994a) draws our attention to a number of factors likely to influence its implementation in Europe (see page 5). He identified cultural diversity as an important factor. In this section cultural diversity will be viewed from the angle of multi-cultural teams and how managerial leadership is influenced by national culture. In the last decade the development of global markets has created numerous cross-cultural contacts, and the ensuing dialogue has formed the basis for transacting global business (Adler, 1997). This has implications for the development of culturally diverse teams, where people from different cultures relate to each other, aided by the power of new technology when it comes to communication systems. The output of culturally diverse teams can be impressive if diversity is well managed. It is said that the potential of diverse teams is not fully realised unless one pays particular attention to the way these teams are managed (Kandola, 1995).

To operate successfully across cultures it is important to be able to recognise cultural differences and be adaptable (Marx, 1999), as well as viewing the organisation as international in orientation. To satisfy the latter it would seem necessary to be aware of political currents likely to affect international trade, to have a management and organisation system tuned into the demands of world markets, and management development activities that nurture an appropriate international outlook. Speaking of management development, one may well ask what type of managerial leadership is appropriate in particular cultures. As a broad principle one can acknowledge that culture influences leadership style (Koopman *et al.*, 1999). More specific associations will now be examined.

In some cultures leaders are respected when they take strong decisive action, whereas in other cultures consultative and participative decision-making approaches are more valued. According to Den Hartog *et al.* (1999), in a culture where authoritarian leadership is valued it would be pointless acting in a way more characteristic of a participative or democratic leader. But in a culture that endorses a more nurturing and humanistic leadership style, being sensitive and considerate as a leader could be functional. Using Hofestede's framework, examined above, masculine cultures are probably more tolerant of strong directive leaders than feminine cultures. In the latter case it is more likely that there is a preference for more consultative, considerate leaders. Also, in 'high' power distance cultures, as defined by Hofestede, authoritarian leadership styles may be more acceptable. In this type of setting dominance and overt wielding of power may be considered appropriate. By contrast, in more egalitarian societies and cultures leaders may be more prone to emphasising less social distance between themselves and their followers, thereby striving for equality with others (Den Hartog *et al.*, 1999).

House (1995) reflects on the North American cultural influence on theoretical developments in managerial leadership, and concludes that the following slant is apparent. There is an emphasis on individualistic rather than collectivist approaches; rationality takes pride of place over ascetics, spiritual values or superstition; reward systems assume more of an individual rather than group character; people are more self-centred than altruistic in their motivation; the responsibilities of followers rather than their rights receive emphasis; and the primacy of work in people's lives and the sanctity of democratic values are conspicuous.

■ Organisational culture

It is apparent from Hofestede's and Trompenaars' work and the literature generally on cultural diversity that national cultures impinge on practices within the organisation. That provides a cue to direct our attention to a study of organisational cultures. Organisational culture finds expression through the thoughts, intentions, actions and interpretations of members of the organisation (Meek, 1992). Schein (1990) defined organisational culture as a pattern of basic assumptions that a given group has invented, discovered or developed in learning to cope with its problems of external adaptation and internal integration. This pattern has worked well enough for the group to be considered valid and therefore is to be taught to new members as the correct way to perceive, think and feel in relation to those problems. An alternative definition provided by Moorhead and Griffin (1998) states that organisational culture is a set of values, often taken for granted, that help people in an organisation understand which actions are considered acceptable and which unacceptable. Often these values are communicated through stories and other symbolic means.

Culture vs climate

Is there a difference between culture and climate within the organisation? Some argue that climate is a sub-set of organisational culture, and that in reality the difference between climate and culture is not pronounced (Furnham, 1997). Others can see a noticeable difference, as follows: climate is concerned with the current atmosphere within the organisation (Denison, 1996), as manifested in communication and reward systems and leadership style, etc. Organisational culture is based on the history and traditions of the organisation with the emphasis on values and norms underpinning the behaviour of employees, and it is more difficult to change in the short term.

Types of culture

Often we refer to organisational culture as strong and weak, as well as a dominant or a sub-culture. Strong cultures are said to be advantageous in promoting cohesiveness, loyalty and the commitment of employees. This is so because the core values of the organisation are widely shared and eagerly adopted by large numbers of employees. Strong cultures exert powerful behavioural compliance, expressed as high agreement amongst members about what the organisation represents. However, looking at the organisation from a perspective of diversity, a strong culture could be disadvantageous because insufficient attention is paid to the diverse strengths and the backgrounds people can bring to the organisation.

A dominant culture, referred to as the organisation's culture, reflects the core values that are shared by the majority of the employees. This could be referred to as the distinctive personality of the organisation. A sub-culture, found in departments, divisions and geographical areas, reflects the common problems or experiences of employees in these areas (Tushman and O'Reilly, 1996). But equally a sub-culture could consist of the core values of the dominant culture as well as the values of the area to which they relate. There could be differences between one sub-culture and another (Hope and Henry, 1996), and between sub-cultures and the dominant culture. The sub-culture of the dealing room could be different from the sub-culture of another department of an investment bank (see Box 5.1.)

BOX 5.1

The culture of the dealing room

Many dealing rooms in merchant banks and stockbroking firms are dominated by one simple system of values: win or be damned. If dealers make large profits for the organisation the rewards – both in a material and psychological sense – are very significant. Not only is personal remuneration substantial, but also the dealers' status in the firm and the market generally is considerably enhanced. However, if the dealers' performance is poor in terms of profits generated or losses sustained the reverse situation applies. They could feel humiliated and isolated and risk losing their jobs with detrimental personal consequences. Always in the background is greed and fear, in particular fear: fear of losing the job and fear of public humiliation. It is fear that prevents dealers from cutting their losses as well as forcing them to get out of profitable positions early.

Dealers live in a unique corporate 'sub-culture', one that encourages overconfidence and insulates them from the outside world. On the trading floor boldness is looked upon as the most important virtue, and the traders' faith in themselves is boosted by their substantial remuneration package. A moment's hesitation or uncertainty could undermine a transaction. Dealers tend to behave as if they are omnipotent, they brag about the size of their deals, and hero status is bestowed on anyone making large sums of money. Because of the high rewards they are encouraged to take unwise risks.

There is a loss of perspective on outside events, with a tendency for dealers to shield themselves from too much information that could metaphorically lead to paralysis. There is the illusion that the computer screen gives them a window on the outside world, even though it is no more than a series of rapidly changing numbers. Erratic ▶

behaviour is condoned if not encouraged, and shouting matches and foot stomping are part of the scene on the trading floor. The dealers display emotional volatility, and this is accepted as long as they are generating good profits. A dangerous cocktail is the mixture of emotional volatility, overconfidence and access to large amounts of capital. In addition to tightening up procedures, Weaving (1995) suggests the following actions to counteract the culture of individualism, competition and insecurity symbolised by Baring Securities, Singapore, in early 1995:

- Create a culture of teamwork in which dealers help each other and share information. When dealers have bad days colleagues would help them by alerting them to the risk management procedures, coaching them through a bad position, and encouraging them to be more rational.
- Take steps to build the dealers' self-confidence, which should help them admit when they are wrong. With self-confidence they are less likely to fall into the trap of the 'illusion of invulnerability', which is often associated with arrogance.
- Help dealers to recognise their own particular response to stress – e.g. feelings of panic and a deterioration in rational thinking that could undermine good decision making – and train them in how to manage stress.
- Institute good management practice exemplified by a competent approach to offering praise, coaching and the provision of feedback. In the appraisal of performance a broad range of behaviour would be considered, and rewards would reflect behaviour somewhat more varied than a single moneymaking criterion.

(Griffith, 1995; Weaving, 1995)

■ Analysing organisational culture

Culture became an issue in the 1980s with attempts to unravel the secrets of Japanese business. Certain fundamental values in Japanese society, such as social solidarity, respect for elders and a strong work ethic, influenced behaviour in organisations. Generally the Japanese corporate culture is supportive of seniority-based pay, job security, uniformity in dress and facilities (e.g. canteen), importance of duty, careful attention to employee selection and training, and a quality-driven system of organisation and management. However, a direct threat to certain values, e.g. seniority-based pay and job security, has come about as a result of the economic recession in Japan in the 1990s.

In the early 1980s the economic success of Japan was attributed to a mixture of US and Japanese practices by Ouchi (1981) in his Theory Z, as follows: a predominant concern for people; a guarantee of long-term employment; decision making based on shared values and collective responsibility; a 'clan' approach to participation, with strong social pressures to encourage performance; high trust and faith in the managers' ultimate judgement; and non-specialised career pathways. The end result was mutual commitment, that is employees responded to the commitment made by the employer by a pledge of commitment to the organisation.

The corporate welfare and paternalistic aspects of Japanese organisational cultures can be found in a particular ideology. This is the ideology of loyalty to one lord as derived from the Japanese appropriation of Chinese 'Confucian' principles and the feudal legacy (Wilkinson and Oliver, 1992). As stated earlier, in effect societal values in Japan have permeated the fabric of the organisation. It would appear that the best course of action by management in the West, which would like to import and use Japanese management practices, is to adapt them to their particular circumstances rather than transplant them in their entirety.

The relationship between organisational culture and performance in the United States was emphasised by Peters and Waterman (1982) when they associated certain management practices with success. In essence these were: adopt an action-oriented and decisive management, identify and serve the customers' needs, encourage independence and entrepreneurial flair with assistance provided by small cohesive groups, involve people at all times in the management of the enterprise in conditions where top management are seen to be in touch with employees, confine the organisation's activities to what it knows best and avoid diversification into unknown territory, avoid complex hierarchical arrangements, and combine central direction with autonomy for the work group.

This research captured the spirit of the times (early 1980s) and offered a US solution to the challenge of Japanese competition. Peters and Waterman felt that the curriculum in business schools, with the predominant emphasis on strategy, structure and quantitatively driven systems, was ill-conceived. To them success rested on a number of factors, such as those mentioned above, which gave more weight to the 'soft' characteristics of HRM – namely staff, style, systems, skills and shared values. Acceptance of the 'excellence theories' propounded by Peters and Waterman would entail paying more attention to leadership, corporate culture, quality, management of change and, of course, HRM in general. It is easy to find fault with the research of Peters and Waterman, in particular the methodology, but it should be borne in mind that this work attracted the attention of top management and succeeded in shifting the focus of management thinking so that much more weight was given to policy issues in HRM (Guest, 1994b).

Another framework of analysis was provided by Deal and Kennedy (1982). Their analysis features 'risk' and 'feedback' as important variables. With these variables in mind culture was analysed as follows:

1 *Tough-guy macho culture* (high risk/fast feedback). In this type of organisational setting you are likely to find entrepreneurial types, who are not very interested in teamwork and are prepared to take high risks. This profile was considered to be applicable to a media or consultancy company at the time the research was undertaken.

2 *Work hard, play hard* (low risk/fast feedback). This is an action-oriented environment where work is viewed as a source of fun. Although there are many solo performers they do rely on supportive teams in a climate of low risk and rapid feedback. This profile could apply to a car dealership or estate agency.

3 *Bet your company* (high risk/slow feedback). The influential people in this culture are those who are technically proficient and show respect for authority in organisations faced with cyclical changes in the economy. The key players are risk takers who rely on slow feedback and were found in industries such as oil or mining.

4 *Process culture* (low risk/slow feedback). The people who function in this environment are low risk takers with an eye for detail, and who rely on well-defined procedures. They put a lot of effort into their work, but are not required to exercise much initiative in conditions of slow feedback. The organisations to which they belonged were located in banking, public utilities and governmental agencies.

With reference to the above profiles, ideally job applicants should give serious consideration to the type of organisational culture most suited to their needs. Equally, organisations should strive to obtain the best fit between the individual and the organisation at the selection stage if the optimum outcome is to be achieved.

There have been attempts to relate culture to the design of the organisation. In this context four types of organisational culture have been proposed (Harrison, 1972):

1 *Power culture*. A small number of senior executives exert much power in a directive way. There is a belief in a strong and decisive stance to advance the interests of the organisation.

2 *Role culture*. There is a concern with bureaucratic procedures, such as rules, regulations and clearly specified roles, because it is believed these will stabilise the system.

3 *Support culture*. There is group or community support for people, which cultivates integration and sharing of values.

4 *Achievement culture*. There is an atmosphere that encourages self-expression and a striving for independence, and the accent is on success and achievement.

A modified version of this typology is proposed by Handy (1985), who acknowledges types 1 and 2 above and adds task culture (e.g. utilisation of knowledge and technical competency in project teams) and person culture (e.g. personal needs and preferences are seriously considered in the assignment of tasks). The typologies examined here can be described as ideal types within which organisations can be placed. Individuals may fit better into one type of culture than another, as would management functions and organisational features. A criticism levelled at this work is the lack of empirical evidence to support it (Williams *et al.*, 1989).

A typology devised by Miles and Snow (1978) recognises the potency of managerial ideology and leadership in influencing and shaping the culture of the organisation. The three-part typology consists of the following:

1 *Defender organisations*. The major objective is to secure and maintain a stable position in the market for the product or service. There is an emphasis on formal systems where planning and control are centralised and there is a commitment to efficiency and cost reduction.

2 *Prospector organisations.* The major objective is to develop new products and exploit market opportunities. To this end there is an emphasis on flexibility, ad hoc systems and creativity.

3 *Analyser organisations.* Careful attention is given to research and development and to steady rather than dramatic growth. There is a tendency to follow rather than lead in the product market.

It is more than likely that different attitudes and beliefs are compatible with the different types of organisational cultures. Also, it is important that structure, strategy and culture blend and harmonise to secure a successful outcome. With regard to strategy, it is known that culture can bolster the strategy of the company and provide the impetus for the development of new products, as has been the case with Motorola, the US corporation. Ogbonna and Whipp (1999) consider the Miles and Snow typology useful when looking at the relationship between strategy and HRM in the UK food retailing sector.

In recent years there was an interest in 'reinventing strategy' as a reaction to downsizing, rightsizing and delayering associated with massive cost cutting (Hamel and Prahalad, 1994). The view is that we should avoid the danger of corporate anorexia and that companies should be energised and stimulated to create new markets.

There are occasions when organisations feel it necessary to reinforce their existing culture and set in motion a series of events or activities to accomplish this objective. Alternatively, there could be a determination to change corporate culture, and this could have significant implications in terms of modification or revision to strategy, structure and processes within the organisation.

■ Changing culture

In recent years many organisations have felt it necessary to change corporate culture to ensure survival or to gain competitive advantage. Often this was prompted by the realisation that the existing culture did not fit the desired future state for the organisation. In Example 5.1 there is an account of action taken to address an inappropriate organisational culture.

EXAMPLE 5.1

Changing culture at Kerry Foods

In the late 1990s Kerry Foods (the Irish food products giant) was growing rapidly as a result of acquisitions. This brought in its wake problems arising from the harmonisation of working practices and changing the nature of jobs (e.g. the job of a van driver delivering food products to retail outlets was changed from merely a delivery role to that of a sales position) in the United Kingdom. There was a desperate need to cultivate a single team ethos within the enlarged organisation because of what was happening in the depots where the drivers congregated and collected the food products for delivery. For example, there was widespread distrust of head office, some depots were performing much worse than others, some drivers would not complete their rounds, absence rates and staff turnover were high, and there were numerous complaints from customers.

It was not surprising in these circumstances for the personnel and training manager of the company to conclude that there was something desperately wrong with the company's culture. She decided to conduct a culture 'health check', drawing on the services of the Department of Economic Psychology, University of Essex, which had developed a cultural audit tool called the Nine Key Factors Survey. Based on nine measures of work culture, a survey was undertaken whereby staff were asked to assess their employer on factors such as fairness, respect, trust, acceptance, team spirit and development. Each factor would receive a rating out of five, and there was also an overall score. The results highlighted problems that needed further investigation.

Out of this investigation came the realisation that, for example, employees were less than enthusiastic about the numerous initiatives which originated from the UK head office in Andover, Hampshire, such as expanding the van delivery role to incorporate sales activity, the advent of Saturday working and the introduction of handheld computers for stock control. In addition, fundamental supervisory and managerial problems were identified in the depots, such as a too relaxed management style or one that encouraged dissent among subordinates. Various training programmes (e.g. induction, leadership, coaching, team building), face-to-face meetings and incentives were introduced to tackle these problems. Some problems were difficult to solve, including trying to create team spirit and loyalty to a remote head office from lone salespeople (van drivers) operating from 27 different depots, but reasonable success has been achieved.

There is now evidence to indicate that employees are beginning to trust the management more than in the past and the business is more successful. Finally, note a concluding comment from the personnel and training manager:

> It has to be accepted that the organisation is a depot-based business, and that it would be futile to impose an inflexible culture on the many depots across the country. One has to recognise that the culture in some depots will be different from others.

(Littlefield, 1999)

Forces in the organisation's external environment could signal the need for a change in culture. For example, in the late 1980s and early 1990s the UK Conservative government took action to unleash market forces within the National Health Service and this had a significant impact, particularly in the case of the culture of Hospital Trusts. The Labour government that came to power in 1997 is also intent on changing culture by means of encouraging the formation of 'joined-up' working and clinically led teams with the spotlight on the patient. Joined-up working can result in a team drawing members from health and social services departments and government agencies to focus on the needs of a service user. So, instead of a service user going from hospital to social housing and then outpatient therapy in turn, their overall care plan would be developed incorporating all the services, so that for the user the provision is 'seamless'. This entails the various providers collaborating over how arrangements should be made and how funding is organised. It is also a challenge to the attitude and power of the professionals involved who are used to holding sway in their own domain.

In Trompenaars' (1993) terms this represents an attempt to move from an individualistic to a collectivist culture. Apart from the external environmental stimulants, the force for cultural change could come from within when senior executives apply new approaches to management, such as total quality management and process re-engineering (these approaches will be discussed later in the chapter). Once it has been established that there is a need for change, a first step would be to analyse the existing organisational culture. Next it would be necessary to envisage the desired end state as far as culture is concerned. Certain commentators see the need for strong leadership to permeate the total organisation, where 'heroes' recognise the need for change and put in place change agents and construct symbols of change in order to create the necessary momentum (Deal and Kennedy, 1982). The major emphasis in cultural change and development is on trying to change the values, attitudes and behaviour of the workforce.

How does one go about changing culture? According to Schein (1985) the organisation can rely on the following 'primary' and 'secondary' mechanisms to change culture. These cultural change mechanisms will now be considered.

Primary mechanisms

(a) Matters to which leaders pay most attention

If senior managers place much emphasis on, for example, the control of expenditure or the importance of service to the customer, and this is visible to employees, then a powerful message is transmitted about the significance of this type of activity. Sometimes it may be necessary to mount workshops or discussion groups to get a key message across to all employees, as British Airways did with its 'Putting People First' initiative, which is dealt with in Example 5.2.

(b) Leader's way of reacting to crises and critical incidents

This could be reflected in the type of situation that is seen as a crisis situation (e.g. a relatively high materials' wastage rate in the manufacturing plant) and the nature of the leader's response to the crisis (e.g. an urgent determination to tackle and solve the problem).

(c) Role modelling, teaching and coaching by leaders

Role modelling occurs when, for example, junior staff copy the behaviour of their seniors and integrate such behaviour into their own pattern of behaviour. This could apply to mannerisms and behaviour such as ways of interacting with valued clients or customers. With regard to teaching and coaching, working closely with people offering guidance and reassurance in a supportive climate has much to commend it and has value in promoting commitment. There is reference to coaching in the context of management development in Chapter 10.

In (a), (b) and (c) prominence is given to the hierarchical role of the leader exercising the right to lead. Some question this type of cultural leadership and point out that if we want cultural change to be effective then there should be wide agreement and ownership amongst people about the desired change (Torrington and Hall, 1998).

(d) Criteria used for allocating rewards

Recently the visibility of performance in the job as a criterion in the determination of rewards has been apparent. At one time loyalty to the organisation received greater emphasis as a criterion than is the case today. If the relationship between performance and rewards is highly visible there is likely to be an expectation that it is functional to strive for improved performance. There is a discussion of performance-related pay (PRP) in Chapter 9, and PRP was used by British Airways to reinforce the training interventions it deployed to bring about cultural change; these are described later in the chapter.

(e) Criteria used for employee selection, promotions and termination of employment

The criteria that would apply under this heading relate to what selectors consider important characteristics in hiring staff, the most appropriate work behaviour to secure career advancement, and what to avoid in order to reduce the likelihood of being made redundant.

Redundancy could be used to terminate the employment of employees on a compulsory basis when, for example, performance is unsatisfactory. An alternative way of shedding labour is to offer voluntary redundancy, or early retirement, particularly to those who might have difficulty in fitting into the new culture. It stands to reason that instituting redundancy measures can have a major impact on the lives of those who leave the organisation, but it can also adversely affect those who stay. For example, if there is a lack of fairness or compassion in the implementation of the redundancy scheme, resentment can arise and have a negative effect after the change in culture has taken place. The legacy of this type of managerial behaviour could sour future relations between management and workers.

As regards employee selection, the organisation could take a conscious decision to recruit workers with attitudes deemed appropriate in the light of the company's culture. This approach has been adopted particularly by Japanese companies setting up operations on a 'greenfield' site. Nissan UK used a rigorous and lengthy selection process when selecting its new workforce (Wickens, 1987). This practice was at variance with the much less exacting traditional practices for hiring shopfloor workers. Nissan's intention was to select a group of employees with values and attitudes compatible with the company's culture. It would appear that the type of person likely to be suitable would be one who is basically cooperative, flexible and certainly not the stereotypical rabble-rouser!

Similarly Cisco Systems, a high technology company, puts considerable effort into bringing about a cultural match between job applicants and the organisation. One means of achieving this is through intensive interaction between the candidates for the job and current employees, normally through a Web site (Welch, 1999). Two of the Web site's more innovative features are a link to the Dilbert cartoon Web site – popular with disaffected programmers – and a chance for an applicant to pair up with a friend, who is a volunteer employee from within the company. This way potential recruits can learn at first hand about the company (Donkin, 2000). It therefore offers the opportunity to discuss objectives of the job, the aspirations of the potential candidate and the organisational background of the job. This system allows the organisation and the candidates to develop a more detailed cultural understanding of each other than would be possible under the more traditional methods. Selecting people who are culturally compatible with the organisation in this way can help to counteract the subsequent problems of changing culture.

The point to bear in mind is that the organisation endeavours to shape behaviour when implementing HRM techniques that utilise the criteria referred to in (d) and (e). An important consideration is the visibility of these criteria in the various decision-making forums.

Secondary mechanisms

(a) Structures, systems and procedures

There could be a fortification of existing structures, systems and procedures or a significant change in them so that the organisation is repositioned to face the future with greater confidence. For example, the desired change might be to create the post-entrepreneurial organisation (e.g. flexible and free from cumbersome bureaucracy) as suggested by Kanter (1989) and discussed in Chapter 3. Such a transformation, if successful, could bring about a fundamental shift in people's attitudes and behaviour at work.

With regard to changing people's attitudes and behaviour so that they will fit comfortably with the emerging culture, it is suggested in Chapter 10 that training and development have a part to play. For example, in teamwork training people are given the experience of working cooperatively in activities away from the actual work situation. This provides them with an opportunity to encounter the attitudes and processes associated with teamwork, and perceive each other's strengths and weaknesses. There is a view that it would be more productive to concentrate on changing behaviour initially in training sessions in the expectation that attitudes will follow the new or changed behaviour. This approach was adopted in equal opportunities training programmes because early attempts to develop awareness and acceptance of the need for equal opportunities were seen as unsuccessful in challenging entrenched biases. Subsequently the emphasis switched to training programmes that highlighted appropriate behaviour (e.g. unbiased interview techniques in selection and promotions). The hope is that the new experience will pose a challenge to the biased attitudes, leading to the development of more appropriate attitudes.

Another example of a behavioural change was the 'Smile Campaign' mounted by a major supermarket as part of a customer service programme. All front-line employees were expected to put on a smile for customers and could face a reprimand if they did not do so (Ogbonna, 1992). In order to motivate employees to undergo the suggested behavioural change a competition between stores was introduced. Senior managers visited stores before making a judgement on which store offered the best level of customer service. Apart from being profiled in the company's magazine, the winner received a financial reward. Here is an example of the importance of the provision of feedback on performance and the allocation of extrinsic rewards (referred to in 'Primary mechanisms' (d), above) as part of a strategy to bring about changes in attitudes and behaviour within an organisation.

(b) Artefacts, façades and physical spaces

These are aspects of the physical environment that convey images, which make an impact. For example, a certain impression is created when a person attending a job interview walks into the reception area of the company and perceives an expensively furnished setting. Another manifestation of the physical environment likely to capture the attention of the person and convey a message is the number of open spaces, the layout of the offices and the nature and distribution of office equipment. When organisations change situations identified in (a) as part of a cultural facelift they could also change certain aspects of the physical environment so that they blend with the changes made. They may also change their logo (the symbol of corporate identity) if the old one is out of keeping with the changed circumstances.

(c) Stories and legends about important events and people

There could be stories and legends containing a mixture of fact and fiction about heroic deeds in the past that may have contributed in a significant way to the company's success, or alternatively saved the company from disaster. The message is that present employees must not lose sight of dedication to duty and the need to continue with unselfish commitment to the success of the organisation. Where accounts of management incompetence or greed circulate perhaps the expectation is that these are things we should learn from and avoid now and in the future.

(d) Formal statements of philosophy and policy

These could include mission statements, which are explicit articulations of the direction in which the organisation is going and the values to which it will adhere. These statements should reflect reality and ideally should be reinforced with reference to their practical significance in a discussion forum.

■ Culture change initiatives

Three initiatives or interventions worthy of note are quality circles (QCs), total quality management and business process re-engineering. Before examining these initiatives our attention could profitably be diverted to events at British Airways throughout the 1980s and subsequently in connection with cultural change. These are described in the case study in Example 5.2.

EXAMPLE 5.2

Cultural change at British Airways

In the early 1980s British Airways (BA) faced considerable problems – loss making, poor reputation for service to the customer and poor industrial relations. After the appointment of Lord
King as chairman staff numbers were cut from 60,000 to 38,000 by means of voluntary
severance and natural wastage. There was a pruning of the number of routes and the sale of
surplus assets (e.g. aircraft). There were, however, limits to cost cutting because fuel prices
and airport charges that formed a considerable proportion of total cost were beyond the control of the organisation. Given this constraint competitive advantage had to be gained from
other sources.

During the initial cost-cutting exercise staff training was reduced, but in 1983 the people
factor was given prominence as a means to overcome the demoralisation following the rationalisation programme. At this time it was felt that the organisation lacked an appreciation of
what the customer wanted. This led to an initiative called 'Putting People First' whereby
12,000 customer-contact employees were put through a two-day course, the aim of which
was to increase people's self-esteem. The belief was that if employees felt good about themselves they were more than likely to feel good about dealing with other people.

In addition to the confidence-building exercises and stress-reduction programmes employees were encouraged to set personal goals and to take responsibility for seeking what they
wanted out of life. The overall programme represented a considerable investment for the
company. On an ongoing basis employees were involved in activities concerned with the development of ideas for improving customer service using forums resembling quality circles. Also,
as a means to generate a greater feeling of belonging and to promote shared interests, profit
sharing was introduced.

Although considerable changes had taken place it was still felt that the management style
was too restrictive. Therefore, in 1985, a new programme called 'Managing People First' was
introduced, in which 2,000 managers participated over a week. The key themes were motivation, trust, vision and taking on responsibility. A short time later a third major initiative was
introduced, called 'A Day in the Life'. This was intended to dismantle some of the barriers
between different groups in the organisation that could act as impediments to change. In
order to increase understanding and to encourage collaboration there were presentations to
staff on the nature and function of work activities right across the organisation, and the chief
executive or one of the directors was present at these sessions to indicate top management
support.

Staff surveys and customer feedback conveyed that a considerable change in the culture of
the organisation had taken place. There was a significant increase in customer satisfaction
and profitability. However, there was not a unanimous positive reaction to the changes within
the organisation. Some staff felt there were conflicts between caring and customer service
values and the pursuit of profits. Subsequent programmes, such as 'Fit For Business', focused
more on commercial skills and activities.

But in the mid-1990s the company experienced financial problems caused by a loss of customers, particularly for business class seats. This necessitated further cost cutting, the use of
lower cost aircraft on long-haul flights and the formation of a cut-price airline – Go – as a subsidiary company. In 1997 there was a serious industrial relations problem, which manifested

itself as a strike by the cabin crew. In its attempt to create a major transatlantic alliance British Airways was engaged in negotiations with American Airlines in 1999. Other airlines (e.g. Virgin Atlantic) objected to this proposal, and the regulatory bodies questioned it. BA also considered a major alliance with KLM (the Dutch carrier), but the talks to bring this about ended in failure. The problems encountered by the company in the 1990s, particularly the lack of profitability and the substantial fine by the EU because BA used its dominant market position to offer travel agents monetary rewards for putting custom its way, led to a substantial fall in the share price of the company. Ironically, in 1999 BA decided to resurrect and fortify a previous initiative to seek the support of staff and customers. The new initiative was called 'Putting People First Again'.

(Hopfl, 1993; Needle, 2000)

This case illustrates HRM acting strategically. To start with there was a business problem expressed as poor standards of service resulting in a loss-making situation. The solution to the problem was seen as the need for a culture change, coupled with the development of appropriate employee attitudes and values. The HRM function was active in facilitating the total process, which was perceived as long term. The initial change process concentrated on the reduction of costs, with substantial cuts in staffing costs. However, it was felt necessary to go beyond the pruning of expenditure. In fact it was considered necessary to bring about a profound cultural change in order to improve performance.

The process of defining the current culture at the beginning of the programme appeared to be problem centred but was intuitive in many ways. An in-depth study of culture at the outset was not undertaken. The process of change revolved around training and development activities, although other HRM activities, such as reward management (e.g. profit-related pay), also played a part. The change was active over a decade and is still continuing in various forms. In effect it represents a long-term investment. It is difficult to quantify in financial terms the outcome of the various training and development interventions, but what is obvious is the belief in the value of the culture change and the commitment of top management. This has had the effect of sustaining the change process.

In between the various stages of cultural change and development there was an opportunity to collect relevant information. This activity influenced matters to be considered at the next stage of the process. Amongst the aspects of culture subjected to change were the attitudes of employees, including their attitudes to customers, management styles and their understanding of the activities of different groups and functions within the organisation. The experience has left British Airways with a greater capacity to handle change and development in the future.

Returning to the theme raised in the opening of this section, the three initiatives or interventions – QCs, TQM and BPR – will be discussed shortly. But first something should be said about quality. The control of quality was an original US idea enthusiastically taken on board by Japanese business and subsequently adopted by both US and UK organisations. The central idea is that quality becomes the concern of all employees and should be totally immersed in the management process. The latter is characterised by delegated authority and empowerment in all activities connected with quality. The needs and expectations of customers are an overriding preoccupation for those charged with responsibility for quality. It is suggested that one reason for the greater uptake of the idea of quality in Japan was due to the greater scarcity of resources and the resultant need to eliminate waste and maximise getting things right first time (Oliver and Wilkinson, 1992).

Quality circles

The QC is a group joined by shopfloor workers to solve problems related to barriers to quality improvement, cost reduction, working conditions, health and safety, etc. The group, normally led by a team leader, consists of 5 to 10 volunteer employees who meet regularly (weekly or fortnightly) to identify and solve problems of the type described above. In order to equip the QC members to sharpen and develop their problem-solving skills, they are offered training programmes covering topics such as problem definition, statistical analysis and teamwork and communication skills. In Japan the QC was viewed favourably as a factor in its industrial success, and was imported to the west in the late 1970s.

It is claimed by some commentators that QCs have a beneficial effect on a number of fronts – e.g. communication, participation, job satisfaction and personal growth – which leads to increased quality and efficiency. For instance, Dale *et al.* (1998) believe that QCs represent an advanced form of employee participation which is associated with favourable employee attitudes and productivity. It is suggested that social needs are satisfied in QCs because an outlet is provided for the expression of grievances and irritations, and instant recognition is provided for the accomplishments of members. All this could have a beneficial effect in terms of a sense of dignity, morale and group cohesiveness. However, there is evidence to challenge these claims. It is suggested that the significance of the QC in Japan has been overrated because the difficulties addressed were relatively trivial; in fact a rather small percentage of 'quality' problems were confronted (Schonberger, 1982). The alleged benefits of the QCs have also been challenged in the United Kingdom. There were low levels of participation – not more than 25 per cent of eligible employees joined QCs – and widespread indifference and often active opposition on the part of employees (Hill, 1991).

Total quality management

TQM is a major management philosophy that embodies the important aim of satisfying customers' requirements as efficiently and profitably as possible, to improve performance continually as situations allow and to ensure that all work activities achieve the corporate objectives and are completed right first time. Quality is seen as the key to the organisation's success, and the success of any policy on quality lays firmly on the shoulders of every employee. To underpin this approach to management would probably require a mixture of soft (e.g. customer care, participation, training, teamwork and performance) and hard factors (e.g. production standards and techniques, and quantitative analysis in the assessment of quality). The proponents of TQM would see it as a total system that fundamentally affects the culture of the organisation rather than as a 'bolt-on' technique, which was often attributable to QCs. In the case of QCs the training and cultural change techniques necessary to embed the circles in the values and attitudes of employees were rarely instituted. But TQM is strategically driven by top management and almost prescribes involvement of all employees in matters connected with quality in their jobs. Since TQM emphasises commitment, trust and self-control within a unitarist perspective it is consistent with HRM. Also, the introduction of TQM gives HRM the opportunity to play a more strategic role in the organisation, such as the creation and maintenance of a supportive culture. It is interesting to note that generally there is a lack of HRM comment in the TQM literature, which tends to be concerned with the technical design of systems and solutions (Wilkinson and Marchington, 1994). Nevertheless, Guest (1992) sees quality improvement as inextricably linked to HRM in the following ways:

- Training and development is the normal technique for communicating the importance of quality.
- Because the quality and commitment of the employees is crucial in improving the quality of the product or service there is a need for systematic recruitment, selection and training.
- Top management commitment to TQM is a function of the quality and development of management.
- Adherence to quality takes root in a process of employee involvement and a flexible mode of operation, and this is likely to be more compatible with an organic type of organisation imbued with high trust.

The experience of an organisation that adopted TQM as a key feature of a corporate culture the company wished to establish is reported in the case study in Example 5.3. Although TQM has its supporters as an effective intervention in changing and developing culture it has been the subject of criticism. It is argued that it is questionable whether employee empowerment or greater autonomy is a reality. On the basis of a case study of an electronics manufacturing company where TQM was adopted it was clear that problem-solving teams worked on problems identified by management, and the implementation of the solutions and any deviations from the standard format for the execution of a task led to the exercise of management control (Sewell and Wilkinson, 1992). Putting TQM into practice is no easy matter. It has been suggested that there is a high failure rate in the application of TQM in Europe (Zairi *et al.*, 1994). In the United States the results of a study showed that there was a lack of managerial skill in handling it, a resistance to change on the part of those involved, and a recognition that it took longer than expected to produce results (Lorenz, 1993).

EXAMPLE 5.3

TQM at Bosch

Bosch, a supplier of car components and electronic products to many of Europe's leading car manufacturers, introduced TQM when it opened its first manufacturing plant in the United Kingdom on a greenfield site in Wales in 1990. Many of the company's customers had specific quality demands so it was necessary to have a corporate culture in which quality was firmly ingrained. The values forming part of the culture included a quality product to secure global competitive advantage, continuous improvement of the employees' skills, improved quality of operations and productivity, and ensuring that the company met its responsibilities to customers, employees, suppliers and the local community.

High on the list of priorities was the continuous improvement of employee skills, production methods and productivity, and relations with customers. There was an emphasis on team-working and team development. This was understandable because the company believed in synergy as applied to the efforts of people – that is, the effect of the group working in concert is greater that the sum of the individual contributions. Teams would be used to tackle problems, to enhance commitment and to further the cause of quality improvement.

The customer–supplier (employee) relationship was emphasised across the board. The supplier would endeavour to deliver to the external customer the appropriate product or service and then ensure that it was delivered 'right first time, on time, every time'. An internal customer is an employee who is a recipient of the company's internal output or service and is entitled to quality customer care. He or she is not the recipient of the finished product or service of the company, but is, for example, the next person on the production line.

The company considered it important that constant feedback flowed from both customers and management to employees to enable them to maintain and improve their standards of performance. The staff newspaper was also used as a vehicle to provide general feedback and reinforcement.

(Fowler *et al.*, 1992)

Business process re-engineering

BPR has been defined as 'a radical scrutiny, questioning, re-definition, and re-design of business processes with the aim of eliminating all activities not central to the process goals' (Thomas, 1994). As a process of change that questions the way activities are carried out in the organisation BPR focuses on core business (i.e. activities that add value), leaving non-core activities to be contracted out. A special characteristic of BPR from an organisational design perspective is that it advocates a departure from the rigid compartmentalisation of processes in hierarchical organisation arranged on a functional basis, which can lead to unacceptable delays in processing tasks (e.g. executing orders from customers), to acceptance of the cross-functional project team approach, which is similar in some respects to matrix organisation and project management. It poses a direct challenge to the division of labour and the need for hierarchical control.

The proponents of BPR point to advantages in terms of speed of response, quality, delayering and the scope to apply information technology to handle the complex interdependent and cross-functional processes. In the early 1990s IBM introduced a new management structure after the arrival of its new chairman and chief executive. Shortly afterwards the focus was on business processes, i.e. the way the company carried out the multitude of tasks related to forming and maintaining customer relationships. The main justification for the company's adoption of BPR was to satisfy the needs of customers more effectively (Kehoe, 1994). An application of BPR to a US insurance company appears in Example 5.4.

In this case job enlargement and job enrichment (both explained in Chapter 9) were experienced by those who participated in the new system. This would suggest that some form of empowerment took place, but this is not always the case. For example, a high street outlet in the United Kingdom, Argos, instituted change processes, which resulted in the simplification and deskilling of tasks.

EXAMPLE 5.4

BPR at Mutual Benefit Life

Before BPR was introduced the company dealt with new applications for insurance by using a complex administrative process in which applications went through 30 steps, 5 departments, and were handled by 20 people who performed simple repetitive tasks. The total process could take any time from 5 to 10 days to complete.

After the implementation of BPR the situation changed radically. All new applications were dealt with individually by case managers, with the exception of the most complicated cases. The case manager had at his or her disposal an information technology workstation utilising a database and an expert system, which was invaluable as an aid to decision making. The end result was that the time taken to process each application was reduced by three to five days and the administrative capacity to handle applications nearly doubled. A reduction in staff amounting to 100 posts led to considerable savings.

(Hammer, 1990)

There are some parallels between BPR and TQM, since both interventions include major organisational and cultural changes. Both require vision and commitment from top management as well as gaining the commitment of employees. Some recent applications of BPR have taken root in greenfield sites. This has inbuilt advantages, as we saw in the Bosch case earlier, because the company can select a workforce compatible with the culture it wishes to adopt and avoid the problems connected with changing the outlook of an existing workforce. First Direct, an autonomous offshoot of Midland Bank (now HSBC), set out to establish a new system of banking involving processes different from traditional banking, and considered it more appropriate to recruit a new workforce with terms and conditions of employment and industrial relations practices different from those in the parent company, but more functional from its own point of view.

It would appear that BPR does not draw on a particular mix of HRM practices. The prevailing circumstances within an organisation are likely to determine the most appropriate mix. However, the following HRM practices are likely to occupy a prominent position: recruitment and selection, job redesign and rewards, training, team building, transformational leadership, and counselling. Opponents of BPR are quick to point out that its claims to success are wildly exaggerated and they would no doubt get some satisfaction from the fact that the Mutual Benefit Life Corporation, referred to by Hammer earlier in Example 5.4, collapsed shortly after the appearance of his article in 1990. They would also point out that there is very little in BPR that has not been incorporated in other management and organisational approaches, such as matrix organisation and TQM.

Some argue that it is a cost-cutting and restructuring technique at a time when the prevailing management emphasis is switching to growth. In other words its focus is on corporate mechanics, not on vision or strategy, and left to its own devices it will drive out all strategies except cost minimisation (Lloyd, 1994). A scathing attack on BPR comes from Case (1999), who in observing that its popularity amongst management is on the decline goes on to say that it has an exploitative dimension to it.

Other techniques

A technique used recently by a UK insurance company – Eagle Star – to change culture is known as 'WorkOut' (see Example 5.5).

EXAMPLE 5.5

Using 'WorkOut' to change culture: Eagle Star

When Patrick O'Sullivan joined Eagle Star as chief executive in 1997 he confronted a high degree of inefficiency and complacency within the company. The system of creating reserves was inadequate, the pricing in the marketplace left much to be desired, the marketing function was unduly influencing risk assessment decisions, information technology was completely disconnected from the business and was consuming large amounts of resources and going nowhere, the actuaries and underwriters were not talking to each other, the finance function was not well integrated into the business (it was a reporting function that did senior management's bidding), and the chain of accountability was deficient. The new chief executive was alarmed to find that only his predecessor and a few of his senior staff were aware of the seriousness of the company's plight. Generally the employees – who were getting more and more rewards (e.g. flexitime, benefits and bonuses) – thought the company was wonderful to work for.

In his first three months the new chief executive visited 40 sites and addressed more than 90 per cent of employees, telling them about the seriousness of the situation affecting the company and the changes that were being contemplated. He experienced subtle resistance from a layer of senior and middle managers, and the rest of the staff were rather cynical. O'Sullivan was convinced that the technique 'WorkOut' could be used to bring about change.

He knew that General Electric, USA used WorkOut successfully when he worked in the past for a subsidiary of that company in Europe. It is claimed that WorkOut could shorten the decision-making process as well as improving it, and enhance responsiveness to customers' needs by using the collective intelligence of the entire company, not just the management elite. The employees are encouraged to come forward with well-prepared and properly costed proposals, and these are presented to 'town meetings' where senior managers are present and are expected to listen to the proposals for change. A WorkOut could consist of groups of 50–100 employees from a cross-section of business units, and three days can be allocated to solving problems. There is likely to be heated debate in these forums and the key decision makers (i.e. the senior managers) are required to give a 'yes' or 'no' answer there and then. If they give a 'yes' answer then implementation will take place over a two to three month period, but if the answer is 'no' the senior managers will have to offer credible reasons why the proposal(s) cannot be adopted.

The WorkOuts in the company started in 1998 with the Eagle Star Direct Group, who were considered to be an innovative team, and they responded positively to this technique. Members came together for three-day WorkOuts and worked long hours without receiving any overtime payments, even though they would normally expect to receive such payments in their jobs. The problems they confronted were response times, and concrete proposals were put forward to increase productivity. Although O'Sullivan acknowledges that much work has to be done in perfecting the technique, he considers WorkOut has been a key factor in turning round Eagle Star. Following a merger in 1998 the company, which is part of BAT Financial Services, is now in the same stable as Zurich Financial Services. O'Sullivan has used WorkOut to bring together Eagle Star and Zurich, two companies with different corporate cultures.

(Bolger, 2000)

■ Culture and HRM

A link between HRM and culture is emphasised when it is suggested that an important role of HRM within high performance work organisations is the development of 'core' organisational values to inform the strategic direction of the business (Gennard and Kelly, 1994; Huselid, 1995).

HRM adopts a unitarist position, which espouses the view that it is in the interests of organisational members to work together towards the achievement of common goals without the intrusive influence of conflict. It takes the view that it is to the benefit of employees, in terms of rewards and job security, for the organisation to achieve its goals successfully. In taking this stand HRM is supporting a particular view of organisational culture, which could be seen as management driven, where conflict does not exist and common interests prevail.

This could pose a dilemma because HRM also espouses a flexible approach to job design. Adopting this approach, which has the ingredients of a pluralist perspective, could mean employees experiencing greater control over their work, including greater responsibility for the outcome of their effort, as well as greater group autonomy through, for example, quality circles and autonomous work groups. Apart from specific initiatives in job design HRM is partial to the removal of layers within the organisation, which has the effect of pushing decision making further down the organisation. This results in reducing managerial control over employees. In addition, HRM expects effective and dedicated performance from members of the organisation when it stresses the need for employees to be creative and innovative in pursuit of higher performance standards, and to commit themselves to hours at work over and above their contractual hours.

Therefore the challenge for HRM is to reconcile the unitarist perspective with the pluralist perspective of greater individual and group autonomy. The reconciliation of these two positions is unlikely to be an easy task, and begs the following question: can we create an organisational culture in pluralist conditions where there can be reasonable harmony between the interests of the organisation and the interests of employees to pursue objectives based on self-interest, which may not be in congruence with company objectives?

There have been a number of criticisms of the role of culture in HRM. Above it is acknowledged that, in the pluralist perspective, managerial control is removed to a certain extent, and subordinates are empowered, thereby creating conditions for a greater diversity of views. In such a climate is it realistic to assume that a uniform culture with strongly held shared values and beliefs can coexist with 'deviant' values held by individuals? According to Willmott (1993) the conditions for the expression of heretical views, or the adherence to competing values by individuals or groups, could be severely limited if the uniform culture is strong. Referring to strong cultures to which organisational members subscribe, alluded to earlier, it is suggested that a disadvantage could be reduced flexibility and adaptation to changing environmental conditions because people subscribe to cultural norms more suited to the previous conditions than to the changed conditions (Legge, 1989). However, one should not be left with the impression that, generally speaking, weak culture is synonymous with flexibility. It may be that the metaphor of relative strength is not the best way to conceive cultures.

Other critics draw our attention to the distinction between the 'practitioner' literature and the 'academic' literature in the way organisational culture is dealt with in HRM (Mabey and Salaman, 1995). Those espousing the practitioner view are seen as simplifying the complex nature of culture and adopting initiatives to control the environment within which people work in order to enhance performance. By contrast the academic perspective appeals to social anthropology to capture the complexity of culture by focusing on the rituals, behaviour, beliefs and language of participants. The views expressed in the academic literature are not sympathetic to the views found in the practitioner literature. We would call for a reconciliation of the opposing views and for the goodness of both approaches to be preserved. This may require practitioner-oriented literature to acknowledge a degree of complexity and tension between competing options rather than espousing the best way of doing things. Conversely, in the academic literature, the needs of practitioners to decide on a course of action should be given due weight, on par with critical comment on policies and practices.

Commitment

A commentary on HRM and culture would not be complete without a serious comment on organisational commitment, which is a key concept in HRM. It is one of the four 'Cs' in the Harvard Model (discussed in Chapter 1) and amounts to a certain degree of identification with the stated aims, objectives and values of the organisation as well as involvement on the part of employees. In attitudinal and behavioural terms this could be reflected in their desire to stay with the organisation, and putting more than adequate effort into the achievement of business objectives. Employees are more likely to be committed to their employing organisation if they feel confidence in their employer's commitment to them. It should be said that real commitment is unlikely without mutual trust.

At one time western companies expressed a strong interest in developing the type of commitment shown by Japanese workers. Values at the heart of the Japanese workers' commitment, apart from its reciprocal nature, are as follows:

- work ethic – seen to work hard, and long hours spent at work;
- conformity – a high need to belong, and not to be isolated from one's community;
- avoidance of shame – failure to discharge duties in accordance with normal social rules can bring shame, loss of face, and could result in isolation.

It would be difficult to transplant these values in their pure form to a western context. In any case commitment is likely to receive a battering in the age of the leaner, fitter and delayered organisation, where opportunities for advancement and security of employment are not what they used to be.

■ Conclusions

It should now be clear that the organisational culture and attempts to change and manage it are legitimate concerns of HRM. Culture is closely linked to strategy and structure and influences activities such as recruitment, selection, appraisal, training and rewards, which are covered in subsequent chapters. Changing culture is a prolonged and costly process. For example IBM, having failed to read correctly developments in the microcomputer market at one stage, subsequently embarked on major cultural change through a different type of leadership and questioning many of the old values, a process that continues to the present day. Likewise, the former Rover Motor Car Company spent 15 years trying to gain acceptance for its changed philosophy of management. In HRM terms the latter is based on mutual commitment, which has the potential to increase cooperation and performance and lead to competitive advantage.

Theories of culture have been criticised on a number of grounds. For example, it can be asked if all individuals in an organisation (or nation) really share the same culture. Equally questionable is the view that an organisation can really change the deeply held values of employees. Nonetheless the policies adopted by the organis-ation, and management action, reflect organisational culture. The combined effect of policy and management action, coupled with the way employees are treated on a daily basis within the organisation, can lead to employees making judgements about the organisation's culture and their place in it. Culture is not just the rituals and ceremonies – it is also reflected in the basic processes of organisational life. Therefore it is crucially important for managers to bear these issues in mind when performing their normal activities. The way managers use power, express emotion, make decisions, involve and reward others will create the setting for the formation of attitudes and commitment of the employees.

References

Adler, N. (1997) *International Dimensions of Organizational Behaviour*, 3rd edn, Cincinnati, OH: South Western College Publishing.

Belbin, R.M. (1981) *Management Teams: Why they succeed or fail*, London: Heinemann.

Bolger, A. (2000) 'How Eagle Star was saved by a high flier', *Financial Times*, 30 June, 16.

Case, P. (1999) 'Remember re-engineering? The rhetorical appeal of a managerial salvation device' *Journal of Management Studies*, 36, 420–41.

Dale, B.D., Cooper, C.L. and Wilkinson, A. (1998) *Managing Quality and Human Resources: A guide to continuous improvement*, Oxford: Blackwell.

Deal, T. and Kennedy, A. (1982) *Corporate Cultures*, London: Penguin.

Den Hartog, D.N., House, R.J., Hanges, P.J., Ruiz-Quintanilla and Dorfman, P.W. (1999) 'Culture specific and cross-culturally generalizable implicit leadership theories: are attributes of charismatic/transformational leadership universally endorsed?', *Leadership Quarterly*, 10, 219–56.

Denison, D.R. (1996) 'What is the difference between organizational culture and organizational climate? A native's point of view on a decade of paradigm wars', *Academy of Management Review*, 21, 619–54.

Donkin, R. (2000) 'Recruitment: common sense makes a comeback', *Financial Times* (Appointments Section), 5 October, XII.

Fowler, A., Sheard, M. and Wibberley, M. (1992) 'Two routes to quality', *Personnel Management*, November, 30–4.

Furnham, A. (1997) *The Psychology of Behaviour at Work*, Hove: Psychology Press.

Gennard, J. and Kelly, J. (1994) 'Human resource management: the views of personnel directors', *Human Resource Management Journal*, 5, 15–32.

Goffee, R. (1997) 'Cultural diversity', in *Mastering Management: Module 6 Organizational Behaviour* (240–6), FT/Pitman Publishing.

Griffith, V. (1995) 'Hero one day, villain the next', *Financial Times*, 3 March, 13.

Guest, D.E. (1992) 'Human resource management in the UK', in Towers, B. (ed.), *The Handbook of Human Resource Management*, Oxford: Blackwell.

Guest, D.E. (1994a) 'Organizational psychology and human resource management: towards a European approach', *European Work and Organizational Psychologist*, 4, 251–70.

Guest, D.E. (1994b) 'Human resource management: opportunity or threat?', in Indoe, D. and Spencer, C. (eds), *Survival and Quality, Annual Course Proceedings 1994, Educational and Child Psychology*, 11, 5–10.

Hamel, G. and Prahalad, C.K. (1994) *Competing for the Future*, Boston, MA: Harvard Business School Press.

Hammer, M. (1990) 'Re-engineering work: don't automate, obliterate', *Harvard Business Review*, July/August, 104–12.

Handy, C. (1985) *Understanding Organisations*, 3rd edn, London: Penguin.

Harrison, R. (1972) 'Understanding your organization's character', *Harvard Business Review*, May/June, 119–28.

Hill, S. (1991) 'Why quality circles failed but total quality management might succeed', *British Journal of Industrial Relations*, 29, 541–68.

Hofestede, G.H. (1980) *Culture's Consequences*, Beverly Hills, CA: Sage.

Hofestede, G.H. (1994) *Cultures and Organizations: Intercultural cooperation and its importance for survival*, Maidenhead: McGraw-Hill.

Hopfl, H. (1993) 'Culture and commitment: British Airways', in Gowler, D., Legge, K. and Clegg, C. (eds), *Case Studies in Organizational Behaviour and HRM*, 2nd edn, London: Paul Chapman.

Hope, V. and Henry, J. (1996) 'Corporate culture change: is it relevant for the organizations of the 1990s?', *Human Resource Management Journal*, 5, 61–73.

House, R.J. (1995) 'Leadership in the 21st century: a speculative inquiry', in Howard, A. (ed.), *The Changing Nature of Work*, San Francisco, CA: Jossey-Bass.

Huselid, M.A. (1995) 'The impact of human resource management practices on turnover, productivity, and corporate financial performance', *Academy of Management Journal*, 38, 635–70.

Kandola, R. (1995) 'Managing diversity: new broom or old hat?', in Cooper, C.L. and Robertson, I.T. (eds), *International Review of Industrial and Organizational Psychology*, 10, Chichester: Wiley.

Kanter, R. (1989) *When Giants Learn to Dance: Mastering the challenge of strategy, management, and careers in the 1990s*, London: Unwin.

Kehoe, L. (1994) 'Down in the dirt to clean up IBM', *Financial Times*, 5 December, 8.

Koopman, P.L., Den Hartog, D.N. and Konrad, E. (and others too numerous to mention) (1999) 'National culture and leadership profiles in Europe: some results from the GLOBE study', *European Journal of Work and Organizational Psychology*, 8, 503–20.

Legge, K. (1989) 'Human resource management: a critical analysis', in Storey, J. (ed.), *New Perspectives in Human Resource Management*, London: Routledge.

Littlefield, D. (1999) 'Kerry's heroes', *People Management*, 5 (6 May), 48–50.

Lloyd, T. (1994) 'Giant with feet of clay', *Financial Times*, 5 December, 8.

Lorenz, C. (1993) 'TQM: alive and kicking in the US', *Financial Times*, 23 July, 15.

Mabey, C. and Salaman, G. (1995) *Strategic Human Resource Management*, Oxford: Blackwell.

Marx, E. (1999) *Breaking through Culture Shock*, London: Nicholas Brealey.

Meek, V.L. (1992) 'Organizational culture: origins and weaknesses', in Salaman, G. (ed.), *Human Resource Strategies*, London: Sage.

Miles, R.E. and Snow, C.C. (1978) *Organizational Strategy, Structure, and Process*, New York: McGraw-Hill.

Moorhead, G. and Griffin, R.W. (1998) *Organizational Behaviour: Managing people and organizations*, 5th edn, Boston, MA: Houghton Mifflin.

Needle, D. (2000) *Business in Context: An introduction to business and its environment*, 3rd edn, London: Business Press, Thomson Learning.

Ogbonna, E. (1992) 'Organization culture and human resource management: dilemmas and contradictions', in Blyton, P. and Turnbull, P. (eds), *Reassessing Human Resource Management*, London: Sage.

Ogbonna, E. and Whipp, R. (1999) 'Strategy, culture, and HRM: evidence from the UK retailing sector', *Human Resource Management Journal*, 9, 75–90.

Oliver, N. and Wilkinson, B. (1992) *The Japanization of British Industry: New developments in the 1990s*, Oxford: Blackwell.

Ouchi, W.G. (1981) *Theory Z: How American business can meet the Japanese challenge*, Reading, MA: Addison-Wesley.

Peters, T. and Waterman, R. (1982) *In Search of Excellence*, New York: Harper & Row.

Schein, E.H. (1985) *Organizational Culture and Leadership*, San Francisco, CA: Jossey-Bass.

Schein, E.H. (1990) 'Organizational culture', *American Psychologist*, 45, 109–19.

Schonberger, R. (1982) *Japanese Manufacturing Techniques*, New York: Free Press.

Sewell, G. and Wilkinson, B. (1992) 'Empowerment or emasculation? Shopfloor surveillance in a total quality organization', in Blyton, P. and Turnbull, P. (eds), *Reassessing Human Resource Management*, London: Sage.

Thomas, M. (1994) 'What do you need to know about business process re-engineering?', *Personnel Management*, 26, 28–31.

Torrington, D. and Hall, L. (1998) *Human Resource Management*, 4th edn, Hemel Hempstead: Prentice Hall.

Trompenaars, A. (1993) *Riding the Wave of Culture. Understanding cultural diversity in business*, London: Nicholas Brealey.

Tushman, M. and O'Reilly, C.A. (1996) *Staying on Top: Managing strategic innovation and change for long-term success*, Boston, MA: Harvard Business Press.

Weaving, K. (1995) 'Sweeping fear from the floor', *Financial Times*, 3 March, 13.

Welch, J. (1999) 'British firms lag behind surfing USA', *People Management*, 5, 13.

Wickens, P. (1987) *The Road to Nissan*, London: Macmillan.

Wilkinson, A. and Marchington, M. (1994) 'TQM: instant pudding for the personnel function?', *Human Resource Management Journal*, 5, 33–49.

Wilkinson, B. and Oliver, N. (1992) 'HRM in Japanese manufacturing companies in the UK and USA', in Towers, B. (ed.), *The Handbook of Human Resource Management*. Oxford: Blackwell.

Williams, A., Dobson, P. and Walters, M. (1989) *Changing Culture*, London: Institute of Personnel Management.

Willmott, H. (1993) 'Ignorance is strength, freedom is slavery: managing culture in modern organizations', *Journal of Management Studies*, 30 (4), 515–55.

Zairi, M., Letza, S. and Oakland, J. (1994) 'Does TQM impact on bottom line results?', *TQM Magazine*, 6, 38–43.

Chapter 6

Employee resourcing: human resource planning

Human resource planning (HRP) is an activity that directly links HRM to organisational strategy. It is concerned with setting out the size, quality and nature of the workforce in order to meet corporate objectives. Increasingly there is a need for flexibility in planning, and resource-based strategies (discussed in Chapter 2) put people centre stage in the strategic planning process. There is a need to be able to meet the demands of the business environment and also to be able to motivate and develop employees. These twin demands mean that HRP has to focus both internally and externally – making the most of external opportunities and enabling current employees to progress and develop their skills. Hence there is a strong link between HRP and recruitment and selection and training and development.

Having read this chapter, you should:

- understand the role of HRP in an integrated approach to HRM;
- be aware of the issues in achieving a balance between the demand for, supply and utilisation of labour;
- be aware of some of the analytical techniques of HRP;
- understand the impacts that changes in external factors, such as legislation and demographics, can have on HRP;
- know what the different types of flexibility are, and have an appreciation of how they can be applied;
- have an understanding of some of the current critical issues and developments in HRP.

Employee resourcing, the process of acquiring and utilizing human resources in the organisation, consists of a number of specialist activities that need to act in harmony to ensure that human resources of the right quantity and quality are available to meet the overall objectives of the company. The specialist activities referred to are human resource planning, which is dealt with in this chapter, and recruitment and selection, which are examined in Chapter 7. These activities are operationalised in the context of strategic human resource management, a topic discussed in Chapter 2. As was stated then, strategic human resource planning is an approach that links the management of human resources to the organisation's overall strategies for achieving its goals and objectives.

A starting point for human resource planning is to assess the future needs of the organisation for employees, noting the blend of skills required. As stated earlier, human resource planning is part of the framework set by the interaction of strategic human resource management and corporate strategy. By contrast, traditional manpower planning was concerned principally with making sure that the organisation had the right number of employees in the right place at the right time. Human resource planning has not rejected this perspective but it has changed our understanding of it. In traditional manpower planning a strong quantitative bias was evident, with an orientation towards dealing with 'hard' problems and their solution. But in human resource management, with its strong emphasis on people as a key resource, there is the recognition that the 'hard' problem approach has to be supplemented by the 'soft' problem approach. In the latter case qualitative issues connected with employee creativity, innovative practices, flexibility, messy problems and so on are taken very seriously.

The anchor of human resource planning comprises three facets, as follows:

1 demand for human resources, which can be gleaned from the strategic human resource plan;
2 utilisation of human resources in a cost-effective and efficient manner;
3 supply of human resources manifested in the current number of employees (internal supply) and the potential pool of suitable applicants external to the organisation (external supply).

There is a dynamic interplay between the three facets mentioned, and the overall process is mediated by happenings within the organisation (internal environment) and forces external to the organisation (external environment). Both environments generate turbulence where change is omnipresent and has to be managed.

■ Demand for human resources

Demand for human resources can be defined as the number of staff required to meet the organisation's future needs as well as the composition of the workforce in terms of the necessary skills. For example, an expansion of the organisation's activities could result in recruiting extra staff with the appropriate skills. On the other hand an organisation may be planning to reduce staffing levels because of an anticipated fall in the demand for the company's product(s). Of course rationalisation of staffing levels could also be prompted by other considerations, such as scope to cut costs, or improve working practices, which offers the opportunity to maintain the existing output, or in some cases to increase output, with fewer employees. As was mentioned earlier, competitive forces emanating from the external environment can have a material bearing on the magnitude of the demand for human resources. This could be reflected in a reduction of staffing levels as well as changing the character and skills associated with the jobs that remain, and is illustrated in Box 6.1.

This illustration shows how organisations need to devise and carry out strategies in order to confront threats from the external environment. The increased competition from building societies, coupled with customer expectations of low charges and quality of services, brought about a need not only to reduce costs but also to maintain levels of service. A method to achieve this was greater use of new technology. As a consequence there has been a reduction in staffing levels in order to avoid overstaffing. This has resulted in a significant reduction in demand for human resources, and led to a preoccupation with the quality of the human resources. For example, it was felt that the staff needed new information technology skills, and to develop their abilities in customer relations, sales and knowledge of the products and services offered by the bank.

BOX 6.1

Developments in the banking sector

Increased competition from building societies, the effects of losses on bad debts, low inflation and a low interest rate environment put considerable pressure on banks to cut their costs. The traditional approach to banking was paper and labour intensive. The use of cheques, for example, reached its peak in 1991. In order to be processed, a cheque would be dealt with initially at the bank receiving it and would pass through a number of people before ending up at the home branch of the customer who wrote the cheque. In order to reduce costs a strategy has been adopted to change the labour-intensive processes of banking through the introduction of new technology.

Since 1991 the use of cheques has been declining and banks commissioned national advertising to encourage customers to use card transactions. By 1993 70 per cent of cash withdrawals were made from automatic teller machines. Much of the need for 'backroom' activity and paperwork was removed by the introduction of new technology, and most of the major banks became involved in rationalisation programmes to reduce staff numbers in branches. The industry employed 400,000 people at the beginning of the 1990s and Brian Pitman, Chief Executive of Lloyds Bank, predicted that there would be 100,000 job losses during the 1990s (Hamilton, 1993).

The jobs that remain will be more concerned with sales of financial services rather than carrying out banking processes, which are no longer labour intensive. In some areas employee reward is being linked to sales targets.

The traditional approach to calculating the demand for human resources is to make use of ratios. An example of a simple ratio is: a ratio of 4:1 is used in a research and development department within a company. In this particular situation that means four scientific officers to one technician. The company decided that an extra four scientific officers would be appointed, in which case it must set aside funds for a new technician as well.

A first step when using ratios in the example given is to decide on the number of new scientific officers that the company requires. To assist with this task data are collected and projected into the future, and this can be presented diagrammatically using trend analysis (see Figure 6.1).

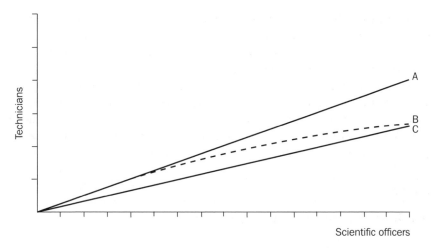

Figure 6.1 Staff ratios: A = constant ratio of 4:1, scientific officers:technicians; B = variable ratio – 'economies of scale'; C = constant ratio of 6:1, e.g. because of the introduction of new technology.

Projection A in Figure 6.1 shows a constant ratio. This means that in every situation the work of four scientific officers will require the work of one technician. Projection B indicates that in certain circumstances the ratio may be variable. In this case there are 'economies of scale', which means that although the first 4 scientific officers need a full-time technician, in a larger department of 20 scientific officers, 3 rather than 5 technicians are needed. This could occur because of efficiency gains from the technicians working as a team, or from them specialising, and becoming expert in particular tasks. Projection C indicates achieving a different ratio because of implementing a change, for example the introduction of new technology, which results in each technician being able to service 6 scientific officers.

This type of analysis, as Torrington *et al.* (1991) point out, can also be used to plot the number of employees needed against projected demand for production. For example, there could be a ratio of 4 scientific officers to 1 million units of production per annum. Therefore, if production were to be raised from 4 million units to 6 million units, the complement of scientific officers would need to rise from 16 to 24 (where a constant ratio was applied).

The use of ratios in calculating the demand for human resources was more prevalent when the influence of trade unions was pronounced. They were used in union–management negotiations on staffing levels. However, in the competitive conditions of the 1990s a more flexible approach was called for. This meant assessing particular requests on the basis of merit. A more flexible approach may involve achieving the same level of output with a reduced number of staff through gains in productivity, the introduction of new technology, or it may involve changes to job design such as job enlargement.

In the heyday of manpower planning statistical forecasting techniques were based on assumptions of stability and absence of radical change when predicting future demand for labour. Such an approach would now be unrealistic given the likely future turbulence and uncertainty in markets. When considering the demand for human resources in an HRM framework a preoccupation with customers and quality in conditions of change is very much in evidence (Bramham, 1989; Hall and Torrington, 1998). Although formal human resource planning techniques are still used by some large companies they lack refinement and accuracy, and the whole process appears to be studded with pragmatism (Storey, 1992). Nowadays planning needs to possess the characteristics of speed and response if it is to be successful. Managerial judgement seems to be asserting itself in the process of establishing demand for human resources where the likely future shape of the organisation and the range of skills required exert much influence on the final outcome (Torrington *et al.*, 1991; Sisson and Timperley, 1994). At the present time the relevant questions appear to be: 'what are the business needs?' and 'what is the ideal complexion and size of the human resource factor to meet those needs?'

■ Utilisation of human resources

Establishing the demand for human resources cannot be achieved without considering the way employees' skills and talents will be used. Utilisation of human resources impacts directly on the demand for staff. For example, a company improves its systems of work as part of a programme to make better use of its employees. As a consequence there are now more staff than are needed to process the workloads. The end result could be a need for fewer staff, and could lead to voluntary or involuntary redundancies. However, if opportunities exist elsewhere within the company there could be a redeployment of all or some of the staff who are superfluous to requirements. An increasing trend has been the use of computer-aided design and production in manufacturing. This trend has reduced the number of human resources needed to carry out processes, which used to be labour intensive. It has also had an effect on the quality of employees required, since people with particular skills are needed to create and maintain the systems.

Another trend has been the use of teamworking arrangements. Small groups of employees take responsibility for the total production of goods or services where individuals had previously specialised in small sections of the production process. This has an implication for the skill levels of the employees, as in a team they need to be able to carry out a wider range of tasks to complete the process. This type of utilisation of human resources is linked to quality approaches and the devolvement of responsibility from supervisors and middle managers to the teams that actually carry out the work.

There has been a long tradition of trying to foster efficiency and effectiveness of the operations of an organisation through work study and related management services techniques. The basic approach is to subject to detailed analysis the way tasks are undertaken and then to make recommendations for the improvement of systems and the better utilisation of staff. The forerunner of present-day work study was the research undertaken by Taylor (1947), the father of scientific management. He examined the tasks undertaken by employees in order to establish how wasted time could be eliminated and how human effort and work techniques could be better used. His approach was to observe employees engaged in the performance of tasks and to document and analyse their movements. On the basis of his analysis he postulated action strategies for improving techniques, making better use of time, and introduced training and incentives, with a view to increasing productivity. Taylor's intentions were felt to be more partial to the interests of management and detrimental to the interests of workers according to commentators such as Braverman (1974).

An example of a present-day work study exercise carried out in a secretarial pool of a buildings and estates department of a local authority is shown in Example 6.1. A number of outcomes following the adoption of the recommendations of this work study report can be identified. Work was redesigned and systems were changed. Secretarial pool operators spent less time correcting small mistakes and more time on producing finished reports to the required standard. The changes also had an impact on the way the professional members of staff worked. This resulted in a reduced demand for staff in the secretarial pool.

EXAMPLE 6.1

Work study in a secretarial pool

The department produced a large amount of documentation. This included plans, reports on the state of buildings, repairs and maintenance needed, tender documents for contracting outside building work, orders and invoices. Most of the work was carried out by professional and officer-level employees, but the word processing was largely carried out by the secretarial pool, which was staffed by 20 people. Their work was checked by the professional staff and was edited before being sent out.

A management services analysis was undertaken of the output produced. A sample of the work was taken and the number of key strokes (letters, punctuation marks, use of the space bar, etc.) needed were counted for the sample. The results from the sample were extrapolated to give an estimate of the number of key strokes needed for the total output. This was compared with the typing/word-processing speeds required of staff recruited to the secretarial pool. The result was that 60 per cent of those currently employed should have been able to produce the total output if they were to work constantly at the rate of which they were capable.

However, at times of high pressure the pool could not deal with the workload and temporary staff were needed to supplement them. It was important to discover the reason for the disparity between the actual and the potential outputs. Staff were interviewed and it was found that a considerable amount of time was spent editing reports and documents. This required going through the document in great detail and picking out specific changes. The result was that it could take two hours or more to make a relatively small number of key strokes while editing. Some documents were edited several times. This raised the question of why there was so much editing. Editing followed changes made by professional staff once they had seen a typed copy of their documents. The changes were mainly related to the originator of the document wanting to see a material change rather than errors made by the secretarial pool being corrected.

A 'right first time' approach was introduced to the department and the result was that the need for editing was substantially reduced. Professional staff were also given greater access to word processors so that they could edit their own work. As a result the secretarial pool received less work, and what they received could quickly be put into the official format and produced to the required standard. The initial analysis showed an overstaffing rate of 40 per cent, but further investigation has been required to understand the reasons behind the problems. Over a period of time reductions of 30 per cent were made in the secretarial pool through natural wastage and relocation of staff within the authority, and the need for use of temporary staff was removed.

A close reading of the case will convey certain weaknesses of objective methods in a work study exercise designed to examine the utilisation of human resources. If the initial raw data had been used for decision making with respect to staff reductions there would have been a reduction in operators of 40 per cent. In exercises of this nature it is necessary to go behind the raw data, and try to detect the reasons for what is happening. In such circumstances the factors at play can be deep rooted at both psychological and social levels. These can relate to factors of performance and motivation (which are addressed in Chapters 8 and 9) and factors relating to the individual's resistance to change (which were addressed in Chapter 4).

Prominence was given earlier to the role of work study as a technique to quantify the utilisation of human resources. But a question to ask is: does this technique live up to the expectations of its adherents? Some people would harbour certain reservations. Workers can disguise their capacity to produce when they are being observed and assessed. Naturally they are very conversant with the various facets of the job, and when they are assessed by the work study practitioners in order to set standards of work and output it could be in their interest to under-perform. By so doing they create a situation whereby softer targets or standards are allocated to them.

In contemporary reflections on the scientific management approach, of which work study is a part, there has been a challenge to the 'carrot and stick' approach where control by management features strongly. An approach more acceptable to a human resource management perspective would be to concentrate on worker motivation, where the emphasis would be on creating enriched jobs and greater self-control so as to provide employees with more scope for self-fulfilment. It is in this climate that appraisal systems that focus on personal/self-assessment have emerged which seek to encourage people to realise their potential. Performance management is discussed in Chapter 8. Finally, making a judgement about human resource utilisation currently involves a greater recognition of the importance of the qualitative approach (i.e. obtaining soft data from managers and workers about the reasons behind what is done and future intentions), though the quantitative approach highlighted in the case in Example 6.1 is still relevant.

■ Human resource supply

The next stage of human resource planning is to evaluate the supply of labour. This is done by reference to the amount of labour needed as a result of having calculated the demand for labour (examined earlier in this chapter). The approach to human resource supply has two parts: internal and external supply.

Internal supply

When reference is made to the number of employees already employed by the organisation we speak of the internal supply. The first step is to report on key characteristics of the internal supply as follows:

- age;
- grade;
- qualifications;
- experience;
- skills.

Before conducting exercises, such as the above method of profiling, policy decisions taken by the organisation with respect to expansion or contraction should be kept firmly in focus. For example, if contraction is contemplated (e.g. downsizing referred to in Chapter 3) it may be decided that employees aged 50 and over could be considered for early retirement. Therefore it is felt necessary to profile staff by age and grade. However, when this exercise is completed and the analysis shows that a substantial number of senior and middle managers are over the age of 50, it would appear necessary to reconsider the policy on early retirement, because releasing a large number of managerial staff over the age of 50 could strip the organisation of most of its experienced managers.

If conditions suggest that an increase in the supply of managers from within the organisation is needed then the organisation has to pay attention to 'succession planning'. This calls for an assessment of the actual performance of the person in their position, with that person's potential for promotion firmly in mind. It normally entails a formal plan to broaden the person's knowledge and experience of many aspects of work in a particular area, and/or training in skills at the technical and human relations levels. One has to guard against the misuse of succession planning where it is seen to disadvantage certain groups.

Where the decision about which individuals gain access to this form of development is a matter of managerial judgement it is important to ensure that there is parity between the judgements of different managers. Conscious or unconscious bias on the part of the manager could result in criteria being used that unfairly discriminate against particular groups. For example, if a manager regards an aggressive or 'macho' style of management as preferable this may give unwarranted advantage to men over women in terms of who is seen as having the potential to make a good manager.

Traditionally, upward movement was a feature of career progression (the linear approach). As organisations move to flatter structures (see Chapter 3), with fewer layers of management, the potential for gradual movement upwards is reduced, and lateral moves (e.g. moves to different positions in a work group at the same level) are entertained. Obviously this can create greater employee versatility as new skills are learnt and familiarity with new roles within the group or team grows. Metaphorically, career ladders give way to career climbing frames, where sideways and sometimes downward moves become increasingly a feature of employee development within organisations.

An organisation could be contemplating a reduction in the internal supply of labour because of a reduced demand for the services of all those currently employed. It is felt that labour is superfluous to requirements in one or more sections. A variety of conditions could have contributed to this state of affairs, including the advent of new technology that has reduced the labour intensiveness of operations. A programme of redundancy is mounted because reliance on natural wastage would not be good enough to get rid of the surplus. It is also important for management to control the outward flow of skills, experience and knowledge from the organisation rather than leaving this solely to the choice of individual employees, as the outcome may be the loss of important skills and the retention of employees who are not as valuable to the organisation.

The law on redundancy must be considered by the organisation because there are legal provisions which state that the company must make every reasonable attempt to find a comparable position for an employee whose job ceases to exist. Therefore, if a situation arose where the organisation is reducing staffing levels in one section, and expanding numbers in another, those whose positions are redundant should receive first consideration for the newly created vacancies over those external to the organisation.

In some situations it is inevitable that the staffing of an organisation will have to be 'downsized', or redundancies made. This is a difficult process, not only for the individuals directly involved but also for others who may have had friendships with those made redundant, and who may fear for their own future security. From an HRM perspective the organisation should seek to minimise the negative impact of staffing reductions by managing the process professionally. This will often include 'outplacement' – a process through which the organisation will help employees facing redundancy to find other jobs. The following activities may be included in the provision of an outplacement service (Graham and Bennett, 1998):

- counselling for the individuals facing redundancy;
- helping employees to discover their aptitude for alternative types of work, for example through the use of psychometric testing;
- offering training in new and relevant skills;
- using corporate networks (for example, with supplier organisations) to identify vacancies;

- support for job search, for example through helping employees to compose a CV and providing stationery and postage;
- allowing employees to take time off from work to seek other employment and attend interviews.

Although such services may be regarded as a cost it should be borne in mind that there is some moral responsibility for employees, and from a public relations perspective such an approach can cast the organisation in a favourable light with the employees who remain.

Inevitably during the process of collecting and analysing data on the internal supply of labour we encounter the staff turnover rate, which could indicate that the organisation has problems. The formula used to compile this rate was given in Chapter 1. The rate in itself is relatively uninformative, but what is useful is the comparison of rates across sections or departments. For example, if in a department of 50 staff 10 left in the previous year, that is a rate of 20 per cent. This may signal grounds for concern if most other departments in the organisation have a rate of 5 per cent or less. In certain industries a high staff turnover is normal. For example, catering staff and kitchen workers have a tradition of staying in a job for a relatively short period of time.

It is always a good idea to establish the reasons why the turnover rate is on the high side (or exceptionally low). Reasons for high turnover can include a local competitor offering better conditions and benefits or general dissatisfaction in a department due to, for example, job insecurity or very poor management. Similarly, it is a good idea to learn more about a group of employees who entered the organisation together. An example of such a group is a cohort of graduates recruited as trainee managers. The progress of the group could be analysed at regular intervals to see how many complete the training, how many achieve certain levels of performance and grades, and how many leave the company. Cohort analysis using statistical techniques can be used to explore the extent of wastage or loss due to turnover. One such technique is Bowey's (1974) stability index, which takes account of the length of service:

$$\frac{\text{Sum of months served (over 'N' period) by staff currently employed}}{\text{Sum of possible months service (over 'N' period) by a full complement of staff}}$$
$$\times 100 = \% \text{ stability.}$$

This formula measures the experience of current staff as a proportion of the maximum experience that could have been gained over the period ('N') being examined if all the staff had been in constant employment for the whole period.

The following example may serve to clarify the use of this index. A group of 20 management trainees is recruited by an organisation, and after two years Bowey's stability index is to be calculated. The sum of the possible service/experience in months is:

20 (people) $\times$ 24 (months) = 480 person months.

This supplies the figure for the bottom of the equation (the denominator).

The current management trainees have the following profile: 5 have served 24 months, 5 have served 12 months and 10 have served 6 months. This indicates that some members of the cohort have left and been replaced during the 2 years. The 15 members of staff who have less than 24 months' experience are replacements. The total number of months served by the current employees is 240. If these figures are inserted into the equation (240/480 × 100) the stability is 50 per cent. This would indicate that the group is not very experienced – it has amassed only half the possible experience it could have gained in the time period. This level of staff stability would be likely to be seen as relatively low.

Further analysis may be undertaken to establish the pattern of leaving. A wastage or stability rate may be distorted by a disproportionately high (or low) number of people passing through one particular position or a specific job type. If this were found to be the case it would indicate that there might be a problem with the particular job or position, which is not general to the whole department. It would be important to discover the reasons behind this phenomenon.

Quantitative techniques, such as Bowey's stability index, are a vital part of the planning of the internal supply of labour. However, they should not be viewed as the ultimate explanation but as a starting point for further explanation. As mentioned earlier when focusing on the application of quantitative techniques we need to go behind the statistics and try to establish the reasons for a particular result or trend. With regard to cohort analysis, what contributed to a high rate of turnover in a particular situation? It could be that employees are leaving to take up better posts elsewhere, or to broaden their experience, or to escape from an unpleasant atmosphere within the organisation.

This type of qualitative information can be obtained from 'exit interviews' with those leaving the organisation. Exit interviews are probably best conducted by a human resource specialist who is likely to be seen as less threatening and as someone to whom one can divulge frank views. A departing employee is often able to voice criticisms about many facets of the organisation and its management, views one would not expect to hear from a person who plans to remain in the organisation. The latter may be reticent about voicing criticism because of a belief that such action would be damaging for their career and future remuneration. Of course a departing colleague could also express complimentary views. Therefore the exit interview provides useful information not readily available from other sources.

External supply

If the organisation cannot draw on an internal supply of labour when extra staff are needed it will need to recruit from the external labour market. The external supply of labour will be discussed with reference to the following:

1 tightness of supply;
2 demographic factors;
3 social/geographic aspects;
4 the type of employee required.

Tightness of supply

A tight supply of labour arises where there are relatively few external candidates with the requisite abilities to do the job. By contrast, a loose supply indicates a large number of able candidates are available. Given the current relatively low level of unemployment in the United Kingdom one might conclude that the external supply of labour is low (tight). Though it is useful to think of external labour supply in quantitative terms, such as low or high, the picture is more complex when viewed qualitatively. For example, the particular skills and abilities required by the organisation are not necessarily found among the unemployed.

Guest (1994) reports that expertise in some areas of information technology is in very tight supply. According to the Federation of Recruitment and Employment Services (cited in Guest, 1994) demand exceeds supply by 3:1 for IT staff. This has resulted in companies engaging in gazumping, i.e. offering higher salaries to potential recruits than the recruits had already agreed with competitor organisations, in order to attract the supply of labour they need. In addition, attractive opportunities for career development could be offered. In the late 1990s the IT sector was still an example of a segment of the labour market where skills were scarce with an abundance of employment opportunities, and this accelerated mobility and led to substantial increases in rewards. Where the organisation experiences difficulty in attracting people with the necessary skills it may resort to the use of subcontractors or consultants to overcome the shortage. This could be a one-off arrangement or alternatively a continuing relationship.

An alternative to recruiting people with the necessary skills is to recruit people with potential and train them to the required standard. This does involve the cost of training and carries the risk that their potential will not be realised. It can be time consuming to train people and, particularly for small organisations that do not have training systems already established, this course of action could be prohibitively expensive and difficult. However there are advantages to training people internally. It can lead to an increased sense of commitment on the part of the employees, the training could be directly related to the organisation's needs, and it is a form of investing in people and treating them as assets. There is more detailed discussion of training in Chapter 10. Apart from the strategies mentioned, labour shortages could be met by attracting certain groups back to work, for example married women with children, and then providing appropriate conditions (e.g. hours that coincide with the school day). The increase in flexible employment practices, such as the latter, has been one of the reasons for an increase in the proportion of women in the workforce. Between 1986 and 2000 the number of women in employment in the United Kingdom grew from 10 million (out of a total of 24 million) to 12 million (out of a total of 27 million). In 1986 3.9 million of the women employed worked part time, and by 2000 this figure had risen to 4.7 million (out of a total of 5.7 million part-time workers) (Office for National Statistics, 2001).

Demographic factors

Demographic changes (e.g. the number of young people entering the labour force) affect the external supply of labour. In 1982 there were 3.7 million young people in the age group 16–19; in 1994 the figure was 2.6 million (Skills and Enterprise Network, 1994). This change (approximately one-third) will affect the supply of labour to organisations that have traditionally recruited young people and trained and developed them by the use of the training process and exposure to the organisation's ethos or culture. The stated demographic change will alter the age composition of the workforce, and will force employers to review their recruitment policies. The outcome of such a review could be to give more consideration to employing older workers who will constitute a higher proportion of the work force than hitherto. Reflecting on these statistics in 2001, one is now in a position to conclude that the declining birth rate was countered by a recession in the early 1990s and the shedding of labour throughout the 1990s, as a result of widespread programmes of rationalisation and cost cutting by organisations.

The composition of the workforce is also likely to experience a change in its gender composition. The Labour Force Survey (Office for National Statistics, 2001) shows women making up 44 per cent of the working population, compared to 41 per cent in 1986. Employment rates amongst women had risen from 47 per cent in 1959 to 69 per cent by 1999. This trend of an increasing proportion of women in employment will put pressure on organisations to become more 'family friendly'. In the future progressive organisations are likely to employ more women and older workers. This will entail the application of appropriate strategies of recruitment, retention and training.

Another factor to note is EU legislation, which has increased the potential mobility of labour within the EU. Under this legislation workers are free to undertake employment in other member states. On the demographic front it should be noted that the proportion of young people in the population will decline even more sharply in Germany and Italy. It could be that this will result in a net movement of skilled workers out of the United Kingdom to take up positions in Europe (Hendry, 1994). However this predicted outcome is subject to varying influences, e.g. linguistic skills, culture and economic growth.

During the economic recession of the early 1990s the predicted effect of demographic changes was not too evident, as observed above, particularly when the unemployment level among school leavers and graduates is noted. (In 1992/3 the 16–19 age group had an unemployment figure of 18.8 per cent, and the 20–24 age group a figure of 15.6 per cent. These compare with an overall rate of 9.9 per cent; Skills and Enterprise Network, 1994.) However, when the recovery in the economy is well established the effects of the demographic changes could be felt. Recognizing the implications of the demographic changes for the organisation, B&Q, a UK do-it-yourself store, created a personnel policy to employ older people (see Example 6.2).

Reflecting on the B&Q case one feels that certain prejudices about older workers are unfounded. In particular, older workers are able to learn as effectively as younger workers given the right conditions. Sickness absence is not higher than that for younger workers, and the profitability of the organisation is not adversely affected.

EXAMPLE 6.2

B&Q and the 'grey revolution'

The DIY store, B&Q, had traditionally recruited school leavers to serve in its shops. Demographic changes prompted the personnel department to initiate a policy of employing older workers. This 'grey revolution' (Jetter, 1993) started with a new store in Macclesfield where all the recruits were over 50.

Recruitment took place through advertisements in the national press and two open days held locally. It was felt that older people would have more experience of DIY and would be able to encourage customers who were unsure of their abilities. The initial training was lengthened from four to eight weeks to allow for slower learning. However this was found to be unnecessary, and it was reduced to the normal period.

The selection policy was thought to contribute to above-average profits, a massive reduction in 'unattributable stock loss' and a very low absentee rate. Staff turnover was 50 per cent below average and customer satisfaction was significantly higher. The manager felt that there was a collective determination to prove that older people can perform.

Subsequently, organisations have started to take these issues seriously. For example, the Halifax has been developing an approach to removing ageism since 1995. In order to do this there has been a focus on recruitment and selection, training and communication, and on becoming an employer of choice (see Example 6.3).

EXAMPLE 6.3

Anti-ageism at the Halifax

The Halifax provides banking and mortgage lending services through a national network of high street outlets in the United Kingdom. In 1995 it included the issue of ageism in its equal opportunities policy and in 1998 an initiative to renew the impetus was launched. Business needs were the driving force behind the initiative, as Tyrone Jones, equal opportunities adviser put it: 'Today's demographics are tomorrow's business' (quoted in Glover, 2001: 40). In other words, it is necessary for financial organisations to reflect features of their clientele in their workforce if they are to maintain market position. A measure of their success is that the Department for Employment and Education's award for Age diversity in employment was won in 2000 by the Halifax.

For a long time Halifax had equal opportunities policies, and it was believed that managers were not being deliberately biased in their decision making, but nonetheless it was important to take action to ensure that unconscious biases were not impacting on both the recruitment and management of older workers. Since 1999 road shows have been used to communicate and promote the benefits of age diversity to managers. This is an issue that is addressed in training sessions, and more than 90 per cent of employees have now participated in a video-based training programme, 'Fair's Fair', which deliberately positions age as a business (rather than a personnel) matter.

There has also been development in the area of recruitment and selection. As Inji Duducu of the personnel department says 'the present skills shortage is focusing managers' minds and making them realise that they cannot persist with their prejudices' (quoted in Glover, 2001: 41). Age-related questions have been removed from application forms, and guidance is given to interviewers to avoid such questions. Selection criteria have been changed to prevent discrimination against the older worker. Older workers are targeted and are growing and thriving in a number of areas. Recently a new member of the legal department was appointed at the age of 60. Even in sales, which has been seen as a 'young person's profession', older workers have been found to be very effective. They are sensitive when it comes to arranging loans and are able to give a sense of comfort and certainty to customers who are inexperienced and may be applying for their first mortgage. The Halifax has been active in seeking out people who are changing careers and has used a number of techniques, including open days, to encourage this trend. In addition, the graduate training programmes have been designed to encourage new mature graduates over the age of 25.

Avoiding age discrimination is not confined to the older worker. Effort has also been put into building bridges with schools and the provision of work experience for young people. The aim is to remove age barriers and focus on skills and attributes that people can bring to the environment which provides financial services to all sections of the community.

(Glover, 2001)

Social/geographic aspects

The external supply of labour is influenced by socio-geographic factors. In certain parts of the United Kingdom (e.g. north of England, Scotland, Wales), where rapid decline of the older industries has taken place, there are large pools of labour with skills. This has prompted industrialists to consider moving their operations to these areas. Amongst the other factors influencing a company's decision to move to an area where an adequate supply of suitable labour exists are the quality of the transport system and access to the market for its output.

Many Japanese companies that have invested in the United Kingdom have done so in greenfield sites where there is high unemployment (Wilkinson and Oliver, 1992). For example Komatsu, which manufactures earth-moving vehicles, set up its operation in the north-east of England. In the case of many of the Japanese consumer electronics companies, the company was not attracted by skills, which already existed in an area, but was more concerned to recruit inexperienced labour. The selection process has been principally concerned with testing candidates' teamworking ability and their attitude to cooperative modes of working, as well as numeracy and dexterity skills.

Type of worker

The category of worker is another variable to consider when discussing the external supply of labour. Graduates and professional staff are more prepared to move location for a job than blue-collar skilled and semi-skilled workers. As was stated earlier, freedom of movement of labour within the EU is now enshrined in legislation, but in practice it is management and professional workers for whom mobility is a greater reality because of the attractive remuneration packages on offer. Initiatives have been taken by the EU to increase mobility in the labour market (Hendry, 1994). These initiatives include promoting common vocational standards, transferability of qualifications and student exchanges.

■ Internal vs external supply

Using the internal supply of resources as a source of labour has certain advantages over the external supply. Those already employed in an organisation are well placed to understand the way things are done and how the different parts of the organisation fit together, and to appreciate the nature of the culture. The people responsible for selecting internal candidates for vacant positions have access to more comprehensive information relating to their abilities, track record and potential achievement than they would have if they were selecting people originating from the external labour market. Drawing on an internal supply of labour to fill vacancies, whereby the internal candidate receives a promotion, sends a powerful signal to employees that the organisation is committed to their advancement and development.

However, one must be aware of certain disadvantages associated with drawing on an internal supply of resources. Although there may be more information about internal candidates at the disposal of selectors, it is not always free of bias. Also, there is greater likelihood of more negative information about internal candidates being available, while external candidates are better placed to conceal information about their past failures and difficulties. Finally, internal candidates could be steeped in the culture of the organisation: if this culture is risk aversive and conservative, it could act as a constraint when innovative practices and initiatives are required of the successful candidate. An external candidate could feel less inhibited where the introduction of fresh ideas to work practices and job performance is highly desirable. But for this to happen it may be necessary to change the corporate culture.

One way in which companies bring about a change in culture is by tapping the external supply of labour (Brown, 1998). This could be reflected in an attempt to create a workforce with values and attitudes compatible with the desired corporate culture. For example, Toshiba aimed to increase cooperation and flexibility on their shopfloor. This was done by carefully wording their recruitment literature, which referred to 'assembly operators' rather than to specific jobs, and through the use of a video shown to candidates offering themselves for employment so that they could engage in self-selection if they felt comfortable with the projected organisational environment on screen. Therefore candidates with a flexible attitude, who were prepared to take on a variety of tasks, were selected rather than people who wanted to assume only one specific and fixed role.

■ Labour markets

In recent years pressure has been mounting from the EU and international bodies, such as the OECD, to take on board flexibility in labour markets and working practices. As a result of high levels of unemployment, high social costs (such as generous benefits and pensions) and long working hours in some parts of the EU, Member States have been encouraged to embrace work sharing initiatives, part-time working, and to reconsider the balance between work and non-work, and the division of labour by gender within households (EC, 1995). It is apparent that much of the ensuing restructuring has been driven by a desire to cut costs, and in the words of Legge (1998), by the urge to extend the scope of managerial regulation of the employment relationship. As Japan tries to cope with its economic problems there are some indications that labour markets are becoming more flexible (Tett, 2000). However, in the United States, where flexible employment took off in a big way in the past, there is recent evidence in an authoritative report by the Economic Policy Institute (a Washington think tank) to suggest that the proportion of workers in temporary or part-time jobs has declined due to the progressive return of full-time employment over the past five years (Taylor, 2000).

In this section we shall have something to say more specifically about flexibility, a topic also considered in connection with developments in restructuring in Chapter 3; in addition, there will be comment on the changing composition of the EU labour force. Flexibility can be construed as consisting of at least five components, as follows:

1 *numerical flexibility* – use of part-time and temporary workers whose numbers and hours can be varied relatively easily and cheaply to meet organisational needs;
2 *distancing flexibility* – the use of contract staff or self-employed freelancers who are provided with a contract for service but are not employees of the organisation;
3 *functional flexibility* – employees possessing skills that cut across functional areas within an organisation; it implies a certain degree of versatility with an emphasis on both the acquisition and updating of appropriate skills through on-the-job training;
4 *temporal or working time flexibility* – relates to the more intensive use of labour, or the closer matching of organisational requirements with staffing levels – e.g. moves to seven-day working, shiftworking and overtime;
5 *financial flexibility* – linking rewards more closely with individual or organisational performance, and including incentives such as performance-related pay, share options and share ownership schemes (Murton, 2000).

Although there are advantages attached to restructuring based on flexibility, some argue that greater flexibility has meant job insecurity, lack of status and reduced bargaining power for workers (Legge, 1998). Others point out the partial nature of flexibility schemes. For example, Ford UK achieved some flexibility in its assembly line operations by getting rid of demarcation lines and redefining jobs in such a way as to reduce 500 differently defined assembly jobs to a mere 50. However, Ford UK failed in the early 1990s to obtain union agreement to accept both quality circles and a formalised system of employee involvement at a time when employee involvement achieved some success in Ford USA (McKinlay and Starkey, 1992). The reader is asked to refer to Chapter 3 for further observations on the concept of flexibility.

Atkinson and Rick (1996) report that temporary work is increasingly being used as a stepping stone to permanent employment, with at least 20 per cent of employers using it in this way. The advantage of this approach is that it gives the organisation the chance to judge the individual on the basis of their performance in reality, rather than as hypothecated through recruitment and selection techniques such as interviews and in-tray tests. It also gives employees a chance to judge whether or not they will fit into the organisation. The downside, however, is that if the match between employee and organisation does not work out, for the employee the job ends.

Clearly, flexibility can have both advantages and disadvantages. Emmott and Hutchinson (1998) summarise survey evidence on employee attitudes to flexible working as follows:

Advantages:
- the ability to combine work with outside interests, e.g. caring responsibilities or hobbies;
- greater job satisfaction;
- improved motivation;
- less tiredness.

Disadvantages:
- unequal treatment in terms of pay and benefits;
- reduced career development opportunities;
- limited training opportunities;
- the 'psychological contract' is threatened;
- increased job insecurity;
- increased stress.

According to Emmott and Hutchinson the majority (nearly 75 per cent) of part-time employees work part time because they do not want a full-time job, and this figure rises to 80 per cent for women.

An important component in the flexibility debate is the changing composition of the EU workforce, though the impact of this change differs between Member States. Over the last couple of decades there has been a decline in the number of jobs in the manufacturing sector and this has had an impact on the available opportunities for men in the European labour market, particularly full-time jobs. By contrast, the job opportunities for women have increased in all countries in the EU, a trend that is likely to continue (EC, 1995).

Although much has been written about the flexibility of home working, in the UK there was no increase in the number of home workers (i.e. those who mainly work in their own homes) between 1996 and 2000, with the figure constant at 0.7m (Office for National Statistics, 2001). However, a survey of 2,500 employers and 7,500 employees by the Institute of Employment Research and IFF Research (Skills and Enterprise Executive, 2001) found that many employees wanted flexible working arrangements, and 62 per cent of organisations allowed some level of flexible hours. Men were found more likely than women to want flexitime, compressed hours and annualised hours. Women were found more likely to want term-time working or reduced hours.

■ The individual and the organisation: change and careers

The concepts of stable identity and form, both of organisations and individuals, are one of the fundamental assumptions of traditional human resource planning. While it has long been acknowledged that organisations will change and people will develop, the assumption was that it was possible to plan for the future through analysis of the past and present. As organisations changed the changes could be accounted for by changes in demand for employees, and development of individuals would be accounted for through career management. However, in the social and economic environment of the late twentieth and early twenty-first century change has been such that prediction based on an assumption of stability has been challenged in a radical way.

Changes in organisations

The drive for productivity, particularly in competitive organisational environments, has had a significant impact on HRP (O'Doherty, 1997). Traditionally, if a department lost people through turnover, promotion or retirement, it would be reasonable to assume that they would be replaced in the human resource plan. From the 1990s onwards it may be more realistic to assume that the vacancies would not be filled because of the need to control costs, increase productivity (and hence shareholder value) (O'Doherty, 1997). Similarly, efforts to increase employee performance, for example through quality initiatives and high commitment management, have often been associated with reduced supervision, which leads to cost savings. So in HRP terms the focus is on utilisation rather than supply of labour.

In addition the nature of utilisation has also been changing. Traditionally the focus would be on developing the way that currently employed staff worked. However, with structural changes that have resulted in 'permeable boundaries' between organisations (creating alliances, close relationships with suppliers, such as just-in-time procedures and outsourcing), the workforce on a particular task may be drawn from different organisations. Such arrangements rely on contracting between organisations, and so the planning for labour supply becomes part of the overall contracting arrangements of a contingency nature undertaken by the organisation.

One example is taken from the film and television industry (Lash and Urry, 1994), where in an organisation such as the BBC the planning of a major project such as a drama series does not necessarily use in-house design, production, editing, technical and facilities staff. The planning of such a project will involve a temporary network of many staff drawn together for a particular purpose and time period. The choice of people is often made through reputation and personal contact. The nature of contracts, working requirements and conditions will relate to the individuals' ability to negotiate, and there is a lack of standardisation of plans and arrangements (O'Doherty, 1997).

Career management

In a unitarist definition of HRM (see Chapter 11), career management, which is also discussed in Chapter 10, has been seen as the 'organizational processes which enable the careers of individuals to be planned and managed in a way that optimizes both the needs of the organization and the preferences and capabilities of the individual' (Mayo, 1991). While career management has traditionally been available to managerial and professional employees there have been attempts to incorporate a broader range of employees in 'people-centred' approaches, which seek to define jobs around the individual rather than exclusively the converse (Bratton and Gold, 1999). In such models counselling sessions, typically between the manager and the employee, will seek to find matches between the organisation's needs for human resources emerging from the business strategy and the individual's aspirations and competences. Clearly this requires managerial competency in career counselling, and achieving a balance in which it is likely that some of the employee's aspirations will not be achievable within the existing opportunities provided by the organisation. In addition it requires the organisation to be flexible enough to meet some of the aspirations of the employee if the scheme is to retain credibility and enhance the motivation of staff. Traditional career counselling models (e.g. Verlander, 1985) tended to focus on manager-led interactions. More recently the focus has swung towards individuals driving their own progress, with an emphasis on personal development plans, learning centres and career workshops (Bratton and Gold, 1999). However, in organisations where delayering has greatly reduced the chances for upward progression the experience of many is, of necessity, that the career is not available to be managed in the mode envisaged by Mayo (1991).

Notwithstanding this problem, some organisations have sought to enhance employee choice, acknowledging that the choice to have a traditional career may be limited. One such example is the retailer Tesco (Prickett, 1998) which, facing a problem of high staff turnover (33 per cent in 1997), began a programme of staff retention. Managers attend core skill workshops in stores along with staff who are earmarked for potential promotion. Individuals have career development plans and are encouraged to move between functions. Movement is also possible geographically, and following the expansion into Europe more than 100 British managers were working in eastern European stores. However, measures are not confined to management and training has been more generally available and jobs and practices in stores have been analysed in order to eliminate unnecessary bureaucracy. For example, traditionally a service desk employee would have to ask a manager before allowing any refund, but this regulation has now been relaxed because it was thought to be a waste of time and demotivating for staff. Additionally, the company employs many female workers, and steps have been taken to enable career breaks and return to part-time management jobs. The company includes sections that operate 24 hours, 7 days a week, and so efforts are made to enable working mothers to organise their shifts around the needs of family life where it can be accommodated (Prickett, 1998).

The impacts of such measures is that planning becomes an interactive process in which employees and the organisation seek to accommodate each other to some extent. It should be noted, however, that the apparent flexibility, which benefits employees, might exist to a greater extent in policy and the use of rhetoric than in the reality experienced by employees (Legge, 1998). For example, in the case of Tesco, flexibility is available in shift patterns 'as long as it can be accommodated'. At the end of the day organisations are unlikely to accommodate employees to an extent that will significantly impact on their profitability.

In other examples there is a high degree of flexibility for professional employees who are able to manage their careers as portfolio workers. One example of a group of highly skilled workers in Reuters is given in Example 6.4.

EXAMPLE 6.4

The Usability Group in Reuters

Reuters is the world's largest news agency, with 1,400 journalists operating in most areas of the globe. One of its focuses is servicing financial centres and stock markets through the provision of up-to-the-minute financial information and computerised financial trading technology. Reuters' terminals supply both general and financial news in addition to investment reports to over 200 exchanges and 4,000 subscribers such as banks in 150 different countries. The market for supplying such information is highly competitive, with organisations such as Bloombergs Financial Services and Dow Jones providing alternatives. In this context, it is vital that customer satisfaction is maintained at an exemplary level. In order to achieve such customer satisfaction Reuters established the 'Usability Group'. The task of this group is to test the efficiency and user friendliness of new information services and computerised financial transaction products with customers.

The first human resource plan for the Usability Group was to have a multi-function team of 22 staff, made up of professionals in software, artificial intelligence, ergonomics, IT and graphics design as well as psychologists and project managers. The group would review new products from their various expert positions and would run the products through 'usability testing'. The latter involves customers working with the products under controlled conditions, and their experience is analysed from multiple perspectives. The outcome of reviews and testing are fed into the design process, and modifications to products occur as a result.

At the time of the submission of the first human resource plan to the board there was a significant downturn in the market and as a result the board handed the leader of the putative group the challenge of setting up a flexible 'virtual' team, rather than committing to long-term employment costs. The group was set up with 3 core staff and others were brought in on a short-term contractual basis to work on specific projects. This gave the group flexibility, and when a project called for a particular professional emphasis a team of the appropriate profile could be built.

Over time the team has expanded to have about 50 'virtual members' with about 18 core members. The virtual members are located around the world and typically contribute to projects through IT links. Of the core staff only 5 are direct Reuters employees. The others are seconded from other organisations or are agency workers. Project teams are led by the group member with the most appropriate expertise regardless of their position in the hierarchy or employment status.

This approach is very flexible, and it is regarded as highly successful by Reuters. It enables the group to call on the services of world experts who would not restrict their activities to a single organisation. However, there were potential difficulties. As group members have 'portfolios' of work that take them to different, sometimes competing, organisations there were problems of confidentiality and openness within the team. Considerable effort was put into team building at the outset, and ground rules, including complete openness, were established. Anyone who cannot live with the ground rules will not remain a member of the team.

Reuters Usability Group was in a fortunate position of being attractive for portfolio workers to have on their c.v., and appropriate funding was available to the group. The work is seen as cutting-edge and it has had a significant impact on Reuters' products. Perhaps because of these attractive features the human resource planning and utilisation of group members on a flexible basis has been efficient and effective both for Reuters and for the team members.

(Beech, 1997)

■ Conclusions

Human resource or manpower planning has always been an area of interest in personnel and human resource management. Emphasis has been placed on different parts (hard and soft) of the planning process at different times in its history. The approach taken has largely reflected the business environment and the state of development of the subject. It is important to strike a balance so that no area of the planning process is neglected.

The current focus is on the need for flexibility in planning so that organisations are able to adapt to situations steeped in change. The impact of information and communication technology (ICT) on organisations has been pronounced. It has enabled arrangements such as teleworking, and increased the substitutability of some employees (those whose jobs can be replaced or changed significantly by

ICT), while at the same time increasing the value and scarcity of others (typically the ICT professionals). As we have seen in the case of Reuters, where there is power on both sides of the employment contract, accommodating the needs of employees and employers in a flexible way is becoming the vogue.

The focus is increasingly not just on planning but also on managing the nature of contractual arrangements through flexible accommodation, sub-contracting and outsourcing. Through such arrangements the organisation can spread the risk of failing to find future business, which it formerly absorbed when taking on permanent employees. Whether the focus for a particular organisation is on cost control and outsourcing, or developing staff through career management, there is a need for proactive HRM. At both ends of the scale there is a need for effective selection decision making – who to sub-contract to, or whose career to support. Although there has been a swing towards 'managerial judgement' and away from more traditional quantitative approaches, it is important to optimise the decision-making process, and this does not imply simply moving to the exclusive use of intuitive judgement, it means contracting the space reserved for intuitive judgement.

HRP is concerned with proactively analysing the external environment and making the best possible use of employees. In these ways HRP can provide an input to the organisational strategy by outlining the possibilities and costs of current and potential workforce configurations. It maps out the implications of strategic decisions for subsequent HRM activities such as recruitment and development. HRP can therefore be seen as an important linking factor between strategy and operation.

References

Atkinson, J. and Rick, J. (1996) 'Temporary work and the labour market', Institute of Employment Studies, Report 311.

Beech, N. (1997) 'Learning to build customers into facilities management: the case of Reuters', *International Journal of Facilities Management*, 1, 51–9.

Bowey, A. (1974) *A Guide to Manpower Planning*, London: Macmillan.

Bramham, J. (1989) *Human Resource Planning*, London: IPM.

Bratton, J. and Gold, J. (1999) *Human Resource Management: Theory and practice*, London: Macmillan.

Braverman, H. (1974) *Labour and Monopoly Capitalism*, New York: Monthly Review Press.

Brown, A. (1998) *Organizational Culture*, London: Pitman.

EC (1995) *Employment in Europe*, Luxembourg: Office for Official Publications in the European Communities.

Emmott, M. and Hutchinson, S. (1998) 'Employment flexibility: threat or promise?', in Sparrow, P. and Marchington, M. (eds), *Human Resource Management: The new agenda*. London: Financial Times/Pitman.

Glover, C. (2001) 'Generation Xtra', *People Management*, 7, 40–2.

Graham, H.T. and Bennett, R. (1998) *Human Resources Management*, London: Financial Times/Pitman.

Guest, D. (1994) 'Gazumping comes to the jobs market', *The Times* (Business Section), 22 July, 32.

Hall, L. and Torrington, D. (1998) *The Human Resource Function: The dynamics of change and development*, London: Financial Times/Pitman.

Hamilton, K. (1993) 'Axing the bank clerks', *Sunday Times* (Business Section), 10 October, 4.

Hendry, C. (1994) 'The Single European Market and the HRM response', in Kirkbride, P.S. (ed.), *Human Resource Management in Europe*, London: Routledge.

Jetter, M. (1993) 'The wisdom factor: B&Q's employment of older people', in McIntosh, M. (ed.), *Good Business*, Bristol: School for Advanced Urban Studies.

Lash, S. and Urry, J. (1994) *Economies of Signs and Space*, London: Sage.

Legge, K. (1998) 'The gift wrapping of employment degradation', in Sparrow, P. and Marchington, M. (eds), *Human Resource Management: The new agenda*, London: Financial Times/Pitman.

McKinlay, A. and Starkey, K. (1992) 'Strategy and human resource management', *International Journal of Human Resource Management*, 3, 435–50.

Mayo, A. (1991) *Managing Careers*, London: IPM.

Murton, A. (2000) 'Labour markets and flexibility: current debates and the European dimension', in Barry, J., Chandler, J., Clark, H., Johnston, R. and Needle, D. (eds), *Organization and Management: A critical text*, London: Business Press (Thompson Learning).

O'Doherty, D. (1997) 'Human resource planning: control to seduction?', in Beardwell, I. and Holden, L. (eds), *Human Resource Management: A contemporary perspective*, 2nd edn, London: Pitman.

Office for National Statistics (2001) 'Labour force survey', *Social Trends*, 31.

Prickett, R. (1998) 'Staff value a career path above salary', *People Management*, 16 April.

Sisson, K. and Timperley, S. (1994) 'From manpower planning to strategic human resource management', in Sisson, K. (ed.), *Personnel Management: A comprehensive guide to theory and practice in Britain*, 2nd edn, Oxford: Blackwell.

Skills and Enterprise Executive (2001) *Get a Life, Get a Work Life Balance*, Issue 1.

Skills and Enterprise Network (1994) 'A summary of "Labour Market and Skill Trends 1993/94"', London: Department of Employment.

Storey, J. (1992) *Developments in the Management of Human Resources*, Oxford: Blackwell.

Taylor, F.W. (1947) *Scientific Management*, New York: Harper & Row.

Taylor, R. (2000) 'Labour market: dramatic shift from flexible employment towards regular work – job security back in booming US', *Financial Times*, 4 September, 10.

Tett, G. (2000) 'Time to rectify a period of disappointment', *Japan – Financial Times Survey*, 19 September, 1.

Torrington, D., Hall, L., Haylor, I. and Myers, J. (1991) *Employee Resourcing*, London: IPM.

Verlander, E.G. (1985) 'The System's the thing', *Training and Development*, April, 20–3.

Wilkinson, B. and Oliver, N. (1992) 'Human resource management in Japanese manufacturing companies in the UK and USA', in Towers, B. (ed.), *The Handbook of Human Resource Management*, Oxford: Blackwell.

Chapter 7

Employee resourcing: recruitment and selection

Recruitment and selection are crucial decision-making points in the establishment of the working relationship with employees. The psychological contract is established in part by the expectations that the organisation and employee have of each other from early impressions, and so it is important that the best possible information flows in both directions. Success in selection has been highlighted as integral to high performance models of HRM, and the cost of poor decisions, both for the organisation and the individual, can be extensive.

Having read this chapter, you should:

- understand the role of recruitment and selection in an overall system of HRM;
- be aware of the nature of job analysis;
- know the purpose and make-up of job descriptions and specifications;
- be able to make judgements about the appropriateness of the various sources of recruitment;
- understand the alternative tools of selection – their strengths and weaknesses.

The process of recruitment and selection is the planned way in which the organisation interfaces with the external supply of labour. Recruitment is the process of attracting a pool of candidates for a vacant position, and selection is the technique of choosing a new member of the organisation from the available candidates. These processes incur significant costs, so it is natural for organisations to pay attention to these activities from a cost-effective viewpoint. Placing advertisements and using the services of managers in selection interviewing can be costly, as it can be if the person selected to fill a particular vacancy does not perform satisfactorily in the job. Substandard performance on a production line can lead to having to correct a mistake, and a lack of skill in interacting with a customer could lead to loss of business. Within a work group a poor performer can affect the rhythm and output of the team.

Certain advantages are said to accrue from external recruitment. It offers the organisation the opportunity to inject new ideas into its operations by utilising the skills of external candidates. When internal promotions have taken place, external recruitment could be used to attract candidates to fill positions, that have been vacated by insiders. Also, external recruitment is a form of communication, whereby the organisation projects its image to potential employees, customers and others outside the organisation.

■ Prerequisites to recruitment

Recruitment and selection need to be underpinned by solid preparatory work in the form of job analysis and preparing a job description and job specification.

Job analysis

Job analysis is the process of finding out what is involved in the job that is now vacant. To start off this process one could interview the previous job-holder as well as his or her supervisor and other staff connected with them in the natural course of events. This approach has value in describing the tasks that constitute the vacant post, and highlights the reporting relationship (to the job-holder's superior) and other forms of liaison (e.g. with colleagues). There is also a tradition in job analysis whereby the job holder may be asked to keep a work diary so that a record of how time is actually spent is available.

Smith and Robertson (1993) have put forward the following six-step approach to job analysis, which covers some of the points mentioned above:

1 Utilise appropriate existing documents, such as job descriptions and training manuals.
2 Ask questions of the line manager in whose department the job is located about the main purposes of the job, the tasks involved and how the job relates to other jobs.
3 Ask questions of the person doing the job about the main purposes of the job, the tasks involved and how the job relates to other jobs. In addition, the job-holder could be asked to provide supplementary information in the form of a record (e.g. work diary) of the activity in the job over a set period (e.g. two weeks).
4 If practicable, an observer could be assigned the task of noting what the job-holder does, normally over a period of more than one day and at different times.
5 The job analyst could go through the motions of performing the job in order to obtain the necessary insight, but it should be noted that this approach may not be possible if the job analyst has not got the necessary training or is unable to use the machinery, where appropriate, because of lack of familiarity with its use.
6 The final step is to produce a description of the job.

Other methods are the Work Profiling System, consisting of a computerised questionnaire produced by Saville and Holdsworth (Smith *et al.*, 1989), designed to provide a detailed job description and a profile of the ideal candidate, and the 'critical incidents technique'. The latter is applied in situations when job-holders are asked to describe a number of specific real-time events that have contributed to successful job performance.

Job analysis is not an unbiased source of information (Price, 1997). Subordinates are capable of exaggerating in the sense that they convey that their jobs are more demanding or complex than they really are; they can also be guilty of omission when they remember the interesting tasks but somehow forget the boring ones. Information provided by supervisors could err on the side of understatement, that is jobs are portrayed as being easier and less complex than they are in reality. Misunderstanding could also arise, as frequently supervisors do not have a detailed view of the subordinates' jobs.

When conducting a job analysis exercise one should keep firmly in mind the justification for the job in the light of current and future organisational needs. Corporate strategic considerations should therefore be a guiding force.

Job analysis will normally take place when a position becomes vacant, but as organisations become more flexible it can be an ongoing process of updating so as to enhance the adaptability of the organisation. Job analysis provides the fundamental information, which will subsequently be used in formulating the job description and job or person specification, i.e. information about the tasks that are carried out and the skills and attributes needed to achieve successful performance.

Job description

Having defined the job after analysing it, the next step is the preparation of a job description. This should contain an outline of the job, the tasks involved, the responsibilities and the conditions. A job description is a foundation stone for a number of human resource practices, ranging from selection to the determination of pay and training. But the traditional job description is now being challenged with the advent of the 'flexible' job description. This has become popular for some organisations, particularly those influenced by Japanese management practices in the early 1990s. The flexible job description will normally outline the nature of the tasks, and mention 'competences' and skills required for the job-holders; but it will not specify which team or group they belong to, nor will it state the precise nature of their responsibilities. The reason for the open-ended nature of the job responsibilities is to provide flexibility in the event of changes in the emphasis or direction taken by the organisation.

Note the reference to competences above. The move towards underlining the importance of competences shifts the emphasis away from closely specifying tasks to be carried out towards stating the abilities and skills required of the job occupants. The Consortium of Retail Training Companies, which promotes retailing as a career in the UK, has identified four core competences expected from job applicants: self-confidence and personal strength, capacity for leadership and teamwork, planning and organisational abilities, and analytical and problem-solving skills (Buckley, 1995). By adopting the competency approach it is hoped that the individual and the organisation will utilise the flexibility to adapt to new job requirements and situations. Also, the rigidity imposed by specifying a closed set of duties and responsibilities is removed.

Job (person) specification

Job or person specification describes a process whereby the information contained in the job description is used to assist in profiling the type of person capable of successfully executing the tasks associated with the job. It lists the essential criteria that must be satisfied. However, it should be pointed out that the leap from job description to person specification is never entirely objective – it requires inference or intuition and it offers employers the opportunity to exercise discrimination by ruling out particular types or groups (Ross and Schneider, 1992).

A traditional approach to help with this exercise of matching job applicants and jobs is Rodger's (1952) seven-point plan:

1 physique (health, appearance);
2 attainments (education, qualifications, experience);
3 general intelligence (intellectual capability);
4 special aptitudes (facility with hands, numbers or communication skills);
5 interests (cultural, sport, etc.);
6 disposition (likeable, reliable, persuasive);
7 special circumstances (prepared to work shifts, excessive travel, etc.).

To make the seven-point plan operational would mean specifying essential and desirable characteristics under each of the above headings. More modern interpretations are likely to place emphasis on skills, work attitudes and interests apart from the above factors. In particular, restrictive personality requirements and criteria such as having a 'likeable' disposition could introduce an element of bias into the process, and so tend to be treated very carefully.

An alternative person specification is the five-fold grading system proposed by Munro Fraser (1958):

1 impact on others (through physique, appearance, mode of expression);
2 acquired qualifications (education, training, experience);
3 innate attitudes (quick to grasp things, appetite for learning);
4 motivation (sets goals and is determined to achieve them);
5 adjustment (stable with high threshold for stress, relates well to others).

The central fact to note is that the preparation of a job or person specification is critical as a step in the process prior to recruitment because it tells us about the type of person needed to fill the vacant post. It provides a benchmark on the desirable qualities and important qualifications below which the organisation must not go. In many cases current practices are modifications of one or more of the above systems.

Key result areas

It is now customary to pay attention to making explicit 'key result areas' for the job around the time the job or person specification is prepared. In this approach getting results is heavily underlined, and so the emphasis is on outputs, not inputs. Outputs could be expressed in the form of quality, quantity, time and cost. A feature of 'key result areas' is that objectives are set for the new recruit, in accordance with stated criteria (e.g. quality/quantity of output), and this can provide the basis for subsequent performance appraisal.

Increasingly the language used in job or person specifications tends to reflect recent cultural shifts in human resource management (e.g. creative management of change, performance oriented), so words such as initiate, achieve, stimulate, etc., seem to have wide currency. It is now commonplace to highlight critical competences likely to be associated with successful job performance when specifying the format and content of the job or person specification. A competency has been referred to above in connection with the job description and relates to an underlying individual characteristic such as ability to communicate, solve problems, delegate effectively and act as a good team player. An elaboration of what we really mean by competences appears in Box 7.1. There is further discussion of competences in a training and development context in Chapter 10.

Before leaving the discussion of job or person specification it should be mentioned that the process so far should be considered within a framework of equal opportunity. This means keeping in mind that all job applicants should be given the chance to demonstrate their abilities irrespective of their sex, ethnic origin, disability or age where these factors are considered irrelevant to job performance.

BOX 7.1

Competences

Increasingly organisations are considering competences as an important feature of recruitment and selection, because of their association with good performance in an organisational role. The Training Agency (1989) defined competence as the ability to perform the activities within an occupation or function to the standards expected in employment. The emphasis is on performing with the necessary level of skill to a desired standard, and national qualifications (e.g. Certificate in Management) can act as a means of verification and endorsement to ensure that the standard is achieved. This can be of assistance to selectors. For example, a person with a Certificate in Management is deemed to possess a range of specified competences in a number of areas (e.g. human resource management, financial decision making and information technology).

Of course there will be certain elements of competence not assessed by national awards, and organisations are expected to compensate for this omission when they analyse jobs. For example, London Transport carried out a competency-based analysis of the position of supervisor, and now bases recruitment and selection around such criteria as written and oral communication, planning and organising, customer awareness, quality consciousness and attention to detail. Within these general headings more specific criteria are identified. For instance, a person competent in oral communication is able to convey information and instructions that can be easily understood, and a person competent in planning and organising has the ability to prioritise work and plan or schedule it. The above competences must be kept firmly in mind when assessment of skills is made during the formal selection process.

■ Recruitment

In this section the spotlight will be on (i) how to attract applicants, (ii) the sources of recruitment, and (iii) the shortlisting of candidates, which takes place before the formal selection techniques are activated.

Attracting applicants

Now that the organisation has a good idea of the profile of the candidate suited to the vacant position, the next step is to attract the attention of suitable applicants. The job or person specification will be used as a basis to create a shortened profile of the ideal candidate and likewise the job description will be used to extract information on the duties and responsibilities of the job-holder. This information is then used to advertise the position and to send an 'information pack' to applicants. This is an important stage in the process because the primary aim of the organisation is to attract a sufficient number of good candidates. It should be noted that it is disadvantageous to attract too many candidates, because sorting out large numbers of applications is time consuming and costly. It is also disadvantageous to attract too few applicants because the organisation is faced with insufficient numbers, which limits choice.

Sources of recruitment

How does the organisation go about finding suitable applicants? A number of options are open to it. Before exercising these options a decision will be made on whether to handle the process internally or externally. In certain situations the personnel department or human resources function has the resources and competency to mount a recruitment campaign. One might expect this to happen where the job is fairly routine and applicants are in plentiful supply, but it could apply to other situations as well. Where the internal function does not have the expertise and confidence to provide the service reliance could be placed on an external provider. External recruitment could run concurrently with activity to advertise vacancies internally, thereby encouraging internal candidates to apply.

The following are examples of situations where the organisation uses external recruitment.

Job centres

A job centre is a free external service, which the organisation could find to be of great assistance. It will advertise the job and help with shortlisting suitable candidates. This can be most helpful where there is a large pool of available candidates.

Recruitment agencies

These agencies are likely to have a list of suitable applicants on their files, and charge a certain percentage of the salary attached to the job for making these available to the organisation. They will be responsible for advertising the vacant position and shortlisting candidates. The obvious advantage to the organisation using the services of recruitment agencies is the saving of time; and the small organisation without an adequate personnel or human resource function has the advantage of having specialist advice and assistance. The disadvantages are the costs involved and the fact that control of such an important process is outside the organisation. Another drawback might be that some agencies do not adhere to the organisation's equal opportunities policy and its implementation in a way the organisation would do when dealing internally with job applicants.

Executive search agencies

When the organisation wishes to fill a very senior position, or a highly specialist position where applicants are in short supply, it may resort to the use of executive search agencies. These agencies charge very high fees, but organisations using them believe that the benefits outweigh the cost. To derive benefits will certainly necessitate providing the search consultant or headhunter with a thorough job specification related to the vacancy.

Casual callers

These are respondents who read vacancy notices at, say, a factory gate, and could be attracted by the image of the company as an employer. They may show a reluctance to register with a job centre or agency, or to respond to a newspaper advertisement.

Friends or relatives of existing employees

The advantage of introductions through friends or relatives already employed in the organisation is that the prospective employee gets an insight into the nature of the job and conditions within the company. However, it is important to bear equality of opportunity in mind because if certain groups (such as ethnic minorities or women) are under-represented in the current workforce they may also be under-represented in the friends and relations of the current workforce.

Schools, colleges, universities

Organisations that have traditionally taken on young people directly from the education system have operated a number of processes to recruit from this source. These include the 'milk round', where employers visit universities publicising their vacancies and interviewing final-year students. Some employers have built up links with schools, encouraging visits and supporting education. Other employers, such as the Royal Navy and some large electronics companies, have funded the education of students on the understanding that the graduates or diplomats will work for the organisation following completion of their courses.

Advertisements

A popular source of recruitment is an advertisement in national, provincial or local newspapers, or specialist magazines or journals. The organisation could liaise directly with the media or use the services of advertising agencies. The latter, which receive their commission from the media, can offer advice on advertising copy and choice of media, and may be better placed than the typical organisation to book advertising space at short notice.

It is important to give serious consideration to the contents of the advertisement. There should be an emphasis on the necessary qualifications and experience, duties and responsibilities, the organisation where the job is located, salary (unless negotiable), method of application, and closing date for applications. Any special requirements such as non-standard hours or travel arrangements might be included to facilitate a prospective applicant's decision. The advertisement is effectively projecting the image of the company, and as such it is a selling document – it is selling the company and the job in order to elicit a good response. The language used in the advertisement and the style of presentation should have intrinsic appeal. In the final analysis it should be uppermost in the recruiter's mind that the potential applicant has the choice to apply or not to apply. Therefore what appears in the advertisement should assist rather than hinder the applicant in deciding whether or not they are interested in joining the organisation.

One should recognise cultural differences in the approach to recruitment advertising. On this theme Price (1997) draws a distinction between the French and the British scene, as follows:

> British recruitment marketing normally features salaries and benefits but French equivalents are vague in this respect, reflecting different approaches to rewards (Barsoux and Lawrence, 1990). UK companies base pay on job requirements; in France it depends on the candidate's qualifications. French advertisements define educational requirements in detail, sometimes indicating the number of years of study after the Baccalaureate as the main heading. Attendance at specific Grandes Ecoles may be requested. Management in France is regarded as an intellectual rather than interpersonal matter. Hence recruitment is geared towards cleverness (Barsoux and Lawrence, 1990). Instead of the managerial buzzwords, such as dynamic, energetic, and high calibre, found in British advertisements, French equivalents seek out les éléments les plus brilliants. The nuance is telling.

Telephone hotlines

In most cases the first major contact between a candidate and the organisation after receiving the appropriate information will be a written submission in the form of either a completed application form or a curriculum vitae (CV). An alternative first contact is a telephone 'hotline'. This may be publicised through an advertisement, and candidates will be encouraged to contact the organisation to discuss the vacancies, conditions of work and so on. This has the advantage of facilitating a speedy response and can encourage a larger pool of recruits, which may be important if there is a tight external supply of labour.

Open days

Some organisations use open days to encourage recruitment. Potential candidates are invited to come into the organisation to meet managers or team leaders, and to see what working for the organisation involves. This allows people to decide whether or not they are attracted to the vacant positions and to the organisation, and it can encourage them to enter the next phase of recruitment. As with telephone hotlines, open days can be useful where there are a number of similar vacancies and a relatively tight supply of labour.

Internet

The use of the Internet as a mechanism of recruitment has been increasing, and over 50 per cent of major UK employers now use it as a significant part of their recruitment strategy (Welch, 1999). Applicants can gain information about the organisation, its vacancies and processes of application via the Internet. In some organisations this has been taken further. One example is Dell, which uses the Internet to enable applicants to 'shadow' current employees via desktop web cameras. This gives the applicants an understanding of what it is like to work for Dell. A problem encountered by Dell, and other popular computer-based companies, is oversubscription for their vacancies. The company attempts to limit this by providing online self-screening so that candidates can determine whether or not they are fundamentally suitable for the position. Another example is Cisco Systems, which recruits exclusively through the Internet. It is possible to interact with current employees via email, and informal conversations enable candidates to assess the nature of the organisation and whether or not they would fit in (Welch, 1999). Issues regarding the implementation of online recruitment are discussed in Example 7.1.

EXAMPLE 7.1

Online Recruiting

British Airways has a high level of technology use, and employees are expected to use the web as a basic tool of the job. It follows that the web should be a central mechanism of recruitment for the organisation. While there used to be a number of separate micro sites advertising different types of post, including jobs for graduate trainee pilots, IT staff and engineers, there is now a discrete site encompassing all occupations. This is the result of a recruitment strategy that deliberately focuses on online processes and which seeks to represent the BA brand in a coherent way. The focus is on BA as an employer of choice, which candidates should expect to have to compete to join. However, the power is not concentrated only in the hands of BA. There is an emphasis on providing information. This is done in a number of ways, as follows:

- advertisements of the BA vacancies;
- details of the required skills;
- profiles of current BA employees;
- explanations from current employees of what it is like to work at BA;
- electronic application forms;
- simulations and games.

The aims are to present BA clearly, so that candidates can judge whether or not they would fit in with the style of the organisation, and to attract the best candidates. The graduate management training programme 'Leaders for Business' now recruits exclusively through electronic media. BA was warned that this would reduce the number of applications, and the number fell from the usual 12,000 to 5,000, but the view of the organisation was that the quality of applicants was very high, and that there was no difficulty in filling the places. Similarly, a recent advertisement on the web for 147 customer-service agents was successfully filled through online recruitment alone. The web is not only functioning as a source of recruitment but also as a means of filtering out potential candidates. BA is not uncomfortable with this on the grounds that in areas such as graduate recruitment and IT professionals one would expect candidates to be web literate. For many jobs traditional media, such as newspaper advertisements, are still used in conjunction with the Internet. The expenditure on newspaper advertisements has been reduced, however, with a typical advertisement appearing in one outlet rather than four as was often the case in the past. The result of this is that the development of the Internet for recruitment has been cost neutral.

The BA jobs site includes a flight simulator. Although the feature is regarded simply as a game by BA the simulator is being used by about 30,000 people per day, and so is obviously popular with the public. This fun factor is part of the drive to make the site 'sticky' for potential candidates.

It is not expected that online application will totally replace traditional methods, but for BA the jobs' web site combines communicating corporate image with up-to-date recruitment and information provision to candidates.

(Merrick, 2001)

Recruitment experts are predicting that the lengthy process of applying for a graduate appointment by filling in a complicated form will be consigned to the dustbin. Instead most employers are expected to adopt online application systems, though at present only a small number of companies (e.g. KPMG, Deutsche Bank, Merrill Lynch) are going down this road.

KPMG, the professional services firm, gets more than 8,000 applications a year for the 650 places on its graduate-appointment programme, and it is now asking universities to inform students that it is going online, pointing out that there are benefits to both the recruiter and the candidate from adopting this approach. The national director of graduate recruitment at KPMG is reported as saying that 'the entire graduate application process has been redesigned to take advantage of the speed, accuracy, and flexibility of the Internet. Also the cost per hit will be much lower.' He expects the online system to halve the paperwork and quadruple the speed of the process.

Online recruitment offers employers an abundance of information at their fingertips – how many people applied, their profiles, their progress, which universities they attend – and this information can be circulated widely within an international firm such as KPMG. The national director of graduate recruitment at KPMG goes on to say that this 'means we can identify good applicants and get them to the offer of employment stage quickly. After all the sooner we can focus on outstanding candidates the more likely we are to get them.'

Job applicants will also save a lot of time because an online application will take much less time to complete than a paper application. But it should be noted that the onscreen form incorporates some kind of test or assessment, so it is important to be prepared and read the instructions carefully. It is claimed that the online recruitment process is much fairer because it is more objective: 'Whatever a candidate's name, racial origin or accent, the computer will score him or her impartially.' Another advantage, according to the spokesperson from KPMG, is that 'online recruitment systems are so efficient that instead of a rejected candidate getting the standard type of reject letter, they can be told why they failed'. KPMG developed their approach with consultants in online recruitment systems and occupational psychology.

(Eglin, 2000)

Evaluation of sources

Recruitment is an expensive and time-consuming process, so its effectiveness needs to be monitored. A basic approach is to establish whether vacancies are filled at acceptable cost, with people possessing at least the minimum qualifications, or whether a sufficient number of applicants were attracted by the organisation's efforts to gain their attention (Iles and Salaman, 1995). A slightly more elaborate approach is advocated by Wright and Storey (1994), who suggest that the following data could be collected:

- the number of applicants who completed application forms;
- the number of candidates, whose applications are processed at different stages in the recruitment process, including those who get on the shortlist;
- the number of candidates recruited by the organisation;
- the number of successful candidates who are still in the organisation after six months.

As a general principle, it would be desirable to obtain evaluative data or information from those involved in the recruitment process, including staff who dealt with initial inquiries in response to the advertisement, as well as from both successful and unsuccessful candidates. Obviously it is unlikely that the unsuccessful candidates would be forthcoming in this type of exercise; however, they could be asked to comment if they contacted the organisation requesting information on the reasons why they were not selected.

Shortlisting

The outcome of the recruitment process is to produce a shortlist of candidates whose background and potential are in accordance with the profile contained in the job or person specification. If there are a large numbers of applicants this can be a time-consuming process. Those engaged in the shortlisting exercise will hopefully be making good use of the information provided by candidates on a well-designed application form, although in some situations candidates are asked to submit a CV instead of completing a pre-printed form.

An advantage of the CV is that it allows candidates to state their qualifications, experience, etc., in a way that reflects their written communication skills. However, one should be aware of the fact that some candidates may receive professional help with the preparation of a CV. A problem with a CV as opposed to a standard application form is that the candidate specifies the information to include or exclude, whereas with the application form it is the organisation that controls events and requires information relevant to organisational needs. The application form could be considered more reliable, because all applicants are forced to divulge information under set headings.

With regard to what is expected of job applicants, practice varies between countries. For example, as a general principle, there could be a request in advertisements in France for a handwritten letter of application to accompany a CV and photograph. The emphasis on handwriting could be due to the use of graphology in the selection process (see page 163). It is said that French CVs are shorter and more factual than the Anglo-Celtic type, and contain little or no personal information such as hobbies and leisure pursuits. In Japan an official family registry record, a physical examination report, and letters of recommendation, as well as a CV and photograph, are expected (Price, 1997).

Whatever approach is adopted the organisation will be looking for information on the person's age, marital status, nationality (which can reflect the need for a work permit), education, qualifications, training, experience, present salary, special qualities, state of health, leisure interests and reasons for leaving the present job; and the candidate is normally given the opportunity to provide any additional relevant information. Some employers provide less elaborate application forms for applicants seeking manual work. Although the application form is designed with selection firmly in mind, the completed form also serves another purpose. It can be used as an input to the personnel records of the successful candidates who join the organisation. At this stage additional information, such as the national insurance number, may be required. In the not too distant future the traditional application form could become obsolete (see Example 7.1 above.)

■ Selection

Selection is referred to as the final stage of the recruitment process when a decision is going to be made on who the successful candidate will be. As you can imagine, this is an important decision and should be made in an impartial and objective way, drawing on some or all of a number of selection techniques as follows:

● interviews;
● psychological tests;
● work-based tests;
● assessment centres;
● biodata;
● references;
● graphology.

Interviews

Interviewing, either on a one-to-one basis or by interview panel, could be considered the most popular selection technique. Interviews offer the opportunity for a genuine two-way exchange of information that can be useful in judging whether or not the interviewee will relate well to colleagues and fit into the culture of the organisation. According to Shackleton and Newell (1991), 90 per cent of their sample of organisations always used at least one interview in their selection process. Some of the basics of conducting interviews are highlighted in Box 7.2.

Interviews are said to have low validity but they continue to remain popular (Lewis, 1985). (The issue of validity will be examined later in this chapter.) The crux of the matter with conducting interviews is not the irrelevance of interviewing as a selection device; it is the widely held view that the process itself is carried out in a flawed way. So what are the dysfunctional aspects of selection interviews?

- Subjective, unsound judgements are made by untrained interviewers.
- There is a tendency for interviewers to arrive at a judgement early on in the interview, and this could be perceived as unjust by the interviewee who picks up this impression from the nature of the questioning and body language.
- Where interviewers have prior unfavourable biases about interviewees, there is the danger of highlighting negative data about the candidates so that it fits the biases. The 'halo' effect is where the interviewers are positively disposed towards interviewees because they like or are attracted to them. The result is that the interviewers look more benignly on the answers of the candidates instead of judging the raw content of what they say. The 'horn' effect is the reverse of this, where interviewers are predisposed to 'hear the worst' in what the candidates are saying. If a number of interviewers are involved (e.g. a panel interview), it is hoped that such individual biases will be reduced.
- There are many times when a consensus view does not emerge from a panel of interviewers, simply because interviewers see different things in the same interviewee.

What can be done to mitigate the worst effects of the selection interview, and improve its overall standing?

1 Set in motion a training programme for those who conduct interviews, be they managers, supervisors or 'personnel' specialists, using closed-circuit television. In such a setting the trainees would receive coaching in good practice.
2 Ensure that the appropriate documentation (i.e. job specification, job description, completed application form or CV) is circulated to the interviewer or interview panel members well in advance, and carefully studied before the start of the interview.
3 The venue should be suitable for conducting interviews, and the furniture in the interview room should be appropriately arranged.
4 A reasonable amount of time should be allocated for the interviews, and generally each interviewee should receive the same time allocation.

BOX 7.2

Interviewing

1 *Be clear on the objectives of the interview*. The main objective is to foster an effective two-way exchange of information between the interviewer and interviewee. The process can be thought of as 'a conversation with a purpose'.

2 *Decide who should conduct the interview*. The advantage of one-to-one interviews is the possibility of building up a good rapport between interviewer and interviewee. The disadvantage is the possibility of unchecked bias on the part of the interviewer. Panel interviews mean that more than one interviewer hears the information supplied by the interviewee, and so the process may be less biased, but if panels are too large it can be intimidating for the interviewee.

3 *Conduct careful advance preparation*. Questions should be well planned, and if it is to be a panel interview an appropriate division of labour between panel members should be agreed. The physical layout of the room should be welcoming, and all distractions such as telephone calls should be banished.

4 *Structuring the interview*. The interview should have a clear structure, with major topics being clearly identified and dealt with in a coherent way. This makes more sense to a candidate than a random selection of questions ranging over diverse topics. The interviewers need to decide how much structure they are going to impose, and what degree of freedom will be given to the candidates to lead the conversation.

5 *Framing the questions*. The key areas identified in the job description will need to be covered, but in addition interviewers will want to get beyond the 'stock' responses of candidates. This requires open questions to establish a topic, for example, 'could you tell us about your experience of leading teams?' and following the response with 'probing' questions, for example, 'could you give us more detail on what you actually did to motivate the team members?'

6 *Managing the climate of the interview*. A good interviewer is able to monitor the reactions of the candidate, and to put them at their ease. This enables them to speak more openly, and a better exchange of information to take place.

7 *Gathering and exchanging information*. Good questioning and active listening are necessary to bring out the information required. It is wise to keep a record of the key points of answers the candidate gives as the interview progresses. It is important to maintain attention throughout the interview, otherwise crucial points may be missed, and bias can creep into the decision-making process.

8 *Controlling the interview*. Some candidates will talk too much, others too little. The interviewer must make sure that questions are directly answered (repeating them if necessary) and that the time spent on the various topic areas is suitably controlled.

9 *Closing the interview*. The candidate should be invited to give any information they have not so far offered, and the interviewer should check that they are clear on what happens next (e.g. further selection testing, or a letter from the HRM department).

5 Where appropriate, open-ended, job-related questions, which require more than a yes/no response, should be asked of interviewees. The information received can be summarised and relayed to the interviewee to check that a correct understanding has been gained.

6 Normally towards the end of the formal questioning the interviewee should be given the opportunity to ask his or her own questions, and be free to make observations.

7 Complement the information gleaned from the interviewee with the outcome of psychological tests (where used), and references (preferably written). (There is a discussion of tests and references later in the chapter.)

8 Using panel rather than one-to-one interviews can reduce the amount of individual interviewer bias (such as the halo and horn effects), and can yield more information than where one interviewer is trying to take in all the information being disseminated. However, interview panels should not be so large that they become intimidating for the interviewees. Between three and five interviewers would be seen as normal.

The selection interview is a process that is evolving on a continuous basis. The discussion above concentrated on the structured interview, with some manifestations of an unstructured emphasis when the interviewee has been given a modicum of control to ask questions and raise issues. This can be a useful approach to encourage a genuinely two-way exchange of information.

One particular approach to interviewing is called the situational interview (Latham *et al.*, 1980). Here critical on-the-job incidents are identified and recorded following a job analysis exercise. Questions are then prepared to elicit the views of the interviewees on these events. For example, an interviewee is asked: 'what would you do in a particular situation?' The answers are entered on a form and rated on a five-point scale. Studies by Latham *et al.* (1980) and Latham and Saari (1984) have shown the situational interview, which is akin to the structured job-related interview, to be more valid and reliable than unstructured interviews. In recent years the superiority of the structured interview over the unstructured interview has been advocated. Boyle (1997) speaks highly of the structured interview as a selection method when it is used by trained interviewers using systematic assessment procedures to target key skills and attributes identified by job analysis. However, some interviewers who are more attached to a discursive style complain that the structured interview is too constraining.

Another development in the selection interview that is worthy of note is the patterned behaviour description interview (Anderson and Shackleton, 1989). The interviewer probes major life change events in order to ascertain the interviewee's reasons for taking the reported career direction. The aim is to create a 'picture over time' to help with predicting the candidate's likely reactions to future career challenges and changes. Patterns of behaviour could relate to educational choices, ways of approaching particular problems and opportunities at work, and decisions about career development. A pattern may emerge in which candidates are either more proactive or reactive to situations, or information may be gained on whether they deal with problems aggressively, assertively or passively. The emerging pattern is compared with the pre-established desirable pattern of behaviour.

A more recent development is 'competency-based interviewing' (Johnstone, 1995). Instead of looking at what the candidates have achieved, the focus is on how they achieved the results they claim. With competency-based interviewing the interviewer is looking for specific traits reflected in past achievements. To identify those traits interviewers are instructed to look for STARs – an acronym that stands for situations, tasks, actions and results. This is likely to unfold as follows: first, examine the job specification to establish what the job requires. For example, a managerial job could require the exercise of leadership skills, or the ability to make a presentation at a senior level, or skills in promoting interaction in teams. Having identified the relevant roles, the candidates are asked whether they played such roles or found themselves in such 'situations' in the past or previous job. Once interviewers have found an appropriate situation in the candidates' past the next step is to identify the 'tasks' they were responsible for, followed by identifying the 'actions' they took if a problem arose, and finally what effect or 'result' the action(s) had.

Psychological tests

Two of the more important psychological tests (often referred to as psychometric tests) used for selection purposes are intelligence tests and personality tests. The justification for considering both intelligence and personality tests in the field of selection is the belief that scores on those tests have some validity in predicting future job performance.

Intelligence testing

If an organisation gave intelligence tests to recruits, which took the form of tests of numerical and verbal ability, and found from experience that good test scores were associated with good subsequent performance in the job, then we could conclude that there is a high correlation between a particular test of intelligence and job performance. Tests of verbal and numerical ability, with questions on vocabulary, similarities, opposites, arithmetical calculations, etc., are often referred to as general intelligence tests. When people score highly on these tests they are said to have a good capacity to absorb new information, pass examinations and pick up things quickly and perform well at work. But it should be noted that a particular test might only be valid for a particular type of job or activity.

Apart from general intelligence tests, there are aptitude tests and attainment tests. Aptitude tests can measure specific abilities or aptitudes (e.g. spatial ability, manual dexterity, numerical ability, verbal ability) and are used to gauge the person's potential. It should be noted that individuals differ markedly in their ability to do certain things – for example the ability to learn to do tasks requiring eye–muscle coordination. Attainment tests, which are sometimes called achievement tests, measure abilities or skills already developed by the person. For example, a word processor operator could be tested for speed and accuracy on a typing test prior to the interview for a secretarial post.

In the last few years the concept of emotional intelligence has been recognised as an important concept capable of practical use (Goleman, 1998). It is concerned with the person's emotional and social skills, and consists of emotional attunement or self-awareness (being in touch with one's feelings and able to empathise with others); emotional management (being in control of one's emotions – e.g. anger – so that one is not overwhelmed by them); self-motivation (able to delay gratification of a need, such as waiting a while for a reward rather than taking it immediately); and self-management skills (well able to handle situations). Those scoring high on the factors described above could be considered good at handling personal relationships and diffusing difficult or explosive situations. There are now measuring instruments on the market to gauge emotional intelligence (Watkin, 1999), such as the Emotional Intelligence Inventory (Hay McBer) and the Emotional Intelligence Questionnaire (NFER-Nelson).

Personality tests

There is a recognition that personality has a bearing on the competence of the individual to perform effectively at work, and that personality defects can nullify the beneficial aspects stemming from having the appropriate aptitude or ability. It goes without saying that a highly motivated, psychologically well-adjusted employee is of greater value to a company than an employee who is emotionally unstable and demotivated.

As a broad statement we could refer to personality as that part of us that is distinctive and concerned more with our emotional side and how it is reflected in our behaviour. In a recent major theory called the 'Big Five' factor theory (see Table 7.1), five basic dimensions of personality are introduced. This theory can be used to illustrate personality characteristics.

By contrast, intelligence is concerned with the cognitive or thinking side of us, though, of course, there are some areas of overlap. For example, in Cattell's (1963)

Table 7.1. The 'Big Five' personality dimensions and representative traits

Dimensions	Traits	
	Desirable	Undesirable
Extraversion (1)	Outgoing, sociable, assertive	Introverted, reserved, passive
Agreeableness (2)	Kind, trusting, warm	Hostile, selfish, cold
Conscientiousness (3)	Organised, thorough, tidy	Careless, unreliable, sloppy
Emotional stability (4)	Calm, even tempered, imperturbable	Moody, temperamental, nervous
Intellect or openness (5)	Imaginative, creative, intelligent	Shallow, unsophisticated, imperceptive

Source: Hampson (1999)

16 personality factors (16PF) inventory or test, one factor refers to intelligence, and the same applies to intelligence in the model in Table 7.1.

After the administration of a test such as Cattell's 16PF, a profile of the job applicant is produced. There are a number of personality inventories on the market with the same basic aim as Cattell's 16PF, such as Saville and Holdsworth's occupational personality questionnaire. When personality is assessed using one of the published tests, the next step would be to compare the resulting profile with some standard profile believed to be appropriate or relevant to the job for which the candidate is being considered. Obviously a good fit would be advantageous, but one must be aware of the extreme difficulty of creating the standard or ideal profile of a job occupant. When a person is completing a standard personality questionnaire the organisation would like to think that honest responses are given, and that the respondent avoids giving socially acceptable answers. In practice there could be problems meeting these conditions, as there could be difficulties in establishing clear links between certain personality traits and job outcomes (good performance). The characteristics of a good psychological test should be noted:

■ The measuring device is able to discriminate between individuals.
■ The test is reliable and valid (this will be explained later).
■ The test is properly standardised, whereby it has been used on a significant sample of the population to which it is related, allowing individual scores to be compared with norms derived from that population when interpreting the results.

Certain assumptions underlie the administration of psychological tests: there is the belief that there are significant differences in the extent to which individuals possess certain characteristics (e.g. emotional stability, intelligence, motivation and finger dexterity); there is a direct and important relationship between the possession of one or more of these characteristics and the ability of the person to do certain jobs; selected characteristics can be measured in a practical sense; and finally an evaluation can be made of the relationship between test results and job performance.

Those who argue that psychological tests have advantages are likely to cite the following:

■ Tests provide quantitative data on the person's temperament and ability that makes it possible to compare individuals on the same criteria (e.g. emotional stability, intelligence).
■ Tests are based on comprehensive theoretical foundations that underpin various behavioural patterns; they are reliable and valid and allow us to draw distinctions between people.
■ Tests are fair because they prevent corruption and favouritism in the selection and promotion of people.
■ Test data can be referred to again at a later stage to see how good it was in predicting actual success in the job (Furnham, 1997).

Critics would be keen to cite the following disadvantages:

- Those tested may lack the ability to give responses that reflect their true feelings, so their responses are meaningless.
- Questions in the test booklet could be misinterpreted due to a lack of understanding on the part of some subjects, and this affects the accuracy of the response.
- The performance of an individual tested is not what one might expect because the person is feeling unwell.
- There could be some individuals who try to confuse the situation by giving irrelevant and stupid responses.
- There could be others, particularly in personality tests, who are intent on creating a false impression; this amounts to faking in order to project a good image (certain action can be taken to reduce faking!).
- Tests fail to measure certain important personal characteristics (e.g. trustworthiness).
- Tests are unfair because they disadvantage members of particular racial and gender groups.
- Tests are invalid because they do not measure what they are supposed to measure, and test scores are not good at predicting the testee's work performance over time.
- There are certain weaknesses in the way testers administer tests, such as lack of skill in interpreting the results, and using inappropriate 'norms' (the figures to which the raw scores are related).
- Given the widespread use of tests nowadays, subjects could be motivated to get hold of copies of them to obtain practice at tackling the questions. If so, performance in the real tests may reflect prior preparation more than the candidates' true ability (Furnham, 1997).

Whatever the shortcomings of psychological tests, there has been a growth in their use in the field of selection. In the mid-1980s 65 per cent of organisations in one survey never used personality tests (Robertson and Makin, 1986); in another survey that figure fell to 36 per cent in the early 1990s, with 27 per cent of organisations using them for more than half their vacancies (Shackleton and Newell, 1991). By 1996 it was reported that for organisations with more than 100 employees, 59 per cent were using psychological testing for managerial positions (Scholarios and Lockyer, 1996). The size of organisation seems to be an important variable in mediating the use of tests. In a further study 59 per cent of large organisations (employing more than 2,000 people) used personality tests and 74 per cent used aptitude tests; the figures for middle-sized companies were 41 and 62 per cent respectively. In small firms (employing fewer than 20 people) 9 per cent used psychological tests for managers, and there was little evidence of psychological testing for non-managerial workers (Scholarios and Lockyer, 1996). In short, there has been a growth in the use of psychological testing, but this has been most pronounced in managerial positions and larger organisations.

Other issues

To conclude the section on psychological tests, other issues – tests and job performance, impact of culture, and integrity and ethics – will be briefly examined.

Tests and job performance: The value of selection test scores to predict future job performance has been the subject of much debate in recent times, with challenges to the validity of such exercises (Blinkhorn and Johnson, 1990). Later Blinkhorn (1997) continued to express profound reservations about the usefulness of psychometric tests, as did Barrett (1998) who has also closely studied this subject. Some people might object to the narrow focus, when personality test scores only are used, because of the failure to consider other relevant factors that influence behaviour, e.g. demands of the immediate environment. Others point out, again in the context of personality, that there can be a danger of recruiting the same or similar personality types and producing a situation where there is a lack of variety in the personality composition of work teams.

There is now evidence of developments aimed at putting forward alternatives to conventional psychometric tests. Robert McHenry of OPP and Steve Blinkhorn of Psychometric Research and Development felt it necessary to develop tests that measure people's ability to apply knowledge. The new range of tests are called Aptitude for Business Learning Exercises (ABLE), and it is their hope that these tests will be superior to conventional tests when it comes to predicting the performance of those tested and reducing the disadvantages alleged to be suffered by ethnic minorities who have taken tests. ABLE rests on the notion that people are given concepts to learn and are then tested on their ability to apply the concepts. There are plans for further developments of this series of tests, such as assessing a person's motivation to do particular tasks, and the ability to think strategically and analyse business decisions (Rogers, 1998).

Impact of culture: There are variations across national boundaries with regard to interest in and acceptance of testing. Italy does not permit the use of tests in selection. In Sweden and Holland applicants have the right to see the test results before the employer sees them, and can destroy the results in the event of a withdrawal of the application (Arnold *et al.*, 1998). The results of a recent study by Feltham *et al.* (1998) indicate that personality tests make little allowances for cultural differences between countries. On the basis of this revelation Feltham and his colleagues embarked on a project to get rid of cultural incompatibility in a test used in practice. Finally, those interested in the selection of expatriates, a topic discussed later in this chapter, should note that the effectiveness of personality tests used in selection may be questionable when it comes to predicting candidates' capability to adjust to different cultures (Dowling *et al.*, 1994).

Integrity and ethics: The issue of ethics is becoming increasingly important in organisations, and as a consequence there are now tests to measure integrity (Baldry and Fletcher, 1997). Integrity in this context could cover a variety of issues including theft, fraud, malingering, absenteeism, inadequate effort and so on. When integrity tests were first introduced in questionnaire form in the selection process they were generally considered an alternative to the polygraph (the lie detector). The application of integrity tests is fraught with difficulty, and if used should be carried out with extreme caution. In the final analysis a decision to reject an applicant because he or she poses a high risk to engage in dishonest or deviant behaviour is a decision difficult to justify on the basis of a score on a single integrity test.

Porteous (1997) raises what he considers to be important ethical considerations about the use of tests generally in selection. Among the issues he examines are the following:

1 Tests should be filed securely and only administered by qualified users.
2 Conditions for the administration of the tests should be suitable, and candidates ought to be put in the picture as to what is in store for them – it would be beneficial if they had the chance to try sample questions before the actual test.
3 The tests should be up to date by reflecting changes in jobs and the calibre of applicants presenting themselves, and the tests should be relevant to the job under review.
4 There should be a connection between the test result and at least some aspects of the person's performance in the job.
5 Candidates should receive sensitive feedback on their performance in tests (particularly intelligence tests) when they are unsuccessful, because of the association with failure.
6 The test results of unsuccessful candidates should be destroyed, or the anonymity of the candidates should be protected if the results are retained.

Work-based tests

When an organisation needs to assess the level of candidates' competence in particular areas behavioural tests can be used. These are sometimes referred to as 'in-tray' tests because the candidates are presented with a representative sample of the work they would be doing if appointed – i.e. a sample of what they might find in their 'in-tray' – and they are required to undertake the typical tasks associated with the job. The quality of their work is then assessed. Normally the test will have a time limit. Candidates will have to prioritise the work they are presented with and carry out as many tasks as they can. For a secretarial position, this may include typing sample correspondence, dealing with enquiries (presented verbally or in writing) and so on. As an extension of this approach applicants could be presented with a series of hypothetical situations, and then asked how they would respond. This is similar to situational interviewing. Another example of work-based tests is evident in the selection of social workers, where candidates join in the examination of hypothetical cases to decide on the appropriate programme of action or care. A further variant of the work-based test arises in situations where an assessment is made of the individual's performance in a group setting. In this case two or more applicants meet to discuss a particular topic. Subsequently, their performance in the discussion is assessed.

Work-based tests are used extensively in the UK, with 47 per cent of small organisations (employing fewer than 20 people) using work sample tests for skilled manual workers, and 51 per cent employing more than 100 using them (Scholarios and Lockyer, 1996).

Work-based tests are valuable in that they provide evidence of the candidate's competence in actually carrying out specific tasks. However, as the situation of the test is simulated, rather than real, certain factors may affect the performance of candidates. Candidates may perform poorly if they are nervous or lack the background information and experience they would have if they were actually in the job. There is a further question to raise and that is what is being assessed? Work-based tests concentrate on the current competences of candidates. However, where the organisation is concerned with flexibility and the future potential of candidates – a stand that would be compatible with an HRM perspective – it would be necessary to use other selection techniques as well.

Assessment centres

Assessment centres, which are events rather than places, use a variety of selection methods in order to increase the likelihood of making a good decision. The methods used include the interview, psychometric tests, and individual and group exercises such as role playing and task simulations, including in-tray exercises referred to earlier.

Before assessment commences the organisation should ensure that the relevant job or person specification and competences are spelled out and are available. The assessment takes on an individual form when psychometric tests are administered and the candidates are interviewed individually. But an important part of the assessment centre is the evaluation of the candidates' interactive and interpersonal skills in a group exercise. This is done by a number of trained assessors, many of whom are line managers within the organisation. One reason for having a number of assessors is to minimise bias in the assessment process. Also, a number of assessors are needed to observe closely the behaviour and interactions of the various candidates. Because a number of methods are used, and it is an intensive process, it stands to reason that the overall exercise is time consuming (say two or three days) and costly.

Normally one finds that assessment centres (or development centres when applied to management development) are used by large organisations to select key staff, and this could include graduate entrants. The cost of mounting an assessment centre for selection purposes is justified if it is effective in channelling a flow of able employees into the organisation. A spin-off of the assessment centre could be the provision of feedback to candidates who have gone through the process that helps them to build on their strengths and tackle their weaknesses. It should be noted that assessment centres have high validity as a selection device.

Over the years there has been an impressive increase in the use of assessment centres by larger companies. In 1973 7 per cent of UK companies with over 1,000 employees used assessment centres, as opposed to 37 per cent in 1989 (Bawtree and Hogg, 1989). By 1998 50 per cent of major UK employers reported using assessment centres (Fletcher and Anderson, 1998). Increasingly they are being used with occupational groups other than managers in the area of both selection and career development.

Biodata

When candidates apply for a job in an organisation they normally complete a standard application form or submit a CV. In these documents one would expect to find certain 'biographical' information related to age, education, personal history, and current and past employment. When one uses biographical information or biodata in a systematic way as a selection tool a questionnaire is used to collect information on a large number of successful performers in the job, and the data are then correlated with the data from candidates. From this exercise could materialise an awareness of biodata (e.g. a certain type of qualification) that is associated with career success. Particular features of a person's biographical profile could receive a higher score than others because of such features' prime importance in influencing good performance. The basic assumption of this approach is that if we know enough about people's life histories we can improve selection by being better able to predict the likely future performance of candidates.

To operationalise the biodata approach the specially designed questionnaire, with weighted items, is used for each candidate. A score is given for responses under each item, and individual item scores are then summed. This technique can be used at the shortlisting phase or later at the time of a structured interview. The discriminating factor in either case is the score given.

There are certain advantages stemming from the use of the biodata approach. It is a useful technique when it is necessary to screen a very large number of applications in response to an advertisement. It is relatively objective and underlines the importance of using a systematic approach to compiling biographical information as a means to improving selection decisions. An obvious disadvantage is the large amount of time needed to ascertain the key biographical items in the first instance, as well as the cost of such an exercise.

There are certain potential dangers in the use of biodata. The features of personal background, which are accorded the status of highly rated desirable features, might be biased against certain minority groups. For example, bias could occur where the sample of employees from whom the biodata profile is drawn – which forms the standard used to judge the candidates – is an unrepresentative group, or has distinctive features that could unfairly exclude others. For instance, if all the successful performers coincidentally had a particular type of family background, to use this as a discriminating factor would introduce bias.

A study found that 20 per cent of organisations used biodata as a selection device for some vacancies, but only 4 per cent used it for all their vacancies (Shackleton and Newell, 1991), and by 1997 there was still little evidence of a broader spread of the use of biodata (Wilkinson, 1997). Finally, there is evidence to support the usefulness of biodata in selection (Brown and Campion, 1994). However, one should be vigilant at all times about the strength of the relationship between particular biodata items and outcomes, such as good performance on the job, and be prepared to make adjustments to the questionnaire items when circumstances make it necessary.

References

A candidate for a job is normally asked to nominate more than one referee. One function of a reference is to provide confirmation that the information provided by the candidate is true, another is to provide a character reference. Normally a reference is taken up when the applicant appears on a shortlist and is seriously considered for the particular job, though there are times when a 'long' shortlist is prepared and a reference has a part to play in the production of the final shortlist. Some candidates are not too keen for a potential employer to approach their current employer with a request for a reference unless a job offer is on the table. They may not want their present employer to know that they wish to move on. Others might positively welcome their current employer being approached, even though they have not received a job offer, because they feel that being considered seriously for another job of some significance is something they would like their current employers to hear about.

References are considered to be an important input to the selection process where honesty and moral rectitude are crucial considerations. But there are cases where the information contained in references is of doubtful value, particularly when referees provide little beyond confirmation of the dates of employment. Obviously references have greater value when informative data on the candidate's track record are provided and the contents of the application form are verified. A reliable form of reference is one that has been prepared specifically in response to a list of relevant questions posed by the potential employers.

A drawback of references as a selection device is that the applicant nominates the referee(s), and he or she is unlikely to choose a person who will provide a negative assessment. In practice referees are often hesitant to express negative views about a person in writing; although some would feel less inhibited if asked to provide a reference over the telephone. Generally the validity and reliability of references are rather poor (Hunter and Hunter, 1984; Reilly and Chao, 1982), but they are still popular in the United Kingdom. Shackleton and Newell (1991) found that 74 per cent of the UK organisations surveyed always used references as opposed to 11 per cent of organisations in France.

Graphology

Graphology is a technique that makes predictions about future performance on the

---

BOX 7.3

Graphology in selection

Exponents of handwriting analysis believe that graphology can show the potential and ability of a person not apparent from the normal scrutiny of a CV or completed application form. The British Institute of Graphologists claims that analyses from trained graphologists are generally described by clients as extremely accurate and compare favourably with other methods of personality assessment, such as psychometric testing.

A graphologist will require a candidate to submit at least a page of spontaneous writing in fountain or ball-point pen, preferably on unlined paper. The content of the submission is unimportant, but the writer is told not to copy a piece of text as this impedes the flow of writing. Precise rules are followed to measure the writing size, slant, page layout and width of letters and pressure on the paper. These measurements are interpreted to reveal the emotions and talents of the writer. Apparently the degree of pressure on the page conveys the writer's level of energy. Nowadays, more than 75 per cent of French companies use graphology as a standard selection procedure, and its use by Swiss companies is even higher. Companies in countries such as Germany, Austria, Belgium, Holland and Italy also use graphology regularly. Job advertisements in Continental European newspapers frequently ask for handwritten letters, and applicants expect their handwriting to be analysed. Therefore it is not surprising to find many Continental European companies having in-house graphologists on their staff.

(Altman, 1995)

---

basis of handwriting analysis. The basic premise is that applicants reveal their personality characteristics through their handwriting. Employers using this method would ask candidates to submit handwriting samples for analysis. Generally, handwriting analysis would not be used alone as a method of assessment; where it is used it is more likely to be one of a number of techniques selected to provide a total profile of the candidate (McGookin, 1993).

Although not very popular in the United Kingdom, it has greater acceptance in France (Shackleton and Newell, 1991) (see Box 7.3). Drawing inferences about the personal qualities of people from an analysis of their handwriting has been challenged as a reliable form of assessment. A report by the British Psychological Society expressed serious reservations about its effectiveness as a selection device (McLeod, 1994).

■ Selection of expatriate employees

In recent years concern has been expressed about the management of repatriation of employees who work for large companies on overseas assignments (Forster and Johnsen, 1996). It is claimed that UK expatriates have had to face harsh conditions on their return by having to cope with downward mobility and even redundancy;

also, it seems that UK companies have adopted a 'sink or swim' policy to returners and their families. Given the importance of this topic to multinational companies, it would be wise to raise certain issues impinging on the selection of expatriate employees. A prominent theme in the international recruitment and selection literature is that of expatriate failure. This could be defined as the premature return of an expatriate manager to the home country before the period of assignment is completed. One can conclude that an expatriate failure represents a selection error, compounded in some cases by poor expatriate management (Dowling *et al.*, 1994).

In an interesting review of the relevant literature Dowling *et al.* (1994) examine a number of issues connected with expatriate success and failure, and these are issues that selectors should seriously consider. Amongst the traits and characteristics identified as predictors of expatriate success are: technical ability, managerial ability, cultural empathy and ability to function in a foreign environment, language ability, diplomacy, adaptability (self and family), positive attitude and maturity, and financial stability. The major factors contributing to failure are said to be: lack of adjustment, inability of spouse to adjust, and personal or emotional problems. With regard to failure to adjust to and cope with a foreign environment, one should always consider national differences.

In addition societal trends, such as dual career families, must always be given serious consideration because they can impede the organisation's efforts to attract the best candidates for an overseas assignment. For example, a first-rate manager, with a spouse who has an interesting and stable position, is reluctant to take a foreign posting because of the disruption that is likely to ensue if he or she accepted the position. The issue of gender in the selection of expatriates is said to be an important variable. There is evidence to indicate that women are less likely to be considered suitable for international assignments, and are less willing to relocate in order to advance their careers (Brewster and Scullion, 1997; Harris, 1995). In the case of married women, or women in long-term relationships, with or without children, could personal attachments be a factor to explain the evidence stated in the previous sentence?

■ Validity and reliability

Validity measures how successful a selection technique is in predicting the future performance of the job occupant. Before we can measure validity, criteria have to be established as to what constitutes successful performance in the job, and also what constitutes successful performance during, for example, the interview process or test. Measuring performance on a psychometric test, for example, is not too difficult, but measuring performance when another selection device is used (e.g. the interview) is much harder. Statistical methods are used to relate measures of performance during the selection process to measures of subsequent job performance.

A valid selection process could be expressed as follows: those who score highly on a selection test perform better on the job than those registering lower test scores.

A statistical relationship showing the correlation between test scores and indicators of performance could amount to +1 (a perfect positive correlation) or the opposite −1 (a perfect negative correlation), and 0, where there is no evidence of correlation and no predictive value (i.e. the selection method is no better at predicting performance than reliance on pure chance). In practice, a very good figure for correlation would be 0.5–0.6, and a range between 0.3 and 0.4 would be acceptable. Finally, one should realise that ascertaining the validity of a selection method is by no means an easy task, and psychologists use different types of validity.

The reliability of a test is the extent to which it measures consistently whatever it does measure. For example, all candidates for a job are subjected to the same tests and are questioned by the same interview panel, and if the procedures remain the same the selection methods are said to be reliable. If a test is highly reliable, it is possible to put greater reliance on the scores individuals receive than if the test is not very reliable.

An example of an unreliable test is as follows: a person is examined on two separate occasions, using a finger dexterity test. He or she scored highly on the test on the first occasion, and was placed near the top of the group. However, without any material change in factors affecting the individual that person scores badly on the test on the second occasion and is placed near the bottom of the group.

Reliability of tests is something one might consider in the context of the implementation of an equal opportunities policy. It is important that all candidates have an equal chance to express themselves and show their competences.

■ Fairness

If standards of fairness were universally accepted in the selection process it would be commonplace for all applicants to be provided with equal opportunity to gain employment. Such an ideal is difficult to attain, as practice bears witness to a number of situations where people are discriminated against in the selection process on the grounds of, for example, race, colour, sex or disability. There is a view that some racial and ethnic minorities do not do as well as other applicants in many tests of intelligence and aptitude, and as a result are not selected at the same rate. The difference in the selection rate is usually referred to as 'adverse impact' (Kellett *et al.*, 1994). On this theme one should recognise that a good test is not unfair simply because members of different societal groups obtain different scores. However, it has to be acknowledged that despite relevant legislation (e.g. race relations) and guidelines, unfair discrimination still exists.

■ Cost effectiveness

It is important that the selection techniques used are cost effective. As was mentioned earlier, the cost of a selection decision mistake can be very high and this has to be balanced against the cost of extensive procedures to minimise mistakes. Consequently, many organisations will use assessment centres (which are costly) for managerial jobs and other positions considered important, but would not incur the same cost for lower level positions in the organisation. Similarly, biodata and psychological tests can be expensive to set up and use because the services of specialist professionals will generally be required. As a result they tend to be used for more senior positions.

■ Debate in recruitment and selection

The traditional approach to recruitment and selection discussed in this chapter is referred to as the 'systems approach' (Graham and Bennett, 1998). In this approach it is a matter of defining the ideal candidate who most closely fits the ideal profile for the job. A number of problems have been identified with this approach. First, it assumes there is 'one best way' of doing the job, and this assumption is often based on what happened in the past rather than what is likely to happen in the future. It is argued that the systems approach underestimates the degree of change affecting jobs in today's organisations (Newell and Rice, 1999). Secondly, it presents a fairly static view of the individual, whereas it has been argued that people change and develop over time, and when they take up a new job there is evidence that they can change quite dramatically as a result of the new experience (Iles and Robertson, 1997).

In line with these criticisms, Scholarios and Lockyer (1996) identified two key challenges to recruitment and selection practice. First, there is a question over how far fixed or constant criteria associated with successful job performance can be identified. Fixed criteria would be based upon a firm understanding of the contents of the job and the ability to predict the stable elements of the position. However, HRM lays emphasis on processes, such as empowerment, delayering and functional flexibility, that are likely to lead to change, some of it unpredictable, and so there may be problems in establishing such criteria. In the future job-holders may be required to undertake activities that are not currently envisaged, and so which remain outside established criteria. Secondly, it is argued that a suitable alternative to the systems model of recruitment and selection (which has a tendency towards fixed criteria) has yet to be found (Scholarios and Lockyer, 1996).

In response to problems such as these the processual approach has been proposed (Newell and Rice, 1999). Under this approach neither the job nor the individual are regarded as fixed entities. Negotiation between the individual and the organisation are envisaged over the nature and content of work, and the adaptability of the organisation to individuals' needs. However, it should be noted that companies that have actively pursued such approaches, for example Cisco Systems, Dell (referred to in this chapter), and Reuters (referred to in Chapter 6) are highly profitable organisations and are dealing with sections of the labour market where demand exceeds supply.

The processual approach to recruitment and selection has as its starting assumptions the view that both the job and the individual can (and are likely to) change over time. Hence the approach should not be one of ensuring the most accurate fit between the job and the individual, but rather there should be a process of exchange and negotiation (Herriot, 1984) in which both parties get around to understanding their current and future needs and values. Newell and Rice (1999) argue that the analysis used in the processual approach should not be restricted to one level, but should examine the person–job fit, the person–team fit, the person–organisation fit and the person–environment fit, and should do so flexibly through keeping the nature and design of the job as open as possible for as long as possible in the recruitment and selection process.

The procedure for implementing the processual approach would be a series of 'episodes' in which increasing amounts of information are exchanged between the individual and the organisation, and through which both adapt to the expectations of the other, in such a way that a psychological contract of mutual understanding is arrived at. This could be operationalised, for example through informal contacts between existing employees and potential candidates over time, as is the case of Dell and Cisco Systems mentioned earlier (Welch, 1999). These contacts could then be more formalised in the selection procedure drawing on traditional methods such as interviews and work-based tests.

Although this approach may sound attractive there can be drawbacks. First, if the organisation remains flexible to the extent specified above, appointments will not necessarily complement its strategic direction and business needs. Secondly, the process can become very convoluted, involving a number of ongoing conversations with rival candidates through which criteria that would act as 'common denominators' to judge between them would not necessarily be clearly identified. Thirdly, allowing this degree of openness with a fair number of potential candidates is likely to greatly increase the costs (in terms of employee time) compared to more traditional approaches to recruitment and selection.

As increases in the flexible use of the workforce occur, recruitment and selection need to adapt to changing circumstances. This can entail speedier approaches to attracting temporary workers and the use of specialist agencies. It is important that these changes do not reduce the quality and fairness of the procedures.

■ Conclusions

The processes of recruitment and selection interact with other systems. In particular they are part of the way human resource plans are implemented and they provide input to the training and development functions of the organisation. As recruitment involves advertising, publicity and corresponding with members of the public it needs to be implemented in a way that supports the image of the organisation.

Employee selection has attracted considerable research and scholarly attention. As a result there has been extensive critical debate about the effectiveness of selection methods. There is now a wide range of techniques available, and the human resource manager should be aware of each technique's strengths and weaknesses so that the best method for the job and the organisation can be chosen. Scholarios and Lockyer (1996) conclude that evidence from surveys over the last 20 years indicates that the use of sophisticated multi-method selection is confined to larger companies, in the main because of the prohibitive costs of more sophisticated methods for smaller companies. They argue that the 'classic trio' of application form, references and interview remain the most popular methods of selection for most vacancies.

Traditionally human resource managers have felt that their expertise in this area is an important part of their professionalism. Increasingly, however, organisations are devolving aspects of recruitment and selection work to line and functional managers. This means that there is a change in focus from providing a high quality, inclusive service to providing support so that other managers can carry out the process legally, effectively and efficiently.

The use of the Internet in recruitment and selection has been increasing, although for many organisations it is mainly a tool for recruitment and a supplement to advertising rather than a fully fledged selection device. It can offer effective access to information, but ultimately the human decisions of who will best fit the job and work environment have to be made, and most people feel that face-to-face interaction is an important part of making that judgement.

References

Altman, W. (1995) 'The write way to a job', (Business Recruitment Feature), *London Evening Standard*, 24 January, 34.

Anderson, N. and Shackleton, V. (1989) 'Staff selection decision making into the 1990s', *Management Decision*, 28, 5–9.

Arnold, J., Cooper, C.L. and Robertson, I.T. (1998) *Work Psychology: Understanding human behaviour in the workplace*, 3rd edn, London: FT/Pitman.

Baldry, C. and Fletcher, C. (1997) 'The integrity of integrity testing', *Selection and Development Review*, 13, 3–6.

Barrett, P. (1998) 'Science, fundamental measurement, and psychometric testing', *Selection and Development Review*, 1 (14), 3–10.

Barsoux, J.L. and Lawrence, P. (1990) *Management in France*, London: Cassell.

Bawtree, S. and Hogg, C. (1989) ' Assessment centres', *Personnel Management*, Factsheet 22, October.

Blinkhorn, S.F. (1997) 'Past imperfect, future conditional: fifty years of test theory', *British Journal of Mathematical and Statistical Psychology*, 50, 175–85.

Blinkhorn, S. and Johnson, C. (1990) 'The insignificance of personality testing', *Nature*, 348, 671–2.

Boyle, S. (1997) 'Researching the selection interview', *Selection and Development Review*, 13, 15–17.

Brewster, C. and Scullion, H. (1997) 'A review and agenda for expatriate human resource management', *Human Resource Management Journal*, 7, 32–41.

Brown, B.K. and Campion, M.A. (1994) 'Biodata phenomenology: recruiters' perception and use of biographical information in résumé screening', *Journal of Applied Psychology*, 79, 897–908.

Buckley, N. (1995) 'Retailing', in Career choice, FT surveys, Financial Times.

Cattell, R.B. (1963) *The 16PF Questionnaire*, Champagne, IL: Institute for Personality and Ability Training.

Dowling, P.J., Schuler, R.S. and Welch, D.E. (1994) *International Dimensions of Human Resource Management*, Belmont, CA: Wadsworth Publishing.

Eglin, R. (2000) 'Online recruiting is just a click away', *The Sunday Times*, Appointments Section, 5 November, p B14.

Feltham, R., Lewis, C., Anderson, P. and Hughes, D. (1998) 'Psychometrics: cultural impediments to global recruitment and people development', *Selection and Development Review*, August, 16–21.

Fletcher, C. and Anderson, N. (1998) 'A superficial assessment', *People Management*, 44 (5), 44–6.

Forster, N. and Johnsen, M. (1996) 'Expatriate management policies in UK companies new to the international scene', *International Journal of Human Resource Management*, 7, 177–205.

Furnham, A. (1997) *The Psychology of Behaviour at Work*, Hove: Psychology Press.

Goleman, D. (1998) *Working with Emotional Intelligence*, London: Bloomsbury.

Graham, H.T. and Bennett, R. (1998) *Human Resources Management*, London: Financial Times/Pitman.

Hampson, S. (1999) 'State of the art: personality', *The Psychologist*, June, 284–8.

Harris, R. (1995) 'Organizational influences on women's career opportunities in international management', *Women in Management Review*, 10, 26–33.

Herriot, P. (1984) *Down from the Ivory Tower*, Chichester: Wiley.

Hunter, J.E. and Hunter, R.F. (1984) 'Validity and utility of alternative predictors of performance', *Psychological Bulletin*, 96, 72–98.

Iles, P. and Robertson, I. (1997) 'The impact of personnel selection procedures on candidates', in Anderson, N. and Herriot, P. (eds), *International Handbook of Selection and Assessment*, Chichester: Wiley.

Iles, P. and Salaman, G. (1995) 'Recruitment, selection, and assessment', in Storey, J. (ed.), *Human Resource Management: A critical text*, London: Routledge.

Johnstone, H. (1995) 'Beat the interview blues' (Business Recruitment Feature), *London Evening Standard*, 8 March, 46.

Kellett, D., Fletcher, S., Callen, A. and Geary, B. (1994) 'Fair testing: the case of British Rail', *The Psychologist*, January, 26–9.

Latham, G.P. and Saari, L.M. (1984) 'Do people do what they say? Further studies of the situational interview', *Journal of Applied Psychology*, 65, 422–7.

Latham, G.P., Saari, L.M., Pursell, E.D. and Campion, M.A. (1980) 'The situational interview', *Journal of Applied Psychology*, 65, 659–73.

Lewis, C. (1985) *Employee Selection*, London: Hutchinson.

McGookin, S. (1993) 'Graphology: a waste of money', *Financial Times*, 19th November, 12.

McLeod, D. (1994) *Graphology and Personnel Assessment*, Leicester: The British Psychological Society.

Merrick, N. (2001) 'Wel.com aboard', *People Management*, 7, 26–32.

Munro Fraser, J. (1958) *A Handbook of Employment Interviewing*', London: Macdonald and Evans.

Newell, S. and Rice, C. (1999) 'Assessment, selection and evaluation: pitfalls and problems', in Leopold, J., Harris, L. and Watson, T. (eds), *Strategic Human Resourcing: Principles, perspectives and practices*, London: Financial Times/Pitman.

Porteous, M. (1997) *Occupational Psychology*, Hemel Hempstead: Prentice Hall.

Price, A. (1997) *Human Resource Management*, London: Thomson Business Press.

Reilly, R. and Chao, G. (1982) 'Validity and fairness of some employment selection procedures', *Personnel Psychology*, 35, 1–62.

Robertson, I. and Makin, P. (1986) 'Management selection in Britain: a survey and critique', *Journal of Occupational Psychology*, 59, 45–57.

Rodger, A. (1952) *The Seven-point Plan*, London: National Institute of Industrial Psychology.

Rogers, A. (1998) 'Psychometric tests go on trial', *The Sunday Times*, 9th August, 7.7.

Ross, R. and Schneider, R. (1992) *From Equality to Diversity: A business case for equal opportunities*, London: Pitman.

Scholarios, D. and Lockyer, C. (1996) 'Human resource management and selection: better solutions or new dilemmas?', in Towers, B. (ed.), *The Handbook of Human Resource Management*, 2nd edn, Oxford: Blackwell.

Shackleton, V. and Newell, S. (1991) 'Managerial selection: a comparative study of methods used in top British and French companies', *Journal of Occupational Psychology*, 64, 23–36.

Smith, M. and Robertson, I.T. (1993) *The Theory and Practice of Systematic Personnel Selection*, 2nd edn, Basingstoke: Macmillan.

Smith, M., Gregg, M. and Andrews, R. (1989) *Selection and Assessment: A new appraisal*, London: Pitman

Training Agency (1989) *Training in Britain: A study of funding, activity, and attitudes*, London: HMSO.

Watkin, C (1999) 'Emotional Competency Inventory (ECI)', *Selection and Development Review*, October, 13–16.

Welch, J. (1999) 'British firms lag behind surfing USA', *People Management*, 5, 13.

Wilkinson, L.J. (1997) 'Generalizable biodata? An application to the vocational interests of managers', *Journal of Occupational and Organizational Psychology*, 70, 49–61.

Wright, M. and Storey, J. (1994) 'Recruitment', in Beardwell, I. and Holden, L. (eds), *Human Resource Management*, London: Pitman.

Chapter 8

Employee development: performance management

Performance management incorporates the review of past performance and the setting of objectives for the future. It should be regarded as a fundamental managerial activity that to some extent formalises the everyday processes of feedback between manager and employee. Various approaches to appraisal can be adopted and the choice of system will reflect the style and culture of the organisation. Some will be top down and judgemental, others will be more open and developmental. In either case it is important that a sound basis is established for other associated elements of HRM practice – training and development and reward management.

Having read this chapter, you should:

■ be aware of the purpose of performance management and appraisal;
■ understand the different techniques that can be applied in performance management;
■ know the alternative perspectives and the implications of these for implementation of a system;
■ have an awareness of some of the key skills of appraisal;
■ be able to compare and contrast different examples of good practice;
■ understand some of the considerations of performance management in an international context;
■ be able to critically reflect on the purpose, nature and outcomes of performance management.

Frequently judgements are made, both formally and informally, about the performance of employees at work. In an informal system we are aware that superiors are continually making judgements about their subordinates' performance on a subjective basis. By contrast, superiors could resort to using formalised appraisal techniques when assessing the performance of subordinates, and these judgements are considered to be more objective. In formalised systems the terms 'performance appraisal' and 'performance management' are used. Both refer to a process whereby managers and their subordinates share understanding about what has to be accomplished, and the manager will naturally be concerned about how best to bring about those accomplishments by adept management and development of people in the short and long term. Also, performance would be measured using the techniques discussed in this chapter and it would subsequently be related to targets or plans. In this way the subordinate receives feedback on his or her progress.

Table 8.1 Distinguishing characteristics of organisations with formal performance management

Performance management organisations were more likely to:

- have mission statements that are communicated to all employees;
- regularly communicate information on business plans and progress towards achieving these plans;
- implement policies such as total quality management and performance-related pay;
- focus on senior managers' performance rather than manual and white-collar workers;
- express performance targets in terms of measurable outputs, accountabilities and training/learning targets;
- use formal appraisal processes and presentations by the chief executive as ways of communicating performance requirements;
- set performance requirements on a regular basis;
- link performance requirements to pay, particularly for senior managers.

Source: Williams (1998)

However, a distinguishing feature of performance management is its integrating strength in aligning various processes with corporate objectives: for example, the introduction of performance-related payment systems and the mobilisation of training and development resources to achieve corporate objectives (Bevan and Thompson, 1991). When defining performance management recently in a British context, Williams (1998) stated that it was a logical progression in the history of the development of appraisal systems and can be seen as a set of interventions with the aim of harnessing the contribution of the employee's performance to organisational performance.

Following a survey by the Institute of Personnel Management (now the Institute of Personnel and Development) in the early 1990s, a list of characteristics, which distinguished organisations with formal performance management from those having other policies for managing employee performance, was produced. This appears in Table 8.1. It should be noted that a relatively small number of the organisations surveyed had performance management policies which would match the list of characteristics (Williams, 1998).

■ Aims of appraisal

The following aims might be considered when examining a performance appraisal system:

- Set targets, which are acceptable to those whose performance is going to be appraised and do so in a climate characterised by open communication between superior and subordinate and strive for partnership in action.
- Use reliable, fair and objective measures of performance, compare actual with planned performance, and provide feedback to the appraisee.
- Where performance is sub-optimal, after going through the previous step, signal the need to specify and agree with the appraisee a personal improvement plan

that could be based on an assessment of the person's training and development needs.

■ Provide an input to succession planning.

■ Make provision for the allocation of both extrinsic rewards (e.g. performance-related pay) and intrinsic rewards (e.g. opportunity to enhance one's skills) following the assessment process.

■ Place emphasis on the use of good interpersonal skills in the appraisal process, so that frank exchanges are encouraged, and recognise that the appraiser and the appraisee have the opportunity to influence each other.

■ Validate the effectiveness of the selection process and previous training.

■ Obtain information on the quality of management and organisational systems from the appraisee.

■ Subscribe to desirable outcomes in the form of employee fulfilment, full utilisation of the individual's capacity, change of corporate culture (where appropriate), and the achievement of organisational objectives in conditions where there is harmonisation of individual and organisational objectives.

■ Recognise that performance management is at the heart of the general management process.

■ Appraisal techniques

Certain techniques are available to evaluate the performance of the employee. This section briefly reviews the major techniques used.

Written report

The appraiser writes a narrative about the strengths, weaknesses, previous performance and potential of the appraisee, with suggestions for improvement. It is important that the appraiser is perceptive with reasonable writing skill.

Critical incidents

The appraiser highlights incidents or key events that show the appraisee's behaviour as exceptionally good or bad in relation to particular outcomes at work. This exercise would depict desirable behaviours as well as behaviour that signal a need for improvement.

Graphic rating scales

This is a popular appraisal technique and, unlike the written report and critical incidents techniques, it lends itself to quantitative analysis and comparison of data. A set of performance factors is identified, including such characteristics as quality of work, technical knowledge, cooperative spirit, integrity, punctuality and initiative. The appraiser would go through the set of factors rating them, for example, on a scale 1 to 5 where the highest number would denote the best rating. This technique is economical in the time devoted to its development and use, but it does not provide the depth of information provided by the other techniques described above.

A variation of the graphic rating scales is the 'behaviourally anchored rating scales', where descriptions of the type of behaviour associated with each point on the rating scale is clearly stated. Behaviourally anchored rating scales specify job-related behaviour associated with each performance factor along a continuum. The appraiser then selects the appropriate point on the continuum for each performance factor. For example, an appraisee, who is a middle manager, is rated as 4 under the performance factor referred to as 'leadership'. The statement of behaviour associated with this point on the continuum or scale is 'exceptional skill in directing others to great effort'. By contrast, a rating of 1 on the same continuum could be described as 'often weak in command situations; at times unable to exert control'.

Multi-person comparison

This technique, which is a relative rather than an absolute measure, is used to assess one person's performance against one or more other individuals. It comprises three well-established approaches, as follows:

- *Individual ranking*. This approach orders appraisees from the best to the worst performer with no provision for ties.
- *Group ranking*. This approach requires the appraiser to place appraisees in particular categories that reflect their performance. For example, a person who performed exceptionally well would be placed in the top 10 per cent, while a person who performed very poorly would be placed in the bottom 10 per cent.
- *Paired comparison*. This approach allows for the comparison of each appraisee with every other appraisee. Appraisees are paired and each person is rated as either the stronger or the weaker individual. When the exercise of paired comparisons is completed, after all appraisees have been paired with each other, each appraisee is given an overall ranking score, which reflects the stronger points. Although this approach permits everybody to be compared with everybody else in a particular organisational setting, it can be difficult to handle when large numbers are involved.

Multi-person comparisons can be used in conjunction with one of the other techniques in order to mix the best features of the relative and absolute measures. For example, a graphic rating scale could be used alongside an individual ranking approach.

Multi-rater comparative evaluation

One example of this technique is an assessment centre, which was examined in Chapter 7 in connection with selection. One can adopt a comparative evaluation approach in an assessment centre, using multiple raters. When used in the context of management development it is often referred to as a 'development centre', where the appraisal of managerial abilities and skills with a view to establishing the suitability of subjects for promotion can take place over a few days. The total appraisal process consists of interviews, psychometric testing, simulations of relevant work activities, peer appraisals and appraisals by trained assessors.

Another example of the multi-rater technique is the 360-degree feedback system. This technique uses ratings from several people (e.g. superiors and their counterparts from other departments, customers or clients, and consultants) and is potentially useful because of the wide range of performance-related feedback it offers, more so than the traditional evaluation techniques. It considers qualitative issues in performance (e.g. leadership qualities) apart from quantitative issues, such as increases in output. Eventually a feedback report is produced and this is discussed with the appraisee at a feedback session (see Table 8.2 on issues to consider in the feedback interview).

For the 360-degree feedback process to be effective the corporate culture must be supportive of this type of appraisal (Warr and Ainsworth, 1999). It should be noted that given the range of appraisal data available from this technique the potential for appraisers to make remarks perceived as threatening is high (Clifford and Bennett, 1997); if this is the case, the operation of the 360-degree appraisal system could be impaired.

Management by objectives

Back in the 1970s management by objectives (MBO) became fashionable. MBO stressed the link between individual performance and departmental performance and in doing so advanced the notion that 'subordinates should play an active role in the appraisal process in order to achieve a degree of commitment to the achievement of targets. The necessity for this approach had been pointed out many years before by Peter Drucker in his classic book *The Practice of Management*' (Lundy and Cowling, 1996), and this gave credence to appraisal being a two-way process

Table 8.2 Feedback interview

- Be thorough in preparation for the event.
- At the outset state the primary purpose of the interview.
- It is advantageous if the appraiser is seen as a person who has credibility and authority.
- A positive emotional disposition on the part of both the appraiser and the appraisee is desirable.
- The focus should be on issues rather than personality.
- The appraiser ought to praise good performance early on in the session, as this could create a less defensive appraisee.
- The appraiser should be helpful to the appraisee.
- If criticism is voiced by the appraiser, it should be done without hostility in words and gestures.
- The appraisee should be given the opportunity to comment on his or her performance.
- The appraiser ought to articulate what is required of the appraisee in the future at the end the interview.

rather than top down. In MBO objectives are formulated and agreed at the beginning of the period under review, and the appraisee is given the necessary assistance and training to facilitate the achievement of those objectives. At the end of the period there will be an appraisal of performance and new objectives are set.

Self-appraisal

As a rider to the discussion of the major appraisal techniques, which are frequently used by superiors in evaluating the performance of subordinates, consider for a moment the practice of self-appraisal in the context of employee development. Michelin, the tyre manufacturer, introduced on a pilot basis a self-appraisal scheme as a means of empowering workers, enhancing teamwork and raising awareness of quality. The pilot scheme covered 30 workers who were asked to complete appraisal forms on which they evaluated themselves against criteria such as attendance, productivity, quality, safety, teamwork and commitment.

The completed appraisal forms were then used as a basis for a discussion with the managers of the participating workers. Freeing the managers from form filling meant they had more time for communication with their subordinates. It was concluded that the workers who participated in the self-appraisal scheme were not backward in coming forward with criticisms of themselves, more so than if the managers conducted the appraisals. It is the company's intention to expand the scheme (Huddart, 1994).

■ Different perspectives

There are two main perspectives on the performance appraisal process; one is evaluative and the other is developmental (Anderson, 1992; Harris *et al.*, 1995). An evaluative appraisal amounts to making a judgement about the appraisee and this follows a historical analysis of the latter's performance over the period under review. The judgement is made after comparing the appraisee's performance against previously established objectives or targets, or against all operational items on the job description. This type of appraisal could be linked to the allocation of extrinsic rewards, such as pay.

A development appraisal sets out to identify and develop the potential of the appraisee with the spotlight on future performance, and could be linked to career planning and management succession. A major aim is to establish what type of knowledge and skill the individual should develop. After identifying the appraisee's development needs, appropriate development objectives can be established. Because it is necessary for the appraisee to be open and frank about his or her perceived personal limitations and difficulties encountered in performance, it is necessary for this type of appraisal to be imbued with a high level of openness and mutual respect between the appraiser and the appraisee; there ought also to be an avoidance of restrictive bureaucratic control. The two performance appraisal perspectives stress the need for feedback on both good and bad performances and underline the importance of indicating future personal development. By doing so they acknowledge the part played by motivation in feedback sessions; for example, being recognised for good performance or being told where there is scope for improvement has real motivational significance. Further discussion of the evaluative and developmental perspectives follows.

Evaluative appraisal

Performance factors were briefly referred to earlier when examining appraisal techniques. Here we will have something more to say about them. When engaged in performance-related behaviour the employee is concerned with the behavioural, social and technical aspects of the job. The appraiser, normally the immediate supervisor or manager, with perhaps assistance from a human resource specialist, has to establish what aspects of employee performance should be examined, and what combination of objective and subjective appraisal techniques should be used.

In research undertaken by Income Data Services, London (an independent research body) (IDS, 1989) it was concluded that the performance factors most usually appraised were as follows:

- knowledge, ability and skill on the job;
- attitude to work, expressed as enthusiasm, commitment and motivation;
- quality of work on a consistent basis with attention to detail;
- volume of productive output;
- interaction, as exemplified in communication skills and ability to relate to others in teams.

Other performance factors that were less commonly used consisted of the following items: flexible mode of operation, ingenuity in tackling problems, capability to act with little supervision, skill at managing others, conversant with job requirements, track record at meeting performance targets, attendance record and punctuality, ability to plan and set priorities, and awareness of health and safety regulations. Obviously there is an overlap between some of these factors and key factors listed above (e.g. job knowledge, ability and skill).

Those involved in the appraisal of performance will pay a lot of attention to the choice of both performance factors and techniques. They will be interested in the outcome of the appraisee's performance. This could be something tangible, such as a quantitative record of the employee's output, or more qualitative, such as the display of appropriate behaviour. What should be avoided is the recording of personality traits, which are not related to actual behaviour on the job.

A feature of the evaluative appraisal is the link between the outcome of the appraisal process and pay or financial benefits (IPM, 1992). Proponents of this association are likely to point out that it is equitable and has real motivational effect. Employees are likely to consider the appraisal process as being significant because good performance is recognised and rewarded, but poor performance is not rewarded. Also, a performance-oriented culture is fostered (Anderson, 1992). By contrast, opponents of the process of linking pay to appraisal feel that the purpose of the performance review is blurred, that it is almost tantamount to a pay review, and that performance appraisal should be separated from a review of pay.

According to Anderson (1992), pay assumes a position of overriding importance when it is linked to performance: appraisees try to extract from their boss performance targets that are easily attainable; the appraisee's behaviour is too narrowly focused on those targets to the detriment of a broader view of performance in order to receive good ratings; appraisees show an inclination to conceal negative information about their performance; and those charged with performance appraisal give appraisees a higher ranking when they know a lower ranking would disadvantage them in financial terms.

When looking at the relationship between pay and performance appraisal it is wise to consider the influence of culture. In an organisational culture supportive of individualism and achievement there could be firm expectations on the part of employees that the appraisal process should coincide with the review of pay. An example of such a culture would be the dealing arm of a stock broking firm (see Chapter 5, Box 5.1). The dealers are likely to welcome a situation of loose organisational control with a minimum amount of guidance from above. The outcome of the appraisal process would form an input to the activity connected with the determination of rewards. It is unlikely that the organisational culture would be supportive of conditions where performance appraisal and the review of pay take place at different times.

There are circumstances where, at the target-setting stage, the performance appraisal process is used to transmit organisational values or culture. The latter could then be reinforced at the evaluation of performance stage when acceptable behaviour in which the organisational values are enshrined is recognised and rewarded. A company subscribing to this viewpoint could be concerned with encouraging appropriate behaviour (e.g. reliability, cooperativeness, able team player, good attendance record, enthusiastic, efficiency conscious and being a good example to others in improving methods and practice) with less emphasis on actual output. This was the approach adopted by Polaroid in its appraisal process when determining who should be promoted (Townley, 1989).

It appears that compliance is exacted from the subordinate in return for some advantage or reward when the evaluative appraisal is used, and the process has ingrained in it images of a power relationship between the superior and subordinate. Such an arrangement could run counter to a system of industrial relations where collective bargaining has taken root. In such circumstances there could be trade union resistance. Now we seem to have moved into territory where the performance appraisal system is seen as a medium of management control and manipulation. However, not everybody would take that view because there is a body of opinion which considers that the appraisal process can create a performance culture that gives due recognition to the individual's actual and potential performance and development needs.

Development appraisal

In this type of appraisal the interview features prominently, with the emphasis on the future development of the appraisee. The provision of open and constructive feedback is used to create the right motivational disposition. In practice the appraisee could gain sight of the appraisal forms and say what he or she thinks of the performance of the person carrying out the appraisal (the appraiser). We now appear to be moving towards emphasising a partnership between the manager and the subordinate in the appraisal process. The importance of personal objectives, which flow from corporate objectives, being agreed by both the appraiser and appraisee as realistic and challenging is strongly advocated, with the rider that appraisal techniques should be appropriate measuring devices of actual perform-ance and kept under review (Williams, 1991).

One should also note the reinforcing qualities of solid feedback in an appraisal session when good behaviour is praised and deficiencies identified, though this is something that should happen on a periodic basis and not just once a year. Where deficiencies have been found steps should be taken to prepare a per-formance improvement plan to help the appraisee rectify the deficiencies and build on his or her strengths; self-development should be encouraged in these circumstances.

There is no doubt about the status of the development appraisal: it is an inte-gral part of the management process. It is suggested that counselling should be coupled with the normal deliberations associated with running the appraisal process. This occurred at IBM in a climate supportive of employee development, with the added dimension of determining merit pay (Sapsed, 1991). Introducing pay determination into the development appraisal is unlikely to be the normal practice in organisations that subscribe to the basic tenets of assessment aimed at development. Apart from counselling and developing a relationship of mutual trust and respect, the manager might give serious consideration to empowering subordinates so that they have the opportunity to stretch their capabilities in a problem-solving context.

Given the developments in HRM, whereby ownership of the appraisal process has moved from the personnel function to the appropriate manager, it is impera-tive that the latter is trained in operating the techniques of appraisal. When using the appraisal data to diagnose development needs the manager will be expected to use counselling and communication skills, including effective listening, and per-haps, in appropriate circumstances, inviting the appraisee to practise upward appraisal (see Box 8.1). If the manager is found wanting in the utilisation of these skills, this could signal the need for a skill-based management development experi-ence for the manager. Where a number of different but complementary appraisal techniques are used, as found in a development centre (discussed earlier), man-agers could find themselves rubbing shoulders with a number of other suitable assessors.

Before looking at the problems associated with appraisal, we shall turn our

---

BOX 8.1

Upward appraisal

This is a bottom-up approach to appraisal, whereby subordinates rate superiors, and has been used by organisations such as British Petroleum (BP), British Airways and Cathay Pacific. It is felt that subordinates are well placed to gain a solid view of the strengths and weaknesses of their boss. A representative view could materialise from the combined ratings of a number of subordinates. For this system of performance management to work well requires it to be efficient and equitable in an appropriate cultural setting. For example, a prerequisite is that the organisation feels it can trust employees to be honest, fair and constructive. Also, there should be a firm belief in the value of two-way communication within the organisation.

Upward appraisal is not without its problems. One has to recognise that some subordinates could feel somewhat inhibited when asked to offer a frank and fair view of their superior for fear of reprisal. Others might show an aversion to rating at either the upper or lower ends of the rating scale, instead they settle for the unadventurous middle point of the range. Sometimes the suggestion is made that subordinates should come forward with anonymous ratings, and therefore might feel less inhibited. However, there could be a downside to such an approach when subordinates avail themselves of the opportunity to be vindictive towards a superior who has been putting pressure on them to reach exacting performance standards.

Finally, subordinates would need training on how to conduct appraisals, and from the organisation's point of view it is desirable that subordinates' ratings are acted upon. The latter could necessitate a significant change of corporate culture.

(Furnham, 1993)

---

attention to two cases dealing with the use of performance management. In Example 8.1 two different cases of good practice are presented. In both the purpose is to pursue the organisation's strategy through developing employees' understanding of their role in corporate performance, and their place in the organisation's culture. However, the organisations take different routes to this goal. For Barclays Bank the answer is a formal but frequently implemented system with quarterly reviews, objective setting and feedback on attributes, or competences.

By contrast Humberside Training and Enterprise Council, with its focus on development, takes a highly flexible and informal approach to 360-degree feedback in order to reinforce a culture of empowerment and responsibility taking by employees. It is clear that there is not a single best way of conducting performance management, and the onus is on the organisation to establish the right approach in its own circumstances. Considerations in making the decision on what type of approach to adopt will include an understanding of the employees, the culture, the nature of the business and the purposes of the performance management system.

EXAMPLE 8.1

Good practice in performance management

The mortgages section of Barclays Bank employs about 800 people in the north of England. It operates in a very competitive market in which aligning the commitment of employees to organisational objectives is seen as crucial. All employees are on the same system, which focuses 50 per cent on objectives ('what you do') and 50 per cent on attributes ('the way you do it').

Business objectives were developed on the basis of the corporate strategy, and were translated into departmental objectives. In order to achieve buy-in from employees, they are facilitated by team leaders to develop their own Key Responsibility Areas, objectives and measures that reflect the departmental objectives. The aim is to set expectations, and to include measurable outcomes in the objectives. Where possible, the nature of exceptional performance is specified. One of the dangers with setting objectives is that they can be filed away and neglected. In order to make the objectives a 'living document', a quarterly review is conducted in which the individual's 'achievement log' is updated. The frequency of reviews enables changes in business priorities to be reflected in the individual's aims.

'Attributes' are the behaviour and qualities that are expected from employees who are performing effectively. An 'attribute library' of 18 attributes, such as 'delivering results' and 'attention to detail', is subdivided into dimensions reflecting jobs at different levels in the organisation, and performance bands. Eight attributes are selected as core to a particular role, and these are assessed in the quarterly review.

The review consists of a self-assessment and a reviewer assessment. Feedback is delivered in writing and the attributes library specifications and objectives are used as benchmarks to judge the employees' performance. Ratings on the scale 'exceed', 'meet', 'fall short' and 'fail' are communicated. In addition the individual is required to gain feedback from six other people during the course of a year. Where there are deficiencies in performance development plans are drawn up.

(Bratton and Gold, 1999)

Humberside Training and Enterprise Council (Humberside TEC) is a public sector body concerned with the stimulation of business and provision of training in an area in the north of England. It employs 200 people. A fundamental part of the strategy is to stimulate and facilitate business activities by others, and the style and approach of its employees is fundamental to its success. The performance management system seeks to reinforce an organisational culture that will inspire employees to be effective facilitators who take responsibility for their own actions. An unstated but clear objective is to avoid the pitfalls of traditional bureaucracies.

Feedback from employees about a previous performance management scheme indicated that the most valuable part of the process was the face-to-face feedback, and the least valuable part was the form filling. Taking this message to heart, the new scheme is paperless. There are no strict rules about the running of appraisals, and people are trusted to develop suitable approaches, although the clear intention is that feedback should be sought from a 360-degree system, which was explained earlier in the text, and that each individual should have at least one appraisal per year. The purpose of appraisal is to improve performance and help people learn and grow.

Typically feedback is given in groups. It was found that group sizes above seven were less effective as the feedback became mainly generalities, but in suitable sized groups clear feedback and behavioural examples could be given. Any written material produced belongs to the appraisee, and there are no files or records. The outcome is that the process is one of dialogue rather than recording.

Employees say that the system is effective, noting that the feedback they receive may not be that different to the feedback they had formerly received from managers in a top-down approach, but they add that hearing six other people say the same thing has a much stronger effect. Employees are also expected to take responsibility for their development plans emerging from the feedback meetings.

Initially employees tended to select a 'safe' group of friends to give them feedback. But as confidence has grown in the system people have started to select more challenging groups to give feedback, knowing that this can provide an effective stimulus for changing behaviour and learning. Employees report that this is reinforcing the culture of empowerment, and that communications have greatly improved.

The managing director of Humberside TEC argued that everyone involved in the 'three-dimensional perspective' on performance takes something out of the process. Further, it has the advantage of being very flexible, so that it can change as individuals develop and the business changes. The process has enabled individuals to reflect on their practice and be involved in planning their training and development. It has also thrown up a number of discoveries for the organisation as a whole as it seeks to become a learning organisation.

(Storr, 2000)

■ Problems with appraisal

Appraisal has many strong points when it is well conceived and executed as a process for providing systematic judgements to support pay reviews, promotions, transfers and the provision of feedback on actual performance, with pointers to performance improvement through changes in attitudes, behaviour and skills. Also, as mentioned earlier, it provides an opportunity for counselling and can sow the seeds for personal development. However, one has to acknowledge a number of potential problems associated with performance appraisal as follows:

1 Poorly designed appraisal forms are compounded by some irrelevant items.
2 Insufficient time is devoted to preparing for the event, completing the appraisal forms and ensuring the necessary training is undertaken.
3 Inadequate interview and counselling skills are used by the appraiser.
4 Feedback given to subordinates is deficient in a number of respects.
5 Action strategies (e.g. training) that stem from the appraisal are not seriously entertained.
6 There is unreliable judgement because of subjectivity on the part of the appraiser, despite efforts to minimise it. One way to minimise subjectivity and promote objectivity is to make sure that there are explicit, previously agreed performance criteria against which judgements are made. Also, a senior

manager could take responsibility for overseeing a number of appraisals to check that differences between the ratings that individuals receive are not due to appraiser bias.

7 Related to point 6 is the appearance of other imperfections. These include invalidity and unreliability (the measure is not measuring what it is supposed to be measuring or it is unreliable), ratings are either too lenient or too severe, and the evaluation is distorted by personal likes and dislikes.

8 Target setting and use of techniques leave much to be desired.

9 Where the appraiser acts as both judge and counsellor, this could give rise to confusion as well as leading to certain difficulties for the appraisee. For example, the appraisee is subjected to an evaluative appraisal at which past performance is assessed and rewards determined, and then there is a switch to a development appraisal; in such circumstances there could well be a reluctance on the part of the appraisee to be open and frank about past mistakes and problems. Randell *et al.* (1984) argue that the solution to this problem would be to arrange different meetings for the different types of appraisal, with a different appraiser for each meeting. The development appraisal might be conducted by a manager from another department or by a human resource specialist in training and development.

10 In connection with ownership and rewards, Lundy and Cowling (1996) cite an IPM-sponsored study (Fletcher and Williams, 1992) in which the following weaknesses in performance management practice in the United Kingdom were identified:

> There was frequently little indication of a real sense of ownership of performance management among line managers, and therefore no depth in commitment. Too many managers perceived it as a top-down process with no feedback loop operating, there was a widespread perception that performance management was 'owned' by the HR department, and there was a lack of thought and imagination when tackling the issue of rewards.

■ International considerations

In this section some important issues are considered when taking a snapshot of performance appraisal in an international context. Technical competence is a necessary but not sufficient condition for successful performance in international management positions. Amongst the matters to consider are cross-cultural interpersonal skills, sensitivity to foreign norms and values, understanding of differences in labour practices or customer relations, and ease of adaptation to unfamiliar environments. It follows that cultural sensitivity has to be considered in the practice of performance appraisal. In Japan, for example, it is important to avoid confrontation to 'save face', and this custom affects the way in which performance appraisal is conducted. It is said that a Japanese manager cannot draw attention in a direct sense to a mistake or error attributable to the subordinate. Instead the emphasis right at the beginning is to focus on the strengths of the subordinate followed by a general discussion of the work, and then explain the consequences of the type of error or mistake made by the subordinate without identifying the actual mistake or the person making it. From this discourse the subordinate is supposed to recognise the mistake and put forward suggestions to improve his or her work (Dowling *et al.*, 1994).

Pepsi Cola International, with operations in over 150 countries, used 'instant feedback' as one of five aspects of its common appraisal system, which allows for modification to suit cultural differences and local circumstances. In utilising the process of instant feedback the following national differences were noted (Schuler *et al.*, 1991):

> Americans use it because it fits a fast paced way of doing business. In most Asian cultures ... feedback is never given in public, and in some Asian cultures head nodding during an instant feedback session does not signify agreement, it merely denotes that the message has been heard. Some Latins will argue strongly if they do not agree with the feedback, and some Indian nationals will ask for a great deal of specific information.

It is no easy task to devise a performance appraisal system for multinational companies that caters adequately for employees consisting of expatriates, host country nationals and third country nationals. Producing documentation and ways of operationalising the system, so that it will not disadvantage a particular group, could prove to be a Herculean task, but it has to be seriously addressed if effectiveness and equity are to be achieved.

These issues are being tackled by Alliance UniChem, a merged organisation that needed to bring together people from different cultures. Their approach was to implement a package that combined 360-degree feedback with the ability to communicate simultaneously in different languages (see Example 8.2).

EXAMPLE 8.2

360-degree feedback in an international setting

In 1999 UniChem, the UK pharmaceuticals company, merged with Alliance Santé of France to form Alliance UniChem. The company then employed 17,000 people in several European countries, becoming the second-largest pharmaceuticals business in Europe. Pre-merger, neither organisation had well-developed corporate HR functions, but HR was chosen as the first area to tackle following the merger as it was seen as being essential to thriving in a market characterised by low profit margins. A central HR department was established in Paris and its top priority was to encourage people to cooperate effectively across cultural boundaries. A main thrust of their approach to achieve this end was the introduction of a new 360-degree performance appraisal package.

The proposal to set up 360-degree appraisal was not met with general acceptance. The method was virtually unheard of in three of the countries (Italy, Spain and Portugal) and in France it was viewed with suspicion as an 'American tool'. However, the board was convinced

that the process was important because it recognised the need to develop multi-cultural management in the group and it wanted to be able to move managers between countries so that
they would get a more holistic and integrated understanding of the business. Integration was
important because the previous style had been for entrepreneurial managers to lead their own
business units, whereas now there was a need to bring them together to drive an organisation
on a completely different scale.

The system was based on four key values that came out of the merger: excellence, service,
innovation and partnership. Competences were drawn up in each area as the basis for feedback. Because the system allows for translation, it is possible for an individual to receive feedback from someone in a different country on the same system, even if they do not have any
shared language. The system was developed to operate in five languages; it includes targets
and records of individual progress. Development activities on each competency are devised
through suggestions from the employee, the system and the manager. Alliance UniChem sees
this development of a set of common behaviours as fundamental to getting employees to
focus not just at the national level, but on the needs and goals of the organisation as a whole.

(Johnson, 2001)

■ Some critical issues

Reflect for a moment on the meaning of performance management. Though the
term performance management is open to a number of interpretations, in the
United Kingdom it has come to take on a particular meaning. It denotes a system
where the level of intervention is that of the individual employee, and the overall
intent is to align individual performance with organisational performance. But this
is a unitarist view, and it fails to recognise the plurality of interests (i.e. varied
interests that are part of organisational reality – see Chapter 11). We should not
expect it to be an easy task to align individual performance with goals that are possibly conflicting and contradictory. Performance management should be owned and
driven by line managers, though in practice not enough is done to make this happen
(Williams, 1998).

It appears that traditional performance appraisal, with appraisal pay bolted on,
is alive and kicking in many organisations. This reflects an outmoded theory X view
of motivation (McGregor, 1960), but it has appeal, in terms of control, to a number
of practitioners operating in a climate where expenditure is continually pruned. An
alternative view – Theory Y (McGregor, 1960) – would be preferable as it is more
expansive in accommodating diverse needs and interests, and would embrace the
following progressive activities: good communication, job enrichment and
empowerment, participation in goal-setting, frequent feedback, a broad view of
performance to include behaviours/competences, a broad view of reward, and the
promotion of employee well-being. However, to implement such a scheme could be
costly (Williams, 1998).

Sometimes the question is asked if performance management is a phenomenon
more appropriate to the private sector of the economy than to the public sector.

Rocha (1998) maintains that appraisal is now a key constituent of the 'new public management', which emphasises economy and efficiency in public organisations. Redman *et al.* (2000) maintain that the 'individual performance review' should continue to have an important role in human resource practices in the National Health Service. But Fletcher and Williams (1996) express concerns about the suitability of the culture in local government organisations, which they call collaborative organisational cultures, to a performance management system that brings in its wake increased competition between colleagues. However, in 2001 one could take issue with Fletcher and Williams' position; it would be easy to concede that the growth of new public management is likely to provide conditions compatible with the implementation of performance management.

■ Conclusions

Performance management has an evaluative and developmental dimension to its make-up, and is crucial in both linking rewards to performance and providing a platform for the development of employees. Overconcentration on the assessment of performance can work to the detriment of effort aimed at establishing the development needs of the individual in an open and honest way. The manager, as an appraiser, may encounter difficulties in reconciling the roles of 'judge' and 'mentor'. Managers need to develop the skills of coping with such tensions in their roles. In some organisations this problem is solved by having different managers carry out performance and development appraisals.

Appraisal provides the context in which managers can seek to ensure that there is acceptable congruency between the objectives of the individual and those of the organisation. Although one recognises the part played by performance management in the determination of rewards, we believe that, if treated as a way of providing feedback on progress and of jointly agreeing the next set of aims, the appraisal can have a positive effect on individual motivation. This view is substantiated by the research linking HRM practices to corporate performance (see Chapter 2).

For many organisations it is important to ensure that employees are fully aware of the corporate objectives and the part they can play in fulfilling these objectives. This can be achieved with relative formality, as in the case of Barclays Bank, or more informally, as in Humberside TEC (see Example 8.1). Either approach can be highly effective, but it is necessary for the approach to fit with the style and culture of the organisation and its members. Performance management is a chance for the organisation to learn about what employees are really doing, and to understand what will motivate them in the future. Innovations such as 360-degree feedback, and in some cases the use of computerised systems, can help facilitate this learning process. The issue of enhancing mutual understanding through such learning is particularly important in international settings where there is a possibility of misunderstandings across cultures, and in some cases having a system that can cope with translation between languages (as in the case of Alliance UniChem, see Example 8.2) is a positive advantage.

References

Anderson, G. (1992) 'Performance appraisal', in Towers, B. (ed.), The *Handbook of Human Resource Management*, Oxford: Blackwell.

Bevan, S. and Thompson, M. (1991) 'Performance management at the crossroads', *Personnel Management*, November, 36–9.

Bratton, J. and Gold, J. (1999) *Human Resource Management: Theory and practice*, 2nd edn, Basingstoke: Macmillan.

Clifford, L. and Bennett, H. (1997) 'Best practice in 360-degree feedback', *Selection and Development Review*, 13, 6–9.

Dowling, P.J., Schuler, R.S. and Welch, D.E. (1994) *International Dimensions of Human Resource Management*, 2nd edn, Belmont, CA: Wadsworth Publishing.

Fletcher, C. and Williams, R. (1992) 'The route to performance management', *Personnel Management*, October, 42–7.

Fletcher, C. and Williams, R. (1996) 'Performance management, job satisfaction and organizational commitment', *British Journal of Management*, 7, 169–79.

Furnham, A. (1993) 'When employees rate their supervisors', *Financial Times*, 1 March.

Harris, M.M., Smith, D.E. and Champagne, D. (1995) 'A field study of performance appraisal purpose: research vs administrative-based ratings', *Personnel Psychology*, Spring, 151–60.

Huddart, G. (1994) 'Firm runs self-appraisal', *Personnel Today*, 17 May, 1.

IDS (1989) *Common to All*, IDS Study no. 442, December.

IPM (1992) *Performance management in the UK: An analysis of the issues*, London: Institute of Personnel Management.

Johnson, R. (2001) 'Double entente', *People Management*, 7, 38–9.

Lundy, O. and Cowling, A. (1996) *Strategic Human Resource Management*, London: Routledge.

McGregor, D. (1960) *The Human Side of Enterprise*, New York: McGraw-Hill.

Randell, G., Packard, P. and Slater, J. (1984) *Staff Appraisal: A first step to effective leadership*, 3rd edn, London: Institute of Personnel Management.

Redman, T., Snape, E., Thompson, D. and Ka-ching Yan, F. (2000) 'Performance appraisal in an NHS hospital', *Human Resource Management Journal*, 10, 48–62.

Rocha, J.A. (1998) 'The new public management and its consequences in the public personnel system', *Review of Public Personnel Administration*, 18, 82–7.

Sapsed, G. (1991) 'Appraisal the IBM way', *Involvement and Participation*, February, 8–14.

Schuler, R.S., Fulkerson, J.R. and Dowling, P.J. (1991) 'Strategic performance measurement and management in multinational corporations', *Human Resource Management*, 30, 365–92.

Storr, F. (2000) 'This is not a circular', *People Management*, 38, 38–40.

Townley, B. (1989) 'Selection and appraisal: reconstituting social relations', in Storey, J. (ed.), *New Developments in Human Resource Management*, London: Routledge.

Warr, P. and Ainsworth, E. (1999) '360-degree feedback: some recent research', *Selection and Development Review*, 15, 3–6.

Williams, R. (1991) 'Strategy and objectives', in Neale, F. (ed.), *The Handbook of Performance Management*, London: Institute of Personnel Management.

Williams, R. (1998) *Performance Management* (Essential Business Psychology Series), London: Thompson Business Press.

Chapter 9

Employee development: reward management

Fostering a motivated workforce lies at the heart of HRM. If people are motivated towards appropriate goals then the likelihood of organisational success is enhanced. Motivation theory has developed over time, and a good understanding of motivation is necessary if we are to manage rewards effectively. There are several different systems of payment and reward, some of which can be used in combination, and others provide alternative choices. Ultimately, what gets rewarded will be a focus of attention for employees, so it is important that their focus is directed on to behaviours that will be advantageous for the organisation and its members.

Having read this chapter, you should:

- have knowledge of the methods for determining the nature and level of rewards;
- understand the various types of reward system – their applications, advantages and disadvantages;
- have a perspective on the issues for reward management in the international environment of multinational companies;
- understand the pertinence and application of motivation theories to reward management;
- be aware of current issues of debate in reward management.

The purpose of managing the system of rewards within the organisation is to attract and retain the human resources the organisation needs to achieve its objectives. To retain the services of employees and maintain a high level of performance it is necessary to increase their motivation, commitment and flexibility by a variety of means, including appropriate management style, competitive compensation package and supportive culture (Armstrong and Murlis, 1994). In effect the organisation is aiming to bring about an alignment of organisational and individual objectives when the spotlight is on reward management. To achieve that aim requires a flexible reward strategy – a product of the corporate plan and the human resource plan – that is capable of responding to internal influences (e.g. demand for skilled employees, resources available to meet the costs of labour) and external influences (e.g. government policy (minimum wage), and the rewards offered by competitors).

In an HRM context reward management is not restricted to rewards and incentives, such as wages or salaries, bonuses, commission and profit sharing, which relate to extrinsic motivation. It is also concerned with non-financial rewards that satisfy the employee's psychological needs for job variety and challenge, achievement, recognition, responsibility, opportunities to acquire skills and career development, and the exercise of more influence in the decision-making process. The non-financial rewards can be equated with intrinsic motivation. Later in the chapter there will be a brief examination of motivation theories. A valid question to ask at this stage is how the organisation determines the level or magnitude of reward.

■ Determination of rewards

Traditionally, many reward systems have been determined by collective bargaining whereby management and employee representatives (usually trade union officials) negotiate wage rates for large groups of employees. In certain UK organisations, such as hospitals in the National Health Service and local authorities, pay grades were established for groups of employees on a national basis. For example, a nurse assuming a particular set of responsibilities in the south of England would be on the same grade as a nurse shouldering identical responsibilities in the north of the country despite differences in the cost of living between the two regions. However, it should be noted that there is a special cost-of-living allowance for those working in London.

Underlining this approach to wage determination is the use of a technique called job evaluation. Job evaluation could be described as a process used at the level of a company or industry to determine the relationship between jobs and to establish a systematic structure of wage rates for those jobs. It is concerned with 'internal relativities'; that is, that individuals doing the same type of work would receive equal rewards. Job evaluation is only concerned with the assessment of the job, not the performance of the job occupant, and it goes without saying that the preparation of reliable job descriptions is a prelude to embarking on administering job evaluation schemes. Job evaluation measures differences between jobs, and places them in appropriate groups and in rank order. Schemes of job evaluation can be classified as either the quantitative or the non-quantitative approach, as follows:

Quantitative   – factor comparison;
              – points rating.
Non-quantitative – ranking;
              – job classification.

Factor comparison

Different jobs are ranked against agreed factors such as minimum level of education, level of skill, task difficulty, supervisory responsibility, level of training and decision-making responsibility. These are referred to as criteria, each with a scale 1 to 5, against which jobs are placed in rank order. A factor comparison system is more applicable to the evaluation of clerical and administrative positions than to more senior positions with pronounced problem-solving characteristics.

Points rating

Job evaluation systems based on points rating require an analysis of factors common to all jobs and at one time were widely used. The factors commonly used include skill, responsibility, complexity and decision making. Each factor is given a range of points to allow the award of a maximum number of points. The relative importance of a factor is the weighting it receives, which is determined by the number of points allocated to it, and is related to the level at which the factor is present in the job. For example, the well-known Hay-MSL system identified nine factors common to all jobs at different levels, as shown in Table 9.1.

Levels 1, 2 and 5 are key indicators for senior jobs, and 3, 4 and 5 are key indicators for all other jobs. In the evaluation of jobs using the Hay-MSL system three characteristics are considered, namely 'know-how', 'problem solving' and 'accountability'. When jobs are matched against these criteria a numerical exercise is undertaken and points are awarded. Generally, the more important the job the greater the number of points.

To make schemes, such as the above, operational requires a lot of preparation and effort. Although these schemes help in the design of graded salary structures, whereby the scores obtained by a particular job under each factor are aggregated, and have the appearance of objectivity, they can be highly subjective. Among the disadvantages of the points rating system are the following:

- The evaluation of all jobs, or even just 'benchmark' jobs, can be a complex, time-consuming and costly exercise. Benchmark jobs are a small number of jobs covering the range of jobs subjected to evaluation and considered by the evaluators to represent a good example of the right relationship between pay and job content.
- The assessment is static and not dynamic because the analysis refers to a moment in time.

Table 9.1 The Hay-MSL system

Level	Factor
1	Purpose
2	Accountability
3	Activities
4	Decision making
	Context
	Relationships
5	Knowledge
	Skills
	Experience

Ranking

This procedure involves comparing jobs on the basis of, for example, knowledge/ skill, discretionary features of decision making and task complexity, and then arranging the jobs in order of importance, or difficulty, or value to the organisation with the appropriate levels of pay. To begin with the most and least important jobs are identified, followed by ranking all jobs within this framework. In this hierarchical arrangement 'benchmark' jobs are established at key points and the remaining jobs are put in position around them. Establishing the position of the most and least important jobs is relatively easy but deciding on the position of the middle range jobs can be difficult. In a ranking exercise it is important to be aware of the potential for the introduction of bias or prejudice on the part of evaluators, and to avoid the pitfall of assessing the performance of the job occupant rather than evaluating the job itself.

Job classification

Jobs are placed into a number of grades in which differences in skill and responsibility are accommodated. These differences embrace areas within a job such as required knowledge, training and type of decision making. A definition of a job grade should be sufficiently comprehensive so as to permit a comparison of a real job description with the corresponding grade definition. The job classification approach with a predetermined number of grades and a pay structure to match is relatively straightforward and inexpensive. However, using the job classification approach with a large number of grades can take a long time and it cannot cope with complex jobs, often found at the more senior levels, which do not fit comfortably in one grade.

Other systems

A more recent system is the single factor approach called 'competence and skill analysis'. The competence or skill requirements of a job are analysed using an appropriate technique. The relevance of the individual's competence to the needs of the organisation is emphasised simply because there is no point in rewarding employees for knowledge and skills that have no operational significance for the organisation. This approach has particular value in situations where the deployment of skills has a material bearing on outcomes, as in the case of the jobs of scientific and professional staff, and could be suited to modern conditions of flatter organisational structures where there is an emphasis on flexibility, multi-skilling and teamwork.

This system, as a non-analytical approach to job evaluation, would be difficult to use in equal value claims and is likely to be unsuitable when used in organisations with firm bureaucratic structures. (An equal value claim arises when an employee asserts that his or her job, though different, is equal in nature to a job that has been given a higher rating. The first legal case in the United Kingdom governed by the Equal Pay Act 1970 (amended 1984) was Haywood v Cammell Laird Shipbuilders, where a cook's work was found to be equal to that of a printer, carpenter and thermal insulation engineer.)

Over the years implementation of the Act has become highly complicated, with cases typically involving expert witnesses on both sides. Pickstone v Freemans plc (1988 IRLR 357; HL), for example, took nine years to reach a decision and was won in the end because the tribunal agreed with Pickstone's expert witnesses rather than those of Freemans. Other complicating factors include access to rewards beyond the immediate payment, for example to pensions, and questions over extending the time limits on entitlement to back pay (currently two years) where an employee wins a case (Newman, 2001). Ways of streamlining the system, for example through appointing assessors to help tribunals come to decisions without referring cases to higher courts, are under consideration, but any new system could not be in contravention of the right to a fair trial established under the Human Rights Act 1998.

Advantages and disadvantages of job evaluation

The advantages and disadvantages of job evaluation should be acknowledged. As to the advantages, it is said to be an objective, fair (free from managerial influence) and logical approach in the determination of a pay structure. Murlis and Fitt (1991) view job evaluation as a good way to improve objectivity in the management of vertical and lateral job relativities with respect to pay, though they are prepared to admit that it is not a totally scientific process. With regard to objectivity, the point should be made that this could be undermined if job descriptions were prepared subjectively. It is worth noting that job evaluation is often viewed favourably by industrial tribunals as a foundation for a reward system that is visible and amenable to adjustment when correction is necessary.

As to the disadvantages, there could be a problem where the objectivity of the evaluators is questioned; it could also be costly to install and maintain. In connection with maintenance, it should be noted that upgradings following the evaluation could mean extra expenditure but savings on downgradings may not follow where protected grade status exists for current employees. The validity and reliability of job evaluation is called into question. One particular bone of contention is that the initial choice and weighting of 'benchmark' jobs is arbitrary (Armstrong, 1999).

Wickens (1987) is critical of the rigidity of job evaluation systems and of the attitudes that underpin them. He feels they result in a level of bureaucracy that runs counter to the notion of flexibility and adaptability ingrained in HRM thinking. Job evaluation operates on the assumption that there is a collection of tasks performed by a job occupant working in a stable reporting relationship in a traditional bureaucratic organisation. But as new organisational forms emerge, epitomised by delayering and flattening of structures, employees will be required to be more flexible and versatile in the work domain. This rules out a job demarcation mentality and introduces a recognition of the need for flexible job descriptions and acceptance of frequent changes to job boundaries. In such circumstances the level of stability required by job evaluation no longer prevails. This could herald the advent of simplified job evaluation systems, for example Nissan's 15 job titles.

Another matter to consider in connection with traditional job evaluation systems is that while it may seem equitable to offer the same reward to different individuals doing the same job on a particular grade, one has to recognise the possibility of variations in their performance. Therefore, one can challenge the fairness of a system that dispenses a uniform rate to workers irrespective of their level of performance. Apparently, a criticism more valid in the past than at the present time is that job evaluation reinforced discrimination, particularly sexual discrimination, amongst employees (Cowling and James, 1994). This arose when greater weightings were given to factors supportive of men, e.g. physical strength or having completed an apprenticeship, while aspects of women's work, such as dexterity or caring, received a lower weighting.

External influences

The 'internal relativities' emphasis outlined in the previous section when examining job evaluation is no longer the overriding consideration when it comes to the determination of rewards. It appears that external market and environmental conditions are now of greater importance. Over the past decade the political environment has had an impact on the determination of rewards. Since 1979 employment legislation in the United Kingdom has weakened the power of the trade unions. The system of the 'closed shop', where everyone doing a particular job governed by a trade union agreement is required to join the same union, is illegal. A large number of employers have taken steps to move away from collective bargaining systems to more individualised reward systems. Performance-related pay, which will be discussed later in this chapter, is a good example of this trend. It is a payment system that takes into account the quality of performance on the job instead of being specifically related to a wage or salary grade.

External competitiveness, rather than internal equity that is associated with job evaluation schemes, is now a live issue in the determination of rewards. This is evident when organisations set out to adopt market-driven reward systems where the rate for the job reflects the rate required to attract recruits rather than being based on a payment system that is underpinned by an internal grading structure.

There are a number of 'sources of information' on the levels of pay and employment conditions amongst organisations employing (and hence competing for) employees of particular types, such as specific professions in the labour market. These would include official national statistics on incomes and economic data, incomes data services from private agencies, company surveys whereby HRM specialists solicit relevant information on remuneration from their counterparts in other organisations, groups of organisations that are committed to the exchange of information on remuneration on a frequent basis, and data collected from external job advertisements and external job applicants.

It is important to compare like with like, and to do so necessitates the preparation of a job description, and not reliance on a job title alone. Of the sources of information listed above, it would appear that well-conceived exchanges of information on pay between companies are highly effective if they are based on reliable job descriptions. Apart from the competitiveness of the remuneration package on offer, one should endeavour to ensure that it is fair. Finally, the role of performance appraisal, which has been discussed in Chapter 8, should be considered in the context of the determination of rewards.

■ Types of reward system

There are a variety of schemes on offer, such as the following:

1 time rates;
2 payment by results;
3 individual/group performance-related pay (including profit-related pay);
4 skill/competency-based pay;
5 cafeteria or flexible benefit systems.

Time rates

When a reward system is related to the number of hours worked it is referred to as a payment system based on time rates; this is common in collective bargaining. Time rates can be classified as an hourly rate, a weekly wage or a monthly salary. Time rates became an issue recently with the establishment of the national minimum wage in the United Kingdom (see Box 9.1).

Traditionally, factory workers received a weekly wage and it is common for office workers to receive a monthly salary. By contrast, part-time employees receive an hourly rate. As stated earlier, jobs have grades attached to them following job evaluation, and each grade has a particular level of pay associated with it. Within a grade it is common to have an incremental scale in which employees move along on the basis of one point each year until the maximum of the scale is reached. This system rewards experience rather than performance; in effect the employee receives an incremental award normally on an annual basis for serving time in the job. Time rates place the main emphasis on the value of the task (the work system process) as influenced by job evaluation, and not explicitly on the value of the skills and abilities the employee brings to the job, or on the quality or quantity of performance.

A stated advantage of the time rates system is that it is open to inspection and is equitable in the sense that employees doing the same job will be on the same grade, though there could be differences in income owing to staff being on different positions on the incremental scale. Other advantages are the following:

■ The system encourages the retention of human resources by creating stability, staff knowing that there are gradual increases in rewards within given grades.

BOX 9.1

The minimum wage

In 1999 the minimum wage was set at £3.60 an hour for employees over 21, and £3 for those aged 18 to 21. From the 1 October 2001 it is £4.10 an hour for adult workers (aged 22, or over) and £3.50 an hour for workers aged 18 to 21. It applies to most workers in the United Kingdom, including home workers, commission workers, part-time workers, casual workers and pieceworkers. Extra money paid to workers who work overtime or do shift work is not included. The Contributions Agency and the Inland Revenue are charged with ensuring the minimum wage is paid, but there is no separate agency to police the system. The Low Pay Commission will monitor how the system operates in practice. Refusing to pay the national minimum wage is a criminal offence, which can result in a fine of up to £5,000. Dismissing a worker because he or she becomes eligible for the national minimum wage will count as unfair dismissal.

The trade unions are worried about the effectiveness of the system to force compliance with the minimum wage. There is a view that it could lead to job losses, but equally certain categories of workers (e.g. women in part-time employment) could benefit. With regard to job losses, shortly before the minimum wage was implemented on 1 April 1999, a poll of more than 2,200 small businesses carried out by Peninsula Business Services, a Manchester law consultancy, revealed that 65 per cent of respondents expect that the introduction of the minimum wage will lead to job cuts or a reduction in recruitment and 67 per cent expect the minimum wage to have a negative financial impact on their business. The results of a recent survey of companies by Income Data Services would challenge the expectation with regard to job losses. There was no evidence of job losses in low paying sectors of the economy because of the minimum wage. Where job losses do occur in low paying areas, such as the textiles and clothing industry, the main reason for the contraction in numbers employed was said to be overseas competition.

In the above survey it was also suggested that a growing number of companies are paying a minimum wage of about £4 per hour, higher than legally required, because of the competitive conditions in a tightening labour market. The minimum rate of pay in the public sector lies somewhere between £4 and £4.60 per hour, not far short of the £5 an hour being demanded by many trade unions. It is interesting to note that more companies are paying the adult minimum rate to workers from the age of 18, and some even from 16, instead of 21.

(Department of Trade and Industry, 1999; Oldfield, 1999; Taylor, 1999, 2000)

The rationale is that employee retention and the stability of the labour force offer staff the chance to enhance their skills and efficiency over time with obvious cost advantages.

- The system is relatively easy to administer and allows labour costs to be predicted.
- The system does not emphasise quantity of output to the detriment of quality.

A criticism levelled at the time rates system is that while theoretically costs of output decrease as the competence of employees grows, employees have no motivation to become more productive. For example, a worker receiving a wage of £300 a week increases output dramatically from 200 to 300 units per week. This clearly is to the advantage of the organisation but not to the employee in monetary terms. The reward received by the employee in the example is the same whether the output figure is 200 or 300. This raises the issue of why an individual should want to be a good performer if good and bad performers on a particular grade receive the same pay. Another matter to consider is that the traditional form of progression up the hierarchy from one grade to the next by way of promotion or career development has to be revised in the light of delayering and flatter organisational structures.

Payment by results

One way to address the criticisms levelled at the time rates system is to introduce a payment by results (PBR) scheme. PBR links pay to the quantity of the individual's output. A forerunner of PBR is the piecework system where pay is linked to the number of units of work produced. This was common in manufacturing industry; for example, if the piece-rate is £2 per unit and a worker produces 200 units of output, the income received is £400. Any figure above or below 200 units would lead to more or less than £400. Another example is the commission received by sales representatives, and this depends on sales volume. The rationale usually put forward to support the PBR scheme consists of the following:

- The employee is motivated to put in extra effort because by doing so he or she will receive additional income.
- Although there is an absence of overall equity in the sense that not everybody doing the same job will receive the same level of income, there is fairness in that the level of reward is related to the level of production.
- There are likely to be cost advantages since wages are directly linked to production and less supervision is required.

Prior to the introduction of a PBR scheme method study techniques are used to establish the best procedures to do the job. Then rates of pay are fixed after calculating the time taken to complete the tasks by the employee working at the appropriate or correct speed. As a general principle, in accordance with the British Standards Institution 100 Scale, one could expect that an employee on a PBR scheme working at the correct speed should be able to earn a third more than a colleague on a time rates system (Cowling and James, 1994).

When considering the measurement of output it has to be acknowledged that in certain jobs output cannot be easily measured. Managerial jobs and many jobs in the service sector do not have easily quantifiable output. For example, a swimming pool attendant's pay could not be based on the number of lives saved. In this example the output is not controlled by the worker (the attendant). Obviously the expenditure of effort and the exercise of skill are critical variables when it comes to life saving, but factors such as the number of swimmers in the pool and their levels of expertise are outside the control of the swimming pool attendant.

It is likely that PBR schemes geared to the individual will stimulate the quantity of output, but management must be on its guard in case increased output is at the expense of quality. An example of an adverse impact on quality is a dramatic increase in the scrap rate following an increase in a PBR worker's output in a factory. Therefore, if there is a PBR scheme in operation, there are obvious advantages in having quality control mechanisms firmly in place.

Apart from the question of quality, the following reservations should be noted:

■ As was stated above, it could be difficult to measure output in certain jobs.
■ In the drive to increase production safety standards may be compromised.
■ Passions could be aroused between workers and management if the workers view the PBR scheme as a device to obtain greater effort from them without commensurate reward, and where they have to haggle over money. If workers feel that they have been short-changed there is the inclination to withhold critical information about job performance.
■ In a climate of suspicion and distrust between trade unions and management the trade union representatives may use the PBR scheme, particularly in relation to pay, as a means to put pressure on management and create conflict.

Taking a positive view, it is suggested that PBR schemes can be effective where they are well conceived, where work measurement and output measurement are possible, where good prior communication and consultation with employees have taken place, and where there is a healthy rapport between management and workers (Cannell and Long, 1991).

Performance-related pay

Unlike payment by results examined in the previous section, performance-related pay considers not only results or output but also actual behaviour in the job. The individual's performance is measured against previously set objectives, or compared with the various tasks listed in the job description, using performance appraisal techniques discussed in Chapter 8. Following this assessment, normally conducted by the manager, with or without professional assistance, there is an allocation of rewards. Rewards linked to performance could consist of a lump sum, or a bonus as a percentage of basic salary, with quality of performance determining the magnitude of the percentage increase; or alternatively accelerated movement up a pay scale.

In connection with the last observation, excellent performance might, for example, justify a movement upwards of two points on the scale, while poor performance could result in staying at the current level. Some incremental pay scales have a bar at a particular point, beyond which there is entitlement to discretionary points. To go beyond the bar and benefit from the discretionary points it would be necessary for the individual to receive a favourable performance evaluation. It should be noted that management reserves the right to award discretionary points.

Designing appropriate schemes, which provide satisfactory incentives for employees, is not straightforward, but Fisher (2001) offers the following steps as a guideline:

- Take account of the corporate environment through a research phase, that is analyse business performance over the last five years and classify the contribution of employee groupings (such as departments or teams) to the performance.
- Combine goals with emotions – be aware that people's reactions to incentives will not only be rational but will also depend on how they feel about the situation; for example, employers who use only money as the reward may be perceived as cynical and uncaring.
- Ensure congruency between organisational goals and personal goals.
- Focus on communication – agree a statement of morale, motivation and performance with departmental heads and make sure that the process is properly explained. Use success stories to spur people on. Crucially, it is important to avoid the 'launch it and leave it' attitude amongst managers.
- Provide adequate skills training for employees.
- Respond effectively to feedback from employees.

Certain conditions are said to be necessary for a PRP scheme to be effective (Applebaum and Shappiro, 1991):

- In order to make the measurement of performance a meaningful activity it is essential that there should be sufficient differences between individuals on the basis of performance.
- The pay range must be of sufficient width to accommodate significant differences in the basic pay of employees.
- The measurement of performance must be a valid and reliable exercise, and it must be possible to relate the outcome of the measurement process to pay.
- Appraisers are skilful in setting performance standards and in conducting appraisals.
- The culture of the organisation is supportive.
- The remuneration package offered is competitive and fair, and the organisation is adept at relating pay to performance.
- Mutual trust exists between managers and their subordinates, and managers are prepared to manage with an eagerness to communicate performance criteria and face making difficult decisions.

While the above conditions are supportive of PRP schemes it is possible to encounter conditions, such as the following, which produce a negative impact (Applebaum and Shappiro, 1991; Goss, 1994):

1 No attempt is made to relate individual performance to organisational objectives.
2 Appraisals are not conducted fairly, because either output is difficult to measure or the appraiser is incompetent.

3 Openness, trust, joint problem solving and commitment to organisational objectives are adversely affected by the introduction of PRP schemes.
4 The introduction of PRP schemes produces adversarial conditions when it creates supporters and opponents of such schemes.

Having examined the conditions necessary for the introduction of PRP schemes, and being aware of conditions likely to produce a negative impact, it is legitimate to ask: what are the advantages and disadvantages of such schemes? First we shall note the following advantages of individually based PRP schemes (Goss, 1994):

■ Incentives are linked to meeting targets or objectives, as well as to the quality of performance as perceived by superiors. Linking pay to performance that lends itself to measurement is considered fairer than awarding across-the-board cost-of-living increases, which do not discriminate between high and low performers.
■ Where employee performance can be measured and the amount of money available to reward performance is sufficient to motivate effort, it saves money if the organisation targets rewards on those who perform.
■ High performers are attracted to PRP cultures in the knowledge that pay is linked to productive effort, and that poor achievement is discouraged.
■ Employees receive useful feedback on their performance.
■ There is an emphasis on a results-oriented culture, with the accent on effort directed at activities that the organisation values.

The following could be considered disadvantages of individually based PRP schemes:

■ Behaviour is rewarded, which one would expect to occur anyway in accordance with the employment contract. The argument goes that good performance is expected and provision is made for it, and where there is poor performance it is the job of management to sort it out.
■ Open communication between managers and subordinates could be discouraged, because subordinates are less likely to divulge information on personal shortcomings just in case such disclosures act to their disadvantage.
■ The rewarding of self-centred individualism can undermine cooperation and teamwork, which are necessary for coping with today's climate characterised by complexity and interdependency (Pearce, 1991).
■ The growth of managerial control over subordinates is promoted, with the effect of isolating the individual; this could affect teamwork.
■ Poor performers are punished; this is unfortunate because it is in the organisation's interest to motivate this group in order to improve their performance.
■ The existence of trade union opposition could sour relationships between management and the representatives of the workers. Sometimes trade unions object to the individualistic nature of rewards that run counter to the spirit of collective bargaining, and there is currently a view that too great a part is played by subjective managerial judgement in the determination of rewards. With respect

to the latter, there is the fear that equitable criteria are not applied objectively to all employees.

A number of practitioners have endorsed PRP schemes, including those residing in Japan (see Example 9.1).

EXAMPLE 9.1

Performance-based pay in Japan

Traditionally Japanese companies guaranteed employees a monthly salary as well as a twice-yearly bonus, equivalent to about five months of annual pay. Because Japan is suffering from its worst economic recession in post-war history companies have moved towards performance-based pay. This trend signals a movement towards ending pay often based on age and experience and the beginning of a meritocratic system. A first move seems to be cutting the bonuses, and then supplementing the reduced bonus with an additional amount determined by performance. Fujitsu is already treading the meritocracy path. Since 1995 this company has been paying employees according to performance. Employees are evaluated against pre-established goals, and the evaluation determines the bonus to be paid.

It appears that there is a modest movement towards remunerating top executives on the basis of performance through the use of share option schemes. But executives in Japan do not enjoy the generous rewards of their western counterparts. In Japan one encounters a more egalitarian spirit, reflected in the sharing of corporate profits equally. For example, the percentage increase in the income of the chief executive in Japan is likely to be in line with the percentage rise in the income of the ordinary worker. The introduction of stock options may signal changes in attitudes, but developments in performance-based rewards are likely to be gradual and hesitant.

(Nakamoto, 1998; Nusbaum, 1999)

The motivational significance of PRP schemes has been challenged (Kohn, 1993; Thompson, 1993). The results of a survey of managers at British Telecom indicated that the PRP scheme was unfairly administered and there was scepticism of its effect on performance; in fact the payments made had an adverse effect on performance (IRS, 1991). British Telecom suspended its PRP scheme for managers following a pay comparison study in which it was established that the company was paying its managers between 11 and 14 per cent above remuneration levels for managers in similar jobs in outside organisations (Taylor, 1994). This line of action was driven by the need to keep costs in check and to retain competitiveness. The importance of external comparability in the determination of rewards is evident in this situation.

The difficulties encountered with individually based schemes were also highlighted in a more recent research study carried out amongst Inland Revenue employees. A major finding was that performance-related schemes generated much resentment as employees faced conflict as a result of the quantity of work demands putting pressure on quality. Also, 60 per cent of respondents were not too happy at having individual performance targets imposed rather than being the outcome of discussion. The researcher concluded that group-based schemes might have the edge over individually based schemes (Halligan, 1997).

Group PRP schemes

These schemes, which link rewards to outcomes such as meeting budget targets or organisational profitability, are said to avoid the threat to cooperative modes of working associated with individually based PRP schemes by de-emphasising the individualistic nature of rewards. According to Murlis (1994), team-based pay seeks to eliminate the divisive nature of individually based PRP schemes. The group PRP schemes include the exercise of share options (see Example 9.2) and profit sharing. A group scheme related to profit is called profit-related pay.

EXAMPLE 9.2

Options for senior executives

The use of share options by senior executives of large companies in the United Kingdom is a contentious issue. Much criticism has been levelled at share option schemes. Though the cost of such schemes is not a charge to the company's profit and loss account under current accounting conventions, it is a potential claim on the company's future profits and so reduces the payouts available to the other shareholders. These rewards are inadequately related to management performance and send a poor signal to employees who are not included in the scheme. In many cases executives receive big rewards if their companies do no more than the average growth of the economy. A finding from a survey by the National Institute of Economic and Social Research in the UK suggests that there is little obvious link between the rewards generated by such schemes and company profitability or total shareholder returns.

Share option schemes are attractive to the recipients. If the company's shares increase in value the directors stand to gain, but if they decrease they merely lose a potential profit opportunity. By contrast, shareholders incur genuine losses in the latter situation. Share options fail the key test of a good incentive scheme, which is that the interests of shareholders and managers should be as closely aligned as possible.

There is a growing feeling that share incentive schemes should be reserved for exceptional performance, and not for meeting the requirements of a normal job. Also, it would appear that not enough is done to share the benefits of success throughout the workforce. However, there is an indication of some movement in this direction. For example, Safeway – the supermarket chain – provides a share option scheme for all its permanent employees.

Following the publication of the Greenbury Report in 1995, L Tips (long-term incentives) were considered appropriate. They have been viewed as an alternative to share option schemes for senior executives who can profit from the sale of these shares three years later if targets (earnings per share measured against a comparator group of companies) are met. In 1997 Nial Fitzgerald, the Chairman of Unilever, expressed reservations about the usefulness of L Tips if the stock market became bearish. In the scheme designed by Unilever the company's performance will be based on the real growth of the business and the value it creates above inflation, instead of relying on performance relative to other companies forming the comparator group.

(*Financial Times*, 1995, 1999; Fitzgerald, 1997)

Profit-related pay

The original idea was that by linking pay to profits companies could make their wage costs variable. Employees would be given an incentive to work harder, and in good times would reap the rewards, while in bad times they would share the pain, though it is possible to design schemes so that the employees are safeguarded when profits fall. Companies can use profit-related pay as a bonus paid in addition to existing salary, or by getting employees to swap part of their salary for profit-related pay. A major reason why many companies that use profit-related pay, such as Boots, do so is because it is a more tax-efficient means for paying bonuses.

The tendency now is for schemes to cover all or most employees as opposed to senior grades as in the past. According to the recruitment manager at Boots, 'the scheme gives our workforce a greater stake in the business. It means they switch off the lights at night and don't keep the machinery running, and may have lessened pay claims' (Kellaway, 1993). Profit-related pay may not be suitable for all companies. The companies that have little to gain from such schemes are those with very low paid workers – who pay little tax – or where profits are so volatile that they are impossible to predict. Some companies steer clear of profit-related pay because they prefer incentive schemes based on individual rather than group performance. But other companies, such as Boots and the Halifax Building Society (now a bank and amalgamated with the Bank of Scotland), view profit-related pay as an addition rather than an alternative to individual incentives (Kellaway, 1993).

Amongst the alleged benefits of group profit-related pay schemes are the following:

- Employees identify more closely with the success of the organisation, and this has obvious advantages in terms of commitment and improved organisational performance.
- There is a breaking down or removal of the 'them' and 'us' barrier.
- Cooperation and working together for mutual benefit is encouraged.
- There is an awareness of the link between performance and organisational profitability, leading to a greater awareness of costs and their impact on performance. This realisation is beneficial to the organisation when wage claims are submitted.
- When adverse trading conditions, such as a recession, hit the organisation the element of profit devoted to pay can fall. Such an eventuality is a preferable alternative to laying off employees.
- Group pressure could raise the performance levels of poor performers.

Recent evidence (Freeman, 2001) has indicated that profit sharing and share option schemes may have a positive impact on performance. A study of 299 UK companies between 1995 and 1998 indicated that companies with such schemes involving non-managerial employees tended to strike the right note with employees, giving them information about business performance. Subsequently, company-wide productivity was seen to increase following the introduction of the schemes. Those adopting profit sharing showed increases of 17 per cent value added per worker, and those choosing share option plans recorded 12 per cent value added per worker.

A disadvantage of group-based schemes, where rewards are linked to company profitability, is that the employee may see the rewards as too distant from individual effort, more so because of having to rely on others as well as the influence of external factors (e.g. competitors and markets).

Cases where management rewarded employees for working as members of teams or groups appear in Example 9.3.

EXAMPLE 9.3

Group-based rewards at Pearl Assurance and the Automobile Association in the UK

Pearl Assurance was unable to pass on the cost of significant salary increases to its customers because of the prevalence of acute market competition and economic conditions of low inflation. Therefore it had to give serious consideration to the most appropriate remuneration system in these circumstances. Previously a performance-related pay system was in operation, but when salary settlements were below 3 per cent of payroll cost managers under this system had little scope to use their discretion and reward staff on the basis of merit.

Team-based pay was introduced and it was the job of the heads of the sections or teams to meet and rank the performance of each section, and to determine the pay increase each section was to receive. Then each head was expected to evaluate the performance of individuals as team players and exercise discretion in the award of individual salary increases.

(Trevor, 1993)

At the Automobile Association team-based incentives were introduced following the creation of a flatter organisation structure. The aims of teams of 30 were to provide high quality service and maintain a quick response rate, but it was proving difficult to create team spirit because teams spent much of their time on the road with a high level of individual autonomy.

Targets were set for teams covering such criteria as the number of jobs completed at the roadside, the average time taken to complete the job, and the average time taken to respond to a Relay call when the motorist's car had to be transported to the home or to a garage. The performance of teams was measured against the above criteria, and teams competed in leagues. The winners received tangible prizes, such as outings and vouchers to use in stores, coupled with the intrinsic reward of the status stemming from being the winning team. The winners were announced quarterly and annually.

(Pickard, 1993)

Skill-based pay

The schemes examined above have concentrated on the 'outputs' of work activity, such as volume and quality of production or profit. By comparison, skill-based pay places the emphasis on 'inputs' that consist of knowledge, skills and competencies injected into the job by employees (Donkin, 1998). In the distant past the crafts- man received differentiated rewards at different stages of his career. As he moved from apprentice to master the development of skill was reflected in increased reward. In the not too distant past the growth of mass production systems accom- panied by advances in technology gave rise to the simplification of work and to a significant amount of deskilling, which had the effect of maintaining a steady demand for unskilled workers.

In the current climate the march of new technology has meant that there is a con- traction in the number of unskilled jobs and a growth in the demand for multi- skilled workers. This has been brought about by a team-based approach towards work and the need for flexibility in staffing arrangements. To foster a multi-skill capability in the labour force calls for the acquisition and use of more skills than required hitherto. In order to provide an incentive to employees to broaden their skill base some employers are linking rewards to skills' acquisition and deployment.

According to IDS (1992), before introducing a skill-based system there should be good planning, a fair amount of consultation and employee participation, as well as training directed at the acquisition of new technical skills and teamworking skills. Subsequently rewards would be linked to both skills' acquisition and use, and perhaps also to the level of performance directly associated with the deploy- ment of those skills, if such an exercise is possible. If it is not possible then an organisation can only hope that skills will be utilised in a manner compatible with high levels of performance.

A point to note in connection with skill-based pay is that management is well placed to use rewards to encourage and support changes in behaviour, i.e. acquisi- tion of a broader range of skills, which are necessary to implement contemporary changes in organisational design and functioning. Also, the operation of a skill- based pay system requires attention to the skills to be rewarded, setting the right rate of pay, providing the appropriate level of training, putting in place the necess- ary procedures, and ensuring that sufficient time is invested wisely in the process. It said that skill-based pay schemes are beneficial in terms of job satisfaction and performance (Lawler *et al.*, 1993).

The cases shown in Example 9.4 stress the growing importance of skill-based pay. In the UNISYS case the main emphasis is on the input of skill, but there is also an aspect of performance assessment. In the IBM case the interaction between organisational design and rewards is highlighted.

Cafeteria or flexible benefit systems

These systems are a way of managing rewards that are gaining in popularity in the United Kingdom, and are established in the United States where they are referred

EXAMPLE 9.4

Skill-based pay at UNISYS and IBM

UNISYS moved away from a performance-related pay scheme to a skill (competence)-based pay one. Behaviour was assessed using criteria such as teamwork, customer orientation, innovative practices, accountability and motivation. Employees were assessed using these criteria and were placed in four categories, with different levels of reward associated with each category.

(Huddart, 1994)

IBM introduced changes to its pay structure involving a move towards skill or competence-based rewards and sensitivity to job market pay rates. The rates attached to particular jobs are linked to market pay rates within a system of general job categories. The number of levels of jobs in the management and professional area was reduced from 12 to 4. The newly created levels represent broad bands containing a range of jobs within which individual employees move from one area to another within the organisation. Moving in this way means there is no change to the cost of the remuneration package because the employee remains within a broad pay band.

The new approach to pay has been influenced by IBM's changed philosophy linked to work design and career structures. The 'job for life' culture and automatic annual pay rises have been challenged. The intention is to create a 'human growth' culture where individual competence is recognised and rewarded. This will put pressure on employees to be concerned with their development and employability so as to secure their future with the company.

(North, 1993, 1994)

to as 'flexible benefits'. In Australia they are called 'packaged compensation', and in the United Kingdom they are known as the 'cafeteria' system. Since they are substitutes for pay they must be calculated within an overall remuneration or compensation package. Their popularity in the United States has no doubt been prompted by tax advantages, unlike the position in the United Kingdom, and mainly comprises life and accident insurance, medical and dental care, and care for children. In addition the growing costs of healthcare for companies in the United States motivated them to take flexible remuneration seriously. Companies give employees pre-tax 'flex credits' that they could use to meet the cost of health benefits.

In the United Kingdom flexible benefits have captured the imagination of human resource practitioners as a means of providing employees with a degree of choice over the form that their remuneration takes, and as a useful measure in the recruitment and retention of human resources. According to Debbie Harrison, Human Resources Director, Financial Services Authority in the UK, the beauty of flexible benefits is that you can change your selection each year to suit your lifestyle (Harrison, 2001). A cafeteria system in the United Kingdom could be made up of such benefits as the company car, additional holiday entitlement, private health insurance, membership of social clubs, modification to working hours, special pension arrangements, mortgage loan subsidies and other benefits. Scottish & Newcastle Breweries offer a package covering ten separate benefits, including the company product in the form of wines and spirits. The scheme allows executives earning, say, £50,000 p.a. to increase their salary to £60,000 p.a. if no benefits were taken. Alternatively, the salary could be as little as £37,000 p.a. if the optimum benefits cover was utilised.

Employees exercise choice when selecting a range of benefits from a menu that they consider important and to which they are entitled. Although a number of schemes apply to executive and managerial staff there is evidence to indicate that these schemes are becoming progressively available to other employees (Woodley, 1993). This may not apply universally within an organisation, certainly not for two companies – BHS (retail stores) and Scottish & Newcastle Breweries – that have avoided introducing flexible benefits throughout their workforce, mainly because those further down the organisational hierarchy have fewer benefits, such as company cars, to choose from. At Scottish & Newcastle Breweries a scheme was introduced around 1992 that initially covered 70 or 80 employees with an intention to extend it to all 2,000 managers who have company cars (Donkin, 1994).

BHS was one of the first companies in the United Kingdom to introduce the cafeteria system when a new chief executive, educated in the United States, joined the company in 1990. Details of the scheme appear in Example 9.5.

EXAMPLE 9.5

Cafeteria system at BHS

A first step at BHS was to give top management more say over the composition of their pay and benefits. The scheme started with over 50 managers and by 1993 was extended to 400 managers who were in possession of company cars.

An example of how the scheme works is as follows. A particular male manager earns £35,000 p.a. The cash value of his benefits is £8,115. The latter provides a ceiling for his benefits, from which can be chosen between one and three times his salary level in life insurance cover, selection from four levels of private medical care and from four levels of annual holiday entitlement between 22 and 30 days. In addition there is a choice of a free company car, the opportunity to buy long-term disability insurance, an optical cover plan that subsidises contact lens purchases and eye tests, and a dental care plan. Benefits in excess of his entitlement can be obtained, in which case there is a reduction of the appropriate amount from his salary.

Taking benefits less than his entitlement could mean an increase in salary by an amount equivalent to the reduction in benefits. The only benefit the company insists that managers take is the minimum level of holiday. The human resources manager at BHS is reported as saying that the package on offer has proved popular and that this system of reward 'is a fairly progressive recruitment tool; to be honest people love it'.

(Donkin, 1994)

The following are issues to consider when adopting cafeteria or flexible benefit systems in the United Kingdom (IDS, 1991):

■ Flexibility in the way remuneration systems are determined is necessary because of demographic changes (e.g. using the services of more women and older workers). However, it should be noted that the economic recession of the early 1990s and the continuing high levels of unemployment largely nullified the effects of demographic change. The economic situation improved as we moved into the later part of the 1990s and this called for flexibility. For example, Price Waterhouse (now PricewaterhouseCoopers), an international firm of accountants/consultants, introduced a flexible benefits system in the United Kingdom in 1997 because it was losing too many female employees. But the scheme was designed in such a way as to appeal to all staff (Maitland, 1998).
■ If flexible benefit systems are too individually based there is a danger that teamwork will be undermined.
■ Every effort should be made to communicate the total benefits portfolio.
■ Those who participate in the scheme have the advantage of choosing benefits considered relevant to their needs from a menu that is publicly available. This could have a beneficial effect on commitment.
■ The position of spouses/partners with careers should be considered in order to avoid duplication of certain benefits (e.g. health insurance).
■ When flexible benefits are costed there is greater awareness of the costs of employing people.
■ Full advantage should be taken of the potential of information technology in the administration of schemes in order to keep the costs of operation within reasonable levels.
■ The costs of schemes should be kept under review; in particular the administration of schemes when employees choose benefits that happen to be in great demand as an alternative to underutilised benefits.
■ The tax implications of schemes should be considered. Some of the benefits are not taxed in the UK; for example, holidays, home computer purchase, life assurance – up to a maximum of four times salary – long-term disability, and pension contributions. But other benefits are subjected to tax (Harrison, 2001).
■ The schemes may be more appropriate to situations where non-unionised labour exists. There is a belief that trade unions may consider such schemes a potential threat to standard remuneration packages. In appropriate circumstances it would appear sensible to involve the trade unions in the various deliberations. In the Price Waterhouse scheme referred to above there was widespread consultation with employees, because it was recognised that these schemes are complex and take time to become integrated into the firm's culture (Maitland, 1998). Therefore involvement of employees in this delicate process is necessary.
■ A feature of the schemes in the United Kingdom is their flexibility and individual bias, but in the United States the major attraction seems to be the tax implications and medical insurance cover.

Other matters to consider are that flexible remuneration arrangements are useful for multinational companies looking for ways to manage expatriate costs; that companies get rid of the perks-driven mentality of employees who expect certain entitlements as a right; and that employees who take part of their total income by way of flexible benefits experience a cost advantage (Donkin, 1994). In connection with the latter, it would be more economical to acquire, say, private medical cover through a company's group plan than on an individual basis out of personal disposable income.

■ International compensation

Companies operating internationally face a demanding challenge when devising and operating reward systems compatible with the achievement of the strategic long-term objectives of the organisation. According to Dowling *et al.* (1994),

> the successful management of international compensation and benefits requires knowledge of the laws, customs, environment, and employment practices of many foreign countries, familiarity with currency fluctuations, and the effect of inflation on compensation. Also, it is necessary to have an understanding of why and when special allowances must be supplied, and which allowances are necessary in the different countries – all within the context of shifting political, economic and social conditions.

Since compensation programmes should be used to improve the international competitive standing of the global corporation, it is no surprise to find that flexibility and cost consciousness feature prominently in their delivery.

The following are considered likely objectives of international compensation (Dowling *et al.*, 1994):

- The policy should be consistent with the overall strategy, structure and business needs of the multinational enterprise.
- The policy must be able to attract and retain staff in the areas where the multinational has the greatest needs and opportunities.
- The policy should facilitate the transfer of international employees in the most cost effective manner for multinational enterprises.
- The policy should be consistent and fair in its treatment of all categories of international employees.

Achieving the above objectives is likely to be a complex activity, primarily because of the different categories of employees that have to be catered for – expatriates, third country nationals and host country nationals (local employees). The company will be faced with a decision whether to have an overall compensation policy for all employees, or to deal separately with the different categories of employees. In this respect Hollinshead and Leat (1995) argue that multinational organisations can take one of three broad approaches:

- The '*ethnocentric*' company seeks to export established practice from its country of origin to the other countries it operates in. In such cases the remuneration system is established at the centre, but may have some local variation as market rates are taken into account. The base salary for expatriates and third country nationals would be linked to the salary structure of the relevant home country.

■ The *'polycentric'* company prefers decentralisation because the assumption is that local managers are best placed to formulate reward policies, which will reflect local needs. In this approach there is variability of reward across the company and an emphasis on salary determination at the domestic level. So, for example, the host country salary level could be offered, with significant international supplements (e.g. cost-of-living adjustments, housing and school allowances, etc.). This approach could create problems when the person returns home and reverts to the home country salary levels. Friction or feelings of inequity could arise between third country nationals and expatriates because the former feels that their total package is not up to the level enjoyed by the latter.

■ The *'geocentric'* company is seen as a more developed form than the previous two types. At this stage of development the aim is to combine strengths from both the ethnocentric and polycentric approaches. Managers should be able to respond locally while holding corporate values and objectives in mind. This introduces potential conflicts in seeking to balance fair internal relativities with responsiveness to international market rates. Although such a balancing act may be difficult to maintain Hollinshead and Leat (1995) argue that it is likely to be the most effective approach in the long term for multinational companies.

The Price Waterhouse/Cranfield Survey (Fillela and Hegewisch, 1994) has indicated a number of trends in reward strategies internationally. First, there is a connection between pay determination and approaches to collective bargaining. In Finland, France and Sweden company-level negotiations tend to complement national or industry level negotiations. By contrast, in Portugal, Spain, Turkey and the United Kingdom company-level negotiations have tended to displace higher (national or industry) levels of bargaining. The tendency for companies from the latter countries may, therefore, be towards polycentricism. Secondly, in general there is a trend towards flexibility and away from centralised and collective determination of pay. Thirdly, the operationalisation of this flexibility is increasingly determined at lower levels in the corporation, particularly in the United Kingdom and France, although multi-employer bargaining has persisted longer in the Nordic countries, Ireland and the Netherlands. Fourthly, there is a general trend towards increased variability in pay. In Germany and France this trend has often found expression through profit sharing, while in Italy, Switzerland and the United Kingdom merit- and performance-related pay has been generally preferred (Fillela and Hegewisch, 1994). The greatest flexibility and uptake of cafeteria systems has been in the United States (Hollinshead and Leat, 1995). It should be noted that although it is possible to identify some general trends, variations may impact on their implementation and local culture may be expected to influence the styles of reward that are perceived to be attractive.

As mentioned in the opening sentence of this section, it is no easy task to come forward with well-conceived international packages to motivate employees. This area of reward management could be a hornet's nest. Because of its complexity, ranging from the determination of salary and incentives to considerations concerned with taxation liability, currency fluctuations, pension rights and various allowances, it presents the HR specialists with a stiff challenge.

■ Relevance of motivation theories

Those with responsibility for designing reward systems will benefit from an understanding of motivation theories. Work motivation theories delve into psychological explanations about what motivates people in formal organisations. Therefore motivation and rewards are connected because rewards are given on the understanding that employees are motivated to commit themselves to perform to satisfactory levels at the workplace.

Pay, as an important component of a system of rewards, has been singled out by Thierry (1992) as having psychological and social significance, because it sends a number of messages to employees, quite apart from its status as a desired material reward. Pay says something about the appropriateness of the employee's work behaviour, it is a symbol of recognition and it conveys what the organisation thinks of the person's behaviour. In addition, pay performs the following roles (Thierry, 1992):

1 It satisfies personal needs (e.g. provides an escape from insecurity, creates a feeling of competence and opens up opportunities for self-fulfilment).
2 It provides feedback on how well a person is doing on a variety of fronts and it acts as an indicator of that person's relative position in the organisation.
3 It is a reward for success in controlling others where the individual has a supervisory or managerial position.
4 It conveys a capacity to spend in the sense that pay reflects purchasing power in the consumer market.

In the above situational interpretation of pay it is clear that a reward could mean different things to different people. For example, one person desires a certain level of income to satisfy their security needs, to another person money serves as a means to portray relative success at work, and to a third it is a means to provide spending power compatible with expectations of status. For the greater part of this century researchers in work motivation have stressed the importance of different factors in the motivation of workers, though in some cases there was a convergence of view.

'Economic man'

Money as a major motivating factor was endorsed by Taylor (1947), the founder of scientific management, in the early part of the last century. People were seen to be motivated by self-interest and were keen to accept the challenge to maximise their income. From the organisation's point of view, the opportunity to maximise production rested on creating reward systems (e.g. piece-rates, payment by results) where financial returns (extrinsic rewards) vary with levels of output. The greater the level of output, the greater the level of individual reward.

Human relations

The 'economic man' school of thought gave way to the human relations perspective expounded by Mayo (1949). Following a series of experiments on the social and environmental conditions at work, the importance of recognition and good social relationships at work as motivational factors contributing to morale and productivity was heavily underlined.

Need theories

Next to appear on the scene were the need theories, principally represented by Maslow (1954) and Herzberg (1966). Maslow arranged human needs in the form of a hierarchy with basic needs (e.g. hunger, security and safety) at the lower end, self-actualisation needs at the top, and ego and social needs in the middle. The individual moves up the hierarchy as lower needs are satisfied, and it should be noted that a pressing need is a powerful motivator of behaviour until it is satisfied.

Basic pay, sick pay and pension entitlement could satisfy security needs, and a work environment where hazards are well controlled could satisfy safety needs. The provision of sports and social clubs, which facilitate interaction at work, and works outings, could satisfy social needs. Position in the organisation and symbols of success, such as a valuable company car, have relevance in the context of satisfying status and recognition needs. An experience whereby the individual acquires key knowledge and skills, and successfully completes an exacting and challenging assignment, could contribute to the satisfaction of self-actualisation needs. Finally, adequate pay has significance at the lower end of the hierarchy, although one should take note of the broader interpretation of the psychological implications of pay attributed to Thierry (1992) earlier in this section.

Using concepts similar to Maslow, Herzberg (1966) concluded from his studies that satisfied feelings at work stemmed from a challenging job, extra responsibility, personal accomplishments, recognition from superiors and progress in one's career. These were referred to as real 'motivators'. On the other hand, negative feelings and dissatisfaction could arise from poor relationships with colleagues and superiors, less than satisfactory company policy and administration, poor pay and adverse working conditions. These were referred to as 'hygiene' factors, and if improved could lower the level of 'dissatisfaction' and negativity. Improving the hygiene factors and then building motivators into a job was considered the best way to motivate people. Note the status of pay in the Herzberg model – a hygiene factor – a position challenged later in the expectancy model of motivation.

There is a strong similarity between Maslow's higher level human needs and Herzberg's motivators. Both would be considered when designing or redesigning jobs by way of job enrichment (see Box 9.2).

The notion of job enrichment – attempting to make tasks more intrinsically interesting, involving and rewarding – is updated in the Hackman and Oldham job characteristics model (Hackman, 1977).

This model incorporates the following five core dimensions, which are key factors when designing or redesigning jobs:

BOX 9.2

Job enrichment in action

A job may be enriched by an individual undertaking greater responsibility – e.g. by organising and checking their own work, or by being involved in decisions about planning the work of their unit. Extending the opportunities for making decisions and exercising judgement changes the content of the work. Job enrichment programmes attempt to build in, over time, scope for the development of an individual's skills to provide a sense of personal achievement. This approach frequently affects the nature of other jobs and therefore careful consideration needs to be given to the whole process of reallocating responsibilities, redefining roles and providing the necessary retraining. Over the years there have been a number of instances where job enrichment led to increased job satisfaction and favourably influenced performance.

(Department of Employment, 1975).

In the 1960s ICI was one of a handful of companies in the United Kingdom that experimented seriously with job enrichment. One job enrichment study within ICI examined the role of sales representatives who appeared to be satisfied with their job but were given very little discretion over the way they operated. The following changes were instituted as part of the job enrichment programme. Sales representatives no longer had to write a report on every customer call. Instead they passed on, or requested, information at their own discretion. They were also given total responsibility for determining the frequency of calls to customers, deciding how to deal with faulty or unwanted stock, requesting service from the technical services department and making immediate settlements up to a certain sum in case of customer complaint, if they felt this would prejudice further liability of the company. In addition, they were given discretion to adjust prices on a range up to 10 per cent on the price of most of the products sold, the lower limit being often below any price previously quoted by the sales office. Following the implementation of the job enrichment scheme both job satisfaction and performance increased.

(Paul and Robertson, 1970)

1 *skill variety* (scope for the exercise of different skills and abilities);
2 *task identity* (extent to which the job requires the completion of an identifiable segment of work);
3 *task significance* (extent to which the job has an impact on the life of others);
4 *autonomy* (extent to which the job offers freedom and the use of discretion in performing tasks);
5 *feedback* (extent to which the job-holder receives information on his or her performance).

The five core dimensions are linked with motivation and performance through critical psychological states (i.e. experienced meaningfulness of the work, experienced responsibility for work outcomes, and knowledge of the consequences of work activities). The model recognises that people differ in their levels of 'growth need'. For example, people with a high need for personal growth are more likely to react favourably in a psychological sense when the five core factors are improved.

Overview

The motivational factors discussed above can be classified as intrinsic (e.g. job challenge, skill-based pay) or extrinsic (e.g. pay, performance-related pay, working conditions). Skill-based pay is classified as an intrinsic factor because it refers to the reward an individual receives for the baggage (input) of knowledge and skill the employee takes to the job. The outcome could be the enhancement of competences and personal development. By contrast, basic pay in the form of 'time rates' can be related to the need theories, since they call for fairness and relative security, which in turn can generate social satisfaction at work.

Expectancy theory

Another theory of motivation is expectancy theory (Porter and Lawler, 1968; Vroom, 1964), which could be considered very relevant to reward management (Lundy and Cowling, 1996). People bring to work various expectations about the likely consequences of various forms of behaviour reflected in work performance. For example, if people expect that the expenditure of effort will lead to good work performance and generate a satisfactory outcome in terms of intrinsic and extrinsic rewards, which are valued, and such expectations are realised in practice, then productive effort is likely to be forthcoming in the future. If this scenario was altered, so that the relationship between effort and reward did not stand, it is possible that the motivational disposition of the employee would change and future effort may be adjusted downwards or discontinued.

In more specific terms Lundy and Cowling (1996), drawing on expectancy theory, state that high performance by individuals or teams will only come about if they are clear about their tasks, to which they have a positive attitude, and that they possess the necessary aptitudes, abilities and competences. Effort will then be expended resulting in a high level of performance when people perceive that their energy and effort results in high performance, that high performance will lead to rewards, and that the rewards available are those that they desire. The critical final stage is the receipt of positive feedback, when they obtain the desirable intrinsic and extrinsic rewards.

In practice it may be difficult to implement expectancy theory. For example, profit-related pay attempts to bring about convergence between individual and organisational goals, in the sense that the individual is motivated to achieve organisational goals, for by so doing the employee is achieving personal goals, particularly with reference to extrinsic rewards. However, with profit-related pay employees may not be sure that specific rewards will be the consequence of particular actions because of the involvement of others. But in the quoted example social needs could be satisfied in the process because the organisation is trying to link the interests of employees with those of the organisation. Social needs could also be considered relevant in the context of group- or team-based pay.

Goal setting

The setting of goals is said to have an impact on the motivation of the individuals, provided the goals set are clear, realistic and challenging, but not too difficult, and that the person subjected to them is able to participate in their setting. Other considerations are feedback on performance, goal acceptance and commitment to the goal (Locke and Latham, 1990). Management by objectives, which was mentioned as a performance appraisal technique in Chapter 8, is an example of a process in which there is an emphasis on participation in the setting of goals. An alternative approach to goal setting as described would be for goals to be set and assigned to the individual, but this approach might not have the motivational impact outlined above.

A reward system anchored in extrinsic rewards, e.g. performance-related pay, utilises the concepts of expectancy and goal setting when judgements are made about the extent to which performance meets objectives, and the adequacy of rewards.

Equity theory

This theory is concerned with the equitable nature of reward and has significance when the employee perceives the relationship between effort and reward, as would occur in the application of expectancy theory. In an employment situation one considers two important variables: inputs and outputs. Education, skill, experience and effort would be considered inputs, and salary, fringe benefits and career advancement would be viewed as outputs. People compare each other's inputs and outputs and, if they perceive unfairness, feelings of inequity can arise (Adams, 1963). The latter could have an adverse effect on production and possibly lead to absenteeism and resignation. Apparently, if after engaging in the comparative exercise some employees consider themselves overcompensated, there could be a feeling of unease.

We shall give the final say to Robertson *et al.* (1992) on the issue of the ideal interaction between the organisational environment and levels of motivation, as follows:

- Expectations in terms of performance are translated into specific and hard goals that are attainable.
- Employees are allowed to participate in the setting of these goals, and they have a realistic appreciation of the link between effort and performance aimed at goal attainment.
- Employees are endowed with the necessary competence and confidence to ensure that effort made results in appropriate performance.
- Jobs are designed in such a way as to offer employees variety, autonomy, and frequent and clear feedback on their performance.
- Control systems that regulate people's work are only used as and when necessary.
- Rewards received by employees for successful performance are geared to their individual requirements and preferences, and are perceived as equitable.

■ HRM and rewards

Systems of pay, such as time rates and payment by results, tend to be associated with the more traditional styles of management, while reward systems, such as performance-related pay and skill-based pay, reflect the spirit of HRM and appear to be growing in popularity. It is claimed that HRM is associated with a management ethos of self-interest that was legitimised in the era of the 'enterprise culture' and the growth of Thatcherism in the 1980s (Keenoy and Anthony, 1992). Around this time performance-related pay became popular and it is clearly linked to the enterprise culture.

In a PRP culture the aim is to make employees more like entrepreneurs, i.e. people who earn a direct return on the value they create (Kanter, 1987). This approach to reward would fit into the category of hard HRM referred to earlier in the book, as it assumes that people are motivated by economic self-interest. However, PRP is subtler than this; it can also include 'goal setting' referred to in the previous section. As the goals set can be qualitative as well as quantitative, the issue of quality is addressed (Guest, 1989).

Lawler (1991) maintains that traditional reward systems (e.g. time rates) tend to motivate a large number of people to climb the organisational hierarchy. This arises when rewards are given as a result of progressing within salary grades and scales. But given the advent of flatter organisational structures and flexible work designs – developments that receive the HRM seal of approval – skill-based pay would appear to be more appropriate than traditional reward systems. Skill-based pay is a reward system that credits individuals in a way that benefits the organisation in terms of goal attainment. It is congruent with the aim of HRM to invest in human assets, and it tries to promote flexibility by ensuring that employees are equipped to carry out a variety of tasks. There is also an element of trust involved: given the acquisition of the right blend of skills there is the expectation that employees will motivate themselves to perform to a high standard, though this may have to be complemented by good management. Overall, it is compatible with soft HRM.

■ Conclusions

There is evidence to indicate that British companies are continually preoccupied with pay systems, with change in reward systems being very common (Goodhart, 1994). A number of large companies have been using a third version of performance-related pay since the early 1980s, with bonus schemes and share options for senior executives in a constant state of overhaul and revision. Now there is a more sober and realistic view of what a reward system can achieve than was the case in the 1980s. The view that a company's success rests principally on adopting state-of-the-art pay systems is now considered too simplistic. This is not surprising, because motivation is a complex phenomenon and designing and managing pay systems is a most difficult task.

There appears to be a tendency to address a number of operational issues, such as the tension between individual performance and group commitment in performance-related pay. The delicate connection between performance appraisal and PRP has given rise to experimentation with appraisal techniques, such as assessment by colleagues. Apparently some companies justify their attachment to performance-related pay in order to prevent them giving increases in pay to inadequate or poor performers. Progress is being made in developing skill-based pay and gain sharing. The latter are incentive schemes that give employees who are responsible for initiating specific improvements a return for their contribution. A number of institutional investors would like to see advances in the determination of executive pay, in particular more realistic share option schemes.

The system of 'national rates' for employees is being challenged, and there is a movement away from pay systems that reward managers for loyalty expressed as commitment in terms of length of service, towards rewarding managers on the basis of individual performance and company performance in order to cultivate loyalty. Linking rewards to the success of the enterprise was considered a sensible way to proceed, as it was likely to promote commitment. There is a danger that the commitment of a number of employees could be undermined because of significant income inequality within the company. The weakened state of national bargaining pay systems has resulted in the centralisation of greater power in the hands of top management in matters connected with pay determination. Regrettably, it appears that members of top management have been overgenerous in awarding themselves pay increases at a time when pay restraint is advocated for most employees.

As organisations increasingly operate on an international scale there is a need for consideration of how best to manage rewards internationally. Alternative approaches can be adopted that are focused either on the systems of the country of origin or on localised variation in the approach to rewards. There is some pressure towards localisation, particularly in view of the differences in trends that are discernible in international comparative studies. In addition, we might expect differences in motivation in divergent cultures. In particular, the impacts of expectancy theory will relate to what is valued by the employees, and what is regarded as being of value will vary with culture.

Finally, an unexpected verdict from Professor John Purcell in a recent 'Rewards Debate' should be noted. He stated that reward management interventions do more harm than good in building trust, commitment and motivation (Purcell and Brown, 2000). The reasons behind this statement are that linking pay to business objectives and cascading this down through the organisation may sound like an attractive option for increasing commitment amongst employees, but it contains a contradiction. Not only does it perpetrate the illusion that companies are rational, top-down, directed organisations (rather than being involved in fast and messy change), it also assumes that people need incentives to work in an acceptable way; in other words, they cannot be trusted to work effectively without such a control mechanism. This is a contradiction because as we have seen mutual trust is at the heart of high commitment management (see Chapters 1 and 2). Additionally, according to Purcell, research evidence in the United Kingdom has consistently failed to show a link between individual PRP and performance.

Taking the counter view in the debate, Duncan Brown argues that while reward schemes may not be perfect it is better to intervene than do nothing. Reward schemes cannot, on their own, change culture, motivation and behaviour, but where they are part of an overall HRM strategy, including effective communication and performance management, they can make a contribution to performance. At least, it may be possible to identify and remove what are perceived as barriers to performance where reward schemes encourage focus on inappropriate activities (Purcell and Brown, 2000).

The debate is as yet unsettled, and given the complex web of factors and outcomes in the arena of reward, motivation and performance, it is likely to be ongoing.

References

Adams, J.S. (1963) 'Towards an understanding of inequity', *Journal of Abnormal and Social Psychology*, 67, 422–36.

Applebaum, S. and Shappiro, B. (1991) 'Pay for performance: implementation of individual and group plans', *Journal of Management Development*, 10, 30–40.

Armstrong, M. (1999) *A Handbook of Human Resource Management Practice*, 7th edn, London: Kogan Page.

Armstrong, M. and Murlis, H. (1994) *Reward Management*, 2nd edn, London: Kogan Page.

Cannell, M. and Long, P. (1991) 'What's changed about incentive pay?', *Personnel Management*, October, 58–63.

Cowling, A. and James, P. (1994) *The Essence of Personnel Management and Industrial Relations*, Hemel Hempstead: Prentice Hall.

Department of Employment (1975) (Report), 'Making work more satisfying', London: HMSO.

Department of Trade and Industry (1999) 'A detailed guide to the national minimum wage', London: DTI.

Donkin, R. (1994) 'An option on perks (flexible remuneration systems)', *Financial Times*, 6 April, 16.

Donkin, R. (1998) 'Reward for know-how', *Financial Times*, Recruitment Section, 24 July, 1.

Dowling, P.J., Schuler, R.S. and Welch, D.E. (1994) *International Dimensions of Human Resource Management*, 2nd edn, Belmont, CA: Wadsworth.

Fillela, J. and Hegewisch, A. (1994) 'European experiments with pay and benefits', in Brewster, C. and Hegewisch, A. (eds), *Policy and Practice in European Human Resource Management: The Price Waterhouse/Cranfield Survey*, London: Routledge.

Financial Times (1995) Editorial comment, 13 February, 17.

Financial Times (1999) Editorial comment, 21 August.

Fisher, J. (2001) 'How to design incentive schemes', *People Management*, 7 (1), 38–9.

Fitzgerald, N. (1997) 'Incentive plans under fire', *The Sunday Times* (Business Section), 25 May, 31.

Freeman, R. (2001) 'Upping the stakes', *People Management*, 7 (3), 25–9.

Goodhart, D. (1994) 'In search of wages that work', *Financial Times*, 27 June, 16.

Goss, D. (1994) *Principles of Human Resource Management*, London: Routledge.

Guest, D. (1989) 'Personnel and HRM: can you tell the difference?', *Personnel Management*, January, 48–51.

Hackman, J.R. (1977) 'Work design', in Hackman, J.R. and Suttle, J.L. (eds), *Improving Life at Work*, Santa Monica, CA: Scott Foresman.

Halligan, L. (1997) 'Performance-related pay attacked', *Financial Times*, 10 June, 8.

Harrison, D. (2001) 'Flexible pay deals: Pick-and-mix benefits keep staff sweet', *Financial Times*, 28 March, 18.

Herzberg, F. (1966) *Work and the Nature of Man*, London: Staples Press.

Hollinshead, G. and Leat, M. (1995) *Human Resource Management: An international and comparative perspective*, London: Pitman.

Huddart, G. (1994) 'UNISYS links rises to personal skills', *Personnel Today*, 17 May, 1.

IDS (1991) *DIY Benefits for the 1990s*, IDS Study no. 481, May, London: Income Data Services.

IDS (1992) Skilling Up. IDS Study no. 500, February, London: Income Data Services.

IRS (1991) *Employment Trends 495*, BT managers hostile to PRP, September.

Kanter, R.M. (1987) 'The attack on pay', *Harvard Business Review*, March–April 111–17.

Keenoy, T. and Anthony, P. (1992) 'Human resource management: metaphor, meaning, and morality', in Blyton, P. and Turnbull, P. (eds), *Reassessing Human Resource Management*, London: Sage.

Kellaway, L. (1993) 'Nice little earner (profit-related pay)', *Financial Times*, 23 April, 14.

Kohn, A. (1993) 'Why incentive plans cannot work', *Harvard Business Review*, September/October, 54–63.

Lawler, E. (1991) 'Paying the person: a better approach to management', *Human Resource Management Review*, 1, 145–54.

Lawler, E.E., Ledford, G.E. and Chang, L. (1993) 'Who uses skill-based pay and why?', *Compensation and Benefits Review*, March/April, 22.

Locke, E.A. and Latham, G.P. (1990) *A Theory of Goal Setting and Task Performance*, London: Prentice Hall.

Lundy, O. and Cowling, A. (1996) *Strategic Human Resource Management*, London: Routledge.

Maitland, A. (1998) 'Benefits all round, thanks to flexible work options', *Financial Times*, 21 April, 22.

Maslow, A. (1954) *Motivation and Personality*, New York: Harper & Row.

Mayo, E. (1949) *The Social Problems of an Industrial Civilization*, London: Routledge & Kegan Paul.

Murlis, H. (1994) 'The challenge of rewarding teamwork', *Personnel Management*, February, 8.

Murlis, H. and Fitt, D. (1991) 'Job evaluation in a changing world', *Personnel Management*, May, 39–44.

Nakamoto, M. (1998) 'Performance begins to win a wider audience', *Financial Times*, 22 December, 12.

Newman, C. (2001) 'Imbalance of Payments', *People Management*, 7 (2), 18–19.

North, S.J. (1993) 'IBM trims pay grades in salary shake-up', *Personnel Today*, 9 November, 1.

North, S.J. (1994) 'IBM hives off its payroll services', *Personnel Today*, 31 May, 2.

Nusbaum, A. (1999) 'Salarymen's fat bonus goes west', *Financial Times*, 20 January, 14.

Oldfield, C. (1999) 'Minimum wage to force job cuts', *The Sunday Times*, 21 March.

Paul, W.J. and Robertson, K.B. (1970) *Job Enrichment and Employee Motivation*, Epping: Gower Press.

Pearce, J. (1991) 'Why merit pay doesn't work', in Steer, R. and Porter, L. (eds), *Motivation and Work Behaviour*, New York: McGraw-Hill.

Pickard, J. (1993) 'How incentives can drive teamworking', *Personnel Management*, September, 26–32.

Porter, L.W. and Lawler, E.E. (1968) *Managerial Attitudes and Performance*, Homewood, IL: R.D. Irwin.

Purcell, J. and Brown, D. (2000) 'Pay per view: reward debate', *People Management*, 6 (3), 41–3.

Robertson, J., Smith, M. and Cooper, D. (1992) *Motivation: Strategies, theory and practice*, 2nd edn, Hemel Hempstead: Prentice Hall

Taylor, F.W. (1947) *Scientific Management*, New York: Harper & Row.

Taylor, R. (1994) 'Must try harder', *Financial Times*, 2 February, 9.

Taylor, R. (1999) 'Both sides of industry anxious on minimum wage', *Financial Times*, 29 March.

Taylor, R. (2000) 'Minimum wage is being exceeded', *Financial Times*, 27 November, 4.

Thierry, H. (1992) 'Pay and payment systems', in Hartley, J. and Stephenson, G. (eds), *Employee Relations*, Oxford: Blackwell.

Thompson, M. (1993) 'Pay and performance 2: the employee's experience', *Personnel Management Plus*, November, 2.

Trevor, G. (1993) 'Pearl Assurance', *Personnel Management Plus*, November, 13.

Vroom, V. (1964) *Work and Motivation*, New York: John Wiley.

Wickens, P. (1987) *The Road to Nissan: Flexibility, quality, teamwork*, Basingstoke: Macmillan.

Woodley, C. (1993) 'The benefits of flexibility', *Personnel Management*, May, 36–9.

Chapter 10

Employee development: training and development

If employees are to behave flexibly and effectively they need to acquire and develop knowledge and skills. If employees are to believe that they are valued by the organisation they need to see visible signs that the company has taken their training needs seriously. Training and development are the processes of investing in people so that they are equipped to perform; these processes are part of an overall HRM approach that hopefully will result in people being motivated to perform.

Having read this chapter, you should:

- understand the importance of training and development from a strategic perspective;
- have knowledge of the national training and development scene in the UK;
- be able to identify the key features of management development and career management;
- be able to distinguish the various approaches to training and development, and know the advantages and disadvantages of the alternative options;
- understand the methods of evaluating training and development;
- be aware of the key issues when training employees for international assignments;
- be aware of some of the international comparisons in training and development.

The training and development of employees has become a topic of increased focus for a number of reasons. First, distinctive knowledge has been recognised as a key competence in many organisations, and some see becoming a 'learning organisation' as a process that will enable them to achieve competitive advantage over their rivals. Secondly, change is endemic in many industries, and this may require employees to exercise new skills and to have a positive attitude to change. Thirdly, it is thought that companies whose employees are able to problem solve, understand and react effectively to customers will be able to enhance the perceived quality of their services. Effective training and development underlie achievements in each of these areas.

Training and development are terms that are sometimes used interchangeably. Traditionally development was seen as an activity normally associated with managers with the future firmly in mind. By contrast, training has a more immediate concern and has been associated with improving the knowledge and skill of non-managerial employees in their present jobs. Such a distinction could be considered too simplistic in an era characterised by developments in HRM, because nowadays development of all employees is considered crucial. Such development would be reflected in a commitment to multi-skilling and a flexible mode of operation. There is also the recognition that the human resource is valuable and must be developed if the organisation is to hold on to staff and retain their commitment while they are at work. One should bear in mind that even managers need to be trained in the here and now, because they need current operational skills or competences quite apart from the qualities (e.g. creativity, synthesis, abstract reasoning, personal development) associated with management development.

From what has been said it would be sensible to regard training and development as interactive, each complementing the other. Finally, the logical step is for the organisation to produce a plan for human resource development (i.e. training and development) which will dovetail into the employee resourcing plan (i.e. selection) and the organisation's overall strategic plan. As Keep (1992) points out, training and development of employees is not an option, it is an intrinsic part of the practice of HRM and is an investment in people.

■ Systematic training

In the 1960s training received a fillip with the establishment of the Industrial Training Boards in the United Kingdom. The emphasis was on the acquisition of behavioural skills and what a training programme could achieve. This is referred to as systematic training and it put emphasis on off-the-job training as opposed to the then popular method of 'sitting next to Nellie'. Quite simply a systematic approach would start with a definition of the training needs of employees, that is the attitude, knowledge, skills and behaviour required by the employee in order to do the job adequately. Next the required training necessary to satisfy these needs is put in motion using suitable trainers, and finally there is an evaluation of the training undertaken in order to ensure it is effective.

A more comprehensive description of the training process, according to Armstrong (1992), is the concept of planned training. Planned training is a deliberate intervention designed to bring about the necessary learning to improve performance on the job (Kenney and Reid, 1988), and it includes the following points. Apart from the issues raised above with respect to systematic training, there is reference to the importance of setting training objectives (i.e. what the trainee should be capable of doing after the training course has been completed) and the planning of the training programme, using the right combination of training techniques and locations, in order to achieve the training objectives.

Above the importance of the assessment of training needs was briefly stated. This could be executed on at least three levels, namely organisational analysis, task analysis and person analysis. At the organisational level there is an emphasis on the identification of deficiencies (e.g. poor financial control within the company) that could be remedied by training. Also, at this level the importance of mobilising training so it is congruent with the achievement of corporate objectives is considered important. Here the needs of the organisation are paramount, though the needs of the individual employee could be satisfied indirectly. It would be functional to stress the importance of training in contemporary organisations in order to create a more flexible, committed and loyal labour force, as well as equipping employees with skills so that they can secure another job if their services are no longer required.

Example 10.1 shows how a small engineering firm responded to a major threat to its continued existence by adopting a developmental approach. It has subsequently reaped the benefits, and has not only survived but has moved from a loss-making position in 1996 to one of profit in 2000, with a 150 per cent increase in turnover.

EXAMPLE 10.1

Development at Hindle Power

Hindle Power was a family-owned engineering firm, employing 32 people. Most of its business (75 per cent) came from its contract with Perkins Engines to sell, customise and service their engines in machinery ranging from forklift trucks to crop-sprayers. In 1996 Perkins gave warning that Hindle Power, along with other distributors, would have to meet tougher customer service targets or face having the contract terminated. This provided the impetus for a culture change in which training was featured prominently.

Staff were given considerable scope to determine their own training needs through a new appraisal system, which was designed to help people clarify their career goals. Every employee was able to take up to 26 days training per year, and some made radical moves in their careers as a result. A service manager, for example, having studied for a qualification in business management became a parts manager, in charge of stock control, and his performance is enhanced by his understanding of other parts of the business. In another case a sales manager is currently studying for a science degree. Most people, however, volunteered for training that was directly relevant to their work roles. There was an emphasis on the following areas: business management, customer care, IT skills and induction. Some of the training was formal and involved attendance on courses that offered qualifications. Other approaches were less formal, for example suppliers were invited to run product awareness programmes for staff. As a direct result of training and development 10 of the staff have either been promoted or moved to new posts.

Hindle Power also opened its doors to student interns, and as a result of playing host to marketing undergraduates it developed a database of all its customers and potential users. A survey showed that while 90 per cent of the potential customers had heard of Hindle Power only 40 per cent had purchased any services. Customer care training improved the staff's ability to provide written quotations, and reminders were sent out to add antifreeze to engines. Subsequent to these profile-raising activities, 60 per cent of the potential market became customers.

The employees are now better placed to expand the customer base, and to ensure that existing customers are happy with the level of service. As one put it: 'processes such as problem solving have a real use – I certainly work with more confidence now'. Performance briefings and monthly financial reports have become a normal part of the operation of the business, and the company has gained IIP (Investors in People) accreditation.

By 2000 the workforce had expanded to 49 people, turnover had grown from £6m in 1996 to £15m, and a situation of making losses and being in danger of going out of business had been turned into one of greater security, growth and profit. Business has expanded and a new franchise to sell engine control products for the company Morse has been set up. Additionally, Hindle Power has become Perkins' first UK distributor to sell parts in China. Such developments require a workforce that is adaptable and people who are problem solvers.

Rarely has the link between training and the bottom line been so clear.

(Littlefield, 2000)

At the level of task analysis a first step is to establish that jobs are necessary in the light of corporate objectives. Having established that the jobs are necessary the next step is to identify the necessary patterns of behaviour that are critical for effective performance in the job. The pattern of behaviour would normally include the expression of knowledge, ability, attitudes and competences that are required to do the job successfully. Finally, the third level – person analysis – puts the spotlight on employees needing training. This information could be gleaned from, for example, the records relating to the outcome of the selection and performance appraisal processes and leads to specifying the most appropriate form of training

■ Competition and change

Competitive conditions facing an organisation can lead to changes in working practices, habits, cultures and the redesign of work. To prepare employees for such an eventuality, we can resort to training with the emphasis on development to maintain or enhance the quality of the operations and output. Nowadays words such as flexibility and teamwork enter the organisational vocabulary when talking about change, as we saw in Chapter 4. To promote the cause of teamworking requires training of the team and developing multi-skills so that members can do different tasks within the team. Also, the team leader should be trained in leadership skills.

At the Nissan car factory at Sunderland in the United Kingdom there is a commitment to the development of effective teams, with much authority delegated to team leaders. Nissan identifies a level of competence for each skill and expects employees to master the operations and eventually be able to train others as well. At Lucas (a parts supplier for the motor industry, now part of the US company TRW Inc.) in the United Kingdom there has been an elaborate scheme to provide employees with the capacity to handle change. Multi-disciplinary task forces were created and given training to cope with work redesign, product quality and issues connected with marketing the product and how to improve the service received from suppliers. In addition, a cultural shift took place when the central training function moved from a preoccupation with the delivery of training to 'training development' and took an active interest in promoting open learning centres and a variety of courses (Storey, 1992).

Although top management at Lucas backed the above scheme those further down the hierarchy, such as middle managers and shopfloor workers, did not experience training and development to the extent anticipated. To them what came across was a work environment characterised by pressure and the cutting of costs. This is an example of where employees further down the organisational hierarchy do not share the degree of commitment and enthusiasm held by top management intent on shaping the company's training culture.

In recent years there have been a number of internal and external initiatives in training following developments aimed at improving the competitive advantage of organisations. The major ones that will be examined in this section are training to underpin management processes, such as total quality management, and national schemes to set standards of competencies for all industries.

Quality management

Quality management, and particularly approaches such as total quality management, already considered in Chapter 5 in connection with changing culture, elevates to a position of significant importance the process of improvements in business operations and output. The final judge of its effectiveness will be the customer in the market. Those responsible for quality improvements and TQM will try to ensure that quality pervades all organisational activities. It is the task of every function and every employee to contribute to activities connected with improvements, and quality systems and a quality culture are essential prerequisites (Hill, 1991). Training is at the service of quality improvement programmes by developing employee skills to cope with change, as well as imparting an understanding of quality monitoring techniques.

At Michelin a training programme was mounted to support a quality improvement initiative and this was aimed at improving existing knowledge and skills, and teaching new skills, as well as knowledge of the inspection process. The company tested the trainees on what they absorbed during the training programme and the outcome of this exercise showed that quality improvements had taken place. As a result, skill-based pay was introduced to reflect the new responsibilities (IRS, 1992). In Chapter 8 skill-based pay was discussed as a reward for the acquisition of skills; in effect pay is linked to some extent to the successful completion of authorised training. This is an attempt to underline the importance of training as an aspect of corporate strategy.

National schemes

There have been criticisms over the years of Britain's poor record in education and training. The education system is criticised for not appealing to large numbers of 18-year-olds, who finish their education earlier than many students from some neighbouring countries, and for not providing an educational experience compatible with the needs of industry. Employers have also been criticised for the lack of investment in training. At the national level these criticisms have been taken on board.

The government felt that previous training initiatives (e.g. the Training Boards referred to earlier) failed because they were both too bureaucratic and too centralised. A preferred alternative in the 1990s was to decentralise responsibility for training, making sure that there was participation of industry and commerce in the scheme. Training and Enterprise Councils (TECs) and their Scottish equivalent were set up as the hub of local initiatives. TECs were allocated government funds, which they control, but they are allowed to raise private funds as well. The majority of the membership of a TEC is from commerce and industry; the rest comes from the field of education and training, trade unions and voluntary organisations.

When a TEC makes an assessment of local labour markets it is normally concerned with the potential for economic growth and the level of skill shortages. Business plans, which include overall objectives, targets amenable to measurement and evaluation techniques, are prepared and submitted to the appropriate section of the Department of Employment. Subsequently the TEC receives funds in relation to the plan and previous levels of performance. The funds are used to provide training opportunities for the unemployed, and to advise employers on the assessment of training needs, training techniques and the resourcing of training. The TEC also encourages employers with a common training need to pool their resources to provide training facilities in circumstances where the provision of an appropriate training facility would be too costly for an individual employer. The TEC encourages enterprise initiatives by allocating pump priming funds for approved new ventures. Recently the UK government stated its intention to abolish TECs and replace them with a national skills and learning body, which will give local skills and learning councils the job of coordinating and funding all work-related further education and training (Pike, 1999). It would appear that employers would have less influence under the proposed new system, which is described later in this chapter.

Some time ago the government took a particular initiative in the field of training by setting up a national framework – National Vocational Qualifications (NVQs) – that linked the provision of training in a direct way to skills used in jobs. NVQs were designed to set occupationally based standards, to recognise competence in the workplace and to provide a ladder of achievement. On offer are competency-based qualifications applicable to jobs at all levels within organisations across all industries. The qualifications can be acquired by employees while they are engaged in normal job activities at their place of work. The actual training would be monitored by an accredited tester, normally a manager or supervisor, who is qualified to act in this way. The employee should be able to demonstrate performance that can be assessed. If the employee has met the standard required at a particular level in the NVQ hierarchy a pass grade is given. If the employee does not meet the standards required this signifies a fail and indicates a training need. The NVQs give employees scope to go on developing their skills and experience and hopefully the overall experience will advance the mobility of labour between employers.

Already reference has been made to 'competency'. This is a term used in preference to knowledge and skills on the understanding that competence, unlike the former, has a better relationship with improved performance. The jury is still out on this one! The Training Agency defined competence as 'the ability to perform the activities within an occupation or function to the standards expected in employment'. This definition would include the ability to transfer knowledge and skills to new situations within employment, and takes on board activities such as organising and planning, creative and innovative pursuits, tolerance for handling non-programmed situations, and interpersonal skills used in liaising with fellow workers and clients. Example 10.2 illustrates the use of the 'competency' approach in a training and development context.

EXAMPLE 10.2

Human resource development at Malin Manufacturing Services (MMS)

MMS manufactures pharmaceutical products, which are sold on prescription. The company's mission statement reveals an intention to produce medicines of the highest quality for the benefit of society. To realise the corporate objectives that flow from such a mission statement would require highly skilled and adaptable employees capable of contributing to the success of the company operating in a rapidly changing technical and market environment.

A number of important changes took place in MMS during the early 1990s. There was a delayering initiative in which the number of layers of organisation was reduced, autonomous business units within the organisation were established, a team approach to working was introduced, and there was a shift in attitudes and practices in the area of human resources, where now the importance of the 'bottom line' in the thinking of employees, and organisational flexibility, are heavily underlined.

It was felt that that there should be greater objectivity in the employee development process. Hence use was made of assessment centres, which were discussed as a selection technique in Chapter 7. They have become popular as a mechanism for development-related purposes, but in this context they are referred to as development centres (Industrial Society, 1996). The assessments were made with reference to 12 competences, and where a need for development was diagnosed appropriate development programmes were provided. But in some cases, where there was a failure to meet the criteria, people were made redundant or redeployed.

Competences were also used at the stage of setting learning objectives for employees. These are raised and discussed at the performance appraisal sessions, and training is offered to help correct the deficiency between the current and desired level of competency. Given the importance of flexibility within teams it is necessary for employees to be multi-skilled. To this end training is provided for new recruits and existing employees. In fact the reward system is mobilised to assist with the acquisition of skills, because pay awards are given to employees who have acquired new skills. Overall there is a firm commitment on the part of the organisation to continuous improvement amongst employees.

(Harrison, 1992)

In this case the company's strategy for training and development is connected to the corporate strategy via HRM, and you will notice that an emphasis is placed on the value of appropriate competences for bringing about organisational success in the future. Also, the competency approach is used at different stages – at the assessment of training needs, the setting of learning objectives and the evaluation of training – and the company values the notion of continuous development.

Reservations have been expressed about the competency approach in the sense that it is considered too restrictive. Doubts have also been expressed about whether increasing individual competences enhances organisational performance, that the focus is on discrete areas of a job and not generalised ability in relation to a whole job, and that too little attention is given to the complexity of the process of skill acquisition and the transfer of skills for the benefit of the organisation (Holmes, 1990). There is also the view that the competency approach does not consider management style, bureaucratic structure, corporate culture, the environment, career patterns and personal learning abilities. These factors were identified as being necessary to operate a sound training programme (Training Agency, 1989). The above criticisms are likely to be too harsh when the advanced stages of the NVQ are considered where management training takes place; the earlier stages would focus on operative training and perhaps the criticisms are more valid at this level.

In recent years there appeared to be some unease about the lack of attention to the general skills of numeracy and literacy. There is no requirement for general literacy and numeracy skills to be developed to gain an NVQ award (Steedman, 1998). Therefore, it would be beneficial to have incorporated within the NVQ framework the literacy and numeracy skills currently outside it; this could have the effect of motivating a number of adults low in literacy and numeracy to rectify a deficiency (see Box 10.1).

A national UK initiative, administered through the TECs, is the investors in people scheme. This attempts to relate training and development to business strategy and provides guidance to companies on how to develop their training programmes to nationally recognised standards. The key issue is the adequacy and relevancy of the company's training requirements in the light of business strategy. The IIP is not too interested in detailed prescriptions on the contents of training programmes, and it is not essential to link training to the NVQ scheme. The IIP national standard embraces the following principles (Goss, 1994):

1 There is a commitment by top management to the development of all employees in order to achieve corporate objectives. This will necessitate the preparation of a written but flexible business plan and there will be an indication of how employees will achieve it.
2 There will be regular reviews of the training and development needs of all employees.
3 There will be a specification of the resources available for training and those responsible for providing training opportunities will be identified.
4 Training and development start with recruitment and selection and is a live issue

---

BOX 10.1

Learning and Skills Council

The new Learning and Skills Council (LSC) in the United Kingdom, with a strong
business representation, replaces the TECs and the Further Education Funding Council
and is set to carry out a major reform of post-16 skills and education. The LSC will
consist of 47 local councils or subsidiaries, which will enjoy considerable freedom to
reflect local needs; the national council – which will assume real strategic power – will
oversee the work of further education and sixth form colleges, and work-based training
and education.

It has an ambitious plan to spend more than £2.5bn on training and teaching adults,
especially those with poor basic skills needed by industry and those coming from
disadvantaged areas. A priority is to tackle Britain's chronic record in adult illiteracy and
innumeracy. Those with poor reading, numeracy and writing skills would be introduced
to learning via Internet access points in the workplace, libraries and other public areas.
It is hoped that the LSC will act as a regulator for industrial spending on training,
helping to direct and increase the £20bn spent privately by companies and other
employers, and provide quality assurance so that companies could choose effective
training schemes. Under the new system multinational companies will not have to
negotiate with numerous local councils or subsidiaries; instead they can go directly to
the national council. This arrangement is likely to be an improvement on the old
system. Another important activity to be undertaken by LSC would be to gather high
quality intelligence data in the marketplace to enable it to track skills gaps in industry.

(Kelly, 2000)

---

throughout the employee's stay in the company. It is necessary to conduct a regular training needs assessment and to act on the outcome of this process.

5 There will be an evaluation of the investment in training and development to see to what extent progress has been made and whether improvements in organisational effectiveness have taken place.

In order to be recognised by IIP an organisation is required to engage in systematic planning, to audit its training operations to establish if things are going according to plan and, where necessary, to take appropriate corrective action. Trained IIP assessors will visit the company to evaluate the progress made and report on whether or not to offer recognition.

It appears that IIP's interpretation of training and development closely coincides with an HRM perspective in this area. There is no distinction between training and development and there is a recognition that all employees have development potential. Also, training is something that permeates the thinking and behaviour of managers at all levels, it is not something that belongs to the training function in the organisation, and it is relevant to the efficient operation of the company. Such a view, if upheld, could be protective of training in adverse economic situations.

There have been criticisms of IIP by the Confederation of British Industry (CBI) to the effect that the procedures used are overly bureaucratic and the costs of assessment are too high (Hilton, 1992). But more recently the IIP has reviewed its procedures to make them more flexible and less bureaucratic. The intention is that they should be equally applicable to smaller organisations and there have been more favourable comments from employers. In a report based on a three-year government-funded study and produced by the Institute for Employment Studies at the University of Sussex it was stated that IIP was having a positive effect in the workplace (Bolger, 1996). In the report employers were attributing a number of benefits to their involvement with IIP, such as a more systematic and focused approach to training based on business needs, improved employee communications, a better understanding of business amongst employees and higher levels of motivation and skill among the workforce.

■ Management development

Management development is an activity that sets out to ensure that the organisation has the required managerial talent to face the present and future with confidence. It is concerned with improving the performance of existing managers, giving them the scope for personal growth and development, and makes appropriate provision for the future replacement of managers (i.e. management succession). From the late 1980s there has been a substantial increase in management training and development (Storey et al., 1997). Amongst the objectives for a management development scheme are the following:

- Identify managers with potential and ensure they receive the right experience, training and development.
- Set achievable objectives for the improvement of performance that are amenable to measurement, clearly specifying responsibilities.
- Create a climate where serious thought is given to instituting a management succession scheme, which would be kept under regular review.

Sisson and Storey (1988) suggested that the following key organisational issues should be considered before creating a management development strategy to increase managerial effectiveness:

- *Job definition*: strive for exactitude in defining what is expected of managers.
- *Selection*: be thorough in screening new entrants to the organisation with managerial potential to ensure the acquisition of the appropriate 'raw material'.
- *Identification of development needs*: adopt an enlightened appraisal process in order to assess the precise nature of managerial needs.
- *Training or development*: try to achieve a complementary balance between off-the-job training (e.g. management education) and on-the-job development to meet identified needs.

- *Reward systems:* recognise the significance of compensation packages linked to performance, as opposed to the traditional promotion system.

Over a decade ago it was felt that the spirit of the NVQ scheme could be applied to the development of managers through the agency of the Management Charter Initiative (MCI). This initiative was conceived following the publication of various reports in the late 1980s that were critical of the provision of management education and training in the United Kingdom when compared with other countries. There is an attempt to build on the framework provided by the NVQ, and management qualifications (i.e. Certificate, Diploma, Masters) on four levels are on offer to cater for the needs of supervisors, first-line managers, middle managers and senior managers.

A challenge similar to the one levelled at the NVQs is directed at the MCI approach. For example, the practicality of devising a set of standard competences that adequately capture the full complexity of managerial work across different types of organisations and different industries is open to question. Also, there is the fear that the MCI approach is overly bureaucratic (Goss, 1994). Therefore it is not surprising that some companies have developed alternative but flexible approaches; an example of which is the capabilities model developed by Brooke Bond. This integrates knowledge and skills with the softer things such as attitudes and qualities. If such a development were to take off in a big way throughout the world of work it could adversely affect the widespread acceptance of the MCI approach. A number of the approaches to management development are discussed later in the section on approaches to training and development.

Career management

This activity is complementary to management development and is concerned with planning and shaping the path that people take in their career progression within the organisation. It normally applies to managerial staff, but not necessarily so, and follows an assessment of the needs of the organisation for managers and the preferences of employees for development. Assessment centres, discussed in connection with selection in Chapter 7, could be used to identify managerial talent or confirm that it is still in existence.

The underlying assumption of career management is that, in the context of management succession, the organisation should be alert to providing able people with the training, guidance and encouragement to enable them to fulfil their potential. This view is not shared by all organisations, which would take in 'fresh blood' as and when needed and do not subscribe to elaborate internal promotion policies. Another view is to promote competent people who have proved themselves in their current jobs to higher positions when the opportunity arises. But progressive companies are likely to take a considered, long-term view when they set in motion sophisticated reviews of employee performance and potential and plan job moves on the basis of the outcome of these processes. In this sense a preoccupation with current performance and effectiveness can go hand in hand with considerations regarding future career moves.

It should be noted that the upward and onward view of a career is not always compatible with organisational settings characterised by leaner and fitter companies with fewer promotion opportunities. These issues were discussed in Chapter 6 on human resource planning. With a decreasing number of rungs on the career ladder the reality of the career plateau will face many people earlier than was the case in the past. On the basis of research conducted in the UK finance sector, Herriot and Pemberton (1995) describe the following career development alternatives to promotion, as perceived by managers, but that are not mutually exclusive:

- *Career flexers*: These tend to be young ambitious managers who move about and are likely to accept a variety of interesting jobs.
- *Ambitious careerists*: These managers tend to be confident about their capacity to evolve to higher positions, and are optimistic about the future in this respect. This disposition seems to be more pronounced when they are younger and have spent little time in their existing or previous jobs.
- *Career disengagers*: These managers are more likely to be older employees who are no longer ambitious or find their work interesting, possibly expecting to be made redundant or being able to avail themselves of an early retirement scheme, though they could be found in younger age groups. They would like to cease working full time either abruptly or gradually.
- *Career lifers*: These managers tend to be older and recognise that advancement is a thing of the past, but are overjoyed when told that they can stay on until retirement. They would welcome a loyalty bonus.

Organisations should recognise the variety of career aspirations of managers, including those listed above, and accept the challenge of recasting the traditional career structure and removing the stigma attached to the plateau. Finally, even though the notion of a career for life in an organisation is becoming more remote, this does not absolve employers from commitment to providing career paths for able employees (Herriot, 1992). Herriot maintains that only those organisations that negotiate careers will retain the people they need to face the future with confidence.

■ Approaches to training and development

A large number of methods are available to the organisation when it is considering the training and development of both managerial and non-managerial staff. To start with we shall examine job-related experiences, such as demonstration, coaching, mentoring and job rotation/enlargement/enrichment. Later the emphasis is on formal training methods, self-development (e.g. action learning) and outdoor courses.

Sitting by Nellie (demonstration)

The trainee is shown how to do the job by an experienced member of staff and is then allowed to get on with it. The advantage of this method is that learning is directly related to the job. The disadvantages are that the experienced member of staff (who may not be a training expert) may have difficulty explaining things and empathising with the trainee, and mistakes made by the trainee could be costly. Also, this method does not provide for the creation of structure in the learning process, neither does it provide appropriate feedback, which is required to improve effective performance.

Coaching

This could be considered an improved version of demonstration and has the advantage of interaction between the trainer and trainee. It has key ingredients not associated with demonstration, such as structure, feedback and motivation. The immediate supervisor or close colleagues normally provide advice and feedback about aspects of the performance of employees. Coaching is predominantly about showing people how to apply knowledge they already possess, and it can be particularly useful in generating ideas and getting people involved in the management of change. Coaches set challenging tasks, carry out appraisals, monitor progress and counsel and prepare people for promotion (Conway, 1994). When coaching is used with senior staff it could be geared to the development of soft skills (e.g. self-awareness, greater understanding of interpersonal processes, flexibility and conceptual thinking) so as to complement the more technical skills developed through other forms of training (O'Reilly, 1998).

Mentoring

This is a method of on-the-job training, particularly for aspiring senior managers, which appears to be growing in importance. It normally arises when senior organisational members take responsibility for the development and progression of selected individuals. The trainee (mentoree or protégé) observes the skills displayed by the mentor, usually a senior manager who is not their boss, and copies and adopts the senior manager's behaviour. The mentor provides support and help in the various assignments undertaken by the protégé and can provide an invaluable insight into the politics and culture of the organisation. The protégé can benefit from the continuous dialogue with the mentor who, if influential within the organisation, can exert much influence in securing interesting tasks for the protégé as well as opening windows of opportunities. As a result the mentor contributes to confidence building and the career development of the protégé and provides him or her with a useful informal network within the organisation. Recently the significance of the mentoring system in a corporate culture sense has been underlined. It is said that it provides a channel through which core organisational values and meanings are conveyed and fortified by mentors of the status of senior managers at the twilight of their careers, and absorbed by those who will eventually succeed them (Collin, 1992). The characteristics one would expect to find in a mentor are summarised in Table 10.1.

Table 10.1 Characteristics of a mentor

- The relationship between the mentor and the protégé tends to be open ended with less immediate concern for attaining goals than you would expect to find in situations where a boss sets targets for a subordinate. It is a protected relationship in which learning, experimentation and risk taking can occur and potential skills are developed with outcomes expressed as competencies.
- The mentor is knowledgeable, has the ability to place issues in a broader context, helps the protégé to analyse and understand social interactions at work, has high status and a strong power base in the organisation.
- The mentor is a good listener, is well able to empathise with the protégé, is able to relate well to people and establish rapport with the protégé (which is often based on shared interests) and is willing to use their power to influence events. The mentor should avoid encouraging an over-dependent relationship and recognise the boundaries of his or her capacity to help.
- The mentor is involved and willing to share their expertise with the protégé and promote the latter's self-development, and does not feel threatened by the protégé's potential for equalling or surpassing them in status.
- The mentor has a commitment to developing others, having a genuine interest and pleasure in the protégé's achievements.
- The mentor is willing to challenge, where appropriate, the ideas and judgements of the protégé in order to force a re-examination of the issues, and in the process is providing good feedback. Constructive criticism is just as important as encouragement.

Source: Clutterbuck (2001); McKenna (2000)

Those who have received good mentoring early in their careers are likely to experience certain advantages, such as accelerated promotions, improved income and satisfaction with their careers. However, we must be mindful of its negative aspects, which could be listed as follows (Bell, 1998; Goss, 1994):

- There may be charges of elitism from those who were denied protégé status.
- There may be a certain incompatibility between the mentor and the protégé.
- The protégé may be over-dependent on the mentor.
- The mentor may show an inability to manage the relationship effectively. For example, the mentor lacks the appropriate interpersonal skills, is too patronising, is too interventionist, and is inclined to lavish too much praise.
- Generally, line managers are suspicious of the process and display resistance and lack of cooperation because of its disruptive effect on reporting relationships already established.

The role of the mentor is changing (Bell, 1998). The hierarchical nature of mentoring is changing in the sense that it is no longer necessary for the ideal mentor to be a senior executive. Mentoring could also be conducted long-distance where there is a significant geographical space between the parties, and it can last for a short time as opposed to continuing over a long period of time.

Job rotation

This involves moving people around on a systematic basis in order to broaden their experience. The advantages of this method are that links between departments are fostered, and employees develop flexibility because of the range of activities undertaken. However, a disadvantage is that it does not offer people the opportunity to practise the complete range of skills because of the limited time spent on any one job. Also, a problem could arise when errors materialise because of the inexperience of the transferred employee, and when managers nominate poor performers for the job rotation scheme.

Other job-related experiences

Apart from job rotation, job enlargement could be used to broaden the job experience of the employee. Job enlargement expands a job on a horizontal basis, as opposed to a vertical basis found in job enrichment, which was discussed in the previous chapter. Diversity is promoted by increasing the number of tasks an employee performs. For example, a word processor operator's job could be enlarged to include tasks such as acting as a receptionist periodically and doing some filing. Job enlargement, along with participating in the work of a project team or task group, could be a useful developmental exercise.

Formal training methods

Amongst the methods used are lectures and discussions, together with case studies, role playing and simulation, and programmed learning. Case studies make use of predetermined situations to provide opportunities for the analysis of data and the presentation of solutions without the risks of failure associated with real-world situations. Role playing and simulation offers the trainee the opportunity to perform in situations as if they were real, as in, for example, the training of airline pilots. Programmed learning with the aid of the computer can be used to test knowledge and ability at a basic level to begin with, progressing to more difficult tasks later.

Formal training can take place off the job. There could be long college courses that cater for the overall development of the employee, but are not specifically targeted to the job. This gives the employee the opportunity to think afresh and to meet people with different experiences outside the job. Nowadays open learning courses have become popular. The learner proceeds at their own pace with the help of a pack of course material, but unless certain measures are taken (e.g. provision of tutorial support) the learner can feel somewhat isolated.

There are also short courses. Although certain of these are general in nature, others are specifically targeted to satisfy an organisational need. Formal courses can be expensive, and there is no guarantee that learning is transferred to the work situation. Supporters of on-the-job training would argue that learning on the job is more likely to find its way into work practices.

Self-development

In self-development control and direction are primarily in the hands of the individual, with a focus on learning from experience. This approach does not have to be unstructured experience tantamount to a process of trial and error, with an intention to steer clear of past mistakes. It can be structured with an agreement between interested parties at the workplace on the best way to make it operational; this could include guided reading and specified work activities.

An influential theorist in the field of self-development is Kolb (1985). The learning cycle he postulated is as follows:

1 The individual has a concrete experience, either planned or unplanned.
2 Next there is reflective observation, and this amounts to thinking about what was responsible for the experience and the implications, etc.
3 Abstract conceptualisation and generalisation follow where general principles can be drawn from the experience or incident.
4. The final step is experimentation in new situations, and this forms the basis for the development of new experiences.

The application of the learning cycle would necessitate managers diagnosing the work situations they encounter, evaluating the avenues open to them and finally formulating a strategy to attain their objectives. Ideally a programme of self-development will bear some relationship to career development for managerial staff and both could be linked to organisational needs as gleaned from corporate plans. It would appear that any good system of management development based on self-development must prepare managers to exercise control of events and to take responsibility for outcomes within their domain, and particularly control over their own actions and learning (Pedlar *et al.*, 1988).

Action learning

The basic ingredients of self-development are ingrained in action learning, but in addition it has a social dimension. Basically, the trainee relies heavily on experience of what happens at work and adopts questioning and exploration in a group setting as a mode of operation (Revans, 1971). In action learning the spotlight is on real problems, where the learner or trainee questions the causes of these problems. This is followed by generating solutions that are capable of implementation.

A small group (called a set) is created and members cooperate in a process that amounts to questioning and testing each other until there is a certain amount of clarity about the nature of the problem and the best way to tackle it. Set members are very supportive as they go about the review of individual projects, and they are keen to provide feedback. A climate of mutual support and mutual constructive criticism can be found in a set that works well. Once the deliberations are completed the set disbands, and trainees are expected to be committed to their chosen action strategies following the various questioning and exploration episodes that took place in the set.

A feature of action learning is the challenge to and the criticism levelled at the status quo and traditional practices. In certain organisational cultures such an approach would not be welcome, but it could certainly take root and produce results in organisational conditions where there is a commitment to action learning. It would appear that action learning as part of a management development programme is a useful approach when the organisation is interested in increasing the effectiveness of its managers in a behavioural sense (Lawrence, 1986), but it is not necessarily the best approach to develop technical competence or to assimilate new knowledge about managing people.

An action learning approach has been adopted by the North Western Health Board in Ireland. The organisation was undergoing significant change, and the aim was to develop a training programme for 500 people. With that number a cost-efficient approach was necessary. Self-managed action learning sets have been established, and so far 160 people are taking part. At the meetings the set focuses on the concerns of each person in turn, and the sets have been likened to 'personal think tanks'. Projects are undertaken, and report backs occur at the start of the next meeting.

In order to develop skills in managing the sets, facilitators were brought in for the first two meetings of each set, but thereafter they became self-facilitating. A number of projects have been launched, including developing support frameworks for GPs, measuring user satisfaction in the mental health service and schemes for the reduction of waiting lists. In one example, the consultant clinical coordinator at Sligo General Hospital joined a set including a social worker, a nursing sister, two physiotherapists and an occupational therapist. Just working with the group itself proved to be an insightful process, and his project has resulted in the introduction of a hospital-wide clinical audit system (O'Hara *et al.*, 2001).

A prominent feature of action learning is learning to learn. This amounts to developing a greater understanding of the learning process, and of the trainee's preferred approaches to learning. Earlier we noted that Kolb (1985) recognised that people learn in different ways. Honey and Mumford (1992) in the United Kingdom developed a model based on the work of Kolb. For example, a person may prefer to learn in one of the following ways:

- through new experiences: the *pragmatist* – they are more effective learners when they see a connection between new information and the problems they encounter;
- by observation and reflection: the *reflector* – they are more effective learners when they evaluate and reflect on their own experiences;
- by conceptualisation: the *theorist* – they are more effective learners when they relate information that they receive to concepts or theories;
- by experimentation: the *activist* – they are more effective learners when they are actively involved in tangible or concrete tasks.

The Global Leadership Programme offered by the University of Michigan in the United States, which was designed to provide individuals with a global perspective, was based on the principles of action learning. Over a period of five weeks teams of American, Japanese and European executives would learn global business skills through action learning (Dowling *et al.*, 1994). To build cross-cultural teams the programme made use of seminars and lectures, adventure-based exercises, and field trips to investigate business opportunities in developing countries (e.g. India, China and Brazil).

Outdoor courses

The outdoor training sessions could be on the use of initiative, problem solving and cooperation, and could be used by organisations interested in the development of team building and leadership skills. Invariably there is a sharing of experience by members of the group in the face of adverse physical conditions, such as a challenging mountain climb, and this can contribute to the development of cooperative modes of operation and psychological closeness.

These training sessions can produce good results if attention is given to a number of issues connected with the planning of the course, the operation of the course and relating the course to conditions in the home organisational environment. For example, does the course have clear objectives? Is the course a natural part of the organisation's total training provision? Are the course organisers familiar with the culture and practices in the organisation from which the participants are drawn? Have the course organisers taken the necessary action with respect to safety? In addition, the instructor/trainee ratio should be low and where possible what takes place during the training sessions should be related to the participant's workplace.

One should be aware of potential problems. If some or all of the members of the training course originate from the same organisation but are of different statuses, superiors might feel uneasy about their image in the eyes of subordinates when they have not performed as well as expected. On the other hand, subordinates might act in a predictable organisational way by adopting a typical behavioural pattern (e.g. submissiveness or compliance) where they perceived superiors to be acting officiously. There might be difficulties in transferring the benefits derived from the training session to the work situation because of constraints with respect to implementation. Certain key people in the organisation might feel uncomfortable if those returning were equipped with behavioural skills that enabled them to challenge cherished practices (Lowe, 1991).

There has been a dip in the demand for outdoor courses according to an Industrial Society survey (Hegarty and Dickson, 1995). Some trainers in the late 1990s were keen to get rid of the macho image of training in the great outdoors, and turned their attention to developing minds and building teams rather than testing endurance. The new approach relies on communication workshops, using body language only, and the live arts rather than freezing mud to provide a new source of inspiration to extract the best from employees (Ashworth, 1999). In the case of the live arts, course participants stage their own shows with the help of stage performers and technical staff drawn from the opera, theatre, circus and film. Those who support this approach believe that the arts have a role to play in the release of creativity.

E-learning

E-Learning refers to information and knowledge delivered via information and communication technology (ICT), and is typically associated with the Internet. Learners can operate online to carry out programmed exercises, read material and gain information pertinent to the performance of their job. Technology-based learning is said to have a number of advantages. First, it means that learners can access knowledge at any time convenient to them. Secondly, information can be transmitted to employees at high speed, and regular updates to material are possible. Thirdly, organisations whose workforce is geographically dispersed can enable all employees (or particular groups) to have the same information (Masie, 1999).

However, one should be aware that e-learning may not be suitable for all learning styles and tasks. Particularly, hands-on learning may be necessary for practical topics, and for many learners a social aspect to learning is important. This does not just mean the socialising that is associated with training courses, but the elements of peer feedback and discussion that can provide an important stimulus in learning. In most e-learning packages these aspects are missing. Lloyds TSB (a high street bank) has made an attempt to tackle some of these potential problems. It has made ICT-based training available at 450 centres throughout the United Kingdom, and staff attend planned sessions in which there are pre- and post-course discussions, although the basis of the training input remains technology based (Hills and Francis, 1999).

Similarly, an approach to leadership training has been developed by General Motors, which makes extensive use of technology. After a course had taken place, participants were supported using a database that removed the need for them to remember everything. Information was available as and when they needed it, and they were supported in 'learning by doing'. They had access to other participants who had similar experiences and were able to share their learning and receive feedback. Through enabling such interactions the database built up live examples that participants could use in deciding how to respond to their own situation (Ulrich and Hinkson, 2001).

In a radical move, Pearl Assurance has acknowledged that use of ICT is an area where 'upward learning' can be fostered in the organisation. Pearl Assurance is part of the Australian Mutual Provident Society and managers on a visit to the parent company in Sydney found an answer to problems they were experiencing in integrating the use of the web: 'e-possums'. The e-possums were a group of ICT literate staff who acted as enthusiastic guides to senior managers, enabling them to get to grips with the technology in a way which focused on solutions to problems that were live for the managers. In a sense this is a form of coaching but, in this case, the normal hierarchical arrangement is reversed (McLeod, 2001).

■ Continuous development

It is almost commonplace nowadays to hear the view that training should be a continuing process with the accent on self-development, as mentioned earlier. This is prompted by the suggestion that employees cannot, in a rapidly changing world, rely on the knowledge and skills acquired in gaining their initial qualifications. In 1987 the Institute of Personnel Management (now the IPD) produced a code of practice with respect to personal development and the demands posed by jobs. A starting point is the assessment of the organisation's present and future training needs; this is done by extracting from the corporate plan the pool of employee knowledge and skills required to implement that plan. Predictably the importance of learning from confronting and solving problems at work is underlined.

The role of top management in cultivating a climate of continuous development is given special mention. Top management is admonished to place high on the corporate agenda the frequent formal review of training activities aimed at the development of employee competencies. In the final analysis it should be recognised that it is wise to promote the view that one should make learning a habit and to accept the idea that work problems offer opportunities for learning. Ideally it is hoped that well-conceived continuous development aimed at helping the individual also helps the organisation to achieve its objectives.

■ Learning organisation

The arrival on the scene of the learning organisation is associated with the need to provide for the internal renewal of the organisation in the face of a competitive environment. A learning organisation has been defined as one that facilitates the learning of all its members and continually transforms itself (Pedlar *et al.*, 1988). It is said that a learning organisation has the capacity to respond well to changes in its environment and creates space and formal mechanisms for people to think, to ask questions, to reflect and to learn, as well as encouraging them to challenge the status quo and to suggest improvement (Handy, 1989).

The climate within the learning organisation should permeate all collective activities (e.g. meetings, conferences) where there is an acute sensitivity to what is going on in the organisation and a willingness to experiment in the light of opportunities or threats. The learning organisation is keen to assist people in the identification of their learning needs; such needs would be reviewed regularly along with the provision of feedback on performance to date. Also, there would be a commitment to providing new experiences from which people can learn and a willingness to mobilise training resources. Learning from others could be extended to 'benchmarking', which is an ongoing investigation and learning experience that aims to identify, analyse, adopt and implement the best practices in the company's industry (Garvin, 1993).

In summary, the learning organisation puts the accent on a number of important issues, such as the following:

■ self-development and continuous development that creates able performers;
■ sharing knowledge leads to shared visions of the organisation's future, which could be facilitated by managerial leadership;

- promoting team learning when organisational members get together and share ideas and opinions with each other so as to improve decision making and achieve objectives;
- double loop learning where organisational members use feedback to test the validity of current values and practices, and a desire to keep the total organisational picture in mind with sensitivity to the external environment (Beard, 1993; Senge, 1990).

Finally, some are sceptical about the concept of the learning organisation because there could very well be a clash between the insights and benefits derived from it and those obtained from normal training activities (Price, 1997).

While it would not necessarily be claimed that the following case, Fox's Biscuits in Example 10.3, has achieved 'learning organisation' status, it has nonetheless been able to link training and development to strategy, culture change and employee involvement. The outcome has been significant cost cutting and the enhancement of performance.

EXAMPLE 10.3

Training and Development at Fox's Biscuits

Fox's Biscuits is part of the Northern Foods Group. It produces biscuits at the rate of 12,000 per minute for supermarkets. Up to 1995 millions of pounds had been invested in new technology, but there had been almost nothing spent on training employees to use it. The workforce had a low skills base, and in some cases poor literacy. There were communication problems and although people worked in teams these tended to be insular with little conversation between teams. The result was that there were grey areas surrounding who was responsible for what stage of the process, and so the process could, and did, fall down quickly and frequently. There was a traditional autocratic culture with eight layers of management and little trust between managers and workers.

The training initiative started with basic levels of training for an NVQ in food and drink. The programme allowed individuals a lot of flexibility, and employees were encouraged to work together. This was helpful because, with all the employees working towards the same study goals, they were able to support each other to improve. Employees reported that they were not afraid to admit that there was something they did not know, whereas in the previous culture no one would have made such an admission. People have gained confidence, and many have gone on to further training and education. The teams are now multi-skilled and can cover for each other's jobs, although each person has a 'principal job'. The shift system has been simplified and the layers of management reduced. Five core action teams were established and they receive suggestions from the workforce. Once the ideas are assessed, voluntary action teams work to develop the ideas. There is now a culture of people wanting to be involved, and 60 per cent of staff have joined in the projects.

Over the period, £300,000 has been invested in training. As a result 181 employees have achieved NVQ level 1, 128 have achieved level 2, and 25 have achieved level 3. Absence rates have fallen significantly, and staff turnover has fallen from 11 per cent to 9 per cent.

Suggestions for the year 2000 alone saved the site more than £350,000, thus more than paying back the investment in training in a single year. In 1995, the factory was seen as a poor performer by Northern Foods, but it is now seen as a success and the general manager sums it up by saying: 'Improving capability through developing and involving our people has been the catalyst for our success.'

(Poole, 2001)

■ Evaluation

Eventually the organisation will need to know if its training and development activities are achieving the anticipated results. To put it technically, we are trying to establish the reliability (consistency) and validity (effectiveness in meeting objectives) of training programmes. This will be easier to establish in some areas than in others. For example, outcomes are more tangible and measurable where there is a change in the way a psychomotor skill is performed (e.g. driving a fork lift truck) than when a shift in values or attitudes has taken place. The central point is to establish a relationship between the training methods used and some measure of performance, and this can only be achieved by assessing the trainees' capability after the training has taken place.

We refer to *internal validity* when it is found that the training objectives are met after the trainees are assessed at the end of the training programme. On the other hand, *external validity* is achieved if, after completing the training programme, the trainees' performance is in line with the laid-down standard (Goldstein, 1978).

One would consider a number of issues other than validation in a restrictive sense when evaluating a training programme. The following are indicative of the approaches adopted. At the end of a training session trainees are asked to complete a questionnaire stating which parts of the training were most useful, relevant and interesting. The results of this exercise could be useful to the trainer, and could lead to an improvement next time round. However, the following weaknesses are associated with this method:

■ Positive responses are made because trainees were happy with the training encounter, possibly having been entertained by the instructor. Such responses would not give any insight into the effectiveness of the training session.
■ The trainees feel that the training session was useful and relevant to their occupational sphere, but unfortunately this judgement may be based on a lack of sufficient awareness of their training needs.
■ Because of the close proximity of the evaluation exercise to the end of the training session, there is no information on the transfer of learning to the workplace.

As a means to remedy the last weakness, follow-up questionnaires could be sent to respondents some time after the training took place (e.g. three months). Questions are asked about the extent to which the learning was used in practice in terms of using knowledge, skills and attitudes acquired during the training session. In the responses there could be an indication of impediments or blocks to the transfer of learning. Of course this may not be the fault of the trainee: it could be due to a lack of suitable equipment or software, or where there is resistance from other employees to the material learnt on the course.

Tests of varying kinds, such as examinations and grading of coursework and projects, can be used to evaluate learning, particularly on longer courses. These tests are likely to affect the processes and culture of the group engaged in learning as competitive and secretive tendencies develop following a realisation that a trainee can be given either a pass or fail mark or grade. A less formal version of tests is that of exercises where trainees engage in role playing, or tackle a case study or in-tray exercise. Then they are given the opportunity to evaluate their own performance, subsequently receiving feedback from colleagues and the trainer. It is hoped that the feedback expressed as criticism is constructive. Although tests and exercises play a useful part in informing us about what learning has taken place we are none the wiser about the transfer of learning to the workplace.

Another approach is evaluation at the 'job behavioural level' (Hamblin, 1974). Here the transfer of learning could be evaluated by the manager or training specialist to establish whether or not behaviour has changed as a result of the training. The following include some of the techniques used for this purpose:

- *Activity sampling and observer diaries*: the trainees are observed to see to what extent they are putting into practice the knowledge, attitudes and skills acquired through training.
- *Critical incidents*: key incidents at work are analysed to establish to what extent 'new patterns of behaviour' are present.
- *Self-recording*: the trainees record how they perform certain activities.

Eventually, the organisation will be looking for evidence of how the changed job behaviour influences other employees and the way the company functions. This would mean measuring changes in overall organisational functioning with respect to productivity, output and costs, but such an exercise would be difficult to undertake.

Finally, at the evaluation stage it is worth considering why the training was undertaken in the first place. There could be a number of reasons, such as to rectify a skills deficiency, to project an image as a responsible employer, to convey to employees that the organisation is committed to their development, and as a reward to able performers.

■ Training for international assignments

In order to compete successfully in global markets, multinational companies recognise that it is vital to train and develop expatriates, host country nationals and third country nationals so that high calibre staff are available when required to achieve the corporate objectives. In this section a fair amount of attention will be devoted to issues related to the training and development of expatriates, but later the importance of training and developing the other employees of multinational companies will also be considered.

It would appear that an effective approach to expatriate training and development includes:

- development of expatriates before, during and after foreign assignments;
- development and training of expatriate families before, during and after foreign assignments;
- development of the headquarters staff responsible for the planning, organisation and control of overseas operations.

According to Dowling *et al.* (1994), studies indicate that there are three areas that contribute to a smooth transition to a foreign post: cultural training, language instruction and assistance with practical day-to-day matters.

Cultural training

A major objective of cultural training is to help people cope with unexpected events in a new culture. Cross-cultural training, in addition to task-specific knowledge necessary for the position, enables individuals to adjust quickly to the new culture (Black and Mendenhall, 1990). With regard to expatriates, cultural training seeks to develop an appreciation of the host country so that individuals can behave accordingly. For example, in the culture of the Middle East emphasis is placed on personal relationships, trust and respect in business dealings. In addition there is much emphasis on religion that influences almost every aspect of life. There is an example of a highly paid expatriate who took two miniature bottles of brandy with him into Qatar (a Muslim country in the Middle East). The alcohol was found by Customs, and the person was promptly deported and ordered never to return. It stands to reason that it is important to accept the host country culture in order to avoid getting into difficulties on an international assignment.

One developmental technique considered useful for putting international employees in the right mind-set is to send them on a preliminary trip to the host country. A suitably arranged visit overseas for the candidate and spouse (where appropriate) can give them the opportunity to establish whether they are interested in the assignment and assess their suitability to embark on it. For example, the Ford Motor Company offered a one-week visit to the foreign location for both the employee and spouse, during which time the employee visited the Ford subsidiary company to meet colleagues, consider future challenges and discuss job requirements. The couple were favourably placed to do some viewing of houses, visit schools and get a 'gut' feeling for the new location and its cultural environment. As a result, they derived first-hand experience of some of the cultural differences so that they were better equipped to make more informed decisions about the overseas assignment. There is no doubt that effective and comprehensive cultural training can make it easier to negotiate the transition from the home to the foreign environment and assist with the development of productive expatriates. Such training could prevent mistakes, such as the case of the expatriate who took alcohol to Qatar, referred to above.

Language training

Though English is the language of world business it would be unwise to place an exclusive reliance on English. Clearly the ability of an expatriate to speak a foreign language can improve his or her effectiveness and negotiating ability in a non-English speaking country. As Baliga and Baker (1985) point out, the ability to speak a foreign language can improve the manager's access to information regarding the host country's economy, government and market; in addition, expatriates can fit in socially more easily, whether or not English is spoken by foreign nationals. You could expect to find orientation programmes and local language programmes provided by the company's personnel or human resource function in the host country.

Practical training

It seems logical to assume that some form of training is needed to assist the expatriate's family to acquaint themselves with the normal practical aspects of life in the host country (e.g. transport, shopping, use of banks, etc.), including help with establishing a new support network. A useful method of adaptation involves interaction between the expatriate's family and other established expatriate families. Such a process facilitates the exchange of information, facilitates adaptation, and contributes to building a suitable network of relationships for the expatriate family. If fluency in the host country language is essential for adaptation, further language training for expatriates and their family should be provided after arrival in the host country.

In Table 10.2 the different approaches to preparing managers for international postings are listed in ranked order. 'It is now widely accepted by both academic

Table 10.2 Preparing managers for international postings

(Percentage of respondents ranking an activity as amongst the five most important methods in their organisations.)

Arranging for managers to visit host country	79
Language training for managers	73
Briefing by host country managers	67
In-house general management course	44
Cross-cultural training for managers	42
Cross-cultural training for family	38
General management course at business school	29
Language training for family	23
Training in negotiating within business norms of host country	17

Source: Barham and Devine (1990), cited in Dowling *et al.* (1994).

researchers and HR practitioners that pre-move training and cross-cultural briefings can help expatriate staff, and their families, adapt to living and working in new
environments' (Forster, 2000). Evidence presented by Forster shows that pre-move
training and briefings for a large group of UK employees and their dependants, who
embarked on international assignments in the mid-1990s, had beneficial effects for
most employees and their dependants. However, the dependants rated the cross-
cultural briefings rather negatively.

Contingency approaches

Black and Mendenhall (1989) cite Tung's 1980s' research into a contingency
framework for deciding the nature and level of rigour of training. Tung argued that
the two determining factors in her contingency model were: (i) the degree of the
'interaction' required of the expatriate in the host culture, and (ii) the similarity
between the expatriate's native culture and the new culture. If the expected interaction between the individual and members of the host culture is low and the
degree of similarity between the expatriate's native culture and the host culture is
high, then the training initiatives should be geared to job-related issues, rather than
culture-related issues, and the level of rigour necessary for effective training should
be relatively low. If the reverse situation were applicable, then one would expect
greater attention to be paid to the new culture and cross-cultural skills, as well as
to the task, with a moderate to high level of rigour of training.

Training host country and third country nationals

The discussion above has laid emphasis on the training of expatriates. However, it is
also important to emphasise the importance of training for host country and third
country nationals (Dowling et al., 1994). For example Fiat, the Italian vehicle manufacturer, used staff transfers as part of its training programme, with host country
nationals spending time at corporate headquarters in Italy. Pepsi Cola International
brings non-US citizens to its Management Institute in the United States for training
in the systems the company uses. While there trainees are developing managerial
skills but also being exposed to the corporate culture. It is recognised from the perspective of the parent company that interacting with the foreign employees can
broaden the outlook of corporate staff. It should be noted that the training of host
country and third country executives and managers in the way outlined above can be
instrumental in developing global management teams. Finally, Matsushita arranged
for the company's overseas managers to spend time in Japan working alongside their
Japanese counterparts, though this initiative is not without its difficulties.

■ International comparisons in training and development

It is important to note that any cross-cultural and international comparisons should
be read with a 'health warning' in mind: that is they entail generalisations which

Table 10.3 Organisational expenditure on training and development

Country	Percentage of organisations spending more than 2% of salaries on training
France	80
Sweden	60
Turkey	47
Germany	43
Ireland	40
The Netherlands	40
Portugal	39
Finland	36
Norway	36
United Kingdom	26
Denmark	25

Source: Larsen (1994), cited in Hollinshead and Leat (1995).

are likely to subsume many differences within overall classifications. Having said that, there have been some studies that survey the international scene on training and management development, and it is worth acknowledging them.

Collin and Holden (1997) and Hollinshead and Leat (1995) explore the training cultures in a range of countries. Table 10.3 gives an indication of spending on training and development.

The indication is that there is considerable variation between different countries. The question is why this should be so. According to Collin and Holden (1997) this can be traced to national culture. In France, there is a directed culture with regard to training in that the law requires employers to spend 1.2 per cent of total gross salaries on training. Vocational training is incorporated into the school curriculum, there is a mathematical/engineering orientation, and competition to get into the best schools is strong because the establishment attended can have a significant impact on a person's career. Similarly, in Sweden, there is a directed culture of training. Vocational content is emphasised in schools, there is considerable free adult education and companies are strongly encouraged to train their workers. In Germany, there is a dual system of practical in-company training and theoretical learning with a vocational bent in schools, with the culture broadly directed. The focus is functional, and engineering/industry oriented.

In the United Kingdom the training culture is voluntarist (voluntary participation). Investors in People awards have encouraged investment, and management developing is growing (Storey *et al.*, 1997); however, apprenticeships are declining and there are only about 13,000 apprenticeship places per annum, compared to France and Germany, both of which have over 300,000. The class divide between theoretical and vocational approaches to learning is long established and is still influential, with 'traditional' universities perceived as distinct from 'new' universities that offer more vocational education.

In Japan, the training culture combines directed and voluntarist tendencies. Central and local government set and reinforce training standards. There is a meritocratic/elitist system in which top companies recruit from top universities. There is considerable in-company continuous learning, which is associated with lifetime employment, and there is an emphasis on self-development.

In the United States, the training culture is voluntarist. There is a focus on individual effort and payment, and wide variation between areas and organisations. There is excellent training by top companies, but this is not universal (Collin and Holden, 1997).

Doyle (1997) conducts what he terms a 'Cook's Tour' of management development in a number of geographical areas. The essence of his findings are as follows:

- *United States/United Kingdom*: A rational–functional philosophy dominates and the justification for management development is that it corrects individual 'weaknesses' and contributes to business strategy and performance. There is a focus on developing the generalist manager.
- *Europe* (apart from the United Kingdom): Here there is a weaker conception of management. Rather than being seen as a discrete set of skills and knowledge it is a 'state of being' (especially in France), which is added on to a functional specialism. Development in a functional specialism is primary and generalist training is less important, particularly in Germany.
- *Japan*: As opposed to the Anglo-Saxon approach, it consists of short bursts of intensive activity. In Japan there is a longer-term and more collectivist approach in which the significant factor is the relationship between the boss and the individual. The aim is to nurture growth.
- *Central Europe*: In countries such as Russia, Poland, Hungary and Romania there has been a rush to adopt 'western' practices of management, but in a number of cases western models have failed to translate well into the central European situation, and a clear 'road map' has yet to emerge in these areas.
- *Hong Kong and China*: Similarly, in this large area there has been an importation of 'western' techniques of management. But discursive and group-work methods of western management development do not necessarily translate easily to a culture in which there is a strong emphasis on conformity, social status, the need to 'preserve face' and the unchallenged position of the 'expert'.
- *Developing countries*: Although it is difficult to generalise at this level, there is a question over the extent to which individualistic modes of management development from the west are applicable and transferable to developing countries. For example, in Africa there is an emphasis on group solidarity rather than self-development.

Of course, such generalisations are open to criticism. But they do raise certain questions. First, should it be assumed that the direction of learning should be in one direction – the west outwards? It may be that in an era of internationalisation learning requires to be more challenging and that some of the taken-for-granted aspects of the western approach would benefit from critical analysis. Secondly, if change and uncertainty continue to be the dominant features of global economy, how should organisations develop in order to cope with the pressures of change? The answer is unlikely to be a singular one best way, but finding a developmental path that fits with the local culture is more likely to yield results. Thirdly, the emphasis of HRM is about training for the purpose of organisational performance, and doing so on an individualised basis. There are a number of tensions contained within this conceptualisation, and the question is how these tensions should be resolved. There is a tension between learning directed at self-development and learning to promote organisational performance. Another tension concerns the causal connection between training and development and corporate performance.

While it is assumed that individuals who are developed will perform better, and consequently the organisation will perform better, each of the links in this chain of reasoning can be questioned. It could be that people are developed and yet, because of circumstances in the economic environment, the organisation fails – e.g. because of substitution by technology, or because the potential customers cannot afford the product.

■ Benefits of training

Training, as a vehicle for human resource development, is concerned with improving the skills of employees and enhancing their capacity to cope with the ever-changing demands of the work situation. It could also make a positive contribution to the empowerment of employees. Specific benefits have been identified by Armstrong (1992) and Kenney *et al.* (1990) as follows:

- Training facilitates getting to grips with the requirements of a job quickly, and by improving the knowledge and skill of the worker it allows him or her to better the quantity and quality of output with fewer mistakes and a reduction in waste. The enhancement of the skill base of the employee allows us to build more challenge into the job (job enrichment) with benefits to both the individual and the organisation.
- When the outcome of training leads to greater competency in the execution of tasks by subordinates the manager is relieved from tasks related to remedial or corrective effort.
- Training is an invaluable process when the organisation wishes to introduce flexible working methods and wants to create appropriate attitudes to equip employees to cope with change. Training could be used as a confidence builder in a management of change programme when employees are given help in understanding why change is necessary, how they might benefit from it, and when they are given the skills to participate in the implementation of change.
- Training has significance in a public relations sense in that it has value in projecting the right image to prospective workers of good calibre.
- Where training incorporates safety training as an integral part of the programme the outcome could be favourable in terms of health and safety at work.
- Training could have a favourable impact on the level of staff turnover, and the

costs of redundancy schemes and recruitment of staff could be reduced when displaced staff are retrained.

■ The motivational impact of training is manifest when staff feel a sense of recognition when they are sent on a training course, and after been trained they are motivated to acquire new skills, particularly when rewards follow the acquisition and use of these skills.

■ The value of training in a communication context is evident when core values, such as those relating to product quality and customer service, are disseminated to employees, with the hope that they will be adopted and generate commitment.

■ Identification with the organisation could be fostered when a better understanding of mission statements and corporate objectives is achieved through a training programme.

■ Training aimed at operationalising certain management techniques (e.g. quality circles) could generate certain desirable side effects, such as analytical, problem-solving and presentational skills.

As a means of complementing the above list of beneficial points associated with training one should note the following issues related to the success of training programmes reported by the employers' organisation in the UK (CBI, 1989):

1 Training fosters a common vision throughout the organisation.
2 Training enjoys high status when it is seen to satisfy the needs of the organisation and produces results.
3 It is important that there is in place organisational structure that facilitates the acquisition and nurturing of skills where employee development is geared to the meeting of corporate objectives. Likewise, business systems should be flexible enough to cater for the investment in people, with agreed budgets and clear targets against which performance is assessed on a regular basis. It is apparent that in this climate training is an integral part of corporate strategy. It is certainly not viewed as a peripheral organisational activity with a narrow remedial brief but is seen as a mechanism for fostering employee motivation with implications for the recruitment and retention of staff.

The success scenario outlined above might, in the eyes of some commentators, err on the side of optimism. But one must recognise the formidable constraints affecting a successful outcome. Factors contributing to the failure of training programmes are as follows (CBI, 1989):

■ Management fails to consider seriously the existing and future skills needed by the organisation. (Often one finds that training budgets are all too easily trimmed when the organisation is looking for savings; the belief is that training does not pay off in the short term, and that an investment in training is lost when people leave the organisation.)

■ Management relies too heavily on local or national labour markets to satisfy the needs of the organisation for relevant skills at all levels.

■ Too often a natural response to skill shortages is to poach key employees from other employers even if such action leads to wage inflation.

■ Conclusions

If HRM is to fulfil its aim of valuing human 'assets' it is necessary to invest in them. This implies a positive attitude towards training and development. In organisations where there is a core of knowledge-based workers, development is vital to maintain their ability to add value to the enterprise. This is equally true where multi-skilled workers are required to participate in teamwork. Even in workforces that are relatively low skilled, training and development can have a significant impact. On the issue of flexibility it will be necessary to ask the question: how much investment should be made in temporary workers?

Training and development cannot be seen as a panacea for all organisational ills. However it is clearly important to equip employees with skills and knowledge and to motivate them to utilise their abilities. This is particularly so when it comes to training staff to operate internationally. There is an increased demand for employees to be flexible in their location of work and to be able to operate globally, but it should be recognised that even where there is the willingness to work in this way additional skills, language, knowledge and orientation training will be needed. It is also important for the organisation to be aware of the issues associated with the return of employees to their home country when they have spent considerable time abroad.

Different countries have adopted alternative approaches to encouraging companies to invest in training. Some (such as France) have formalised requirements, while others (such as the United States) have taken a more voluntarist approach. In the United Kingdom there had been a decline in training in the 1980s under a voluntarist approach. In the 1990s, however, this trend was reversed (Storey et al., 1997). Traditionally, when companies experienced financial difficulties the training budget would be the first to be cut. Nowadays some forward-looking companies, when faced with difficulties, actually increase training.

The integration of training and development policies with other areas of HRM strategy is seen as important. If the organisation is planning change, and particularly when that change can have an impact on tasks, skills and organisational culture, the training employees receive will be a determining factor in the success or failure of the change programme. If there is an aim to form closer and more adaptive relationships with customers and suppliers, which is often the case in current forms of organisational restructuring, then employees need to have sufficient training to enable them to understand and solve problems for customers. When an organisation is seeking to pursue a policy of employee involvement then the success of the implementation of the policy will depend on employees having the relevant skills and appropriate attitudes. Clearly there are linkages between training and development and recruitment and selection. The basic question is whether a company should buy in skilled people from the external labour supply or develop its own people internally. Nowadays it is thought that whichever approach is taken it will be necessary to have an ongoing training policy if employees are to keep up to date and if they are to believe that the company is committed to them.

References

Armstrong, M. (1992) *Human Resource Management: Strategy and action*, London: Kogan Page.

Ashworth, J. (1999) 'Management training is changing: dramatic change to the art of team building', *The Times*, 5 February, 26.

Baliga, G. and Baker, J.C. (1985) 'Multi-national corporate policies for expatriate managers: selection, training, and evaluation', *Advanced Management Journal*, Autumn, 31–8.

Barham, K. and Devine, M. (1990) 'The quest for the international manager: a survey of global human resource strategies', *Special Report No. 2098*, London: Economist Intelligence Unit.

Beard, D. (1993) 'Learning to change organisations', *Personnel Management*, January, 32–5.

Bell, C. (1998) *Managers as Mentors*, Maidenhead: McGraw-Hill.

Black, J.S. and Mendenhall, M. (1989) 'A practical but theory-based framework for selecting cross-cultural training methods', *Human Resource Management*, 28, 511–39.

Black, J.S. and Mendenhall, M. (1990) 'Cross-cultural training effectiveness: a review and a theoretical framework for future research', *Academy of Management Review*, 15, 113–36.

Bolger, A. (1996) 'Investors in People: both sides reap the benefits', *Financial Times*, 22 November, 13.

CBI (1989) *Managing The Skills Gap*, London: Confederation of British Industry.

Clutterbuck, D. (2001) 'Human Resources: Mentoring and coaching at the top', Part 13, *Mastering Management Series, Financial Times*, 8 January, 14–15.

Collin, A. (1992) 'The role of the mentor in transforming the organisation', Paper presented at the Annual Conference, Employment Research Unit, Business School, University of Cardiff, September.

Collin, A. and Holden, L. (1997) 'The national framework for vocational education and training', in Beardwell, I. and Holden, L. (eds), *Human Resource Management: A contemporary perspective*, London: Pitman.

Conway, C. (1994) 'Mentoring managers in organisations: a report of a study of mentoring and its application to organizations with case studies', Ashridge Management College, Berkhamsted.

Dowling, P., Schuler, R.S. and Welch, D.E. (1994) *International Dimensions of Human Resource Management*, 2nd edn, Belmont, CA: Wadsworth Publishing Company.

Doyle, M. (1997) 'Management development', in Beardwell, I. and Holden, L. (eds), *Human Resource Management: A contemporary perspective*, London: Pitman.

Forster, N. (2000) 'Expatriates and the impact of cross-cultural training', *Human Resource Management Journal*, 10, 63–78.

Garvin, D. (1993) 'Building a learning organization', *Harvard Business Review*, July–August 78–91.

Goldstein, I.L. (1978) 'The pursuit of validity in the evaluation of training programmes', *Human Factors*, 20, 131–44.

Goss, D. (1994) *Principles of Human Resource Management*, London: Routledge.

Hamblin, A.C. (1974) *Evaluation and Control of Training*, Maidenhead: McGraw-Hill.

Handy, C. (1989) *The Age of Unreason*, London: Business Books.

Harrison, R. (1992) *Employee Development*, London: Institute of Personnel Management.

Hegarty, S. and Dickson, T. (1995) 'Rise and fall of corporate thrills', *Financial Times*, 9 January, 7.

Herriot, P. (1992) *The Career Management Challenge: Balancing individual and organisational needs*, London: Sage.

Herriot, P. and Pemberton, C. (1995) *New deals: The revolution in managerial careers*, Chichester: Wiley.

Hill, S. (1991) 'Why quality circles failed but total quality management might succeed', *British Journal of Industrial Relations*, 29, 541–68.

Hills, H. and Francis, P. (1999) 'Interaction Learning', *People Management* 5 (7), 48–9.

Hilton, P. (1992) 'Shepherd defends training policy', *Personnel Management*, December, 11.

Hollinshead, G. and Leat, M. (1995) *Human Resource Management: An international and comparative perspective*, London: Pitman.

Holmes, L. (1990) 'Trainer competences: turning back the clock', *Training and Development*, April, 17–20.

Honey, P. and Mumford, A. (1992) *Manual of Learning Styles*, 3rd edn, London: P. Honey.

Industrial Society (1996) Report, *Assessment and Development Centres*, London: Industrial Society.

IRS (1992) 'Skill-based pay: the new training initiative', *Employee Development Bulletin*, 31, July, *Industrial Relations Review and Report*, No. 516, 2–7.

Keep, E. (1992) 'Corporate training strategies', in Salaman, G. (ed.), *Human Resource Strategies*, London: Sage.

Kelly, J. (2000) 'Skills Council targets adult illiteracy', *Financial Times*, 11 December, 6.

Kenney, J. and Reid, M. (1988) *Training Initiatives*, London: Institute of Personnel Management.

Kenney, J., Reid, M. and Donnelly, E. (1990) *Manpower Training and Development*, London: Institute of Personnel Management.

Kolb, D. (1985) *Experiential Learning: Experiences as the source of learning and development*, Englewood Cliffs, NJ: Prentice Hall.

Larsen, H.H. (1994) 'Key issues in training and development', in Brewster, C. and Hegeswisch, A. (eds), *Policy and Practice in European Human Resource Management: The Price Waterhouse/Cranfield Survey*, London: Routledge.

Lawrence, J. (1986) 'Action learning: a questioning approach', in Mumford, A. (ed.), *Handbook of Management Development*, Aldershot: Gower.

Littlefield, D. (2000) 'Four-stroke of genius', *People Management*, 6 (3), 52–3.

Lowe, J. (1991) 'Teambuilding via outdoor training: experiences from a UK automotive plant', *Human Resource Management Journal*, 2, 42–59.

McKenna, E. (2000) *Business Psychology and Organisational Behaviour*, Hove: Psychology Press.

McLeod, M. (2001) 'Surfers' paradigm', *People Management*, 7, 44–5.

Masie, E. (1999) 'Joined-up thinking', *People Management*, 5 (11), 32–6.

O'Hara, S., Webber, T. and Murphy, W. (2001) 'The joy of sets', *People Management*, 7 (3), 30–4.

O'Reilly, S. (1998) 'Smart money goes on coaching', *The Sunday Times*, 12 July, 7.14.

Pedlar, M., Boydell, R. and Burgoyne, J. (1988) *Learning Company Project*, London: Manpower Services Commission.

Pike, A. (1999) 'Employers and unions attack new skills plans', *Financial Times*, 14 October, 3.

Poole, C. (2001) 'Smart cookies', *People Management*, 7 (2), 46–7.

Price, A. (1997) *Human Resource Management in a Business Context*, London: International Thomson Business Press.

Revans, R. (1971) *Developing Effective Managers*, London: Longman.

Senge, P. (1990) *The Fifth Discipline: The art and practice of the learning organization*, New York: Random House.

Sisson, K. and Storey, J. (1988) 'Developing effective managers: a review of the issues and an agenda for research', *Personnel Review*, 17, 3–8.

Steedman, H. (1998) 'Basics are essential: vocational training must include literacy and numeracy', *Financial Times*, 26 August, 9.

Storey, J. (1992) *Developments in the Management of Human Resources*, Oxford: Blackwell.

Storey, J., Mabey, C. and Thomson, A. (1997) 'What a difference a decade makes', *People Management*, June, 28–30.

Training Agency (1989) *Training in Britain: Employees' perspectives*, Research Report. London: HMSO.

Ulrich, D. and Hinkson, P. (2001) 'Net heads', *People Management*, 7, 32–6.

Chapter 11

Employee relations

Employee relations, having emerged from industrial relations, is one of the main subjects of research related to HRM. It is concerned with the theory and practice of the relationship between management and workers in an organisational context. Important influences on this area of study include Marxist, structural and critical theories in which workers and organisations are seen as being arranged in opposition, and power is a focus of attention. Although there has been a tradition of adversarial relations between managers and workers in the United Kingdom, HRM espouses a unitarist approach in which their mutually shared interests are emphasised.

Having read this chapter, you should:

- be aware of the main theories and frameworks for understanding employee relations;
- understand models of communication and alternative practical approaches to communicating;
- be able to assess and criticise employee involvement and participation schemes at the macro and micro levels;
- be aware of changes in the relations with trade unions and collective bargaining;
- be aware of trends in international employee relations;
- understand how conflict arises in organisations, and know some of the alternatives for dealing with it;
- recognise the nature of ethics and diversity and their relevance to HRM;
- understand the importance of health and safety in the workplace, and know what the key issues are.

Employee relations ranges widely as an area of study, so it is necessary to be selective in the choice of issues to cover. The following topics will be discussed in this chapter:

- industrial relations vs employee relations;
- communication;
- participation;
- trade union representation;
- international trends and perspectives in employee relations;
- conflict;
- health and safety.

■ Industrial relations vs employee relations

Prior to the advent of HRM, employee relations was often called industrial relations and was concerned with the interactions between the employer (represented by management) and the workforce (typically represented by trade unions). It involved the processes of collective bargaining, negotiation and consultation, and occurred at two levels – the organisation and the industry. Industrial relations tends to be associated in a negative sense with conflict between trade unions and employers and in creating images of bitter strikes and walk outs (Blyton and Turnbull, 1994).

Employee relations, with its milder tone, differs from industrial relations in so far as there is an emphasis on direct communication with the workforce and liaison with employees at the level of the individual; this creates a scene where there is reduced interaction with trade unions (Bright, 1993). However, Purcell (1994) makes the valid point that the adoption of HRM does not in every case result in a radical individualisation of the practice of workplace relationships. While traditional collective bargaining concentrated on pay settlements and conditions of work, HRM approaches based on employee relations have sought to broaden the involvement of employees and take a more participative approach to management through increased communication, thereby impinging on power relationships within the organisation. On the face of it employee relations may be seen as a positive development, but there is always the danger that the rhetoric of HRM may be used to disguise a policy of anti-unionism.

Typologies

A classic way of conceptualising traditional industrial relations was put forward by Fox (1974). He constructed two ideal types: the unitary and pluralist perspectives. There has been reference to this terminology when examining HRM elsewhere in this book. The unitary view has the following features:

- management is the only source of authority and power;
- there is a view of everyone pulling in the same direction, united by common goals;
- conflict and opposition are abnormal and dysfunctional (conflict may be caused either by poor communications, so that workers misunderstand the direction of the organisation, or by the presence of dissidents in the workforce);
- trade unions are viewed negatively, and are discouraged.

By contrast, the pluralist perspective has the following features:

- organisations are expected to contain groups that have divergent interests and perspectives;
- each group (the trade unions and the management separately) have power bases from which they can operate;

- conflict occurs naturally where there is a clash of interests;
- management does not have sole authority, but must compete with other sources of leadership (such as trade union representatives).

Purcell and Sisson (1983) further developed the work of Fox and an extended typology of the relations between organisations and workers can be represented as follows:

1 *Traditional approach*: Workers are viewed as a factor of production, they are excluded from decision-making processes, power is concentrated in the hands of management, and trade unions are excluded or opposed.
2 *Sophisticated human relations or paternalists*: Workers are well treated, and sophisticated approaches to recruitment, selection and training, and generous reward packages are believed to remove any need (or justification) for opposition by workers. Trade unions are unlikely to be recognised by the organisation.
3 *Sophisticated moderns*: Workers, normally via the trade union, are seen as legitimately involved in specified areas of decision making. Some (the '*constitutionalists*') who adopt this view take a legalistic approach to collective bargaining, clearly set out areas where management exercises power and areas where management and workers engage in joint decision making. Others (the '*consultatives*') take a less formal approach, and will bargain with trade unions over a range of issues, which may change and develop over time.
4 *Standard moderns, opportunists*: This approach can be seen to swing between unitarism and pluralism as the situation demands. A firefighting approach is taken to industrial relations. When union power is low management may take control of most of the decisions, but when union power is high a negotiating or consulting approach may be adopted. In large organisations there may be a lack of standardisation across different workplaces, with union recognition and collective bargaining being applied in some but not others.

In terms of the Purcell and Sisson model, HRM approaches would tend towards the sophisticated modern or sophisticated human relations approaches. Some would argue, however, that in reality it is possible for organisations to adopt the language of these types while continuing with traditional and modern organisational practices.

Influence of culture

Poole (1986) argued that the style of industrial relations adopted could be related to culture. He examined three distinctive national cultures: Japan, the United States and Nigeria. Japanese industrial relations were typified as 'benevolent paternalism'. This style was thought to derive from a modified Confucian view in which original virtue rather than original sin was assumed. This led to an emphasis on morality as well as economic success, and the desire of business people to be seen as good moral citizens, hence the tendency to treat employees well.

In the United States the wider culture exhibited an embedded individualism. In organisations this was expressed through unitarism, and through an anti-union approach, which went along with developed communications and information sharing. In the Nigerian case Poole found evidence of a style that combined authoritarianism and arbitrariness with a people-centred paternalism. This led to unions often being ignored or dealt with informally, and strikes occurring in response. (It should be noted, however, that not all researchers in the field of culture would accept that such generalisations at the national level are valid.)

■ Communication

Communication is a process at the disposal of the organisation to keep management and employees informed about a variety of relevant matters. For example, it is important for managers to let people know about the mission statement, if there is one, and the objectives of the company. Also, people are informed of what is expected of them in terms of performance, and how changes in the strategic direction of the company are likely to affect their jobs. It is also important to give employees the opportunity to communicate with management so that their reaction to proposals put to them is heard, as well as having the chance to put forward counter proposals. Good communication, as the lifeblood of the organisation, helps to promote the involvement of employees in the decision-making processes, and in so doing can enhance the individual's identification with the organisation, which in turn can lead to improved performance.

Effective communication involves the sending and receiving of clearly understood messages between management and subordinates in a two-way process. In this respect one should keep in mind the following steps:

1 Have a clear idea of the message to be put across.
2 Ideas should be put across in a suitable form using, where possible, the language of the receiver.
3 Choose the most appropriate communication medium (e.g. telephone/fax, email, meeting, memo or report). Consider building 'redundancy' (i.e. same information in more than one form) into the process when circumstances justify it.
4 Ensure the message gets to the receiver, but it must be recognised that in the final analysis it is the responsibility of the receiver to tune in to the contents of the message.
5 Ensure that the intended meaning of the transmitted message gets across. This is more likely to be established where two-way communication exists.
6 Monitor the reaction of the receiver if a response is required.
7 Elicit feedback from the receiver not obtained in step 5.

Feedback is a two-way process and for it to be open and constructive requires the establishment of the right climate by management. Managing this climate is seen as a vital activity for success, because if employees do not feel they are being dealt with openly and honestly resentment and conflict may arise.

The potential for barriers to effective communication to exist within organisations is great, and sensitivity to these impediments is advocated. These barriers consist of the following:

- The message is distorted because of the use of unsuitable language.
- The message does not get through because of interruptions due to physical noise (e.g. a noisy place of work) or psychological noise (e.g. biases and prejudices harboured by the receiver of the message).
- The message is interpreted selectively by the receiver (e.g. the person hears what they want to hear rather than what is said).
- The receiver of the message arrives at a conclusion prematurely, or becomes defensive as a result of being insulted by what has been said.
- Difficulties arise owing to an overload of information in the message.
- The sender of the message is in the dark as to the views of the receiver because the sender misinterprets the feedback or gets no feedback from the receiver.

The size of the organisation will influence the style (e.g. formal or informal) of communications. The following internal approaches to communication can be used in different circumstances, but equally they can complement each other.

Notice boards and memoranda

Written information (e.g. details of vacancies, forthcoming events) is disseminated in a formal sense to employees generally. In the case of the notice board, obsolete information should be removed and overcrowding the board with pieces of paper should be avoided; also, censorship, either unintentional or deliberate, whereby only certain types of information gets on the board, should be guarded against. A drawback of this medium of communication, which could also apply to magazines and newsletters (examined below), is that it does not provide an immediate reaction where the sender of the message can check that the intended message has been properly received and understood and the receiver can express a point of view. In cases where full attention is not paid to memoranda and notice boards the message fails to get through.

Magazines and newsletters

This medium should strive for a balance in its coverage of human-interest stories and organisational issues. It is customary for magazines to be produced by management, whereas the newsletter may be subject to more employee control.

Consultative committees

These committees consist of both management and employees and are formally constituted with an agreed procedure. Minutes of the meetings are prepared and could be displayed on a notice board. Such committees could be used if there is a tradition of industrial relations within a company.

Presentations

These could be used by top management on a regular basis. In particular a chief executive interested in human relations could periodically visit the various company sites and address the rank and file on such matters as the financial health of the company, present problems and future challenges. This approach was adopted successfully by a past managing director (Trevor Owen) of Remploy Ltd. Presentations give the chief executive the chance to meet all employees over time and, provided people do not feel inhibited in such a setting, they can be a useful mode of communication. The former chief executive of the Body Shop – Anita Roddick – regularly made presentations to people in the various retail outlets of the company using a video recording.

Team briefings

This is a technique originally conceived and promoted by the Industrial Society in the United Kingdom and has been adopted by organisations seeking to extend face-to-face communications. Briefing sessions take place at various levels within the organisation, and observations on important issues discussed further up the organ-isation can cascade downwards. Team leaders address a group, varying from 4 to 14 in size, on a regular basis (monthly or bi-monthly). Information is disseminated on company policy and decisions, and the reasons for them can be explained. At any particular level within the organisation the greater part of the briefing could be devoted to local issues, but circumstances will dictate the amount of time devoted to important issues originating further up the organisation (e.g. the implications of a takeover bid for the company).

Team briefings offer the opportunity for employees to interact in the process of clarifying and understanding decisions and policies and are an example of a more direct form of communication. It is important that part of the session consists of two-way communication so that the organisation is aware of the concerns, ideas and suggestions of the workforce. In such circumstances it would be necessary to have an upward reporting system following the briefing session. Amongst the prob-lems surrounding the operation of team briefings are not having enough to report on a given occasion, the numbers in the team being either too small or too great, and the system not being uniformly applied in the sense that certain parts of the organisation are not taking them seriously. Team briefings can have a favourable impact in improving the status of the supervisor as a provider of information and can create a positive participative climate for resolving problems.

However, in conditions where good industrial relations are absent, team briefing could be viewed by trade unions as a technique used to undermine their influence

(Marchington, 1987). Additionally, although managers often claim benefits for team briefings, employees have a more mixed view. In some cases they reported briefings being rushed or irregular, and in research conducted in 25 companies 77 per cent of employees said that team briefings left their commitment unchanged, and 4 per cent reported that their commitment was actually reduced (Marchington *et al.*, 1989). Finally, it is important that the 'briefer' receives appropriate training.

Attitude surveys

The organisation is keen to feel the morale pulse of its employees and mounts attitude surveys to gauge their attitudes and opinions on a variety of issues. This could highlight areas of concern as perceived by employees. If exercises of this nature are to be taken seriously it is important that management acts on the results, otherwise employees could consider participating a waste of time.

Suggestion schemes

This is a form of upward communication whereby employees are encouraged to put forward ideas and proposals for the improvement of work practices, which in its own right is a worthwhile pursuit. Schemes of this nature normally have a short life.

Communicating with employees is obviously an important process. The results of a survey suggest that 90 per cent of organisations sampled used one or more of the methods outlined above (Millward *et al.*, 1992).

While reflecting on a number of the above communication methods, Ramsay (1996) reviewed a survey of 400 companies and noted that management rate notice boards and memos as relatively poor methods of communication, but nonetheless use them more than any other method. Team briefings, employee opinion surveys and management accessibility (e.g. through 'open-door' policies or management by walking around) are more highly rated. However, such oral and face-to-face approaches are also more time consuming, which is perhaps the reason for their lower level of implementation. Even where they are practised they cannot guarantee effective two-way communication because, as Ramsay argues, such attempts to engender trust may result in a 'catch-22' situation in which the existence of a climate of trust is a prerequisite for employees to speak out.

Ramsay (1996) identified a number of typical problems with communications that hold implications for managerial practice. They are as follows:

- managerial failure to specify the objectives of a communication scheme;
- the loss of momentum after initial enthusiasm;
- the wrong amount of information – too little or too much;
- too much 'tell and sell' in management style, provoking mistrust amongst employees;

- attempts to undermine trade unions, which can backfire;
- failure to specify those responsible for communicating at each level in the organisation;
- lack of training (for example in presentation and communication skills) for both presenters and recipients of information;
- overformality.

Being aware of the complexity of communication, and the issues raised above, is a useful starting point to bring about improvements in this important process.

■ Participation

The level of employee participation has a major impact on the way an organisation works, and is generally related to two key areas, i.e. management style and employee representation or involvement, such as the worker-director of old. The issue of employee involvement is addressed in Box 11.1.

BOX 11.1

Employee involvement

Employee involvement (EI) schemes fall into four categories, as follows: downward communication, upward problem solving, financial participation, and representative participation. Differences between EI schemes can be reflected in the degree of involvement (the extent to which employees have influence over a decision), the level of involvement (e.g. at job, departmental or organisational level) and the form it takes (direct, indirect or financial). These distinctions are discussed below.

Downward communication can involve methods discussed in the previous section, such as newsletters, presentations and videos in which management send messages to employees. Downward communication would be seen as fairly low in degree of involvement because it affords little influence to employees. However, such schemes have the potential to be extensive in terms of the levels, range and direct form of involvement.

Upward problem-solving schemes are those that seek to tap into the knowledge and understandings that employees have developed through doing the job. Schemes can involve small groups in solving specific problems, or can be more general and seek opinion on a broader level, for example through the use of employee attitude surveys. The upward problem-solving schemes can produce a greater degree of involvement than downwards communication, and have the potential to address a range of matters.

Financial participation schemes represent attempts to create clear connections between the performance of the organisation (or unit) and the rewards the individual employee receives. Schemes in which participation occurs can include profit sharing, employee share ownership and bonus payments determined on the basis of corporate ▶

---

or business unit performance. These types of reward system are discussed in Chapter 9 on reward management.

Representative participation schemes tend to be those that give greatest degree of involvement, typically by enabling employees to be part of decision-making bodies. Examples include joint consultative committees, advisory councils and works councils. Such approaches can provide an extensive range of involvement, and send a serious message to the workforce that its views are taken seriously. They also derive from the assumption within management that many heads are better than one, and that better decisions can be made through opening up to more people the traditional boundaries of the managerial prerogative to decide.

One can draw a number of practical suggestions from a serious consideration of EI schemes, as follows:

- Management commitment to the scheme should be firm, and should acknowledge that schemes can be demanding of managerial time and effort.
- Support for the scheme must be secured throughout the management structure, that is not just from the top, but also from the middle and supervisory levels whose actions (or lack of them) will strongly impact on the success (or otherwise) of the scheme.
- The objectives of the scheme need to be well thought through in advance.
- Training in the necessary skills must be provided for all involved.
- Impartial monitoring of the scheme should be carried out in order to record where objectives are met and make changes where they are not.
- Excessive expectations of the scheme should be tempered – EI can make a significant contribution but it is not a panacea.
- Be aware of existing relationships, particularly with trade unions, as a scheme that is thought to undermine their position is likely to meet opposition.

(Holden, 2001; Marchington *et al.*, 1992; Ramsay, 1996)

Macro participation

At the macro level, participation with employees as a collective is governed by procedures related to consultation and negotiation with trade unions and workers' representatives. These issues are also addressed later in this chapter in the section on trade union representation.

A present-day manifestation of macro participation is the type of works council increasingly used by companies. Works councils are committees usually made up of representatives from workers and management, and can be found in a number of European countries. They operate at the organisational level and meet to discuss issues such as employee relations and business matters and to engage in joint decision making (Holden, 2001). For example, in Germany regulations governing recruitment and selection, regradings and dismissals require the agreement of Works Councils (Sparrow and Hiltrop, 1994). The Works Councils Directive came into existence under the Social Chapter of the Maastricht Treaty in 1991, and

Britain used the Social Chapter opt-out to avoid its effect. Therefore, technically, British companies do not have to comply with the provisions of the Directive as far as their UK workers are concerned because of the opt-out clause. However, British companies with operations in other EU member states would be subjected to the Directive for employees working outside the UK.

Companies to which the Directive applies are those with at least 1,000 employees within the 15 EU member states covered by the Directive. They will be required to set up European Works Councils (EWCs) with the express purpose of consulting employees and giving them information about their company's performance and prospects. The alleged advantages of Works Councils are that employees will be better able to understand the pressures businesses face and appreciate the need to adapt to change in a competitive world. Also, EWCs could be seen as a means to cultivate the commitment of employees to the achievement of their company's objectives.

Although not required to do so, some British companies set up EWCs in the United Kingdom. Amongst them are United Biscuits, Coats Viyella and ICI. Electrolux is to include UK employees in its company-wide Works Councils that will cover all its European plants. Interestingly, surprising preliminary evidence from research conducted by the Industrial Relations Research Unit, University of Warwick, suggests that up to 300 British companies could be affected by the directive (Bassett, 1995).

Relying on the views of managers involved in EWCs in UK-owned companies, Wills (1999) arrived at the following judgement: EWCs seem to be taken seriously by UK companies, they are an integral part of corporate communications, and the trade unions may see them as a vehicle to spread best practice in employment, but it appears that EWCs are more likely to be driven by a managerial agenda than a trade union one. Therefore, in the years to come can we expect significant developments in macro participation in the United Kingdom?

Micro participation

At a micro level, the degree of individual participation will depend on the management styles adopted. Forms of participation in HRM tend to be broadly conceived. The Harvard model of HRM (Beer *et al.*, 1984) holds that the various stakeholders in an organisation should be taken into account when making decisions. The stakeholders include shareholders, customers, employees and unions. It is thought that if employees and unions are involved in the decision-making processes they will feel a greater sense of 'ownership' of the decisions made and will be more committed to their implementation. Workers will be more motivated to perform tasks where they have had some input into the determination of work goals and to the way they will be met. Participation can be seen as an important aspect of the way HRM can seek to enhance employee commitment.

Employee participation can be viewed as consultative or delegative. Consultative participation encourages and enables staff to contribute their views, but management retains the right to make the final decision. Delegative participation goes further and allows workers to take on decisions that had traditionally fallen within the managerial prerogative (Geary, 1994).

In previous chapters various types of participative practices (e.g. autonomous work groups and quality circles) have been examined. An analysis of non-unionised organisations on 'greenfield' sites (Guest and Hoque, 1994) found that nearly half had high involvement/high commitment practices and HRM strategies. Less than a quarter had authoritarian and non-participative management styles. With regard to authoritarianism in management, in particular where there is a tinge of abusive behaviour, there are some who believe that this style of management is tantamount to firm management and may be particularly appropriate if good commercial results are to be achieved in certain corporate cultures. Others would argue that the dividing line between this type of management and bullying is rather tenuous. A survey undertaken by the University of Stafford on behalf of the British Broadcasting Corporation (BBC) in 1994 showed that 78 per cent of the 1,137 employees sampled had witnessed workplace bullying, which in some cases amounts to a culture of management by fear and intimidation (Fursland, 1995). Example 11.1 illustrates a case of a management style that may constitute bullying. An example of an organisation – Chelsea and Westminster Healthcare Trust – that is taking such matters seriously and has developed a strong policy on dignity and respect in the workplace is highlighted in the health and safety section later in this chapter.

It would appear that the management style referred to in Example 11.1 is unlikely to be popular as we progress in the twenty-first century. According to an Institute of Management report (1994) respondents in a survey of 1,200 managers strongly maintained that 'authoritarian management styles will be increasingly inappropriate'. Respondents also stated that in 29 per cent of organisations there

---

EXAMPLE 11.1

Firm management or bullying?

A computer analyst with nine years' service resigned from a company in the financial services field, Credit Lyonnais Rouse, London, after being at the receiving end of public abuse from the financial director. Apparently the financial director swore at him in an open-plan office for allowing an old printer to remain on a filing cabinet in contravention of company rules. The case was brought to an industrial tribunal, which heard evidence from the financial director that he was unrepentant, claiming that he gave the analyst 'a severe, well-merited and public reprimand'. From this statement one can conclude that the financial director's behaviour was not an unexpected aberration but part of his management style. The chairman of the industrial tribunal rebuked the financial director, saying that he neither apologised nor sought to make amends for his discourteous behaviour. The computer analyst was awarded £11,000 for 'constructive dismissal'.

(Fursland, 1995)

were moves towards a more cooperative, less coercive style of management, and that in a further 39 per cent of organisations such a style of management was partly implemented. The manager, according to the report, will be a team leader who earns the employee's respect, rather than giving orders, by the beginning of the twenty-first century.

It was felt that 'female attributes' – group orientation, skills connected with building teams and networks of relationships, consensus management, negotiating, interpersonal skills, tolerance and the ability to cope with the demands of several projects at one time – would be needed by successful managers in the future. According to Fondas (1997) such a scenario poses a direct challenge to the often-stated maxim that masculine skills are necessary for managerial success, and puts the spotlight on qualities that women are more likely to possess. It may be helpful for women's prospects if organisations begin to value such skills. From an ethical standpoint one can question the relevance of gender in the workplace. Research has indicated that there is little or no difference in leadership performance between men and women (although women were slightly more effective in areas such as business, education and government, and men in areas such as the military and outdoor pursuits (Eagly *et al.*, 1995). The topic of ethics will be discussed in greater detail later in this chapter.

A particular perspective on managerial leadership, i.e. transformational leadership (Bass, 1990), seems to be compatible with an HRM outlook on organisational life. This type of leadership is executed in a way that empowers and respects people. Leaders are expected to be innovative, creative, charismatic, and visionary risk takers who subscribe to exacting targets and are able to influence their followers to share their inspiring visions of future accomplishments. In the process leaders will be supportive and keen to encourage those subjected to their influence to be entrepreneurial in outlook and bold in seizing opportunities to exploit their talent and make innovative contributions (McKenna, 2000).

Although traditional approaches have focused on the hierarchical relationship between leader and subordinates, another view is that in order to be effective in modern organisations leadership also needs to be 'lateral' and even 'upward'. These issues are discussed in Box 11.2.

BOX 11.2

Vision, strategy and other leadership capabilities

A powerful vision is a precondition for leading a company or a country at any time. It is a persuasive picture of where you want to go, how you want to get there, and why anybody should follow. Herb Kelleher formed Southwest Airlines USA in 1971 to make flying affordable and the company profitable. That vision has guided the company ever since. The airline has some of the lowest ticket rates in the industry. A strong vision in a vacuum is not good enough; it must be considered in a strategic context influenced by intensifying competition and not enough time to achieve corporate goals.

▶

Professional investors and analysts in the City and Wall Street expect top management to produce good performances. Although vision and strategy are essential, they are joined by new critical abilities, namely leading out, leading up and moving fast.

With regard to leading out (lateral leadership), companies require managers who can lead out (not just down to subordinates) as they increasingly outsource services, use joint ventures and construct strategic alliances. In other words, the skill of delegating to subordinates is being supplemented by a talent for arranging work (e.g. outsourcing contracts for information services) with partners outside the company. Such lateral leadership is essential for obtaining results when you have no formal organisational authority to guarantee the desired outcome. Lateral leadership could entail in this case the identification of the service to contract out, dealing with the right outside partners to provide the service, and convincing sceptical internal managers that the arrangement would deliver what they wanted. Lateral leadership requires the following:

- strategic thinking to understand when and how to collaborate in order to gain competitive advantage;
- deal-making skills to secure the appropriate arrangements with outside companies and to ensure that they provide a quality service;
- monitoring the progress of the partnership by overseeing and developing the collaborative contract; and
- change management to spearhead new ways of doing business despite internal resistance.

As to leading up, in conditions of decentralised authority companies place a premium on a manager's capacity to mobilise support from superiors as well as subordinates. Effectively one expects managers to lead their own bosses. Where the manager's manager lacks data the subordinate manager should provide the superior with what is needed. Upward leadership depends upon followers who are ready to speak out, solve problems and compensate for weaknesses at the boss's level, but if it is not done in a subtle way it could be disadvantageous to the person exercising it. When handled delicately, it can be beneficial in career terms to those using upward leadership because it gives them the opportunity to be noticed.

With regard to moving fast, the widespread use of the web has increased the availability of information to buyers and sellers and reduced the costs of transactions between them. Acting decisively and quickly with the help of new technology in changing markets, and modifying strategy in response to changes in the company's competitive position is essential. When competitors of eBay – the world's largest online auction site – began competing in the auction market, the chief executive adopted some of their features on eBay's website, as well as adding new features.

(Useem, 2000)

Cynics might suggest that the rhetoric of progressive management practices belies the reality in today's world characterised by delayering and downsizing or right-sizing, in which job insecurity, occupational stress and poor morale are not difficult to find. Therefore it is not surprising that at times managers are prone to outbursts that one would not normally associate with a more humane management style.

Processes such as employee involvement, upward leadership and a team orientation have an impact on and reflect the nature and distribution of power in the organisation. Hardy and Leiba-O'Sullivan (1998) developed a typology of power, based on a review of the research, that can be informative in analysing such processes. They argue that there are four dimensions of power: overt power in the decision-making arena; power over non-decision making; unobtrusive controls; power as a network of relations and discourses.

Overt power may be derived from control of resources, position in the structure and the control of rewards and sanctions. The location of power is observable, and it can be exercised when there is conflict in order to achieve compliance with the dominant order.

However, the decision-making arenas are not open to all who have an interest in the outcomes. Power can also be exercised in deciding who should be involved and who excluded, what items appear on the agenda, and in forming alliances in order to control the outcome of meetings. In other words, not all power is exercised overtly in making decisions, but much occurs behind the scenes.

A third level of sophistication in analysis reveals unobtrusive controls – those that are not simply observable in the way rewards are controlled, or alliances formed. Unobtrusive controls operate through cultural norms, generally held assumptions and structures that legitimise the demands and interests of some but not others. So, for example, the operation of power occurs in conditions of political inactivity. One should not assume that silence indicates agreement – it may be that those with little power are unable to voice their desires and needs as these would not be regarded as legitimate. Power in this sense operates in unseen ways, and attention should be paid not only to actions and words but to silence and inaction.

Lastly, power can be discerned in the network of relationships and discourses. At this level of analysis power is not regarded as an object that can be owned, or a force that an individual can marshal to achieve his or her ends in a straightforward way. Rather, the concept is that we are all subject to the influence of a web of power relations that resides in every individual perception, action and interaction. Discourses determine what is seen as important and what is ignored, and they determine how people are perceived and the way they are interacted with. Hence certain expectations will be held of leaders, and if they do not live up to these expectations they will be regarded as poor leaders, and will suffer the consequences. Similarly, depending on the social context, the same people could be 'constructed' quite differently. For example, in one setting X would be a conservative, and Y a radical, whereas in another setting X would be regarded as being concerned with quality and Y with the generation of new revenue. The way these individuals are assessed will be based on a deeply embedded, and often unconscious, sets of concepts and relationships that cannot be controlled by any single individual – even those who are apparently powerful.

Hardy and Leiba-O'Sullivan (1998) analyse a case of empowerment, a topic of relevance to team leadership and motivation, using the four dimensions of power discussed above. In empowerment there is some transfer of overt power in decision making from managers to employees; however, there may be limitations to what an empowered team can decide – for example, their overall budget may be fixed, and hence they have only limited power over the 'non-decision-making arena' that sets their own arena of power. Unobtrusive controls may operate through peer pressure on attendance, perception and performance within the team. For example, those who oppose empowerment might be seen as 'dinosaurs' and 'neanderthals'.

Lastly, when power is regarded as a network of relations and discourses, attention is drawn to the complexity and ambiguity of empowerment as experienced by individuals. The same event can be seen as empowerment, exploitation, or even as not constituting change. At this level of analysis it is not that one could check the objective facts to see which version is true. Rather, the different people are operating in different 'realities' that are real to them. So for some empowerment is experienced as a subtle form of control in which management is extracting greater effort from the workers, for others it is the chance to exercise greater self-determination. In a sense both are right and both are wrong simultaneously. Greater effort and performance are required and yet there is greater self-determination. But there are still strong limitations to individual freedom as the organisation will measure output and the manager and peer group will have expectations that, if flouted, will at least lead to social sanctions such as exclusion from the group. However, the immediate control of supervisory management is removed. The challenge for managers in such situations is to recognise these different levels of reality and enable employees to cope with the ambiguities they entail (Beech and Cairns, 2001).

■ Trade union representation

Workers are often represented by trade unions in negotiations with management about pay and conditions, in which case both parties enter into collective bargaining. The latter takes place when employees are members of trade unions that undertake to negotiate on their behalf in matters such as pay grades and systems, working conditions, holidays and other benefits, the content of work and its allocation, and when employers recognise trade unions and their officials as legitimate bargaining agents (Price, 1997). Collective bargaining came into existence because unions felt it was a better system than individual bargaining to increase employees' bargaining power and to challenge attempts by employers to create competition between workers. In return for the best possible deal, the unions required solidarity between their members.

A recent demonstration of a move towards collective bargaining is given in Example 11.2. This was presented as a partnership approach, and it is clear that the union felt they had gained through the deal.

EXAMPLE 11.2

Carlsberg-Tetley and the Transport and General Workers' Union

Carlsberg-Tetley, the beer producers, reached a deal with the Transport and General Workers' Union (T&G), which they saw as being a partnership approach. Collective bargaining replaced the traditional local negotiations for transport workers. This was seen as an indication of the maturity of the relationship between the employers and the union, as previously there was great hesitancy on the part of the employers to enter into collective bargaining on the grounds that, if it were to go wrong, beer transportation would be halted right across the country.

The partnership agreement has led to major changes in working practices, terms and conditions. The traditional overtime pay, bonuses and supplements have been replaced by a standard salary. Workers are now expected to stay till the job is completed. The structure has been simplified with 25 job titles reduced to 4: driver, driver's mate, team leader and warehouse operative. The result was, according to the director of HR, 'substantial and essential cost savings'. These savings were regarded as necessary given the competitive situation the company found itself in. An implication of the agreement was that the company would not be seeking to outsource its transport; however this was not an explicit statement.

It is worth briefly considering the context of this development in employee relations. Other brewers had recently outsourced their transport functions and, given the company's need to cut costs, the T&G feared that the same approach could be taken by Carlsberg-Tetley. It was believed that if transport were outsourced the terms and conditions of employees would deteriorate radically over time.

Although this agreement was presented as a partnership, Carlsberg-Tetley did not have equally good relationships with all unions. They had derecognised the manufacturing, services and finance union (MSF), which represented 400 middle managers, saying that they were in the minority, and that no one had complained. The HR director denied that the company was 'into union bashing'.

(Thatcher, 1998)

In the above case it can be seen that Carlsberg-Tetley also gained considerably in flexibility and cost savings. The impact of contextual factors, such as the industry norm for local bargaining, and the highly competitive situation, had an impact on the agreement. The trade union accepted and was influenced by the need for a change in employee performance. The approach may be represented as the 'sophisticated modern' approach (Purcell and Sisson, 1983), examined earlier, in that the organisation was extending the way in which it worked with the union but, in view of the way it treated other unions, it would be possible to raise the question of whether the company also displayed 'standard modern' tendencies in the way it displayed opportunism.

Should one consider *national cultures* when viewing the dynamics of collective bargaining? According to Dowling *et al.* (1994) cross-national differences ought to be considered when examining the objectives of the collective bargaining process and the enforceability of collective agreements. They go on to say: 'many European unions view the collective bargaining process as an ongoing class struggle between labour and capital, whereas in the US union leaders tend toward a pragmatic economic view of collective bargaining rather than an ideological view'. Such a pronounced distinction between the two continents is less likely to be the case in the early 2000s.

Relations between employers and trade unions can be characterised as either consultation or negotiation, as shown in Table 11.1.

In the case of consultation, the union may be involved in joint consultative committees, whereas negotiation may be conducted through collective bargaining, which, as we have seen, can only take place where the union has been recognised by management as a legitimate representative of the company's employees. Negotiation can take place in a single organisation, or on a wider scale, when, for example, a union can represent workers doing similar jobs in different organisations in the public sector.

HRM has been associated with an opposite trend – a move towards local level bargaining. This is partly because centralised bargaining (e.g. where pay rates and conditions are centrally determined without reference to local conditions) was seen as time consuming, but it also reflects the changing relations between management and unions. Throughout the 1980s a number of changes occurred in the United Kingdom, which affected the nature of the interaction between management and unions, and as a result we have witnessed the emergence of the new industrial relations. A series of factors has contributed to these changes. For example, there was a decline in manufacturing industry, economic recession, high unemployment, a move to flexible job descriptions, the disappearance of job demarcations in the face of flexible working practices, and an increase in the number of part-time workers with the advent of the flexible firm.

Changes such as these bought in their wake more non-union organisations where contact between employers and individual employees (individualised systems) is prevalent, which could be seen as contributing to the weakening of employee power and growth of employer power within the organisation due to the waning influence of collectivism (Hendry, 1995). As a result, it was not surprising that the level of trade union membership fell from 55.4 per cent of the workforce in 1979 to below 40 per cent in 1992 (Marsh and Cox, 1992), and by 1995 this figure had fallen to 32 per cent (Brown *et al.*, 1997). Culley *et al.* (1998) identify one fundamental

Table 11.1 Relations between the parties

Consultation	Negotiation
The views of the trade union are invited by management	Both sides have a right to make an input to the decision
The decision remains within the managerial prerogative	An agreed outcome has to be reached
The decision may or may not take on board the trade union view	The decision is a bargain between the two positions

change in the personnel management/HRM landscape. This has been the decline in joint regulation by collective bargaining. Union recognition has fallen from 60 per cent in 1984 to 53 per cent in 1990. Between 1990 and 1998 it fell a further eight points to 45 per cent. Meanwhile the proportion of workplaces with no union members increased from 27 per cent in 1984 to 36 per cent in 1990, to 47 per cent in 1998. In the words of Culley and his colleagues, this signals a major transformation of the landscape of British employment relations. Some argue that a unitarist view implicit in US models of HRM – i.e. the interests of the employees and the employers should be the same – can result in a considerable reduction in union membership, as was the case in the United States (Beaumont, 1992).

Various pieces of legislation in the United Kingdom have been enacted that have worked against traditional union activity. A secret ballot is required before industrial action can take place, and secondary action (in support of other workers not employed by the same employer) is no longer allowed. 'Closed shops', where all employees are required to join a particular union, are no longer enforceable, and the way of handling those who take industrial action has changed. Prior to the new legislation strikers could be dismissed (as they were considered to have broken the contract to supply their labour in return for remuneration), but everyone striking would have to be dismissed. Individuals could not be singled out; and if one or more strikers were re-employed the others could lodge a complaint with an industrial tribunal. Under the new legislation it is now permissible to dismiss strikers and to re-employ them selectively after a break of three months. These changes have limited the power of the unions and changed the nature of industrial relations.

In the new industrial relations scene management has greater power to impose its will without negotiation or the need to enter into joint consultation. Trade unions, which in the past were opposed to management initiatives, such as increased flexibility and reductions in demarcation lines between jobs, have become less confrontational. The UK Trades Union Congress (TUC) formed the view that properly practised 'soft' HRM is not incompatible with unionism (Monks, 1994). Increasing employee involvement, good communications and treating employees as valued assets rather than factors of production are developments supported by the TUC. An analysis of the 'Workplace Industrial Relations Survey 3' (Monks, 1994) found no correlation between HRM and anti-unionism. It was found that the more anti-union the employer the less likely the employer was to pursue HRM techniques. Wood (1996) argues that there is some evidence to suggest that unionism can coexist with contemporary strategies for bringing about HRM-based changes that are compatible with the demands of the external environment, but adds that a condition for this coexistence is a continual emphasis on negotiation and collective bargaining.

HRM can view unions as a positive factor, assisting in the process of communicating with and involving employees. In some cases this attitude has resulted in single union deals. Single union agreements are those where sole negotiating rights are granted to one union. They are particularly prevalent in companies that set up operations on greenfield sites and in Japanese-owned organisations. In these situations consultation may be carried out through 'company councils', where the employees' representatives are elected by the workforce rather than appointed by the trade union, although there may be some degree of compromise on this arrangement.

Another feature of the new industrial relations are 'no strike agreements'. Normally these have an automatic referral to an independent arbitrator built into the negotiation procedures where there is failure to reach an internal agreement. The arbitration is often of the 'pendulum' form, which means that rather than the arbitrator making a compromise decision a choice is made between the last offer of the employer and the last claim of the union. Because of the normal obligation of the union not to take industrial action while the procedures are in progress, this means that in effect there is an agreement not to strike. However, unconstitutional industrial action may still occur. Single union and no strike agreements represent a more cooperative approach from unions, and in some cases this is reciprocated by positive HRM practices. For example, in Lucas Flight Control Systems (United Kingdom), the union (the Amalgamated Engineering and Electrical Union) agreed with management an extensive programme of reorganisation, including increases in teamworking and skill flexibility, on the understanding that employment conditions for blue- and white-collar workers will be harmonised, and that the working week will be shorter, with no loss of pay.

However, with the change in the power relations between management and the trade unions, some organisations have sought to impose the managerial prerogative, which has produced a negative effect for workers. For example, in the printing industry there has been a decline in collective bargaining, a derecognition of unions and the imposition of 'individual' contracts.

Finally, according to Roche (2000):

> we may be witnessing the end of new Industrial Relations as a working model for unionised enterprises and sectors in advanced economies and as a major explanatory paradigm for comprehending the dynamics of industrial relations systems. A new perspective is emerging in which the growing influence on industrial relations regimes of contingencies of various kinds actually constitutes the trend in advanced economies.

In other words, the tradition of employee representation through trade unions and collective bargaining as the focus of engagement between management and unions is being replaced by new relationships in the workplace, but the replacement is not of a single type. Rather, it is made up of a number of different (sometimes contradictory) trends. In some cases the traditional model is retained, in others there is increased individualisation, and in yet other cases a 'partnership' approach is adopted in which unions take on some of the concerns of the organisation, and work with management in order to maintain the profitability and longevity of the firm.

■ International trends

When viewed over time, it can be seen that there are three directional trends in union membership. Some countries, such as Finland and Denmark have shown

Table 11.2 Trade union membership by country as a percentage of all employees

Trend	Country	1970	1980	1990	1995
increasing	Sweden	68	80	82	83
increasing	Denmark	60	76	71	82
increasing	Finland	51	70	72	81
fairly stable	Belgium	45	56	51	53
fairly stable	Canada	31	36	36	34
decreasing	Ireland	53	57	50	38
decreasing	Australia	50	48	40	33
decreasing	United Kingdom	45	50	39	32
decreasing	Japan	35	31	25	24
decreasing	New Zealand	41	56	45	22
decreasing	United States	23	22	16	15
decreasing	Spain	27	25	11	15
decreasing	France	22	17	10	9

Source: adapted from Bratton and Gold (1999)

increases in membership figures and have reached high levels of union density. Others, such as Belgium and Canada, have remained fairly stable in their levels of union density, and yet others, such as the United Kingdom, France and Japan, have had decreasing rates of membership. There are three broad bands of membership density: high (above 70 per cent), low (below 20 per cent) and medium. Typically those in the upper bracket have shown an increasing trend of membership. Most other countries (with the exception of Belgium and Canada) have shown a decreasing trend. Table 11.2 shows the percentage of total employees who belong to trade unions in various countries. However, although there have been declines in trade union membership density, the proportions of the workforce covered by collective bargaining has generally remained constant, and even in some countries where there is decreasing or low membership density a high proportion of the workforce is still covered by collective bargaining (see Table 11.3).

Table 11.3 The proportion of the workforce covered by collective bargaining

Trend	Country	1980	1985	1990	1994
increasing	France	85	92	95	95
increasing	The Netherlands	76	76	71	81
stable	Finland	95	–	95	95
stable	Germany	91	91	90	92
stable	Spain	–	67	68	66
stable	Canada	–	37	38	36
decreasing	Australia	88	85	80	80
decreasing	United Kingdom	83	76	65	48
decreasing	Japan	28	–	23	22
decreasing	United States	26	20	18	18

Source: adapted from Bratton and Gold (1999)

Different countries have divergent experiences of trade union relations. In the United Kingdom there have been exceptional reductions in coverage of workers by collective bargaining and trade union membership. This could be said to be a causal factor in a reduction of perceived power of employees in the employer/employee relationship (Bratton and Gold, 1999). What has been responsible for this? It could be the outcome of political factors, with legislation limiting trade union power, as well as economic factors. With regard to the latter there is a view that periods of high unemployment create the perception that, if workers were militant, they could be replaced by others from within the labour market, or employers could rely more on new technology.

Claydon (1998) has argued that the political voice of trade unions in the United Kingdom, expressed by the Trades Union Congress, has been increasingly 'productivist', emphasising that 'terms and conditions cannot be improved ... without improvements in underlying economic performance' (TUC, quoted in Claydon, 1998: 182). This tone is more akin to a unitarist approach than the traditional pluralist stance of unions. It has also been argued (Gilbert, 1993) that employers have increasingly developed an antipathy to unions, with fewer feeling the need to use unions to mediate their dealings with employees. Similarly, Kelly (1996) argues, from a review of the available research, that there is a growing readiness on the part of employers to bypass trade unions and reduce the range of issues over which they have influence.

Hollinshead and Leat (1995) offer an analysis of the trends in other countries. They argue that the high level of membership in Sweden can be explained by the 'corporate social partnership', which has been established over many years. This has been reinforced by a partnership between trade unions and what was, until the early 1990s, the dominant political party. Consequently, trade unions have enjoyed favourable legislation and governmental support.

By contrast, the United States has been typified as a 'business movement' rather than a social partnership. It is argued that the lack of a traditional class base and the high degree of opposition to trade unions from employers and government in the United States have led to the situation of low membership and collective bargaining. Where unions have been active they have tended to focus at the workplace rather than industry level. Additionally, they have tended to adopt a conflictual approach, and so HRM in the United States has tended towards a non-union stance in line with the national trend.

In Japan enterprise has been in a dominant position as far as the unions are concerned since the 1950s, and trade unions have generally operated in a cooperative mode rather than the conflictual approach typified by US unions. In France there is the interesting apparent tension between low and decreasing membership and as yet the increasing numbers of employees covered by collective bargaining. According to Hollinshead and Leat (1995) this can again be explained by the political characteristics of the country. In France the trade union movement is politically and religiously fragmented, but it has gone beyond focusing on workplace terms and conditions, and has held broader political aims. In pursuing these aims it has sought to achieve collective bargaining at industry level and to exert pressure on the government, and has had a degree of success in doing so.

■ Conflict

Conflict in organisations can occur at the collective level (i.e. organised) or the individual level (i.e. unorganised). Collective conflict can lead to industrial action including strikes, go-slows and overtime bans. Individual conflict may manifest itself in absenteeism, a high turnover rate or even sabotage. Any of these actions or outcomes is potentially damaging for the organisation, so it is necessary to use methods for resolving conflict at the earliest opportunity.

Collective conflict may occur when there has been a breakdown in collective bargaining, as, for example, in a dispute about pay levels. Disputes can also arise when there is opposition to changes in working patterns and jobs. At one time the trade unions in the United Kingdom were accused of creating the 'British disease', a high level of strike action. However, in recent years the number of days lost due to industrial stoppages in the United Kingdom is not worse than those of its main competitors. In fact the figures fell gradually throughout the 1980s with one or two exceptions (such as the miners' strike in the mid-1980s).

The United Kingdom was placed 7th amongst the 12 EU member states in terms of production days lost due to strikes (Wassell, 1993). Spain, Greece, Italy, Ireland, France and Portugal had a worse record. In a 'militancy ranking' – based on the number of working days lost, the number of reported strikes and the number of workers involved in disputes – the United Kingdom was rated 5th out of 12 EU members (Sparrow and Hiltrop, 1994). Over time there has been a pronounced decline in days lost to strike action in the United Kingdom. This is indicated by the change from a height of 2,917 stoppages with 629 working days lost per 1,000 employees in the period 1970–4, to a low of 334 stoppages with 37 working days lost per 1,000 employees 20 years later in the period 1990–4 (Brown et al., 1997). While the recent trend with respect to industrial stoppages gives ground for optimism, it would be foolish to conclude that the British are experiencing relatively high levels of workplace harmony. It may be that workers are hesitant to take industrial action for reasons connected with the economic situation and the fear of losing their jobs.

Resolving conflict

To continue with the theme of collective conflict, where it is not possible for management and the representatives of the workers to resolve their conflict, a third party could be invited to intervene. A third party could perform any one of three roles, i.e. conciliator, mediator or arbitrator. A conciliator acts as a facilitator when the main parties are trying to resolve the conflict. A mediator also acts as a facilitator, but in addition puts forward recommendations. An arbitrator actually makes decisions to resolve the conflict.

In cases of individual conflict, as opposed to collective conflict, an employee can make a grievance claim where there is a feeling that he or she has been treated unfairly or in an unacceptable manner. The UK grievance procedure, which does not have formal legal status and was more prevalent in the pre-enterprise culture, allows the individual to complain to the immediate superior (e.g. the supervisor) in the first instance. If the matter cannot be resolved, then the complaint will be heard by the next level of management (e.g. the departmental manager). A union or other representative of the employee may become involved at this stage. The case will be heard and evidence may also be called, for example the views of witnesses to an incident that sparked the complaint. The alleged culprit will also be given the chance to submit his or her version of events. The outcome of the process may involve practical ways of dealing with the problem, or alternatively disciplinary procedures may follow. In exceptional cases a third party may be asked to intervene. Normally there is a right of appeal to a higher authority if the complainant is still dissatisfied after exhausting the procedure.

There are occasions where an employer institutes a disciplinary measure because of a belief that the employee is failing to carry out his or her duties adequately or is behaving in an unacceptable way. Where discipline takes the form of terminating the employment of the individual, one may ask if the dismissal of the employee was fair. The UK Employment Protection (Consolidation) Act (1978) states that the employees (with more than two years' continuous service) cannot be unfairly dismissed. If a complaint relating to unfair dismissal is made the employer has to show that the dismissal was fair by proving that the principal reason for dismissal was one of the following:

- lack of capability or qualification to do the job;
- unacceptable conduct of the employee;
- redundancy (the job has disappeared);
- legal restraint (e.g. an employee works as a truck driver but is disqualified from driving;
- another substantial reason (e.g. the employee's spouse sets up a rival company).

In addition, employers must be seen to have acted 'reasonably'. This means that they followed the appropriate set of procedures. The Advisory, Conciliation and Arbitration Service (ACAS) has a model disciplinary procedure, which is adopted by many organisations. The purpose of the procedure is to provide a breathing space for the employee whose performance or behaviour has fallen short of acceptable standards so that the necessary improvement can be made.

Certain principles underlie the procedure. These include that the employee will be given full information, and that careful investigation will take place before any disciplinary action is taken. Before the formal procedure is invoked, particularly where the fault is a minor one, the option of dealing with the problem informally should be explored. This might take the form of a counselling session. However, where it is necessary to use the formal procedure, the employee (accompanied by a friend or representative where appropriate) should be given the opportunity to put his or her side of the case at a forum, which sits at a time to be arranged between each of the stages listed below. The stages of the ACAS procedure are as follows:

1 *Oral warning.* A note of this is kept on the employee's file.
2 *Written warning.* This is activated where there is repetition of the offence following an oral warning, or where the offence is more serious.
3 *Final written warning or disciplinary suspension.* For repeated misconduct where previous warnings have not been effective. (A serious alternative may be suspension without pay).
4 *Dismissal.* Where the employee has failed to comply with the requirements of the final written warning.

For gross misconduct, where the offence is very serious (e.g. theft, fraud, fighting, serious negligence), following an investigation the employee may be dismissed without going through stages 1–3. The employee will normally have the right to appeal against the decision at each stage of the procedure.

Apart from unfair dismissal, which is applicable to cases where the company has employed the individual for at least two years, there is wrongful dismissal. An employee with less than two years' service can exercise a 'common law' right to sue the employer for damages if dismissed wrongly. A case of wrongful dismissal arises when, for example, the employer has not given proper notice, or the behaviour of the employee did not justify such treatment. A case of unfair dismissal would be heard before an industrial tribunal. However, a case of wrongful dismissal would be referred to an ordinary court where the damages awarded could be higher than the maximum stipulated by the industrial tribunals. Always remember that dismissal has to take place before a tribunal or court can act.

When we reflect on the role of grievance procedures and the use of discipline our concern should be to solve a problem and make matters better, and not to be totally preoccupied with the administering of punishment. For example, there is a problem where an employee is persistently late for work. Our aim should be to discover the causes of this behaviour (e.g. lack of motivation, difficult domestic circumstances, travel difficulties, a personal problem), and then to help the employee confront and hopefully remove the underlying cause(s), rather than just dealing with the symptom.

Handling conflict in an organisation is facilitated by the rules and procedures in place. However, we cannot overlook the part played by management style and organisational culture. An aim of HRM is to create a culture in which employees are committed to the goals of the organisation. Where this prevails and is reflected in, for example, increased employee participation, a situation can emerge where employees become more involved in their own 'discipline' (Edwards, 1994). If employees are working in a team, they are not only carrying out the tasks allocated to them but are also interacting with others. In the course of interaction, approved behaviour is likely to be supported, while deviant behaviour could be subjected to sanctions (group discipline). If the team is committed to a goal of achieving high quality work, it is likely to reward team members whose performance meets the requisite standards.

■ Ethics, HRM and managing diversity

Increasingly, ethical issues are being raised as matters of concern in organisations. Issues may range from the micro, such as harassment and bullying (discussed in Example 11.1, page 264) to unfair discrimination in selection decision making (for example in relation to the use of tests as discussed in Chapter 7) through to macro issues such as protection of the environment. While people have a personal view of what is right and wrong there is a cultural dimension, for example the practice of bribery is acceptable in some cultures but not others (McKenna, 2000; Montagnon, 1998). It has been argued by some (e.g. Eccles *et al.*, 2001; Hartley, 1993) that it is necessary to formulate ethical codes of conduct and to reinforce them through measurement in order to persuade organisations to behave ethically. However, this in itself may be insufficient to have a genuine impact and it has been argued that the HRM function should be proactive in raising awareness of ethical issues and the need for consistency between the values and behaviour, particularly in the age of the 'green consumer' and the 'ethical investor' (Pocock, 1989).

An example is provided by the Co-operative Bank. In 1992 it produced a 12-point code which specified that it would not lend money to companies involved in cruelty to animals, the arms trade or environmental destruction. By 1998 the Bank's market share had increased by about 3 per cent and it is thought that this is at least partially attributable to its overt focus on ethical issues. In addition, the Bank has enjoyed considerable loyalty from its workforce, with over 60 per cent of employees having in excess of 20 years' service. Commitment is regarded as a two-way thing, and the Bank has made no-redundancy agreements with staff and placed an emphasis on providing training, annual pay increases and an examination of the balance between work and family life (McKenna, 2000). One can ask how far such policies are genuinely ethical if they also bring economic benefits. This has been a matter of debate in HRM, and Legge (1998) offers an analytical framework that is applicable in such matters of judgement.

The framework includes three alternative perspectives on ethics as follows:

1 *Deontological theory* – derived from the philosophy of Immanuel Kant – is based on a belief in moral laws that describe what is ultimately right and wrong. Ethical behaviour is a matter of doing what is right, for example treating others as we would want to be treated ourselves and operating in a fair and just way.
2 *Utilitarianism* – based on the philosophy of John Stuart Mill – does not accept that there are ultimately right and wrong actions, rather rightness is contingent. Choosing the right action is a matter of calculating what the consequences of alternative actions will be and selecting the one that will lead to the greatest good (or least harm) for the greatest number of people in the circumstances.
3 *Stakeholder theory of justice* – based on the philosophy of John Rawls – argues that justice is neither an ultimate truth nor straightforwardly a matter of calcu-

lation of consequences. An alternative is proposed based on a 'mind experiment' as follows: imagine that people existed, but are not yet in the world – they are able to choose the ethical structure and 'rules of engagement' for society, but do not know in advance their own position, strengths and weaknesses. Rawls believes that people in such a position would choose a system of distribution in which no one would lose out completely, and in which care would be given to all people, no matter how weak. This choice would be made because no individual would know in advance how strong or weak they would be. In application to the organisational world, such thinking emerges as a concern with the needs and desires of divergent stakeholder groups, while maintaining the long-term survival of the organisation.

The different perspectives provide a framework through which the ethical value of HRM policies and actions can be judged. In the case of the Co-operative Bank described above their policy would be ethical in terms of stakeholder justice, but would not necessarily be seen as fully ethical from the deontological perspective as it appears that the 'ethical' policies may have been a means to the end of business success. Ultimately ethical decisions would be the ones taken because they were right no matter what the business outcomes (good or bad). An example of the operationalisation of the ethical framework is provided in Example 11.3.

EXAMPLE 11.3

Ethics and the production of jeans

The different perspectives on ethics lead to different ways of assessing a situation. For example, an ethical question for HRM can be drawn from Abrams and Astill's (2001) investigation of the production of denim jeans. They found that mid-priced jeans being sold in Europe were composed of materials from 13 countries around the world, and while some suppliers were operating a reasonable approach to employment others (in the view of Abrams and Astill) were not. For example, the copper for rivets and buttons was being mined by people working for low wages in poor conditions, and at the cost of environmental contamination in Africa. Similarly, the final product was being assembled and stitched by people working for very low wages under circumstances that would be seen as well below the acceptable standards of health and safety in the United Kingdom.

If we were to think of this situation from the deontological frame it could be argued that this policy of sourcing production at low cost is unethical because it treats people in a way that is always unacceptable. From a utilitarian perspective there would be a number of questions. Although there are bad consequences for some, overall are the interests of the majority served? If so, does the benefit, in human terms, outweigh the costs? If the answers to these questions were yes, then the policy would be seen as ethical. Similarly, from a stakeholder perspective there would be further issues of balance to explore. In particular there is the question of whether some level of employment is better than none. In the mining situation the benefits for the local population may outweigh the costs, notwithstanding the long-term environmental effects. Similarly, although the pay of the production workers is very low by European standards, in their own economic setting it does allow them to live, and the alternative of unemployment would be worse. For the deontological theory perspective it is possible to make a simple assessment of right and wrong. For the other two ethical theories this judgement is contingent on outcomes and degree of balance of the stakeholders.

A question arises – how ethical is HRM? The answer for Legge (1998) depends on what is meant by HRM and which ethical perspective is adopted. The elements of HRM that are concerned with cost cutting and ensuring that workers are flexible on the terms of the organisation are unlikely to be seen as ethical unless they lead to the greatest good for the greatest number. For example, it could be argued that making some people redundant maintains the viability of the firm, without which everyone would ultimately lose their jobs. It is more likely that the developmental side of HRM – encouraging mutuality, investing in people and rewarding them appropriately – would be regarded as ethical from all three perspectives.

Managing diversity

The issue of managing diversity is one that has been raised as a particular ethical issue for HRM. The term diversity emerged from the focus on equal opportunities which was concerned with eliminating unfair bias and using only criteria for selection decision making that were strictly relevant to the job. This would normally exclude criteria based on gender or race.

Managing diversity has broader aims and is concerned with 'creating a working culture that seeks, respects, values and harnesses difference' (Schneider, 2001: 27). Diversity is not a policy of assimilation in which minorities are absorbed into the culture of the majority. Rather it is a deliberate attempt to bring into one organisational setting people who differ in nationality, ethnic origin, gender, religion, sexual orientation, background and so on. The argument for this is based on business logic, and in particular the need to operate in a globalised environment. For organisations operating across national boundaries there are questions of how they are going to be most effective with different groups of employees and different groups of customers. This means having people who can speak the local language and who understand local culture – in Unilever's term being a 'multilocal multinational' (Schneider, 2001). It can also be the case that diverse teams can be highly productive and creative. One example is Intel's development of the Pentium chip, which was undertaken by a 'global product development team'. Following this success such teams have become the norm for Intel.

In order to implement diversity policies Schneider proposes a systematic approach. This starts by gathering three types of measures in a diagnostic phase: employee statistics (such as the make-up of the workforce by gender, ethnicity and disability), internal perceptions (for example running focus groups to gather the perceptions of minority groups and employee surveys incorporating diversity questions) and external perceptions (for example gathering information from customers on how they regard the organisation). Following the diagnostic phase the targets for progress should be set in a meaningful way. For example, terms such as 'diversity' may have little meaning for the workforce, and structuring policies in terms of 'respect' and 'fairness' may be more effective. In addition to policies it is important to identify the behaviours that will support the vision of diversity. For companies such as Barclays Bank, which has been following this process, it has encompassed a culture change, and thus cannot be regarded as a stand-alone activity. Rather there is a need to link policies and behaviours to the recruitment and selection practices and the performance management system. The case of BAE Systems is introduced in Example 11.4. In this case there is a link between managing diversity and quality improvement that incorporates an integrated approach to change.

EXAMPLE 11.4

BAE Systems' diversity policy

BAE Systems employs 120,000 people in four continents. In the United Kingdom it employs 70,000 of whom 12 per cent are women, 5 per cent are from ethnic minorities and 1 per cent are disabled. There are two female managing directors and one female non-executive board member. Traditionally the industry has been white-male centric, but BAE fears that unless it can broaden its appeal it will be difficult to recruit the 2,000 engineers (including ICT specialists) it needs every 12 months. Its aim is to create an inclusive culture that does not demand that minority staff should 'fit in'. The reasoning behind this is that job-holder value (i.e. the value of the job and company to the employee) should be regarded as highly significant alongside shareholder value. BAE believes that if this can be achieved then staff will feel valued by the company and will contribute to its success. In addition, it will make the company attractive to graduates and others who will become sources of recruitment.

The approach has been to integrate the diversity policy with an agenda for change that incorporates the European Foundation for Quality Management (EFQM) business excellence model. A SWOT analysis of the current situation was conducted, and best practices identified. In order to foster behavioural change local implementation teams took responsibility to help move their business units from being 'learners' to 'world class' by progressing through bronze, silver and gold measured standards under the EFQM model. Audits are conducted and achieved outcomes are rewarded.

There is some evidence of improvement on the business profile measures that are important to BAE. In the *Sunday Times* survey of 'employers of choice' they rose from 74th to 25th between 1999 and 2001. At the same time benchmarking against industry norms has shown improvement. In the Opportunity Now Survey of 1999 BAE was 6 per cent below the manufacturing sector's norm, but by 2001 it was 11 per cent above the norm. For BAE the link of diversity to business needs is crucial.

(Benwell, 2001)

■ Health and safety at work

Devoting a short section to health and safety is in no way meant to condone its relatively low position in the pecking order of HRM topics. It is recognised that the health, safety and welfare function within the organisation has been very much the 'Cinderella' of HRM despite the enormous human and economic benefits that can flow from a well-conceived and properly implemented health and safety policy within a company. Under the UK Health and Safety at Work etc. Act (1974) employers have a duty to ensure (so far as is reasonably practicable) that they provide a safe and healthy environment both for their direct employees and for other people (including contractors) who may be affected by the work activities. This means that employers are responsible for the following:

- providing safe equipment for the job and ensuring that it is used in accordance with correct procedures;
- making sure that employees do not undertake dangerous activities;
- checking that all the procedures involved in jobs are safe;
- providing a safe and healthy environment in which to work (including adequate light, heat and ventilation).

Employees are required to comply with the employer's reasonable instructions with regard to health and safety. So, for example, if instructed to wear safety goggles, or to ensure that a guard is fitted when operating a machine, they are expected to comply. The Management of Health and Safety at Work Regulations (1992) were enacted to implement the European Commission Directive on health and safety. Employers are required to perform the following tasks:

- carry out assessment of hazards and risks and surveillance,
- plan and monitor preventive measures,
- make sure that employees have adequate information,
- provide necessary training.

Directives have also been implemented on limiting the manual handling of loads, use of computer (display screen) equipment and the provision of personal protective equipment. A legitimate concern of health and safety practitioners, in association with appropriate HRM specialists, could be the provision of counselling and other services to those who succumb to stressful conditions at work often brought about by a climate of profound change. Such action could lead to people being able to cope better with the demands made on them and could have a beneficial effect on absenteeism and staff turnover.

Traditionally managers have confined their attention to health and safety issues within the workplace, reacting to problems as they arise. Nowadays a number of employers have decided to adopt a more proactive stance in health care. This often takes the form of fitness and health screening schemes designed to change the lifestyle of employees inside and outside the organisation (see Example 11.5, page 284). Another manifestation of preventive health management programmes is the employee assistance programme (EAP) highlighted below (McKenna, 2000).

EAPs – in which employees are counseled on problems ranging from alcohol and drug abuse to financial, marital and legal difficulties – have only taken root in the UK in recent years, but are well established in the US. The main purpose of EAPs is to enhance the quality of the employee's personal life (Berridge and Cooper, 1993), but offering these programmes could be viewed by some companies as a way of projecting a caring image. A main reason why employees use this service is that it gives them the opportunity to address issues connected with relationships, family problems and financial worries. This may not be a surprising development because in many cases traditional support services (e.g. family, church and GP) are not readily available.

Although it is changes in the workplace – e.g. widespread downsizing and restructuring often resulting in greater pressure and more work for those left behind – that often persuade companies to introduce EAPs, many of the problems dealt with by the programmes are frequently unrelated to work (Hall, 1995). Normally the types of problem presented vary according to whether they are discussed face to face or over the telephone. According to Michael Reddy of ICAS (an EAP provider), about half the people calling telephone helplines seek financial or legal help, with less than a third of calls related to work. People may want to talk about drink driving, or social security benefits, or eviction threats by a landlord, or separation, or behavioral problems in children experienced by single mothers, or one partner reluctant to move following the relocation of a job.

SmithKline Beecham (now GlaxoSmithKline), the pharmaceutical company, introduced an EAP programme and found that many of the problems presented were not work-related (e.g. Child Support Agency assessments, or meeting the needs of an elderly parent living far away). The company found that those who participated in the programme were subsequently happier, more punctual and productive. At the Post Office stress counseling was said to be beneficial in terms of a decline in anxiety levels and depression, improved self-esteem, and a reduction in absenteeism.

The question sometimes asked is whether the provider of the service should be from within the organization or from an external source? Some organizations, such as British Telecommunications and the Inland Revenue, prefer an in-house service. However, the use of an outside provider can help reassure staff that their problems remain confidential (Hall, 1995).

A complementary initiative to the EAP is one recently adopted by a hospital trust. Krystyna Ruszkiewicz, Director of Human Resources, Chelsea and Westminster Healthcare NHS Trust is quoted as saying in the June 2001 issue of *Trust News* that the Trust is committed to the physical and psychological health, safety and welfare of its employees:

> The trust believes that all individuals have the right to be treated with dignity and respect at work and affirms that harassment, discrimination, or bullying at work, in any form, is unacceptable . . . We are firmly committed to promoting a working environment free from all forms of hostility, so that staff are enabled to achieve their full potential, contribute more effectively to organizational success, and achieve higher levels of job satisfaction.

The Trust has recently introduced a Dignity at Work Policy, which specifies the different forms harassment can take. In this document there is advice on both formal and informal ways in which staff can tackle the problem. In particular it is said that any employee who believes that he or she is being bullied or harassed

EXAMPLE 11.5

Health care at Unipart

Unipart in the UK spent £1m on preventive health care for its 2,500 employees, and opened a £500,000 extension to its on-site sports facilities, which include squash courts, an aerobics studio and a centre for alternative health therapies. The facilities, known as the Lean Machine, compare very favourably with the best of the private health clubs.

Unipart's approach to revolutionising occupational health is seen as a way to combat stress while staying ahead of the competition. According to Unipart's chief executive, the rapid pace of change means that employees are facing more and more stress, which can have damaging consequences. In the 'Lean Machine' employees have the opportunity to get fit so that they can cope with stress. Also, they receive treatment to deal with some of the problems created by stress, and learn to avoid problems and manage stress through the medium of exercise and therapies.

(Wolfe, 1995)

should avail themselves of the opportunity to discuss the situation confidentially with someone who is impartial, empathetic, and trained in issues of equality.

The Trust is about to recruit a team of Harassment Advisers: 'The Harassment Adviser will be part of a team. The aim is to provide a professional, yet informal and friendly service, which staff can use with confidence, and which is independent of line management systems.' Staff who are interested in this role are asked to come forward, and they will receive special training on a course lasting three and a half days. When trained they will offer confidential advice, guidance and support to any member of staff who feels they are being harassed.

The field of health and safety at work is well provided with regulations and directives with the noble intention to create greater safety awareness and to protect people from hazards in the workplace. Nevertheless, accidents do happen and frequently the cause is human error. Where this is the case the human element in the man-machine system at work is found to be wanting. Mindful of the prominence given to accidents and mental health in the UK government White Paper 'Health of the Nation' in 1992, Glendon and McKenna (1995) have attempted to mobilise applied psychology within an HRM framework to shed light on the human factors in safety and risk management.

■ Conclusions

Enhanced communications are central to HRM. Without effective multi-directional communication it is unlikely that there will be mutuality and commitment between employer and employees. A range of media are available for communication in the modern organisation, but the essence of effective communication remains encoding, transmitting and decoding messages with the minimum of interference. Media such as suggestion schemes and attitude surveys are important for maximising the number of staff who can make an input, but face-to-face modes of communication, such as team briefings, remain vital as they offer a greater opportunity for clearing up misunderstandings and for generating direct feedback.

Participation is another central feature of HRM systems. At the macro level this can include consultative committees and Works Councils. At the micro level decision making on certain issues can be placed in the hands of the workforce. The extent to which there is such delegation is related to the management style adopted. Increasingly there are calls for forms of management and leadership that increase the focus on involving employees, such as transformational, lateral and upward leadership. These approaches include a shift in the location and nature of power. Traditionally, power was in the hands of those at the top of organisations. In flatter and more empowered organisations power may be more dispersed throughout the structure, and it may be exercised through networks and expertise rather than in the setting of organisational rules and procedures.

The emergence of the new industrial relations and HRM is reflected in an increase in the amount of direct communication and an elevation of the status of individualism as seen in the importance given to individually based performance-related pay, which tends to replace collectively negotiated pay settlements in the United Kingdom. These changes, and falling membership, have meant that a response was needed from the trade unions. One type of response that is likely to be on the increase is the merger of unions to form 'super unions', e.g. the creation of Unison in the public sector. The new industrial relations has also seen a more cooperative stance on the part of the trade unions.

The influence of the EU is likely to increase pressure for consultative forums with employees, involving elected members of the workforce rather than trade union-appointed representatives. However, the tradition of management/union relations is not being eradicated. It has been found that although organisations are increasing the amount of direct communication with employees and offering them greater opportunity to engage in participative processes, these developments are taking place within a framework called 'dual arrangements', i.e. alongside existing trade union institutions and procedures (Guest, 1998; Storey, 1992). New flexible and delayered structures, coupled with environments of constant change, call for care and sensitivity in the way conflict is managed, and signal the need to create participative forums to elicit mutual benefits for the workforce and the organisation.

There are different trends in trade union membership and collective bargaining on the international stage, and these can be understood in terms of the model originally proposed by Fox (1974) and subsequently developed by others (Purcell and Sisson, 1983). Certainly, the rhetoric of many UK organisations has moved towards that of the 'sophisticated moderns', who seek to expand employee involvement and who are not averse to the idea of trade unions playing a role. However internationally, for example in the United States, it could be argued that a 'sophisticated human relations' or paternalistic approach is in vogue. Having said that, critics may argue, with some justification, that the practice (as opposed to the rhetoric) of employee relations in different national and organisational settings can move towards 'traditional' adversarial or 'standard modern' opportunistic styles.

Whichever approach is taken, the focus is on improving organisational perform-ance, and this has increasingly been accepted by trade unions. Where the trade unions accept the focus on increasing performance the opposition to efforts by organisations to increase flexibility and productivity is likely to decline. HRM, although unitarist in origin, does not prescribe a single approach to best practice when it comes to employee relations. Pluralism does not seem to be ruled out, at least in practice, by a company adopting a strategic approach to HRM. Rather the approach takes a contingency perspective, that is adopting an approach which is most likely to maximise performance. In adopting a contingent view, however, it is important to maintain consistency between the different strands of the employee relations approach – for example on issues such as employee involvement, and other areas of HRM policy such as selection, training and reward management.

The management of diversity is an emerging field of increasing importance. It has a base in ethics and it can be understood through alternative ethical perspectives. In addition, there are now strong arguments in business logic for encouraging diversity in the workforce in order to match diversity in globalised markets, and to make the most of the available labour market.

While the health, safety and welfare function has been the 'Cinderella' of HRM it is clear that great care and attention should be paid to this field. There are both ethical and business-related arguments for this. On the ethical front it is important that people are properly treated in the workplace and that they are protected from dangers and excessive risks. On the business-related side, prevention is likely to be more cost effective than cure when it comes to accidents, injuries and illnesses that can occur as a result of unsafe processes and products. In addition, the workforce is unlikely to believe that the organisation is committed to them if it does not take care of their health and safety.

This chapter has covered a broad span of topics. It is important to bear in mind the linkages between the different areas. Although some models of HRM have emphasised individualism in employee relations this is not necessarily the HRM prescription. Rather the focus should be on finding the appropriate approach to communications, participation and general employee relations that enhances the connections and commitment between employees and the organisation.

References

Abrams, F. and Astill, J. (2001) 'Story of the blues', *The Guardian* (G2), 29 May, 2–4.

Bass, B.M. (1990) 'From transactional to transformational leadership', *Organizational Dynamics*, 18, 19–31.

Bassett, P. (1995) 'No escape from the worker councils', *The Times* (Business News), 2 March, 32.

Beaumont, P.B. (1992) 'The US human resource management literature: a review', in Salaman, G. (ed.), *Human Resource Strategies*, London: Sage.

Beech, N. and Cairns, G. (2001) 'Coping with change: the contribution of postdichotomous ontologies', *Human Relations*, 54, 1303–1324.

Beer, M., Spector, B., Lawrence, P., Mills, Q. and Walton, R. (1984) *Managing Human Assets*, New York: Free Press.

Benwell, D. (2001) 'Range finders', *People Management*, 36, 36–7.

Berridge, J. and Cooper, C.L. (1993) 'Stress and coping in US organizations: the role of the Employee Assistance Programme', *Work and Stress*, 7, 89–102.

Blyton, P. and Turnbull, P. (1994) *The Dynamics of Employee Relations*, Basingstoke: Macmillan.

Bratton, J. and Gold, J. (1999) *Human Resource Management: Theory and practice*, 2nd edn, Basingstoke: Macmillan.

Bright, D. (1993) 'Industrial relations, employment relations and strategic human resource management', in Harrison, R. (ed.), *Human Resource Management Issues and Strategies*, Wokingham: Addison Wesley.

Brown, W., Deakin, S. and Ryan, P. (1997) 'The effects of British industrial relations legislation, 1979–1997', *National Institute Economic Review*, 161, 69–83.

Claydon, T. (1998) 'Problematising partnership: the prospects for a co-operative bargaining agenda', in Sparrow, P. and Marchington, M. (eds), *Human Resource Management: The new agenda*, London: Financial Times/Pitman.

Culley, M., Woodlands, S., O'Reilly, A. and Dix, G. (1998) *Britain at Work: The 1998 Workplace Employee Relations Survey*, London: Routledge.

Dowling, P.J., Schuler, R.S. and Welch, D.E. (1994) *International Dimensions of Human Resource Management*, 2nd edn, Belmont, CA: Wadsworth Publishing Company.

Eagly, E.H., Karau, S.J. and Makhijani, M.G. (1995) 'Gender and the effectiveness of leaders: a meta analysis', *Psychological Bulletin*, 117, 125–45.

Eccles, R.G., Hertz, R.H., Keegan, E.M. and Philips, D.M.H. (2001) *The Value Reporting Revolution*, New York: John Wiley.

Edwards, P. (1994) 'Discipline and the creation of order', in Sisson, K. (ed.), *Personnel Management*, 2nd edn, Oxford: Blackwell.

Fondas, N. (1997) 'Feminisation unveiled: managerial qualities in contemporary writings', *Academy of Management Review*, 22, 257–82.

Fox, A. (1974) *Beyond Contract, Power and Trust Relations*, London: Faber.

Fursland, E. (1995) 'No place for the bully', *The Times* (Section 3), 12 January, 20.

Geary, J.F. (1994) 'Task participation: employees' participation enabled or constrained?', in Sisson, K. (ed.), *Personnel Management*, 2nd edn, Oxford: Blackwell.

Gilbert, R. (1993) 'Workplace industrial relations 25 years after Donovan: an employer view', *British Journal of Industrial Relations*, 31, 235–53.

Glendon, A.I. and McKenna, E.F. (1995) *Human Safety and Risk Management*, London: Chapman & Hall.

Guest, D.E. (1998) 'Human resource management, trade unions and industrial relations', in Mabey, C., Salaman, G. and Storey, J. (eds), *Strategic Human Resource Management: A reader*, London: Sage/The Open University.

Guest, D. and Hoque, K. (1994) 'The good, the bad and the ugly: employment relations in new non-union workplaces', *Human Resource Management Journal*, 5, 1–14.

Hall, L. (1995) 'More and more companies are using workplace counselling' (Health and Safety Executive sponsored Guide), *Financial Times*, November, 8–11.

Hardy, C. and Leiba-O'Sullivan, S. (1998) 'The power behind empowerment: implications for research and practice', *Human Relations*, 51, 451–83.

Hartley, R.F. (1993) *Business Ethics: Violations of the public trust*, New York: John Wiley.

Hendry, C. (1995) *Human Resource Management: A strategic approach to employment*, London: Butterworth-Heinemann.

Holden, L. (2001) 'Employee involvement and empowerment', in Beardwell, I. and Holden, I.

(eds), *Human Resource Management: A contemporary approach*, 3rd edn, Harlow: Pearson Education.

Hollinshead, G. and Leat, M. (1995) *Human Resource Management: An international and comparative perspective*, London: Pitman.

Institute of Management (1994) *Management Development to the Millennium*, London: Institute of Management.

Kelly, J. (1996) 'Union militancy and social partnership', in Ackers, P., Smith, C. and Smith, P. (eds), *The New Workplace and Trade Unionism: Critical perspectives on work and organization*, London: Routledge.

Legge, K. (1998) 'The Morality of HRM', in Mabey, C., Salaman, G. and Storey, J. (eds), *Strategic Human Resource Management: A reader*, London: Sage/The Open University.

McKenna, E. (2000) *Business Psychology and Organizational Behaviour*, 3rd edn, Hove: Psychology Press.

Marchington, M. (1987) 'Employee participation', in Towers, B. (ed.), *A Handbook of Industrial Relations Practice*, London: Kogan Page.

Marchington, M., Parker, P. and Prestwich, A. (1989) 'Problems with team briefings in practice', *Employee Relations*, 11 (4), 21–30.

Marchington, M., Goodman, J., Wilkinson, A. and Ackers, P. (1992) *New Developments in Employee Involvement*, Employment Department Research Series No. 2, Manchester: Manchester School of Management.

Marsh, A. and Cox, B. (1992) *The Trade Union Movement in the UK 1992*, Oxford: Malthouse.

Millward, N., Stevens, M., Smart, D. and Hawes, W.R. (1992) *Workplace Industrial Relations in Transition*, Aldershot: Dartmouth Press.

Monks, J. (1994) 'The union response to HRM: fraud or opportunity?', *Personnel Management*, September, 42–7.

Montagnon, P. (1998) 'Public turning against the use of bribery', *Financial Times*, 14 October, 7.

Pocock, P. (1989) 'Is business ethics a contradiction in terms?', *Personnel Management*, July/August, 244–7.

Poole, M. (1986) *Industrial Relations: Origins and patterns of national diversity*, London: Routledge & Kegan Paul.

Price, A. (1997) *Human Resource Management in a Business Context*, London: Thomson Business Press.

Purcell, J. (1994) 'Human resource management: implications for teaching, research, and practice in industrial relations', in Niland, J., Verevis, C. and Lansbury, R. (eds), *The Future of Industrial Relations*, London: Sage.

Purcell, J. and Sisson, K. (1983) 'Strategies and practices in the management of industrial relations', in Bain, G.S. (ed.), *Industrial Relations in Britain*, Oxford: Blackwell.

Ramsay, H. (1996) 'Involvement, empowerment and commitment', in Towers, B. (ed.), *The Handbook of Human Resource Management*, 2nd edn, Oxford: Blackwell.

Roche, W.K. (2000) 'The end of new industrial relations', *European Journal of Industrial Relations*, 6, 261–82.

Schneider, R. (2001) 'Variety performance', *People Management*, 26, 26–8.

Sparrow, P. and Hiltrop, J.M. (1994) *European Human Resource Management in Transition*, Hemel Hempstead: Prentice Hall.

Storey, J. (1992) *Developments in the Management of Human Resources*, Oxford: Blackwell.

Thatcher, M. (1998) 'Brewer and union agree national deal', *People Management*, 4, 13.

Useem, M. (2000) 'How to groom leaders of the future', *Mastering Management*, Series, Part 8, 20 November, 8–10.

Wassell, T. (1993) 'Job cutters axe chips away at power of labour', *The European* (Business News), 21 October, 40–1.

Wills, J. (1999) 'European Works Councils in British firms', *Human Resource Management Journal*, 9, 19–38.

Wood, S. (1996) 'High commitment management and unionisation in the UK', *International Journal of Human Resource Management*, 7, 41–58.

Wolfe, R. (1995) 'Healthy workers, healthy office', *Financial Times*, 27 January, 13.

Chapter 12

HRM: critique and developments

HRM is a subject derived from a number of academic traditions, some more critical than others, and this has been instrumental in the shaping of the subject into an entity that can be seen as incorporating divergent views and even contradictions. Similarly, the practice of HRM has developed in different organisational, economic and cultural settings in such a way that it has created a range of practices which provide choice for managers and which need to be actively managed if they are to complement each other. Given the amount of criticism HRM has generated it is important to be aware of some of the main trends and theories, and to understand how such critical engagement has assisted the development of both theory and practice.

Having read this chapter, you should:

- be aware of the theoretical criticisms of HRM;
- be aware of the critical research on the practice of HRM;
- know of the recent research on the implementation of HRM;
- be aware of the issues in the future development of HRM;
- have an understanding of some of the key linkages between HRM and other areas of management.

■ Traditions in HRM

Before examining the various criticisms of theory and practice, it would be wise to reflect for a moment on the different traditions in HRM. According to Bach and Sisson (2000), who use the term 'personnel management' most of the time, HRM has originated from a cross-breed of three perspectives, as follows:

1 *Prescriptive approach*: This is primarily concerned with providing managers with a bundle of techniques, which have been considered at length earlier in this book. The prescriptive approach has received heavy endorsement in the United Kingdom from a professional body – the Institute of Personnel and Development – with a strong vocational orientation, and it is considered the most popular approach. HRM offered personnel management a lifeline when it suggested that personnel management should react to the dictates of corporate strategy. In doing so it solved a dilemma for the Institute of Personnel and Development by

offering the possibility of increased economic efficiency for the organisation coupled with an improved quality of working life for the employees. One could argue that the linking of the competitive advantage of the company to the implementation of HRM policies had some effect in silencing the critics of traditional personnel management.

2 *Labour process*: This sets out to identify the controlling aspect of personnel management and is critical of the prescriptive approach. Managers are seen as agents of those providing capital and they seek to maximise profits by not being averse to getting as much as they can from the workforce and systematically reducing labour costs; though it is acknowledged that managers in their role of employees are themselves subjected to an increased range of controls and new management practices. Personnel managers are viewed similarly, and are accused of using their battery of techniques to exploit the workforce (Braverman, 1974). The ideas of the contributors to the labour process debate could be considered a useful counterbalance to the strictures of the prescriptive school, and they certainly encouraged the emergence of more critical accounts of personnel management – see, for example, Legge, 1995a and Mabey *et al.*, 1998.

3 *Industrial relations approach*: This perspective, discussed in the previous chapter, views personnel management as a system geared to the regulation of employment practices where personnel techniques are mobilised to make a contribution to the continual negotiation of order within organisations.

While the above traditions evolved they drew on the contributions of the social and behavioural sciences and strategic management. There are inputs to the theoretical basis of HRM from academic disciplines or subject areas such as sociology, psychology, labour economics, marketing and strategy, but there is a view that HRM is not a coherent body of thought with predictive qualities that can be tested in a scientific way (Noon, 1992). In HRM there is no one accepted body of theory.

■ Criticisms of HRM

We have now reached the stage where it would be productive to examine briefly the criticisms levelled at HRM and to take note of developments likely to shape its future. HRM has attracted a considerable amount of critical comment and analysis. There has been criticism of both theory and practice.

Criticism of theory

HRM takes on different manifestations in different situations, and some of the aspects of it can contradict each other (Legge, 1989). For example, elements of hard HRM such as performance appraisal linked to performance-related pay do not fit easily with the elements of soft HRM such as developmental and facilitating managerial behaviour. It is not just a matter of the different elements not fitting together in practice; it is that they are driven by different theoretical approaches. The set of assumptions about how people are motivated and managed under hard HRM is opposed to the set of assumptions governing motivation and management embedded in soft HRM. Such contradictions may arise in established subject areas, but they become the subject of intense debate. HRM seems to tolerate their presence, and some would argue that this points to a lack of rigour in the subject. On reflection, the above distinction between soft and hard HRM is not as fine as one has been led to believe. According to Morgan (2000), Storey's hard versus soft models of HRM dissolve into ambiguity when applied to Hewlett-Packard or Marks & Spencer, as both seemed to display qualities of both hard and soft at various stages of their development.

Keenoy (1999) argues that one way of understanding these apparent ambiguities and contradictions is to accept that HRM is a hologram, which when surveyed from different perspectives will be perceived as having divergent or even contradictory characteristics. As Martin (1992) has pointed out, while managers may believe that they have created an integrated culture in which there is shared vision it is possible that other stakeholders in the organisation view things differently. It is not uncommon to find different views of what the organisation is doing, and whether it is operating well or badly, subject to variation at different levels in the hierarchy and amongst different professional groups (Harris and Ogbonna, 1997). Similarly, critical analysts have expressed a number of divergent views of HRM, for example seeing it as a disguised way of exploiting workers, or as a way of apparently empowering employees while actually intensifying surveillance of their work. When observing from a Taylorist viewpoint one would be likely to see (soft) HRM as being a high cost/low performance option. Conversely, when looking at (hard) HRM from a labour process perspective, a view of organisational flexibility as exploitation through power inequity is likely to be arrived at. Such contradictions do not imply that HRM is meaningless. The implication is that it is not a singular object that is subject to one dominant theory.

It has been suggested that HRM is merely a form of rhetoric that does not have a substantial theory behind it (Keenoy and Anthony, 1992). New phrases such as performance-related pay, the enterprise culture and so on do not represent new ideas about practice. It is said that the game plan is not the introduction of rigorously tested concepts but a ploy to solidify management control in organisations. This is also a theme considered by Legge (1995b). She is severely critical of HRM and views it as empty rhetoric serving to conceal the fact that the labour input to the organisation is increasingly treated as a commodity. She contends that HRM is simply promoting a hyped-up version of personnel management, and considers the response of management to the so-called enterprise culture as a ploy designed to justify changes to the employer/employee relationship under the umbrella of progressive HRM. This means that management can adopt a harsh regime in particular situations while pretending that they are subscribing to an inspired vision of the management of people. Sparrow and Marchington (1998) also take a pessimistic view when they maintain that the HRM function is invariably seen as 'in crisis', in a black hole, in uncharted territory.

In addition to the theoretical traditions described by Bach and Sisson (2000) above, recent developments in postmodern theory have had a strong impact on critical theoretical thinking about HRM. Postmodernism has been referred to by some (e.g. Clegg, 1990) as a period in time that is characterised by fast, discontinuous change, and by a breakdown in traditional organisational structures in favour of flexible forms of organisation. The more radical (epistemological) form of postmodernism, exemplified by writers such as Lyotard (1984), maintains that the basis for our knowledge and understanding of the world of organisations has been fundamentally changed. In this sense, postmodernism is contrasted with modernism and 'the enlightenment project' (Alvesson and Deetz, 1999), which have been associated with the philosopher Kant. A belief fundamental to modernism is that knowledge is cumulative, and that it develops through scientific study in which ever-improved theories and getting hold of the facts leads us towards a more perfect knowledge of the truth. So, for example, our current understanding of motivation would be seen as more advanced and closer to the truth that those understandings that were prevalent a century ago.

Postmodernism rejects this general view of truth and knowledge in a number of ways. First, knowledge is not regarded as objective and progressive towards the truth. Rather, knowledge is strongly linked to power (Foucault, 1980) in that what counts as knowledge is determined by how it serves existing power structures. So, for example, the classification of a worker as either motivated or demotivated is a way of codifying knowledge of the individual which can subsequently be used in such a way that it influences reality for that person; for example, in the likelihood (or otherwise) of the future promotion of that individual. Thus a manager's perception of a worker, and the worker's efforts to present certain facets of their behaviour (and hide others) to the manager are related to the power over distribution of rewards.

Secondly, doubt is raised over the existence of objective reality. Modernism seeks to uncover reality as it truly is. Postmodernism argues that we create 'reality', and that much of this creation is to do with image, perception and bias. People do not start their search for the truth with completely open minds, rather they gather representations of reality and fit them into dominant ways of seeing the world (Baudrillard, 1983). For example, from a modernist perspective a manager may have a perception of employees as being basically lazy (Theory X) and as a result will perceive their direct workers as not putting in as much effort as they could. Under a Theory X conception the remedy to this problem is greater control. In such a modernist analysis there is a dominant perspective and the facts of the case are linked through logical sequences (e.g. people in general are lazy, these people in particular are lazy, and the solution is to prevent them being their natural selves). From a postmodern perspective the issues of motivation would be seen as more complicated and as specific to the context and meanings of the local situation. Workers may be regarded as lazy by this manager, but the workers may regard themselves as limited in the actions they can take by the fear they have of reprimand from their boss. Depending on the perspective adopted the workers may be thought of as lazy, hard working, or anything in between, and what you perceive may say as much about your presumptions as the actual activities of the workers. For critical and postmodern thinkers there is no single objective reality – rather there are multiple 'realities' created by the people in a particular setting and hence there is no single truth (or falsehood) and knowledge is regarded as relative. In a postmodern analysis there is no acceptance that there is a set of 'facts of the case' (e.g. it cannot be clearly determined that the people either are or are not lazy, in a sense they may be both simultaneously depending on the social construction of perceptions) and there is no expectation of uncovering single line logical sequences (e.g. by a manager the workers may be identified as lazy, the correct management techniques may be applied, but the workers may react in unpredicted ways) – rather one would expect multiple lines of reasoning (or rationalising) that may be contradictory.

In a conversation with a prominent organisation theorist (Professor John Child) in the UK in August 2001, reported in Box 12.1, it was suggested by him that there are two types of postmodernism.

These theoretical arguments raise certain questions for HRM and the study of organisations. First, they raise problems over seeking to gain objective knowledge of employees and using such knowledge as the basis for decision making. So, for example, in selection decision making, there would be scepticism about managers' ability to genuinely understand the candidates and choose the one who best fits the person specification. Secondly, people are not conceived as essentially rational beings and this has implications for, amongst other areas, performance management. An assumption which underlies typical performance management is that goals can be set for employees which they will understand and pursue in order to gain the rewards that follow from successful completion of their targets. However, from a postmodern perspective it may be expected that employees will not only pursue other goals, they will conceive their official goals in ways which diverge from the meaning intended by management, and will also indulge in behaviour that does not lead to any distinct goals, and from a Weberian perspective (Weber, 1962) would be irrational. Thirdly, one would expect fragmentation of organisational culture (Martin, 1992). Much of the rhetoric of HRM espouses an integrated culture in which there are shared meanings. A labour process view would expect opposition within the culture between managers and workers. A fragmentary view, however, maintains that different groups and individuals may not only disagree with each other on particular points, they may conceive what the point is differently, or not even be aware that they disagree. In a sense, groups will 'talk past each other' rather than disagreeing. This has an impact on many aspects of HRM. For example, in developing a strategy or managing change, the rhetoric of HRM often calls for clear goals and vision. For postmodernists, no matter how clear the manager is in setting a vision, there is always the possibility for 'reading' the situation differently, and the likelihood of really achieving a shared understanding is remote. This has an impact for the potential of achieving congruence and mutuality – two of the most fundamental concepts in models of HRM.

BOX 12.1

Reflections on postmodernism

There are broadly two variants of postmodernism. The first maintains that we have progressed, or should progress, beyond the 19th century belief that the world is advancing and converging towards some eventual state of modern civilisation, underpinned by a bureaucracy in the Weberian mould that applies the same rules fairly and honestly to all and guarantees an acceptable order in society. While recognising that bureaucracy and the standardisation it represented had some virtues, adherents of this postmodern perspective argue that the modern approach fails to accommodate the huge variety of local cultural and material needs in society and the sheer speed at which these are evolving.

The second variant of postmodernism goes much further in the direction of seeking to deconstruct the institutions and organisations (and even the language associated with them) that we have taken more or less for granted in the recent past. It regards these as justifying and maintaining an essentially exploitative social order through the ways in which organisations are constituted and the ideology of corporate capitalism that lulls us into taking them for granted. This variant of postmodernism maintains that what each individual says and does is equally valid, and as such it is fundamentally opposed to any form of organisation except for the purely spontaneous and voluntary.

I find the first variant of postmodernism acceptable and constructive in helping us understand so-called new and evolving forms of organisation, as well as the wider cultural and other shifts in society they reflect. It is broadly the approach that Stewart Clegg adopts in his 1990 book on postmodern organisation. I don't find the second variant acceptable, either academically or in terms of the state of society to which it would lead us, for I believe it is likely to lead us to a kind of Hobbesian world in which everyone would be at war with everyone else. I view the first variant as espousing variety and creativity, and arguing for freedom, whereas I fear that the second espouses anarchy and threatens an eventual loss of freedom, which is ironic in view of its aspirations.

In an assessment of HRM today Storey (2001a) acknowledges that HRM is no panacea for all corporate ills. However, he maintains that it has characteristics worthy of note, which should be considered in our quest for effective ways to manage organisations. He concludes that the HRM domain is lively and vibrant, where ideas are hotly contested. There are many new initiatives, and those who scrutinise the development of HRM are struggling to make sense of the changes and their significance. In a similar vein Bach and Sisson (2000) maintain that even though HRM may not have realised the optimistic expectations in store for it, nevertheless it is probably in a better state than it was previously, with the three traditions considered above – the prescriptive, the labour process, and the industrial relations approaches – continuing to make valuable contributions to our understanding of the field. We would maintain that the postmodern critique should be added to the stated traditions.

Criticism of practice

Early research studies into the practice of HRM found it wanting in a number of respects. For example, Storey and Sisson (1993) found that, apart from a few cases, the uptake of HRM was partial and fragmented. In some studies it was argued that there was little or no new practice to accompany the rhetoric that grew up in the mid-1980s to 1990s (Keenoy, 1990). It was argued that while there had been uptake of certain hard HRM practices (such as performance-related pay), soft HRM approaches to employee development were yet to be commonplace (Keep, 1992). In a similar vein, the results of the Workplace Employee Relations Survey reveal that although there has been considerable 'employment relations' restructuring in the UK few organisations have redesigned these practices in line with the commitment models of HRM. There is still considerable diversity in practice and massive uncertainty about where personnel/HRM is leading (Cully *et al.*, 1998). Reflecting on the economic benefits of HRM, Pfeffer (1998) maintained that practice does not always bear witness to the alleged economic returns obtained through the implementation of key HRM principles – e.g. high involvement, high commitment.

Another difficulty is that, while HRM espouses valuing employees, there are aspects of HRM which have the effect of devaluing employees. With regard to the adoption of flexibility, the 'peripheral' workforce suffers instability and uncertain conditions of employment (Emmott and Hutchinson, 1998; Pollett, 1988). The management of culture can be seen as an attempt to manipulate the attitudes and activities of employees (du Gay, 1997; Willmott, 1993). Similarly, the adoption of customer-centred quality approaches can be seen as another managerial strategy to control the behaviour of the workforce through imposing new constraints and requirements (du Gay and Salaman, 1992). A snapshot of problems in practice brought about by the march of globalisation and technological change appears in Box 12.2 (Maitland, 2001).

In addition to the problems discussed in Box 12.2, Pfeffer and Veiga (1999) have argued that it is difficult for organisations to implement HRM best practice for a number of reasons:

- Managers may be enslaved by short-term pressures that divert them from being able to invest time in managing their people actively.
- Macho norms about what constitutes good management (i.e. a control-oriented approach) are still pervasive in some organisations.
- There may be a lack of trust between managers and workers, and hence a lack of delegation.
- Organisations may fail to persist with the HRM strategies over a sufficient period of time to reap the full benefits.

However, the research evidence is that where HRM is effectively implemented it has a positive impact. The implementation of high commitment work practices has increased, and shown positive results (Wood and Albanese, 1995; Wood and de Menezes, 1998), and case studies of top performing UK companies (Tyson, 1995,

---

BOX 12.2

Difficulties in implementing HRM

In a report prepared by Rajan and Chapple (2001), based on the views of 247 financial and business services companies mainly in the City of London, it is stated that change is being undermined by a lack of flexibility and dynamism amongst the very people who are asked to implement it, namely human resource professionals and line managers. Both have experienced modifications to their roles in recent years, whereby managers are asked to handle people issues (e.g. recruitment and training) and HR professionals get involved in issues connected with corporate strategy. The HR function was also affected by outsourcing and by the application of software/intranets to routine activities.

The change in roles has been met with resistance. Some HR professionals feel that the changes have been detrimental to their professionalism. Many line managers, who are overloaded, are reluctant to take on HR functions. One glaring deficiency is that neither line managers nor HR professionals have been properly trained for their new roles and may not be the right people for the job. An HR director at a retail bank is quoted as saying that: 'HR people will have to be recruited from outside – we need people who have a blend of technical and business skills. Our HR people have been very old-fashioned.' Although senior HR executives are expected to work in partnership with the heads of business units on designing and implementing strategy, the report says that many HR executives do not have the necessary broader business qualifications or experience. Meanwhile line managers have little experience of HR and their priorities are different.

The authors of the report say that:

> more thought needs to be given to developing the appropriate skills of HR professionals and line managers. The majority of senior HR professionals – who work in partnership with line managers – and the line managers themselves, have rarely had any training in leadership skills or business awareness. Their understanding of the big picture is limited as is their ability to inspire trust and motivation.

It is said that the emphasis placed on professional specialisation by the Institute of Personnel and Development is not congruent with the new roles given to HR professionals. The latter are expected to become much more generalist and business oriented. An important conclusion is that both HR professionals and line managers require broad experience built through lateral moves in their early careers. Challenging assignments are likely to become the most significant form of training for HR professionals over the next few years, while line managers are expected to be exposed to a greater extent than before to coaching and learning by doing.

(Rajan and Chapple, 2001)

1997) showed that these companies had a propensity to adopt HRM. Similarly, in broader-based studies that focused on performance, Huselid *et al.* (1997) in the United States and Patterson *et al.* (1997) in the United Kingdom have found telling evidence that soft HRM practices are strongly associated with heightened performance of the firm. Thus, while it would still be reasonable to suppose that not all organisations that use the HRM rhetoric are carrying out the practice – and worse, that some are using the rhetoric as a cover for exploitative forms of management – it appears that there is a growing body of companies, particularly among the high achieving firms, who are developing integrated and effective HRM strategies and practices.

■ Developments in HRM

HRM arose in a set of environmental conditions that included increases in competition, changes in technology and a series of economic recessions. HRM placed an emphasis on flexibility, high standards of performance and the development of employees so that the organisation can survive and flourish. As environmental conditions continue to impact on the organisation we can expect to see HRM developing. Speaking of development, particularly in the context of the study of strategic HRM, Mabey *et al.* (1998) distinguish between the first and second waves.

First wave

The first wave was concerned with a number of central questions. First, did the emergence of HRM represent a substantive change, or was it merely a change in language (Keenoy, 1990)? Amongst the critics of HRM there was a perception that HRM did not bring with it changes in organisational practice, and that the rhetoric of HRM on such issues as employee involvement and development was, in reality, disguising the intention to cut costs and seek productivity increases from the workforce. Secondly, there was a question of to what extent HRM was of strategic importance (Sisson, 1990). HRM claimed to be central to the formulation of organisational strategy, but critics argued that while many directors of companies would claim that they were concerned for people, in reality the key strategic issues were those of markets, products and competition, and the workforce was only a matter of secondary interest. Thirdly, HRM claimed to be a cohesive set of policies, which were integrated (Hendry and Pettigrew, 1986). So, for example, the future direction of the organisation would be directly linked to recruitment and training policies and the approach to job design. Critics of personnel management had argued that it was a disparate collection of policies, which could even work against each other on occasions. Some believed that HRM, despite its claims, was little different to personnel management in this regard.

Second wave

However, subsequent research (e.g. Wood, 1996; Tyson, 1995) indicated that HRM was leading to changes in practice, which were both strategic and integrated. In particular, it has been shown that in the United Kingdom firms in the mid-1990s were increasingly following coherent strategies of 'high commitment management' (Wood, 1996) that entailed enlarging/enriching jobs, introducing teamworking, involving employees in major decisions, and training and development to achieve functional flexibility amongst the workforce (Patterson *et al.*, 1997). Although this is not the only organisational model for financial success, these research findings have represented a significant shift to a second wave in the study of strategic HRM (Mabey *et al.*, 1998), which has the following focal points:

- The significance of the social and economic context of HRM – for example the attention that is paid to the needs and desires of a range of stakeholders.
- The search for conclusive evidence that best practice of HRM results in improved organisational performance.
- The impact of changing organisational structures – for example, network arrangements between organisations, or the use of contractors as part of the 'normal' workforce.
- A focus on knowledge, organisational capability and learning as key themes in both general strategy and strategic HRM.

The study and practice of strategic HRM is an emergent field. It is notable that academic research at the beginning of the 1990s was often critical of the whole concept, and of its possibilities for making any difference in practice. More recent research, however, incorporates a number of streams that are far more positive in their implications for HRM. It could be claimed that HRM is now strongly linked to organisational performance (Huselid, 1995) and it is regarded as a central area of attention for the strategies of successful organisations (Mintzberg *et al.*, 1998).

The requirement for flexibility and speed of response to market changes is likely to continue to increase. This has implications for the practice of HRM. If increases in flexibility create an increase in the peripheral workforce, the result may be that they are relatively untrained and deskilled, since most organisations are reluctant to invest in peripheral workers. If this is allowed to happen, it will be difficult for peripheral workers to be creative and to make a positive contribution to the organisation. There is a need, therefore, for HRM to be involved in seeking a way to invest in this section of the workforce and to ensure that its members have sufficient security.

European Union legislation may have an impact on the management of employee relations. In particular, there may be a push to increase employee involvement in decision making, and curbs could be placed on the power of management through health, safety and social legislation. In order to deal with these changes, HRM will need to be proactive and to establish effective systems of communication and employee involvement.

Many organisations have adopted quality approaches and a customer orientation. This is increasing in the public sector, which has been adopting aspects of HRM. Organisations are likely to continue seeking different ways of working. After the propensity for greed, which was evident in the 1980s with the emphasis on self, gain and competition, the 1990s saw pressures for organisations to act in an ethical way, and this is likely to continue in the present century. Pressures have included consumers becoming more environmentally aware and exerting influence on both political parties and companies to think carefully about the effect of their policies and practices on the environment.

Some organisations are entering into network arrangements where they link with others who may be their suppliers or their customers. Agreements are made that guarantee continuing relations between the companies, and the emphasis is on a high level of trust. In some cases companies have had an open approach to their accounts so that other members in the network will know the financial details and the implications of the deal. This is felt to be an effective way of operating, rather than trying to act competitively and maximise profit at every transaction. It should be pointed out, however, that some companies are not yet ready for this type of cooperation and collaboration.

Increases in trust and a concern for a wider range of stakeholders, such as the local community and those affected by changes in the physical environment, are associated with an ethical approach to the management of people. The concern is to promote employee development, family-friendly organisations and flexibility of conditions that accommodate employees' needs as far as is possible.

However, the developmental and ethical dimensions of HRM practice have to be balanced with business needs and the enhancement of organisational performance. In view of the developments in the theory and practice of HRM, and taking into account the prevalence of complex, demanding and changing organisational situations, it would be inappropriate for HRM to prescribe one best way of doing things. A more appropriate approach would be to support 'reflexive choice making'. This involves understanding the domain of choice. First, one should be aware of one's own reasoned position or perspective, its strengths and weaknesses. This is important so that one is aware of a focal point of attention and blind spots, which will affect the way that situations are perceived. Secondly, one should be aware of the constraints on choice. Thirdly, one should be aware of the possibilities for choice and action, so that informed outcomes can be sought.

Constraints on choice of HRM policy include legislation, national culture and the macro economic environment but there are choices to be exercised when dealing with the general nature of HRM strategy (e.g. adopting a high commitment/involvement strategy), the type of culture the organisation seeks to foster, and the policies developed on HR resourcing, development and employee relations. Similarly, choices can be exercised on the style of leadership adopted and the approach to employee involvement and communications. It is important for the success of the organisation that informed choices are made and that the policies, practices and styles adopted are mutually supporting.

Looking into the future, Storey (2001b) maintains that the real challenge facing managers of human resources is handling diversity in its many forms. From a UK perspective he also says that the adoption of the new European-led social regulation suggests that US-style free market policies will not be acceptable in an unrestrained way. Neither would the adoption of a fully fledged social model, despite the attractiveness of the case made by its adherents. One of those adherents is Sisson (2000), who advocates the European social model as the way forward. Bach and Sisson

(2000) see future trends in the field as following the European HRM model as distinct from the US model, but they accept that the old European social model is in the process of being eroded. Although they would be partial to the adoption of the new European model, which appears rather idealistic, nevertheless they acknowledge that the current reality of personnel practice in the United Kingdom and Europe is closest to the US model. For a definition of the old and new European and US models refer to Table 12.1.

Table 12.1 Models of HRM

The US model has, as its key features, relatively weak trade unions with little collective bargaining facility, which management influences heavily. The outcomes are job insecurity, relatively low pay, flexibility, competitiveness and high levels of employment.

The 'old' European model has, as its key features, strong trade unions and collective bargaining machinery founded on legal regulations based on assumptions about employee rights. The outcomes tended to be job security for those in employment with relatively high pay, but with the downside of inflexibility, lack of competitiveness and unemployment for the many.

The new European model includes as its main ingredients flexibility, security, education and training, direct participation through empowerment and indirect participation through partnership. The outcome includes quality people, quality goods and services, competitiveness and good jobs.

Source: Bach and Sisson (2000)

Integration with other subjects

Developments in HRM increasingly indicate areas of linkage with other management subjects. Some of the key links are as follows:

Marketing

The way the workforce treats customers will impact strongly on customer satisfaction with service quality, and some organisations seek to differentiate themselves from their competitors on the basis of the quality of service their workforce provides. Marketing approaches, which focus on relationships with customers and clients, require a workforce having the appropriate interpersonal skills to build trust with clients. Additionally, such an approach would only be likely to succeed where the employees had sufficient discretion to make decisions when dealing with requests clients may make. This has an impact on job design and the levels of autonomy exercised by employees.

Operations management

This function in many organisations is required to maintain quality standards and to promote continuous improvement, and there is an implication that the workforce must be willing and able to learn and adapt. Similarly, flexible approaches to the manufacture of a product or the rendering of a service require flexible skills and attitudes from the workforce. Job design is a topic of importance in both operations and HRM, and one needs to be aware of both the requirements of the operating system and the scope for enhancing the motivation of employees through job redesign.

Managing financial resources

The HRM connection with the financial systems of the organisation includes the approach adopted towards rewards. Whether it is sharing of profits, share ownership, performance-related pay, skill-based pay or a traditional time-based system, there is clearly a mutual impact between the financial and the human resource systems. In addition there are connections between HRM performance and the financial performance of the firm. HRM introduced a cost-focus to people management (Beer *et al.*, 1984) and more recently in second-wave HRM (Mabey *et al.*, 1998) there has been a focus not just on cost but also on the positive impacts of HRM on productivity and profitability.

General and strategic management

This is an area where there have been many linkages with HRM, and these have been discussed in earlier chapters. In essence there are links between employees' contributions and the organisation's distinctive competencies, the organisation's ability to adapt to its market environment and its ability to develop as a learning or knowledge-centred organisation. There is also the issue of the capability of the workforce to become involved in the development of strategy, which is espoused by the processual school of strategic management considered in Chapter 2.

Overall, recruiting, developing, communicating with and managing the relationships with employees are fundamental to the achievement of objectives in other areas such as marketing, operations, financial performance and the corporate strategy. The organisational activities that constitute these areas take place within the framework of the organisational structure and culture, and as such HRM is intertwined with the other key activities of managing and organising.

■ Conclusions

Although HRM has been strongly criticised over the last ten years its path appears to continue undaunted. This may be because it reflects a number of trends that impact on organisations – knowledge/learning as distinctive competency, the need for flexibility, an acceptance of change, the provision of high quality service and organisational performance through people. The speed and depth of change means that it is prudent to invest in training and development and produce a workforce that is adaptable and knowledgeable (Nonaka and Takeuchi, 1995). Failure to do so can lead to ambitious employees being 'poached' by rival companies and to a lessened ability to compete. Flexibility of operation, whether in manufacturing or service industry, and increasingly in the public sector, has become a requirement of modern organisations. Satisfying the customer and delivering quality is vital to continued good performance. Of course it is always possible to seek change through restructuring the organisation, for example, to form alliances, outsource operations and flatten the hierarchy, but unless the people remain committed to the purpose of the company any such changes will be unlikely to reap their intended benefits.

There are no guarantees that adopting soft HRM practices in order to gain commitment and performance will be effective; as Pfeffer (1998) has pointed out, there may be no one best way. The direction of cause and effect, from individual motivation/commitment, to individual performance, to group and organisational performance, is convoluted and complex, and should not be oversimplified. Hence there is a need for thoughtful and reflexive treatment of people in organisations, taking a contingent approach that does not fall into the trap of treating people in an unfair manner (Legge, 1995a). Although the issues mentioned above are current for most organisations they are also reminiscent of the concerns that were of importance in HRM at its inception (e.g. Sisson, 1990). It may be that over time the issues remain broadly the same, but that circumstances change, and hence there is a requirement to develop in a way that addresses the core issues.

References

Alvesson, M. and Deetz, S. (1999) *Doing Critical Management Research*, London: Sage.

Bach, S. and Sisson, K. (2000) 'Personnel management in perspective', in Bach, S. and Sisson, K. (eds), *Personnel Management*, 3rd edn, Oxford: Blackwell.

Baudrillard, J. (1983) *Simulations*, New York: Semiotext.

Beer, M., Spector, B., Lawrence, P., Mills, Q. and Walton, R. (1984) *Managing Human Assets*, New York: Free Press.

Braverman, H. (1974) *Labour and Monopoly Capital*, New York: Monthly Review Press.

Clegg, S.R. (1990) *Modern Organizations: Organizations in the postmodern world*, London: Sage.

Culley, M., Woodland, S., O'Reilly, A. and Dix, G. (1998) *Britain at Work: the 1998 Workplace Employee Relations Survey*, London: Routledge.

du Gay, P. (1997) 'Organizing identity: making up people at work', in du Gay, P. (ed.), *Production of Culture/Cultures of Production*, London: Sage.

du Gay, P. and Salaman, G. (1992) 'The culture of the customer', *Journal of Management Studies*, 29, 615–33.

Emmott, M. and Hutchinson, S. (1998) 'Employment flexibility: threat or promise?', in Sparrow, P. and Marchington, M. (eds), *Human Resource Management: The new agenda*, London: Financial Times/Pitman.

Foucault, M. (1980) *Power/Knowledge: Selected interviews and other writings 1972–1977*, Brighton, Sussex: The Harvester Press.

Harris, L.C. and Ogbonna, E. (1997) 'A three-perspective approach to understanding culture in retail organizations', *Personnel Review*, 27, 104–23.

Hendry, C. and Pettigrew, A. (1986) 'The practice of strategic human resource management', *Personnel Review*, 15, 3–8.

Huselid, M.A. (1995) 'The impact of Human Resource Management and practices on turnover, productivity and corporate financial performance', *Academy of Management Journal*, 38, 635–70.

Huselid, M.A., Jackson, S.E. and Schuler, R.S. (1997) 'Technical and strategic human resource management effectiveness as determinants of firm performance', *Academy of Management Journal*, 40, 171–88.

Keenoy, T. (1990) 'HRM: rhetoric, reality and contradiction', *International Journal of Human Resource Management*, 1, 363–84.

Keenoy, T. (1999) 'HRM as hologram: a polemic', *Journal of Management Studies*, 36, 1–19.

Keenoy, T. and Anthony, P. (1992) 'HRM: metaphor, meaning and morality', in Blyton, P. and Turnbull, P. (eds), *Reassessing Human Resource Management*, London: Sage.

Keep, T. (1990) 'Corporate training strategies: the vital component?', in Salaman, G. (ed.), *Human Resource Strategies*, London: Sage.

Legge, K. (1989) 'Human resource management: a critical analysis', in Storey, J. (ed.), *New Perspectives on Human Resource Management*, London: Routledge.

Legge, K. (1995a) *Human Resource Management*, Basingstoke: Macmillan.

Legge, K. (1995b) 'HRM: rhetoric, reality, and hidden agendas', in Storey, J. (ed.), *Human Resource Management: A critical text*, London: Routledge.

Lyotard, J-F. (1984) *The Postmodern Condition: A Report on Knowledge*, Manchester: Manchester University Press.

Mabey, C., Skinner, D. and Clark, T. (1998) *Experiencing Human Resource Management*, London: Sage.

Maitland, A. (2001) 'The thin, blurred line in personnel management', *Financial Times*, 25 January, 13.

Martin, J. (1992) *Cultures in Organizations: Three perspectives*, Oxford: Oxford University Press.

Mintzberg, H., Ahlstrand, B. and Lampel, J. (1998) *Strategy Safari*, London: Prentice Hall.

Morgan, P. (2000) 'Paradigms lost and paradigms regained? Recent developments and new directions for HRM/OB in the UK and USA', *International Journal of Human Resource Management*, 11, 853–66.

Nonaka, I. and Takeuchi, H. (1995) *The Knowledge-creating Company: How Japanese companies create the dynamics of innovation*, New York: Oxford University Press.

Noon, M. (1992) 'HRM: a map, model or theory?', in Blyton, P. and Turnbull, P. (eds), *Reassessing Human Resource Management*, London: Sage.

Patterson, M., West, M., Lawthorn, R. and Nickell, S. (1997) *The Impact of People Management Practices on Business Performance*, London: IPD.

Pfeffer, J. (1998) *The Human Equation*, Boston, MA: Harvard Business School Press.

Pfeffer, J. and Veiga, J.F. (1999) 'Putting People First for Organizational Success', *Academy of Management Executive*, 13, 37–50.

Pollert, A. (1988) 'The flexible firm: fixation or fact?', *Work, Employment and Society*, 2, 281–316.

Rajan, A. and Chapple, K. (2001) *Tomorrow's Organization: New mindsets, new skills*, Create Research Consultancy.

Sisson, K. (1990) 'Introducing the *Human Resource Management Journal*', *Human Resource Management Journal*, 1, 1–11.

Sisson, K. (2000) 'The new European social model: the end of a search for an orthodoxy or another false dawn', *Employee Relations*, 21, 445–62.

Sparrow, P. and Marchington, M. (1998) 'Introduction: is HRM in crisis?', in Sparrow, P. and Marchington, M. (eds), *Human Resource Management: The new agenda*, London: FT/Pitman.

Storey, J. (1992) *Developments in the Management of Human Resources*, Oxford: Blackwell.

Storey, J. (2001a) 'Human resource management today: an assessment', in Storey, J. (ed.), *Human Resource Management: A critical text*, 2nd edn, London: Thomson Learning.

Storey, J. (2001b) 'Looking to the future', in Storey, J. (ed.), *Human Resource Management: A critical text*, 2nd edn, London: Thomson Learning.

Storey, J. and Sisson, K. (1993) *Managing Human Resources and Industrial Relations*, Buckingham: Open University Press.

Tyson, S. (1995) *Strategic Human Resource Management*, London: Pitman.

Tyson, S. (ed.) (1997) *The Practice of Human Resource Strategy*, London: Pitman.

Weber, M. (1962) *Basic Concepts in Sociology* (trans. H.P. Secher), London: Peter Owen.

Willmott, H. (1993) 'Strength is ignorance; slavery is freedom: managing culture in modern organisations', *Journal of Management Studies*, 30, 515–52.

Wood, S. (1996) 'High commitment management and organization in the UK', *International Journal of Human Resource Management*, 7, 41–58.

Wood, S. and Albanese, M.T. (1995) 'Can we speak of high commitment management on the shop floor?', *Journal of Management Studies*, 33, 53–77.

Wood, S. and de Menezes, L. (1998) 'High commitment management in the UK: evidence from the Workplace Industrial Relations Survey and Employers' Manpower and Skills Practices Survey', *Human Relations*, 51, 485–516.

Index